Accolade

Stanton Peele has created a revolutionary approach to the treatment of addictions.

— Aaron Beck, M.D., Professor Emeritus,
Department of Psychiatry, University of Pennsylvania
Medical School, originator of cognitive-behavioral therapy

The modern understanding of addiction and recovery begins with *Love and Addiction*.

— Tom Horvath, Ph.D., past President,
SMART Recovery®

The second book (after Andrew Weil's *The Natural Mind*) that really made an impact on me was Stanton Peele's book, *The Meaning of Addiction*, which I read in '86. My experience with great books, whether I was reading John Stuart Mill, or Peele or Weil, is that, you're saying, 'I was thinking that and they came up with the same formulation I've been using.' And then you see that the author took it beyond where your own thinking had gone.

— Ethan Nadelmann, Ph.D.,
Founding Director, Drug Policy Alliance

Peele offers a calm, reasoned, and highly effective alternative to the disease model of addiction and other bad habits. His work is electrifying and profoundly helpful.

— Carol Tavris, Co-author,
Mistakes Were Made (but not by me)

Peele makes it abundantly clear that the disease model of addiction, the ideology that currently reigns over the American addiction treatment industry, is an emperor without clothes. . . . He empowers people to view addiction in a new optimistic light.

— G. Alan Marlatt, Ph.D., past Director,
Addictive Behaviors Research Center,
University of Washington;
Co-author, *Relapse Prevention*

Peele offers a courageous indictment of the destructive mindset that all deviant behavior is a disease. Peele offers mindful alternatives to those suffering from addictions and to professionals seeking to help them.

— Ellen Langer, Ph.D., Professor Emeritus of Psychology,
Harvard University; Author of *Mindfulness*

Stanton Peele is the latest in a long and worthy line of American contrarians unwilling to accept the status quo, especially when it is the product of wishful thinking, not empirical research.

— Peter E. Nathan, Ph.D., past Director,
Rutgers Center of Alcohol Studies

You know I love ya and deeply respect your work and character. But you are a *curmudgeon*! People like Maia Szalavitz and Johann Hari are only saying what you've been saying all along. They're just more pleasant about it.

— Facebook commentator

Stanton's obsessive nature is one of his best qualities. That refusal to accept the status quo and keep worrying away at the issues that bother him—like a dog with a bone—is exactly what he's done for the last forty years and why he continues to be relevant when other, less interesting commentators have fallen by the wayside.

— Peter McDermott, Writer/researcher with extensive
personal experience of drug treatment, UK

Stanton Peele is a liar. He's in total denial of science and has been completely shut out of the scientific community.

—James Milam, Ph.D., Co-author,
Under the Influence (after debating Stanton)

Stanton Peele has been a pioneer behind the idea that addiction occurs with a range of experiences and that a natural process of recovery is required through a harm reduction approach.

— Adi Jaffe, Ph.D., Leading contemporary harm
reduction specialist; Author, *The Abstinence Myth*

Dr. Stanton Peele has been a trailblazer in the addictive behaviors field since the 70s.

— Andrew Tatarsky, Ph.D., Director, Harm Reduction
Psychotherapy Program, New School University

Love and Addiction pre-dated by almost a decade the notion of sex addiction and codependency popularized by authors such as Patrick Carnes . . . and Melody Beattie. . . .

— Wikipedia

You're a national treasure, but what's new about that? I've been saying that for years.

— Dan Hostetler, CEO, Above and Beyond
Recovery Center, Chicago

I read *Love and Addiction* as soon as it was published. Peele and Brodsky view addiction as a normal behavior that has veered out of control and they compare it with dysfunctional human relationships. It was the first book I ever read which analyzed addiction in a way that made sense to me and echoed what I knew from my work. . . . *Love and Addiction* still reads absolutely true as an understanding of addictive behavior all these years later.

— Rowdy Yates, former addicted drug user, Senior Research Fellow, Scottish Addiction Studies Group, University of Stirling, Scotland

I had severe problems with drugs for seventeen years or so. I had gone down the road of twelve-step programs, introduced to me through a drug treatment centre. In 2002, I found your book, *The Truth About Addiction and Recovery*, at my local library. I read it and began to implement the Life Process Program for myself. I returned to school and became a horticulturist. My life is now rich and full. I am married and a father to a six-year-old daughter. I am fit, and I have many interests and hobbies. I just wanted to let you know what a difference you have made to my whole life. Thank you so very much.

— John Rothfuss, Perth, Australia

This book worried me. Dr. Peele is widely read outside the scientific community. The distortions are subtle, the writing is slick, and to a person unfamiliar with the literature, the arguments are very seductive. . . . I would be delighted to hear from readers who have thought about these issues.

— Margaret Bean-Bayog, M.D., assistant professor, Harvard Medical School (who resigned from Harvard and gave up her medical license in 1992), review of *The Meaning of Addiction* in *New England Journal of Medicine*

In my years covering harm reduction, it has long since ceased to surprise me when leading names, authors, scientists and advocates in every area of this field have disclosed Stanton's seminal influence on their thinking about addiction. The groundbreaking nature of his work, dissecting the inadequacies and harms of the disease model, has been matched by his courage in plowing, for many years, almost a lone furrow as an anti-disease theorist in the US. His approach to addiction has, however, among harm reductionists at least, become practically mainstream.

— Will Godfrey, Editor-in-Chief, *Filter*, digital harm-reduction magazine

ETHAN: Stanton, no one takes you seriously any more.
STANTON: Will you read my memoir?
ETHAN: (pause): Yes.

— Ethan Nadelmann, longtime colleague in addiction field

Peele (1985) summarized, 'addiction may occur with any potent experience' . . . until recently, mainstream addiction research has greatly departed from this broad definition of addiction that can encompass any kind of behavior whatsoever. Instead, there has been a clear tendency to over-identify addiction with substance abuse and to distinguish drug addiction in particular as a unique phenomenon, quantitatively and qualitatively distinct from behaviors and habits of everyday life. However, recent evidence in psychology, behavioral economics, and neuroscience seems to increasingly suggest that the qualitative dichotomy is unwarranted and that addiction to drugs shares essential commonalities with motivated or goal-directed behaviors in general.

—Köpetz et al., "Motivation and Self-Regulation in Addiction," *Perspectives on Psychological Science*, 2013

The two keynote conference speakers (at Northern Ireland's 2019 national addiction conference), Stanton Peele and Marc Lewis, really are [at the] top of their game and their work will, I believe, be highly influential on addiction policy in the future.

— Terry Maguire, Slugger O'Toole (opinion portal in UK), "Addiction in a Time of Crisis"

"Having shared speaking platforms with Stanton for some years, I sometimes think of him as a cross between a bullfighter waving a red cape before the leaders of the addictions field and the Trickster of Native American folklore whose actions puncture and deflate prevailing institutions and ideas."

— William White, Author, *Slaying the Dragon: The History of Addiction Treatment and Recovery in America*

A Scientific Life on the Edge
My Lonely Quest to Change How We See Addiction

Stanton Peele

Broadrow Publications
Watertown, Massachusetts

Books by Stanton Peele

Love and Addiction (1975, 2014)
with Archie Brodsky

How Much Is Too Much (1981)

The Science of Experience (1983)

The Meaning of Addiction (1985, 2015)

Visions of Addiction (1987)
edited volume

Diseasing of America (1989, 2016)

The Truth About Addiction and Recovery (1991)
with Archie Brodsky and Mary Arnold

Alcohol and Pleasure (1999)
edited volume, with Marcus Grant

Resisting 12-Step Coercion (2000)
with Charles Bufe and Archie Brodsky

7 Tools to Beat Addiction (2004)

Addiction-Proof Your Child (2007)

*Recover! An Empowering Program to Help You
Stop Thinking Like an Addict and Reclaim Your Life* (2014)
with Ilse Thompson

Outgrowing Addiction (2019)
with Zach Rhoads

◆

To IGNAZ SEMMELWEIS—who introduced antiseptic procedures at the Vienna General Hospital obstetrics ward. Despite his demonstration that maternal mortality fell below one percent, the medical and scientific community rejected his ideas. Semmelweis had a breakdown and died in an insane asylum at age 47. His practices were successfully implemented years later by Louis Pasteur and Joseph Lister.

◆

Contents

We cannot solve our problems with the same thinking we used when we created them.

— Albert Einstein

My name is "Nobody."

— Ulysses to the Cyclops before blinding him

Stanton to younger bartender/musician friend after the friend has had a couple of drinks (and Stanton has had one beer): "I don't care if you drink less, you drink as much but take care of yourself, you quit now or forever, or you mix and match. I just want you to be okay."

Bartender/musician friend: "I know that and I appreciate it."

Stanton: "Of course, if you join AA, we're through."

Friend (laughing): "I know that, too."

Foreword

Stanton Peele has created a very different kind of addiction book—a memoir of his tumultuous career in the addiction field interwoven with his personal life history.

Stanton has formulated and applied (in a wide range of contexts) a conception of addiction—and its prevention and treatment—centered on a person's life experience in their social environment. This has set him in opposition to both the demonization of drugs, leading to persecution of users, and the ostensibly humane but actually disempowering as well as wrongheaded notion of addiction as a disease, as if it existed only in one's brain and body and not in one's mind and soul—and community.

Stanton has fought this battle for half a century as an independent scholar with no institutional position or funding, yet somehow earned a living and raised a family. He's still at it, and with his online Life Process Program, blogs on *Psychology Today* and *Filter*, and social-media presence he enjoys broader exposure than ever before, along with an increasingly receptive audience. Still, mainstream addiction treatment and public policy lag far behind.

Along the way Stanton has suffered as well as inflicted a good many wounds. In his memoir he explores how his upbringing and early experience prepared him for this give and take and gave him the fortitude and, when called for (or not), combativeness to keep going. He lives his life (and teaches his children and grandchildren) the same way he practices his profession—principled, adventurous, purpose-driven, and always "on the edge."

Stanton tells this tale with bold confidence and defiance about his ideas and values, yet with ironic self-awareness when it comes to his rambunctious personality. I have assisted him again as an editorial adviser—and something more, having traveled many of the same roads with him (including coauthoring *Love and Addiction*), going back to our college days when he and I nurtured each other's iconoclastic ways of thinking.

It's been a long, strange trip—but one of consequence, as what follows will show.

Archie Brodsky, Cofounder, Harvard Medical
School Program in Psychiatry and the Law

A Note Regarding References

Because of the sheer number of references throughout this book, we have chosen to house them online. Find them at peele.net/ScientificLife. They appear within the text (they are live links in the ebook) in a lighter typeface, like this: This is a link to a reference source. The online source lists them by page number and repeats whatever is shown in lighter type.

Prologue

How I revolutionized addiction theory and treatment but haven't been allowed into the mainstream of the field—even as my rejection has delayed progress in fighting addiction for decades.

Stanton is one of the world's great iconoclasts, contrarians, and rascals. He provokes people, often for a serious purpose, and sometimes—well, just for the fun of it. For Stanton, the meaning of addiction lies in what really motivates people as opposed to what they think motivates them—the comforting illusions they use to cushion themselves from reality. Stanton's great gift, both innate and cultivated, is to look straight at the truth with as few as possible psychological and cultural blinders . . . nothing can deter Stanton's seriousness of purpose and his willingness, when necessary, to stand alone.

> — Archie Brodsky, "Stanton Peele: Sixtieth Birthday
> Tribute," January 2006 (see Afterword)

Addiction is not a chemical reaction—addiction is an experience, one which grows out of an individual's routinized subjective response to something that has special meaning for him—something, anything, that he finds so safe and reassuring that he cannot be without it.

> — Stanton Peele and Archie Brodsky,
> *Love and Addiction*, 1975

This book is a memoir of my rocky life lived on the edge, partly due to my reckless personality and off-center approach to life, partly due to my off-center but crucial ideas, particularly about addiction, where I am sometimes acknowledged as a pioneer.

This memoir shows how I have spoken presciently about addiction for decades, while it details my life as an outsider. My outsider status has both enabled me to have this vision and allowed my vision to be ignored.

I am bitter about this at times, angry even. I have endured a lot of personal attacks and been denied access to influential venues. On the other hand, I enjoy my life and accept who I am.

More important, I identify with the task I have chosen for myself. I have purpose. I am driven by a set of values and way of thinking that I feel are right, worthwhile, and helpful to the world.

My distinctive outlook, combined with my creativity and talents, has led me to some success in life. I have survived, raised a family, and had a reasonable lifestyle—along with becoming a known brand in addiction.

I have also incurred considerable flack and courted danger that could have unhinged my life, and still might. The worst thing for me, however, is that my ideas haven't gained the scientific, policy, and clinical stature that they deserve, and that the world needs.

◆

Michael Lewis writes about the psychologists, Nobel Prize–winner Daniel Kahneman and his buddy, MacArthur Genius Award–winner Amos Tversky, in his best seller *The Undoing Project*. My book is like Lewis's except that: (a) I'm writing this book about myself; (b) I've never won a MacArthur or Nobel (I *have* won a few prestigious awards); (c) I'm not widely esteemed in the scientific and academic communities; (d) in fact, I've only ever held one academic position (that one was at Harvard, albeit its business school) and that one many decades ago; (e) conventional science still hasn't widely accepted my seminal ideas about addiction.

But people in the addiction field know who I am. I have an almost adulatory Wikipedia entry that says that I was the first one to recognize that love relationships can be addictive and notes my opposition to the disease theory of alcoholism and addiction. This once off-the-wall opposition is becoming a *slightly* more mainstream point of view (in the pages of *Scientific American* and in Wikipedia, for instance), but often with a failure to acknowledge me.

Here is what one distinguished alcohol researcher, William White, said about me and my career:

> Stanton Peele's name is familiar to anyone who has worked in any capacity within the modern addictions field. Stanton is a prominent speaker, commentator, and prolific writer, who, in addition to hundreds of articles and blogs, has authored such books as *Love and Addiction, Diseasing of America,* and *The Truth About Addiction and Recovery.* [The dates for those books are 1975, 1989, 1991. Bill left out my Nobel Prize candidate, *The Meaning of Addiction,* published in 1985. I've written thirteen books—the latest being *Outgrowing Addiction,* which I co-authored with Zach Rhoads in 2019.]
>
> His gadfly attacks on the portrayal of addiction as a disease, abstinence-only treatment, and Alcoholics Anonymous [White is in AA and abstains] make him one of the most polarizing figures in modern addiction treatment, but Stanton Peele has made significant contributions to the addictions field. He was one of the first writers to move beyond a focus on drugs to what came to be called process addictions—destructive relationships with people, sex, food, and work. His biting cri-

tiques of prevailing approaches to conceptualizing, treating, and recovering from addiction and his proffered alternatives have moved discussions of addiction from scientific and professional enclaves to subjects worthy of broader public debate.

And more than any other author writing for the general public, Peele has brought attention to alcohol and other drug problems and their patterns of resolution beyond those seen in addiction treatment or mutual aid fellowships [that means AA].

Having corresponded with and shared speaking platforms with Stanton for some years, I sometimes think of him as a cross between a bullfighter waving a red cape before the leaders of the addictions field and the Trickster of Native American folklore whose actions puncture and deflate prevailing institutions and ideas. Stanton Peele is a lawyer as well as a psychologist, and he revels in a good fight. And that is the challenge in reviewing his written work: *Stanton's persona can dwarf his written words, leaving both his most avid supporters and rabid critics more focused on him and his most inflammatory rhetorical flourishes than the more nuanced points that can be found in his books* [my emphasis].

◆

So, you see, I'm not chopped liver. And you also see my problem (the part in italics).

Bill White is a revered figure in the alcoholism and addiction field. He is also a very nice man. What he says about me is largely true. But the degree to which Bill accepts and recognizes my career is unusual among mainstream addiction and alcoholism theorists. The general reaction to me is far more often rejection. Indeed, my career in the addiction field is largely a string of rejections.

Nor am I the ubiquitous and prominent speaker he describes. Although I have spoken around the world—and the United States and especially Canada—I am now largely absent from North American venues, even ones where radical ideas like my own are discussed.

How and why have I been excluded from these circles, even as many of my ideas—such as that addiction is not limited to drugs, that conventional abstinence-only treatment is highly ineffective, that social context is critical in addiction, and that we need a whole new way to conceive of and deal with addiction—are floating out there in the miasma? That is the question at hand.

◆

Bill White attributes my combativeness to my being a lawyer. That's the least accurate part of his profile. I went to law school in my late forties and became an attorney at age 52. My iconoclastic work in addiction, my offbeat (to put it nicely) personality, and my contentiousness long preceded that midlife endeavor. And I've never really been "a lawyer," as in having a law office and a practice.

That would have been too narrow a path for me, and I was indifferent to its beck and call, resisting my ex-wife's urging me to use my law degree to make some extra money. Typically for me, I went to law school and entered the New Jersey and New York bars so that I could be more effectively combative for my own purposes.

I don't mind disagreeing with powerful people. And I don't worry about being an outsider—in fact, I prefer it. I don't even mind so much being the object of ridicule, anger, and scorn—although it obviously irks me that I am only partly, and in my and some others' view insufficiently, recognized for my original insights and scientific contributions.

How I have become and operated that way throughout my life, with middling success and a fair amount of accomplishments, is a central part of my story.

◆

While I was in South Africa in 1969, I secured a contract with Penguin Books to write *Love and Addiction*, a book that, over time, made me more than a half million dollars as a mass-market paperback. It also presented a new scientific model of addiction, one that has gradually impacted the whole field. Doing those two things at the same time was now, I realize, impossible.

Archie Brodsky (with whom I wrote *Love and Addiction*) and I split with Penguin in England and instead took up with a small American publisher, Taplinger, and its proprietor, Terry Taplinger, who released *L&A* in 1975. But both reviewers and the scientific community scorned our effort (they rarely noticed it at all): "Who can actually believe," critics spat out, "that relationships can be addictive, like drugs?"

In toto, people found my fundamental goal of redefining the scientific concept of addiction crazy. One psychiatrist told Archie and me in 1970, "We already *know* what addiction is." Most everyone agreed. Yet I have devoted my life to this project.

Flash forward. Optimistically, Archie and I thought we might have an easier time marketing my memoir fifty years later. After all, I *had* published thirteen books and innumerable popular and journal articles and blogposts. Moreover, the question of addiction has, in recent years, risen to the top of the list of debatable scientific concepts. And my name—along with *Love and Addiction* and others of my books, like *The Meaning of Addiction* and *Diseasing of America*—is often cited in these debates.

At the same time, through 2020, drug-related deaths have continued to rise rapidly, as they have since the turn of the century. Wasn't now a good time to review where we have been in regard to addiction over the last half-century, with me as guide?

Yet, once again, when we proposed *A Scientific Life on the Edge: My Lonely Quest to Change How We See Addiction*, we were met with skepticism about me, my ideas, my style. And we tried hard! Finally, we found a prominent British academic publisher where an editor was enthusiastic about the book. So I wrote the book you are now reading.

Then the publisher pulled the plug on it. It seems that a book about my life and times, my personal experiences and views of others in the addiction field, one that simultaneously confronts the thorniest issues of how we see addiction and deal with drugs and alcohol, among other things, was impossible.

◆

I fantasize about winning a Nobel Prize in medicine for my practical and theoretical work with addiction. Go ahead and laugh—I can't even get a job at a university! (Economist Gary Becker *did* win a Nobel Prize for his 1988 paper on a "Theory of Rational Addiction." One of the handful of references in his Nobel-winning article is to my book, *The Meaning of Addiction*. Go on—top that!)

My view of addiction is that people get something they need from their addictive involvement—a feeling of control or of self-acceptance or a reduction in anxiety or depression or a way to structure their time, their existence—that they can't find (or believe they can't find) any other way. The addiction thus serves a function for the person, even if its effects are overall negative and self-destructive.

Really, observers tend to see people with addiction in this light—for which they are currently shamed as being biased and benighted, starting at school age. Instead, they are asked—no, told—to believe (per Archie's Foreword) "the ostensibly humane but actually disempowering as well as wrongheaded notion of addiction as a disease, as if it existed only in one's brain and body and not in one's mind and soul—and community."

Here is a version of that modern disease view in 2019 from a drug policy reformer commenting on the major American drug policy reform conference in an article in a national libertarian magazine—"Lessons From The Drug Policy Alliance Biennial Conference." The writer is the chair of the board of Students for Sensible Drug Policy (SSDP):

> As was discussed in the panel *The Overdoses Crisis in Our Backyards*, the medical field treats drug abuse as a "behavioral" issue but doesn't do the same for diabetes or heart disease, both of which can be attributed at times to sedentary lifestyle and poor diet, lifestyle choices that may exasperate a genetic predisposition. Addiction is also genetic, involuntary, and can happen to anyone.

The reformist writer, at a conference to change how we view and deal with drugs, here restates the classic disease idea that even "medicine(!) doesn't see addiction as a genuine disease (as it must)"—ignorant doctors are so blinded by prejudice that they don't recognize that consuming substances compulsively is, "like diabetes and heart disease," the result of "genetic, involuntary" processes "that can happen to anyone." Apropos the topic of the panel, does this mean the Obama daughters are exactly as likely to die of overdoses in their backyards as children raised in impoverished Appalachia or inner-city Baltimore?

And, so, the disease theory says that addiction is a biological disease unaffected by who people are or where they are in life. They certainly can't just quit being addicted, say, by quitting smoking or ceasing to shoot up drugs and moving on in life—you don't reverse diabetes or heart disease by changing your outlook or behavior!

My definition instead sees *all addiction—whether to drugs, or alcohol, or something else—as the result of a cycle of seeking need fulfillment while damaging one's ability to function.* It can and does occur for "anyone," but *much more so* for people in deprived, hopeless social or psychological circumstances, who see little relationship between their endeavors and how they can fulfill themselves. Addressing this disconnect in people's lives is how we can humanely and effectively act to stem addiction, even as most people progress in that direction on their own under ordinary life circumstances (and often even quite challenging ones).

◆

In 1975 in *Love and Addiction*, Archie and I proposed an integrated model of addiction that responds to the inadequacies others increasingly have found in the way the term is conventionally used. Although after 45 years the field has begun to catch up to our critique, those who wrestle with this problem generally have gone about it wrongheadedly, either scrapping the useful and irreplaceable concept of addiction (throwing out the baby . . .) or applying it inaccurately or in an arbitrarily selective way.

The concept of addiction that Archie and I first presented then, and that I reaffirm here, best interprets and explains the data and points to the workable, effective remedies that some clinicians and policy makers are beginning to advocate and practice. In any case, it will take a societal commitment to make those remedies work and to produce results on a large scale. As I said in the summary chapter of my 1991 book (with Archie), *The Truth About Addiction and Recovery*, "The only way we can really do something about addiction is to create a world worth living in."

As I have always asserted, we can understand and remedy addiction only when we understand where addicted people are at in life, both in their in-the-moment experience and in their life situations, which lead to what they seek and get from a drug or other addiction. This understanding is needed to replace addictions, for individuals and in our society, with more positive and sustainable life choices.

Otherwise, we will continue to fail to stem the addiction tide, as we are currently failing, which my approach is needed to reverse. I will give examples of accurate analyses and predictions I have made throughout my career and writings, bringing in names and events as diverse as Lindsay Lohan, the Delray Beach recovery community, Nora Volkow, and the opioids crisis.

◆

This is the story of me, my ideas, my being rejected, and my survival and continued pursuit of truth and acclaim, and the need for my ideas in America and the world.

Stanton Peele
Brooklyn
May 2021

Part I

The Foundation

My mother treated me as a genius, told me to disregard those who minimized or ridiculed my ideas or person. I never lost that protective shield. I can't be deterred—which I think I can safely say at age 75. At some level, I revel in the ample ridicule, the total disregard.

When Stanton was a kid, a teenager, he had a friend, a kind of soul companion at the time, who had filled the walls of his bedroom with pictures of great people: athletes, movie stars, writers, artists, musicians. Sartre and Camus might have been on that wall; Picasso, Churchill might have been there. As Stanton looked at those pictures, he realized how he was different from his friend, and how he would be moving on. As he put it, his friend had invited those illustrious people into his room, where he would be content to commune privately with them for the rest of his life. That wasn't good enough for Stanton; he was entranced by the same people, but he was determined to go out and meet them on their own ground, out in the world where you test your imagination against real challenges and constraints.

— Archie Brodsky, "Stanton Peele: Sixtieth Birthday
Tribute," January, 2006 (see Afterword)

1

I Can't Get No Respect
My unique standing in the addiction world

I see addiction as a completely normal human response, exacerbated to its worse forms by extenuating personal and emotional circumstances, rather than as some special, biological condition created at the level of neural synapses and chemical receptor sites activated by one or more of a changing cast of drugs. It has become a truism in America—steeped in its temperance tradition and our contemporary habit of medicalizing virtually everything—that we regard and treat addiction as a disease that resides solely in the latter, biomedical province.

My views (although not solely those) contribute to my never having held a university or other position in the field of addiction. I have never been acknowledged by the National Institute on Drug Abuse, or even by the leading alternative drug theory groups like the Open Society Foundations or Harm Reduction Coalition. I could never be invited to speak at my alma maters, the University of Pennsylvania or the University of Michigan, including the latter's famed Katz-Newcomb lecture, although I knew Ted Newcomb and Dan Katz, who was my dissertation chair.

True, I have been recognized and acknowledged to some degree by addiction theorists and psychologists. I've even received awards from the Rutgers Center of Alcohol Studies, the seminal American alcohol research group, and Drug Policy Alliance, the leading drug policy reform group in the US.

But, in general, I've been ignored, ridiculed, and attacked—by both popular media and scientific and therapy professionals and organizations—throughout my fifty-year career in addiction.

Me: Nora Volkow (head of the National Institute on Drug Abuse) has never uttered or written my name. Do you think she knows who I am?

Will Godfrey (editor of *Filter* digital magazine): When you write a piece about how Nora Volkow is ruining the world, she's going to be aware of you.

Actually, as we will see, Nora Volkow increasingly refers to my constructs, like love addiction, and explanatory models, like environmental determination, now, more than forty years after I developed them.

Pioneers in a New Understanding of Addiction All Doff Their Caps to Me

In recent years, decades after I personally began and maintained an onslaught on the disease theory of addiction, a series of best sellers supporting my point of view has appeared. They include Maia Szalavitz's *Unbroken Brain*, Marc Lewis's *Memoirs of an Addicted Brain* and *Addiction Is Not a Disease*, and Carl Hart's *High Price* and *Drug Use for Grown-Ups*.

The authors have all noted that I foresaw much of what they saw, for which they all give me due credit.

Maia Szalavitz:

Stanton Peele is a true pioneer of addiction research and theory. His ideas must be reckoned with by anyone who is serious about understanding addiction.

Marc Lewis:[*]

You are the pioneer. You put these ideas out long before anyone else was thinking this way. These ideas continue to reverberate in the addiction world and influence many people, many besides me.

Carl Hart:

I just want people to understand that these ideas are not new. And I'm not the person who invented them. People like Stanton Peele deserve more—most—of the credit.

These notables have recognized institutional positions—Lewis and Hart are professors: Marc of Neuroscience at the University of Toronto, Carl of Psychology and Neuroscience at Columbia University. Szalavitz has been the leading American neuroscience journalist for *Time* and *Vice*. Meanwhile, Andrew Tatarsky, who is director of the leading American training program in harm reduction psychotherapy at New School University, says about me:

Dr. Stanton Peele has been a trailblazer in the addictive behaviors field since the '70s, forecasting new ideas, riding the crest of each new progressive wave in the field, and sounding a call to arms in defense of each new development in the theory and technique for helping people with addictions recover.

---

[*] Marc told me that my 1989 book, *Diseasing of America*, changed the course of his thinking and his work.

Harm reduction is the opposite of the disease theory and abstinence fixation of American drug therapy and policy. *HR places primacy on the person's overall well-being and life functioning, rather than whether they abstain or use.* For some people, harm reduction equates with non-abstinence. I look to it for a more fundamental reconception of addiction (see Chapter 9).

Adi Jaffe, a Los Angeles harm reduction guru, lists me second in the "Top Harm Reductionists" in *Psychology Today* (Andrew Tatarsky was first):

> Stanton Peele has been a pioneer behind the idea that addiction occurs with a range of experiences and that a natural process of recovery is required through a harm reduction approach. Peele has been a leader (and a rebel) in the harm reduction and alternative approach to the addiction war for decades.

Adi is a powerhouse entrepreneur of harm reduction. In recognition of his efforts, in 2020 I wrote him, "Thank God you're changing the world where I've left off." Adi graciously responded, "Thanks a lot Stanton. That means quite a bit coming from you. I am amazed you did this forty years ago . . . can't imagine the pushback."

Tom Horvath, former president of SMART Recovery, said:

> The modern understanding of addiction and recovery begins with *Love and Addiction*. Unfortunately the recovery field and society have been slow to comprehend what Peele and Brodsky wrote. To read this book, again or for the first time, allows one to consider what we might have done about addiction since 1975, but have not done.

Sometimes word of me leaks out to popular publications, as in *The Atlantic*'s list of "10 People Revolutionizing How We Study Addiction and Recovery," including Bill White, Tom McLellan, Nora Volkow, Bill Miller, Keith Humphreys—names that reappear later in this book:

> Few figures in the recovery world have been as controversial as Stanton Peele. While his arguments have been vehemently challenged by many AA stalwarts, Peele, who has authored countless books and treatises on the subject, remained staunchly committed to his thesis that AA is not the only way to treat addiction, and that alcoholism is not a chronic and progressive disease. Most addictions, he believes, are a product of culture and an individual's response to their personal experience. In his view, temperance-oriented cultures like Britain and the United States, who largely believe in abstinence-only cures, tend to suffer much higher alcoholism rates than nations like than France, Italy, and Spain, where people are trained to develop "normalized" attitudes toward alcohol from a young age. Peele's moderation-management methods are lauded by a vocal minority of addiction experts and advocates, but his willingness to challenge AA and the complete abstinence model of recovery, have made him a virtual pariah among hard-core AA enthusiasts.

Like Tatarsky, Jaffe, and Horvath—but unlike Lewis, Hart, and Szalavitz—I am actually involved in treating addiction. Somewhat later in my career (I was 60) I partnered in a residential rehab that morphed into an online addiction coaching program, called the Life Process Program, that is active worldwide.

However much I appreciate the praise of these writers, researchers, and therapists, I think of addiction in a fundamentally different way than they do—that it has to be defined in terms of human experience. Explaining their incomprehension of this idea and its consequences and purveying my view are the purpose of this memoir.

My View of Addiction Has Ascended, My Reputation—Not So Much

Before I discuss how I became who I am and how my career unfolded, I *do* have a brand name. William White wrote about me in reviewing my 2014 book with Ilse Thompson, *Recover!*, in the quote I included in my Prologue:

> Stanton Peele's name is familiar to anyone who has worked in any capacity within the modern addictions field. He was one of the first writers to move beyond a focus on drugs to what came to be called process addictions—destructive relationships with people, sex, food, and work. His biting critiques of prevailing approaches to conceptualizing, treating and recovering from addiction and his proffered alternatives have moved discussions of addiction from scientific and professional enclaves to subjects worthy of broader public debate.

Thanks, Bill!

But this still doesn't capture what I've done for the addiction field—my reconceptualization of addiction. As I stated and showed in *Love and Addiction* and since, "Addiction is not an accidental side effect of consuming drugs. It is rather a direct link people form with an involvement or an experience that offers them essential feelings and emotional rewards that they can't (or don't believe they can) get elsewhere."

Nothing is in itself addictive—*virtually everyone* takes opioid painkillers without becoming addicted. Meanwhile, people form the worst life-endangering addictions to other people, a recognition I pioneered that now underlies an entire industry and professional cadre. The original sex and love addiction groups have since morphed into the Society for the Advancement of Sexual Health, SASH. Although Wikipedia declares me the progenitor of this movement, this disease-oriented group would never acknowledge me.

> **One Strange Story**
>
> Through the 1990s I was regularly invited to speak to the addiction-equals-disease conferences organized around the country by Dan Barmettler's Institute for Integral Development and the *U.S. Journal* (see Chapter 7). The conferences were in Colorado Springs, and I was staying in a fabulous corner room in the famous Antlers Hotel.
>
> At one such conference, an attractive woman came to my room, introducing herself as the fiancée of sex addiction "pioneer" Patrick Carnes. We spent the evening walking around town discussing her and Carnes's marital situation. He was getting divorced; she was previously married to a Jewish Philadelphia physician. We had fun.
>
> I never heard from her again; I've *never* heard from Carnes.

On the other hand, a Scottish former heroin addict and drug researcher called Rowdy Yates said about *Love and Addiction*:

> This book I read as soon as it was published. Peele and Brodsky view addiction as a normal behavior that has veered out of control and they compare it with dysfunctional human relationships. It was the first book I ever read which analyzed addiction in a way that made sense to me and echoed what I knew from my work. Years later, I undertook a study looking at recovered addicts who had been sexually abused as children. One of the researchers we used was a psychotherapist and remarked to me that the relationship they described with their drug(s) of choice sounded exactly like their relationship with their perpetrator. I remembered Peele and Brodsky and pulled it off the shelf. It still reads absolutely true as an understanding of addictive behavior all these years later.

In 2013, for the first time, almost forty years after me, the American Psychiatric Association declared in its diagnostic manual (called *DSM-5*) that behavioral syndromes can be addictions. DSM discounted sexual addiction. The World Health Organization in its comparable, international volume, *ICD-11*, *did* recognize sex addiction. DSM meanwhile recognized *one* behavioral addiction—gambling. (Strange, isn't that, as I will discuss.)

This inclusion or exclusion violates my essential idea: Drug use is not a separate area of human action; it—including addiction—follows the same rules and patterns that any compulsively engaging behavior does.

I Am in the Encyclopedia, or Wikipedia:

> According to Peele's experiential/environmental approach, addictions are negative patterns of behavior that result from an over-attachment people form to experiences generated from a range of involvements. He contends that most people experience addiction to some degree at least for periods of time during

their lives. He does not view addictions as medical problems but as "problems of life" that most people overcome. The failure to do so is the exception rather than the rule, he argues.

Wikipedia recognizes my primacy in this realm in the addiction field:

> When it was published in 1975, *Love and Addiction* pre-dated by almost a decade the notion of sex addiction and codependency popularized by authors such as Patrick Carnes, whose *Out of the Shadows*, one of the earliest popular books to describe sex addiction, came out in 1983, and Melody Beattie, whose *Codependent No More* was published in 1986. *Love and Addiction* pre-dated the current popular use of the terms "sex addiction" and "codependency" to describe disorders of love attachment. However, because *Love and Addiction* was concerned with observing the same condition of addictive human attachments, it has been argued that this is the first book to be written on the subject of codependent relationships.

Wikipedia also recognizes how my approach has become the common wisdom, and at the same time been bent out of shape. Quoting a Canadian psychologist, my entry says:

> That experiences can be addictive was a prescient notion in 1975 as psychology now embraces the concept of the process (or behavioral) addictions such as pathological gambling, compulsive eating, and sex addiction. But it must surely be to Peele's dismay that instead of rethinking substance addiction as a medical illness, psychology has gone and classified the behaviors as addictions in the same medical sense and yielded the solution into the hands of the 12-Steps [and neuroscience].

The Institutional Definers of Addiction Don't Know (or Pretend Not to Know) I Exist

I'm happy that Wikipedia did me right. But it's the exception. And the noteworthies who praise me—Szalavitz, Lewis, Hart, Tatarsky, Horvath—while they are distinguished professionals, are themselves at the periphery of American addiction. The linchpins—like Nora Volkow, the head of the National Institute on Drug Abuse (NIDA), and Charles O'Brien, University of Pennsylvania psychiatry professor and the chair of the committee defining substance use disorders and addiction in *DSM-5*, either don't know my name or choose never to utter or write it.[*]

---

[*] I *have* been feted by some prominent addiction figures—including former NIDA director (1986–1992) Charles "Bob" Schuster and his wife Chris Johanson, a professor at the University of Chicago, and distinguished Penn psychiatry professor Aaron "Tim" Beck, who created what is now America's go-to form of psychotherapy, Cognitive Behavior Therapy. Bob and Chris did research showing that the rewards and environmental alternatives in people's and animals' drug use were more important than the drugs themselves in determining behavior (which I will discuss in Chapter 3). For Beck,

Volkow's and O'Brien's silence doesn't begin to plumb the depths of contempt with which I have been, and continue to be, treated in the field—examples of which I will cite, here and in the Conclusion. Let me begin by noting that none of my fourteen books has been reviewed by a major popular publication.

But one of my groundbreaking works, *The Meaning of Addiction*, was reviewed in the prestigious *New England Journal of Medicine* by a renowned disease and Alcoholics Anonymous proponent, Dr. Margaret Bean-Bayog. Here's how that went:

> This book worried me. Dr. Peele is widely read outside the scientific community. The distortions are subtle, the writing is slick, and to a person unfamiliar with the literature, the arguments are very seductive. . . . Is there any court of appeal from slur and innuendo? I would be delighted to hear from readers who have thought about these issues.

True, another journal review was more complimentary:

> This is a book to be read slowly, to be taken seriously, and to be debated hotly by every professional in the field. This whole subject is one of the major medical, political, and societal problems of our civilization, and we seem unable to find any workable solution.
>
> — John A. Owen, Jr., University of Virginia School of Medicine

But it would be hard to find a more execrable description of me than the one from James Milam in the *Washington Times*:

> Stanton Peele is a liar. He's in total denial of science and has been completely shut out of the scientific community.

I debated Milam at a 1988 government conference by listing a series of questions about whether alcoholism was best regarded as a disease. Let's just say I think I did well. For his part, Milam shocked the audience with a speech attacking Herbert Fingarette, a philosopher who also questioned the disease theory, who wasn't present.

I've never been invited to debate any disease representatives, or been invited to speak in any format, by the government organizations responsible for defining and dealing with addiction: the NIDA or the Substance Abuse and Mental Health Services Administration (SAMHSA).

---

how people thought and interacted overwhelmed the claimed biological bases for mental illness and addiction. Thanks to these prominent figures for their appreciation. But none of them had any impact on my career.

Without changing directions, the field is, belatedly, acknowledging my positions

Despite my being ignored, per the Szalavitz, Lewis, and Hart best sellers (and Johann Hari's *Chasing the Scream* and TED talk—more about Johann later; see Chapter 10), there has been a minor surge, if not in *my* direction, then in my ideas' direction.

In 2018, Marc Lewis published in *Scientific American* blogs: "Why the Disease Definition of Addiction Does Far More Harm Than Good . . . Among other problems, it has obstructed other channels of investigation, including the social, psychological and societal roots of addiction." This was actually the fourth of a series of pieces in *Scientific American*, as Lewis explained:

> Over the past year and a half, *Scientific American* has published a number of fine articles arguing that addiction is not a disease, that drugs are not the cause of addiction (by Carl Hart), and that social and societal factors are fundamental contributors to opioid addiction (Maia Szalavitz) in general and the overdose crisis in particular [these are all points I have made repeatedly for decades]. *The dominant view, that addiction is a disease resulting from drug use, is gradually being eroded by these and other incisive critiques* [my emphasis].

The first referenced of these articles, "arguing that addiction is not a disease," cited the exact evidence that I have been using for forty years to make this case. Which is funny, since every few years since the 1980s I would send a query to *Scientific American* asking if they would be interested in such an article, to which I got no response whatever.

Pieces about new visions of addiction largely, if not entirely, ignore me

None of the articles in *Scientific American* mentioned me or my work.

I should say that in her 2016 best seller, *Unbroken Brain*, Maia did give me credit:

> It was not until 1975, when Stanton Peele and Archie Brodsky published the groundbreaking *Love and Addiction*, that the two ("love" and "addiction") were given a thorough side-by-side psychological examination. Point by point, the authors illustrated how unhealthy relationships—whether with drugs or with people—share the same fundamental qualities.

In fact, a number of people I now know became aware of my "groundbreaking work" only by reading Maia's book.

But that's not so many people. In writing about the "expanding definition of addiction in *DSM-5*" for the National Institutes of Health, two authors trace this development:

The field of addictions has undergone dramatic changes in recent years. In 2001, Constance Holden wrote an article for *Science* discussing the concept of 'behavioral addictions.'

Sigh. The Holden article was written exactly a quarter of a century after *Love and Addiction* and fifteen years after *The Meaning of Addiction* was reviewed in the *New England Journal of Medicine*.

I *do* appear in America's narrative of continuing failure to deal with drugs and addiction. In 2007, for example, *New York Times* reporter Jane Gross took a rosy view of a remarkable development around the massive growth in addiction rehabs on Florida's coast—many who entered the rehabs chose never to leave the place where they were treated.

In Florida, Addicts Find an Oasis of Sobriety

Delray Beach, a funky outpost of sobriety between Fort Lauderdale and West Palm Beach, is the epicenter of the country's largest and most vibrant recovery community, with scores of halfway houses, more than 5,000 people at 12-step meetings each week, recovery radio shows, a recovery motorcycle club and a coffeehouse that boasts its own therapy group.

Recovery communities are springing up outside the walls of rehab centers for alumni seeking the safety in numbers. [Gross then quotes me as the fly in the ointment of the glories of treatment (my usual role). She indicates clearly that I stand alone in my objections—and that I am wrong.]

This society-within-a-society gets mixed reviews from addiction experts. *A few* find it insular and cultish. "Cutting off contact with the outside world, is that a sign of mental health?" asked Stanton Peele, a psychologist and author who challenges much conventional wisdom in the field.

But many more experts note that a recovery community like Delray Beach may provide a promising environment for certain addicts [my emphasis].

Here is that story in the *Times* in 2017, exactly ten years later:

Haven for Recovering Addicts Now Profits from Their Relapses

In a nation awash in opioids, there are few, if any, places where this kind of scene plays out more often than this artsy beach town. Last year, Delray paramedics responded to 748 overdose calls; sixty-five ended in fatalities. In all, Palm Beach County dealt with 5,000 overdose calls.

Unlike other places in the United States that have been clobbered by the opioid crisis, most of the young people who overdose in Delray Beach are not from here. They are visitors, mostly from the Northeast and Midwest, and they come for opioid addiction treatment and recovery help to *a town that has long been hailed as a lifeline for substance abusers*. But what many of these addicts find here today is a crippled and dangerous system, [and they] *fall deeper into addiction* [my emphases].

Of course, Americans have bought this bill of disease-treatment goods for decades, and will continue to do, ad infinitum. We are addicted to it.

Me as Survivor

Nonetheless, I am still out there, fighting and arguing my position, writing books (in 2019 I published *Outgrowing Addiction: With Common Sense Instead of "Disease" Therapy* with Zach Rhoads), regular blogposts, and articles about defining addiction in national, if perhaps secondary, publications: in *Psychology Today*, "Addiction In Society: Blinded by biochemistry" and *Reason*: "Addicted to Brain Scans: The debate about sex addiction reflects a larger cultural confusion."

My first article (with Archie) about addiction appeared in *Psychology Today* in 1974: "Interpersonal Heroin: Love Can Be an Addiction." I'm still burning in the 2020s. I currently write for the cutting-edge digital publication, *Filter*: see my "Disease Model Proponents Are the Climate Change Deniers of Our Field"; "In Defense of the Concept of Addiction"; "Beyond Harm Reduction—Encouraging Positive Drug Use"; and "So We're Drinking Our Way Through the Pandemic—That's What Drugs Are For." Meanwhile Zach Rhoads and I are creating a series of podcasts to recast the disease-recovery narrative as a part of my online Life Process Program.

Say, how does someone get accepted around here?
What's my problem in being positively recognized for my unique contributions to the field of addiction in the United States over half a century? Let's explore that question.

2

Becoming Me
How I grew up like me

CNN's Chris Cuomo and MSNBC's Mika Brzezinski are two TV commentators who weren't easily intimidated when Donald Trump lashed out at them. It would seem that their coolness under fire was encouraged by their parentage: Cuomo's father, Mario, was a three-term Governor of New York, which his brother, Andrew, also became.

For Brzezinski's part—as her husband and cohost of MSNBC's popular show Morning Joe, *former Congressman Joe Scarborough, notes—not everyone was running around the White House as a little girl. Her father, Zbigniew, was President Jimmy Carter's National Security Advisor. Her mother, sculptor Emilie Anna Benešová, is a grandniece of Czechoslovakia's former president Edvard Beneš.*

I am similar to Cuomo and Brzezinski in regards to their sangfroid, although my father never held elected or appointed office. He was a shoe salesman. My mother was an indifferent homemaker who didn't graduate from South Philly High School. But I was never told that I had to accept a philosophy or way of thinking, and I was never prevented from criticizing authority. My parents, despite their lack of education, were free thinkers.

The fact is, we all carry pain, grief and loss. We spend most of our time hiding it, but it's there, it's in you. So you open up those boxes.

—Brad Pitt

Circe offers to remove Odysseus' scars, but he refuses: "How would I know myself?"

— Madeline Miller, *Circe*

Does a Middle-Class Jewish High Achiever Have a Backstory?

Best sellers about addiction are written by people telling their personal stories of addiction, even when they're successful academics and writers who haven't been addicted for decades. Maia Szalavitz begins her best seller, *Unbroken Brain*, with her addiction to heroin and cocaine while she was a student at Columbia—an addiction she gave up in her early twenties and never returned to. Marc Lewis, author of *Memoirs of an Addicted Brain* and *Addiction is Not a Disease*, has a similar tale, culminating slightly later in his life.

Carl Hart, another best-selling writer about drugs (*High Price*), wasn't addicted to drugs—in fact, he says drug users rarely have problems with their use. Carl grew up in Miami's urban ghetto, where he largely avoided drugs (taking crack was like holding a gun to your head, he thought). He went on to be an American success story. A professor of psychology and psychiatry at Columbia, he is the first tenured African American professor in a science in the university's history. (Carl *now* takes drugs, including heroin, which is a story for later, in Chapter 10).

I don't have a story like those. Although my origins are humble and I was somewhat disadvantaged, I was never addicted to drugs or a part of the underclass. But I still had a notable upbringing that enabled me to see things differently and to have the courage of my convictions so as to present my unpopular ideas, no matter what reactions I got.

My story can be considered one of trauma and psychological dysfunction—you be the judge of that. No matter what, however, it's not an average story.

Growing Up Stressed, Independent, and Capable

Here's how I got the insights and guts to know and say what I do about addiction, with at times virtually no support, while my ideas have become more prominent, and been accepted, slowly and imperfectly, throughout my career.

I'll start with my childhood in Philly in a difficult family. Let me quickly jump to one end point: my only sibling, my older brother, committed suicide in middle age. The good news: although Jeffrey didn't make the age of 60 (and Ignaz Semmelweis died well short of 50), I am 75.

I got here with some difficulties.

Have I been traumatized?
Gabor Maté is a famous Canadian proponent of the idea that all addiction stems from childhood trauma. I oppose this point of view not only because

it's untrue, but mostly because it isn't helpful. Gabor is wildly popular in North America. The hate mail I get from his fans rivals what I used to get—and sometimes still do—from AA acolytes. Here's one, written in 2020 in response to a *Psychology Today* blogpost I wrote (with Alan Cudmore) in 2011, "The Seductive, But Dangerous, Allure of Gabor Maté." It is one of hundreds such responses to that blogpost:

> To: POS
>
> Hey Stanton, you're a piece of shit. Not only for disrespecting the brilliant Gabor Maté, but for introducing doubt into one of the strongest philosophies of healing. You have hurt countless people by doing so. Unpublish this article, you fucking asshole.

Hate mail from Gabor's supporters takes this form: insulting me, praising him as a god, telling me to disappear and never be heard from again. What does it say about the spirit conveyed by Maté (whose family escaped the Nazis) that his followers feel free to express themselves this way?

Certainly, per Maté, people in highly traumatic settings are more likely to develop addictions and mental health problems. But most, perhaps remarkably, don't. More importantly, having people focus on their traumatic pasts isn't helpful to them.

Trauma, Trauma Everywhere

The psychological movement to find trauma in people's lives traces back to Freud. It reached its apotheosis in the daycare center hysteria of the 1980s through '90s, highlighted by a trial charging caretakers at the McMartin preschool in a Los Angeles beach suburb of bizarre rituals—including that they killed and buried a child! (Investigators dug up the back yard.) There were no McMartin convictions after the longest criminal trial in American history. Documentary filmmakers, originally convinced of the guilt of the teachers and owners, released the film, "The McMartin Family Trials." It showed the case, as described in the *Wall Street Journal,* "built of false charges of sexual abuse, manufactured evidence, and the attention of a runaway press corps" was a modern witch-hunt. Since this and similar trials in the 1990s, no ritual child torture cases at daycare centers have been reported.

People experience pain, sometimes intense, and search for its source. I understand and sympathize with that urge. More recently, trauma has become an all-purpose cultural tool and microscope people apply to their lives to explain and justify such intense feelings, as well as their emotional conditions. But they are chasing a tail (or tale) by doing that, not helping themselves. And I despise people who feed on that futile pursuit and call it therapy.

Martin Seligman, a pioneering researcher on the learned-helplessness model of depression, and later in his career on the positive psychology of well-being, and John Tierney describe the psychologically successful way most people deal with trauma:

> Our emotions are less reactions to the present than guides to future behavior. Therapists are exploring new ways to treat depression now that they see it as primarily not because of past traumas and present stresses but because of skewed visions of what lies ahead. While most people tend to be optimistic, those suffering from depression and anxiety have a bleak view of the future—and that in fact seems to be the chief cause of their problems, not their past traumas nor their view of the present. While traumas do have a lasting impact, *most people actually emerge stronger afterward.* Others continue struggling because they *over-predict failure and rejection* [my emphases].

Denise Sloan, a professor of psychiatry at Boston University and associate director of the National Center for PTSD, repeated this reassuring truth during the pandemic:

> The most common response to trauma is resilience. In fact, the overwhelming majority of people who endure a life-threatening event recover on their own and never meet criteria for PTSD.

Meanwhile, Gabor doubles down on trauma at his workshops: He asks if anyone there feels they developed an addiction without having been traumatized as a child. Several people raise their hands. Maté then picks one and proceeds to question the "mark" to uncover the trauma they didn't realize, or they deny, they suffered.

This leaves the person sputtering and feeling foolish, while a delighted audience applauds Maté's display of brilliance and clairvoyance. In his process, Maté makes no effort to understand the person's perspective. I ask groups about Maté's famous process: "Is this your idea of how to help people?"

I actually experienced personally Maté's circus act in what I term "My Traumatic Breakfast with Gabor Maté." I had been critiquing his trauma approach, which Gabor isn't used to. So when I scheduled a workshop for British Columbia's provincial psychological association in Vancouver in 2013, Gabor was eager to meet. Although I thought the meeting was to seek some rapprochement (we both, after all, believe that life experience creates the framework for addictions), it turned out that Gabor, seething over my criticism, was lying in wait.

Gabor's circus act is to stare at you and say, "I can see that you have deep pain that you haven't come to grips with."

He pulled his shyster's trick on me at our meeting in a Vancouver coffee shop. As sideshow tricksters know, everyone can think of some trauma or source of pain in their lives (see Brad Pitt's quote at the beginning of this chapter). This undermines the whole idea of traumatized people as a universe unto themselves. Maté thus can upset any human being, since we are all harboring things we don't usually dwell on that can choke us up. Actually, Maté has spread the trauma net to include having parents who work and can't devote all their time to their children. So, even if you weren't abused as a child, according to Maté, not having had an ideal upbringing is traumatic, leaving you susceptible to addiction.

Peter McDermott, a writer and researcher who is a friend of Maia Szalavitz, has been tracking my career (see Afterword for "Letter from an Unknown Admirer"). He observed:

> Stanton's obsessive nature is one of his best qualities. That refusal to accept the status quo and keep worrying away at the issues that bother him—like a dog with a bone—is exactly what he's done for the last forty years and why he continues to be relevant when other, less interesting commentators have fallen by the wayside. I very much doubt that Gabor Maté feels as though he's being slandered—but I bet he wishes Stanton would just shut up. He's hardly the first self-appointed drugs expert to find themselves in that position and I'm sure he won't be the last.

Was my childhood traumatic?

Gabor predicates his trauma-causes-addiction model on Vincent Felitti's Adverse Childhood Experiences model, which lists ten forms of childhood trauma: mental illness, criminality, or substance abuse in the home; a battered mother and/or divorce; psychological, physical and/or sexual abuse of the child; and emotional and physical neglect.

Two-thirds of Felitti's subjects scored at least one of these forms of trauma. But I had none of these ACEs (adverse childhood events). I wasn't ever hit or sexually abused, my parents didn't get divorced, my father didn't beat my mother, and neither of them had a drug or alcohol problem or went to prison. Rather, I was praised and attended to, by my mother especially. Indeed, Sara regarded me as a genius from my first conscious moment.

So did I have an ideal upbringing, as my zero ACE score might suggest?

My father was the most anxious person I've ever known, as a result of which he yelled constantly—not exactly at me, but at the world. In fairness, I need to say that my father was a capable and smart (if largely uneducated) man who was knowledgeable about world events and competent within the small world he inhabited. I learned to value these qualities because of him. Nonetheless, Ted woke up every morning screaming at the universe. At home, he was always becoming angry with everyone in our family because they had failed him in some way.

So I can say that I was traumatized by a kind of psychological abuse. But having only one ACE doesn't put you in a high-risk category, for example for suicide, which was how my brother ended his life at 59. On the other hand, I can quote Mercutio, friend of Romeo in my favorite Shakespeare play (since it explores teen suicide), who, after he was run through under Romeo's blocking arm, said of his wound, "'tis not so deep as a well nor so wide as a church-door, but 'tis enough, 'twill serve."

That level of childhood trauma was enough to create the vulnerabilities in life that I will detail here. I have a tendency to fear that the other shoe is about to fall, since I was always on tenterhooks waiting for my father to be offended by some misdeed of mine or someone else's. It makes me a so-called anxious-attachment type (about which Archie wrote a book, *If This Is Love, Why Do I Feel So Insecure?* with Carl Hindy and Conrad Schwarz).

But I don't fall into an obvious psychiatric category, which is true for so many people with worse traumas than mine. I have been divorced. However, I was with my wife, Mary Arnold, for thirty years and we had three children together. None of my kids has been institutionalized; all have intimate relationships and highly productive careers. I have a Ph.D. and a law degree, sent all those kids to college, and have had a close relationship with my grandchildren.

I have had a fairly middle-of-the road emotional life—no addictions, no obvious mental disorders. I will describe *how* I bettered the emotional circumstances that my father (and my origin family) lived through, and especially those that drove my brother to kill himself. *Moreover, I admire without bounds people who, with even worse childhood and other life circumstances than mine, survive, thrive, and achieve greatness. These are my role models.*

For all that, I can't say that I am a model of mental health. But I am a productive, positive, motivated human being and member of society, and an adventurer of mind, body, and soul. Even in my seventies, I am largely healthy and enjoy life. And I have a purpose.

I Have Purpose

I have a purpose in life—to revolutionize our way of thinking about addiction and to change drug policy and addiction treatment. (See the subtitle of this book.) I have pursued this purpose through thick and thin. I don't lack confidence in myself. I am never afraid to think things through, and I am not intimidated by disagreement and opposition. I bear up well under personal attacks and criticism (a required skill for me).

I realize that other people have skills different from or superior to mine in different areas, including some intellectual skills. But when I recognize unusual ability or intelligence or talent in other people, I reach out to them in order to take advantage of their gifts. As I describe in Part II, my ability to enlist help has been a crucial tool in my life—it's how I got through high school and college, got my Ph.D. and law degrees, passed the bar, published so much, and (sometimes) made a lot of money.

I am also able to read situations, large and small, to put their essential elements into words, and to see links and similarities among them over a wide range of human experience. I think of my mind like a filing system, where I cross-code experiences in terms of their major themes. This is true of virtually every human interaction or mental experience I have, movie I see, book or news article I read, and so on. I know, that's impossible. But I am remarkably good at my internal filing system. And I'm not afraid to ferret out and assert connections in the universe.

Drinking with the Italians

Throughout the latter parts of this book, we will see—time and again—that social learning is critical in addiction and alcoholism. In a cultural context, Italians (and Italian-Americans) regularly show up second lowest to Jews among American ethnic groups in their problem drinking and alcoholism levels. George Vaillant, for instance, an ardent AA supporter, found that Italian-Americans, Greeks, and Jews as a group were a third as likely to become alcohol-dependent over their lifetimes as Irish subjects in Boston's North End.

When Mary and I lived in Oakland and she worked in San Francisco, we went one Sunday to spend the morning with a group organized by the Italian boyfriend of one of her coworkers in a café in North Beach, the Italian enclave in San Francisco. We sat around a table, conversing jovially, drinking *much* more than Mary and I would ever do on our own—even though we skipped rounds.

Mary's friend's boyfriend brought an outside friend who likewise wasn't used to consuming this much alcohol. He began boisterously trying to stick tips into the waitress's blouse. We noticed that the man sitting at the head of the table nodded to the boyfriend. The boyfriend turned to his friend, and said, "Can I speak to you?" They stood up and the Italian-American young man told the young mid-American, "We don't do that here—you're going to have to leave." He was, late in the man's life, teaching the man the drinking customs of Italian-Americans!

Later that year, I gave a talk in Northern California to a conference of AA diehards. I told the North Beach story by way of illustrating the importance of social influence in developing drinking habits. (It was wasted effort with these closed-off disease adherents.) Afterward, Mary admiringly said to me, "I saw exactly what you saw. But I never put it together into a picture." I don't know anyone else who could, most especially the very epidemiologists who study group differences in drinking. Rather, they studiously ignore everything around them in their theories. *My understanding of addiction is instead anchored in my lived experience and life observations, which led me to explore research data and other people's worldviews and other cultures' drinking and drug universes.* Both these epidemiologists and I have worldviews. The difference is that I am mindful of them and factor them into my theories. And I call these experiences to the attention of audiences whenever I speak.

I owe my confidence in my thinking and observations to Sara, my mother—with whom I had plenty of conflicts after my early childhood. But during my childhood I was the apple of Sara's eye. She taught me arithmetic— I taught myself how to read comic books—before I entered kindergarten. Most important, she listened to, and appreciated, my jokes, my ideas.

My mother needed me to be special because her husband and older son disappointed her. Sara expected to be well off. The reality was Ted's crappy shoe store. Sara wanted a world-beating son. She instead got Jeff's insecurities and uncertainty. So she built me up.

Sara with her arm around the more forlorn-looking of her boys. Which kid do you feel she favors?

> ### Jeff and Me at the Shoe Store
>
> At age 9, I was working alone in the store with my brother, age thirteen. A man came in and asked for a pair of shoes for his son. We sold two varieties, one slightly cheaper than the other. Ted had taught us to offer the more expensive shoe first, and then use the cheaper one as fallback.
>
> When Jeff brought out the higher-priced shoe, the guy lowered his voice: "The last time I was here, I was the only customer, like now. So your father said he was able to offer me a bargain he reserved for a few customers." (I could see Ted chuckling to himself as he pulled that line out.)
>
> I foresaw instantly what Jeff was going to say, "We have another style of shoe, but it's not . . . [a special—we offer it to everyone]" "Jeff," I interrupted him. "I know the shoe he means. I'll go get it."

My brother completely lacked a sense of how the world worked and what you needed to say or do in a situation for your own advantage. He deeply resented me. More than four years older than me, he alternated between trying to teach me the advanced math he was learning and pounding my brains out. Sara would never intervene in those fights. Never.

I had to learn to survive on my own. And that was Sara's goal. (Me to Anna: "Who do you think was more spoiled, you or me?" Anna: "Me. But I'm less spoiled than any kid I know.")

> ### Confidence Scenes with My Kids
>
> **Mary:** "I whisper in [infant] Dana's ear: 'You're a genius.' That's what Sara told me to do."
>
> I drove cross-country with Dana when he was seven years old. I gave him long strings of mathematical equations to solve in his head and had him do data presentation slides for me as a teenager.
>
> At age fourteen, Anna took care of a boy with autism after his bus returned him from a special school. The boy sometimes randomly started screaming. **Mary (to Anna):** "Can you help him so he can attend regular classes?"
>
> In high school, Anna won the forensics prize for a comedy reading. **Me:** "I didn't know you were in forensics club." **Anna:** "I'm not. No one was competing in that category, so I asked if I could." **Me:** "Weren't you nervous?" **Anna:** "Dad, it was the most nervous that I've ever been."
>
> **Me,** seeing a big kid push Haley in the park, and Haley punched him in the chest: "Wasn't he kind of big for you?" **Haley:** "So?"
>
> I let Haley as a child steer our car while sitting on my lap—now she's an *excellent* driver who takes command of situations without fear.

The Family Disease

The males in my family are impatient, impulsive. Ted was. Jeff was. My son Dana was. My grandsons are. They have drugs for that now. Mary and I simply refused to drug Dana. Today he is a major e-commerce software engineer who works at a computer hour after hour. I've calmed down somewhat, too. But people instantly note my impatient, jolting personality, even now in my seventies.

And when I displayed what people would later call hyperkinesis, or dyslexia, or ADHD, as a child, my mother told me, and whatever authority confronted us, that it was nothing to worry about. My mother told them—told me—there was nothing wrong with me, that people should instead focus on my great gifts, which overrode my trivial deficiencies.

Sara laughed it off that I reversed "b"s and "d"s, which was later taken as a sign of dyslexia, or a mixed-up brain. "Why is that a problem?" she challenged people. It's as though she anticipated electronic keyboards, where I wouldn't make such mistakes. My mother's view that I could do no wrong extended to behavioral problems I had in school. As a result, I never got down on myself. However, in adult relationships, my lack of a guilt response can cause problems.

My Morning Ride

After my divorce, I had an Anglo-American girlfriend, "Eileen," from a prominent family. (Quotation marks signify the first appearance of a pseudonym.) Her sister was married to a wealthy retired financier in England. Eileen came with me to a conference in England where I spoke, and we visited her sister and husband in their lovely country home. But their home was out of the way. My host, the retired financier, apologized that there were no coffee bars in their small village, and that the only Sunday newspaper he could get delivered was a second-rate scandal sheet.

Sunday morning, still on New York time, I awoke at five o'clock. I went to the garage, got in a car which had keys in it, drove to the nearest large town, purchased a quality newspaper, had a cappuccino, then returned with the paper to Eileen's sister's home. After reading the newspaper, I kept it, although I knew its presence would be noted. Her brother-in-law asked, innocently it seemed, "How did we get this *Guardian*?"

Eileen confronted me, and I confessed. She said, "You drove my sister's Mercedes twenty-five miles on these twisting country lanes, on the left side of the highways and streets, to get a newspaper and a cappuccino?" "Well," I replied, "I got up early. And I didn't think she'd mind." Eileen snarled, "She *wouldn't* say anything. But you believe that what you did is okay? And your explanation is, 'I got up early'?"

> **Did you shut up then?**
>
> Earlier, stateside, when I asked Eileen if it wasn't strange that her family was so politically liberal, yet neither she, her siblings, nor any of their children ever went to an integrated school, she looked crossly at me, then took her breast out and put it in my mouth. **Archie**: "Did you shut up then?"

You can't get me down by criticizing me, or shut me up by bribing or threatening me. I regretted the breakup with Eileen, who was brilliant, whom I liked very much, who took drugs and drank recreationally with me, and who was famously unconventional. If I couldn't form a relationship with her after Mary, then with whom could I relate intimately? (The answer turned out to be a septuagenarian named Alta Ann.)

I can't be made to doubt myself. It can't be done. If it could, I would have given up on my thinking and theories about addiction a thousand times over. I have been on a thousand panels, faced a thousand audiences filled with people almost totally hostile to me (see me here* on *Oprah*). It's hard to endure public attacks—just witness how upset political candidates get from a negative comment or two. But I have a gift—or have developed a skill—at taking incoming flak.

> **I Look for Talent and Seriousness in Others**
>
> One night, stoned on cannabis cookies, Eileen and I were watching TV. Disinhibited by the drugs, Eileen (who *was* a polite Englishwoman) started "doing" me—not only using my notorious hand mannerisms, but riffing the way I do about the media, people, politics. **Me:** "You know, someone can only do me if you're a genius like me." **Eileen:** "My husband thought I was stupid." **Me:** "He and I focus on different things."

I Don't React to Immediate Stress

I'm not stressed by public confrontations. By nature and by training, I'm cool under fire from authority figures and audiences. I've been ambushed by the best—and the worst, including Alan Colmes on Sean Hannity's original Fox talk show, *Hannity and Colmes*, where Colmes was the liberal! (He read the Milam quote about my being a liar whom no one takes seriously that I cite in the previous chapter.) I generally react to such attacks with bemusement.

My wife and I were Democratic rebels in our heavily Republican New Jersey town, Morris Township. At one point, a rebel slate (albeit all

---

* https://peele.net/lib/oprah.html

Republicans*) was elected to the Township Committee and held a slim 3–2 majority. But one of the rebels moved, and the Republican County Committee was charged with selecting his replacement.

They picked an old warhorse, my wife's political enemy, who had been ousted in the last election. One thing held against him was his having purchased Township parkland that abutted his home.

Before he was returned to his place on the Township Committee, I rose and asked if I could question the man, Henry Blekicki. The large majority of people in the packed municipal auditorium were Republican partisans who wanted Blekicki seated and wanted me to sit down and shut up.

"Henry," I asked, beckoning him to microphone at the front of the seething room, "why don't you explain how you purchased part of Frelinghuysen Park?"

Slowly coming forward, Blekicki answered, "The town attorney said it was legal for the Township to sell me the land."

"Henry," I asked, "Do you own the land now?" (A neighbor had sued and made him give it back, since the conditions of the gift of the park by the Frelinghuysen family stipulated that no part could be sold.)

"No," he frowned. "How come?" I asked.

He was put on the Township Committee anyhow. Meanwhile, the mob was screaming for my hide.

When I returned to my seat next to Mary, I was worried about her reaction. She looked up at me and said, "You're the bravest person I know."

The next morning, Mary had changed her mind: "I've decided that you're impervious to people's anger." That wasn't a compliment.

I View Things Differently

I see the world differently than others do. Maybe I even seek such differences and exaggerate the way I see things differently. Peter Nathan, who became head of the Rutgers Center of Alcohol Studies—and whose intellectual integrity I was later to question (See Chapter 11)—wrote of me and my book *Diseasing of America*:

> Stanton Peele is the latest in a long and worthy line of American contrarians unwilling to accept the status quo, especially when it is the product of wishful thinking, not empirical research. In this book, Peele challenges us to examine our most fervently held beliefs on the causes and cures of the addictive disorders— and urges us to modify them, when the impelling logic of the data demands.

---

* The Township went Democratic in the 2018 election.

This is a strong validation from Peter. But my criticizing Peter later for his ethical shortcomings led Barbara McCrady, his successor at Rutgers, to accuse me of disloyalty, as I describe in Chapter 11.

I can tolerate disapproval and rejection. My mother Sara's father, Moishe, was a communist who emigrated from Kiev (now in the Ukraine) before World War I to become a union organizer. My mother styled herself a communist. That didn't translate into anything other than liberal political views and Democratic voting, including a love of Adlai Stevenson.

Sara informed the way I saw the world existentially. I learned that just because everybody believes something doesn't make it right. Actually, the opposite is true: when everyone believes something, it is most likely wrong. This critical perspective was the one from which I viewed the United States, my teachers and schools, and my family. My childhood friend, Danny Frank, who became a dean at McGill medical school and whose family was also leftist, thought the same way—but he kept silent, like many like-minded people I have met.

And that's how I approached addiction from the start.

Overcoming My "Trauma"

When I came to the conclusion (see Chapter 3: "How I Discovered Addiction") that my father, Ted, felt and acted like an alcoholic (even though he didn't drink heavily), it was a way of mastering my family, of mastering my father, of mastering my life. It also created my idea of what it meant to be a man—I saw that panicking or running away from difficult situations only made things worse.

I had already developed unusual feelings of competency in my dysfunctional household. My father's raw emotional reactions to problems, to anything different, were obviously dysfunctional. This was both an insight for my personal life and a way of thinking about addiction. "Why make your life more difficult, more unmanageable, than it already is?" I thought.

"That's what addiction is—you react to your problems so as to cause your situation to deteriorate further." I realized that my father could never do better than

Ted standing behind Jeffrey and me (unnamed younger cousin in front)

to run a shitty little shoe store in a rundown Philadelphia neighborhood (called Kensington, now the center of Philly's heroin market). My mother yearned for someone who had the guts to take on the world, not to run away from it.

That was me.

So, am I the victim, or the beneficiary, of trauma? My attainments certainly are real. So are my problems. As to what this mix has led to, the work must speak for itself.

Sticking Up for the Underdog

My mother, commie that she was, as well as always questioning authority and attacking the big boys, the power brokers, always stood up for the underdog. For one thing, at a time when it was rare, she always upheld the equality of the races. And she never let people pile on someone in her presence. She'd rather stand up to the leaders in the group.

My mother taught me that our social order caused us to fear or to despise whoever was down and out. Accepting that view was to play into the hands of the very people who oppressed us all. We joined them in putting down those worse off than us even though this enabled the people at the top to keep all the big benefits for themselves!

And, so, just as I never hesitated to confront powerful figures, I never feared talking to people whom others despised.

Listening to Madness

Once, Mary and I had a holdover at the Honolulu airport. Cheapskate that I was, I suggested that we go to Waikiki Beach—by bus. When we boarded the crowded bus from the airport, we found ourselves seated a few rows down from a man who was loudly talking to himself. Gradually, detecting my attention to his ranting, he turned fully around and spoke directly to me.

When we got off the bus, Mary looked at me. "You had to listen to him, didn't you?"

Everyone has a story in which they are the main character. The story justifies the person's life. In some cases, these stories have gone off track; the person is deranged. But their story is crucial nonetheless. The man could tell that I was tuned into what he was saying, trying to make sense of his delusional world.

It is now a popular mantra that we shouldn't stigmatize the addicted, the mentally ill, the downtrodden. But that's all hypocrisy. The minute people perceive that someone is even mildly different from them, they run the other way. No one would listen patiently to that man if he were on a midtown Manhattan bus today, no matter how much they tout mental disorders as illnesses. My approach, on the street and in therapy, is to encourage and empower sufferers, not to label and ghettoize them. But I also ask and expect them to behave as reasonably as possible.

Disease theories of mental illness and addiction regularly claim that biomedical models enable us to accept people with problems like these. The reverse is true. Research consistently shows that biomedical ways of thinking about mental illness make us *more* likely to stigmatize people with mental disorders. Worse, these models convince others—and people with problems themselves—that they are unable to change.

We naturally label and stigmatize people who aren't like us. Disease theories are ways of setting ourselves apart from such people, justifying our distaste for them, and excusing our avoiding them. Yet, as the Scottish researcher who reviewed *Love and Addiction* nearly forty years after it was published said, "Peele and Brodsky view addiction as a normal behavior that has veered out of control and they compare it with dysfunctional human relationships."

I am incessantly critical in my thinking about people, which can make relationships painful. But *I naturally view all behavior as human, and seek to understand it in human terms.* I view people, addiction and other psychological syndromes, and social problems as puzzles to be thought through and solved.

I Am NOT Antisocial

While Mary thought I was impervious, she didn't think I was destructive. To our kids' amusement, Mary and I both pick up trash, sometimes in woods cleanups, but even when walking the streets of New York. I *hate* destructive activity, like vandalism. I am the opposite of antisocial. True, I minimize, disregard, and sometimes mock authority. But I do so in the service of larger goals and values, and not gratuitously. I grew up with Westerns and have returned to them throughout my life. I love—and over-identify with—the noble cowboy who rides into town to set the world straight.

The biggest mistake people make about me is thinking that I welcome mayhem and destruction because I defy authority. In grad school, one tortured fellow student said to me: "I just see you ignoring what they tell us to do, sitting in your apartment smoking dope, saying 'fuck all this.'"

Me: "I'm sorry to tell you, that's not me."

On the streets, I'm the one who objects to people's antisocial public behavior—talking on cell phones in theaters and nearby restaurant tables, littering, putting their feet on subway seats, touching works of art in museums. My family and others warn me, and shudder at the prospect, that I'll be beat up—or worse—on the streets or in the subway. But that's never happened. Oh, I have been threatened once or twice. But people often thank me or tell me they admire me for holding people accountable for disturbing other people or contaminating public facilities.

> ### Here I Took a Risk, Like a Western Hero
>
> Two muscle-bound short men grabbed a handful of candy bars from the shelves of one of those candy-magazine shops nestled in New York subway stations. As one man held the candy bars behind him away from the lunging, diminutive Asian proprietor, I grabbed the candy bars and returned them to him.
>
> The thug grabbed some more, and I wrestled them from him. He was looking at me, a senior citizen, and thinking whether he should punch me, when his compatriot said, "Let's go." A woman came up to the proprietor and said, "You should just have let him take the candy—otherwise you could get hurt." She said nothing to me. When I went to buy some peanut crackers, the proprietor charged me the full dollar they ordinarily cost.
>
> And I paid it. We movie heroes don't take credit for being heroes.

My moral commitment is evident in my work. One of my most-cited academic works is "A Moral Vision of Addiction: How People's Values Determine Whether They Become and Remain Addicts." My later books—*7 Tools to Beat Addiction* (2004), *Addiction-Proof Your Child* (2007), *Recover!: An Empowering Program to Help You Stop Thinking Like an Addict* (2014), and *Outgrowing Addiction: With Common Sense Instead of "Disease" Therapy* (2019), as well as my online addiction coaching program—all emphasize the role of life purpose, pro-social values, and maturity in combating addictions. Along with taking personal responsibility, these values involve commitment to a community.

Most essentially, I confront Nora Volkow's dangerous and dysfunctional idea that addiction eradicates free will. I instead emphasize people's potential to change, and that convincing them that they *cannot* change—as the disease theory (including Gabor's trauma version of it) do—is ethically perverse. *Nothing is more despicable to me than to convince someone they are an "addict" and that they are permanently trapped by their addiction.*

But my crusades have alienated me from many. They also ended my thirty-year marriage.

Mary and I spent more than a decade as political and environmental activists in Republican Morris Township. You remember the story of my contesting Henry Blekicki's seating on the Morris Township Committee? That was an example.

Our longest battle was against the construction of a large retirement community proposed by the very powerful Delbarton School, a part of the holy-sounding St. Mary's Abbey, on nearly 200 acres it owned—environmentally pristine land where such development was forbidden. The Abbey, with a cold eye toward political expediency, said that the development would be used to house old monks. But no monks were to live there—those high-end residences were for rich seniors to admire the view. Instead, some small portion of the multimillion dollars in proceeds would be used to shunt retired monks off to a friars' retirement community.

We were leaders in a very well-organized community protest group.

> ### My Criminal Rap Sheet
>
> For one hearing on the development, Mary had made posters she put along the walls, which the committee insisted be taken down. When I protested on her behalf, I was arrested here, for public disturbance and, then, resisting arrest (I fell on my way out). Resisting arrest is a felony! I actually went to trial, where I was convicted of disturbing a public meeting, a misdemeanor that, fortunately, had no consequences for my psychology license or bar membership.

That trial—the whole campaign—created a lot of stress. Although in itself the trial didn't cause our divorce, it set us on the downward spiral that, within a year or two, ended our marriage, with both of our older kids having left home, and only Anna remaining in high school.

Years later, I attended the 2009 press conference at which Delbarton/St. Mary's Monastery announced the sale of their land as open space. The meeting was emceed by Tony Cicatiello, a lobbyist for the monks.

> ### Me, Tony Cicatiello, and Governor McGreevey
>
> In 2002, New Jersey's Democratic Governor Jim McGreevey came for a town meeting to Morris County Community College. The place was so packed that my friend and fellow Township activist Terry and I were sent to an overflow room where we watched the proceedings on a giant closed-circuit screen.

> We could see McGreevey on screen bantering with various local politicians in our heavily Republican county before the event. He suddenly called out, "Tony Cicatiello, our state's biggest lobbyist. Who are you here to represent?"
>
> I bolted from my seat, ran to the entrance to the main auditorium, and said to the woman guarding it, "I need to be in this room." She let me in.
>
> I rushed to the microphone for the Q&A. When I got to the mike, I asked McGreevey, "You greeted Tony Cicatiello (pronounced "chick-a-tello") as the state's most powerful lobbyist. Do you know who he's here representing tonight?"
>
> The entire mood of the auditorium shifted. McGreevey tensed. I told him, "He's here representing St. Mary's Abbey."
>
> An aide brought McGreevey a manila folder. He replied, "I understand that the Township has approved the Abbey's project."
>
> "They still need a special permit to sewer an area designated as highly environmentally sensitive by the State Plan. Is the State Plan appropriate for everybody, or just for people who don't have lobbyists?"
>
> What could McGreevey do but promise to set up an appointment for my team with the head of the NJDEP (NJ Department of Environmental Protection), which I attended with Julia Somers, the peerless head of the New Jersey Highlands Coalition.

One of our troops, Elliott Ruga, recorded the interaction in the auditorium here[*]—see especially the reactions of Tony and the Abbey's prominent attorney, Edward Broderick, who were sitting together in the audience. (Compare my engaging with McGreevey to other commentors at Township meeting.)

That was in 2002. In 2009, the economics of such retirement communities had changed. St. Mary's sought, and won, money from The Trust for Public Land to preserve their acreage as open space. At a public meeting at the Abbey to celebrate the award, Tony proclaimed: "Everyone wins. The monks will secure the money they need to continue to do their work. The people who were concerned about the fate of the property win because it will be preserved. I want to praise the community members for the extremely constructive role they played over the years in bringing about this resolution."

Tony paused. "Except for Stanton, that is," he said to the assembled audience and media, 95 percent of whom had no idea who I was or what he was talking about. (Tony, by the way, once offered me a job.)

---

[*] https://www.youtube.com/watch?v=sMO0WYBVoxo

I Will Never Be Discouraged—Never

In 2017, Ronan Farrow did a special for *The Today Show*, "Is addiction genetic, and should it be treated as a disease?" The segment producer called me, saying that a cameraman had recommended me for a competing view on the "question." Actually, I was being set up as the bad guy. I might have guessed so when the producer argued with everything I said while filming me over six hours in my Brooklyn apartment. As shown, the program featured three generations of addicted women. Along with the one quote of mine the producer eked out, I was labeled a representative of the "medical establishment" who was ignorant of developments in genetics—a ludicrous identification meant to show me up as the enemy of science in helping these women.

In fact, I have written extensively, professionally and popularly, for *Psychology Today* and in blogposts, about what genetic research tells us about alcoholism. The *combined* contribution of any number of genes to addiction or mental illness is very small, and certainly doesn't overwhelm environmental impacts. For instance, the *majority* of identical twins reared apart are discordant for mental illness and alcoholism (when one has the malady and the other does not). Even the *larger-than-average* concordance in such cases has environmental aspects, since reared-apart twins are usually brought up by relatives, or at least people from the same ethnic and social group.

But the most important scientific and practical objection to the concept of genetic inheritance of addiction is that, over their lifetimes, 90 percent of those addicted to a drug or alcohol cease their addictions. Since whatever addictive tendencies people may have inherited do not ultimately determine their fates, why focus on genes? Isn't it better to tell people (children) to exercise care and mindfulness when drinking or using drugs, and to encourage them to develop enough life ballast to offset whatever addictive predispositions they have? Instead, *people all the time tell their kids they are set up to become alcoholics and drug addicts.*[*]

The Human Genome Project and BRAIN Initiative

Do you remember the hullabaloo when the Human Genome Project commenced in 1990? It had the goal of "mapping all of the genes of the human genome from both a physical and a functional standpoint." (Wikipedia) As a nation, we were feverish with the excitement that we were going to

---

[*] From Archie's vantage: "This paragraph is exemplary. If there's any hope that people will read and be influenced by this book, this paragraph shows why and how."

learn the genetic sources of human personality, behavior, and—most assuredly and importantly—mental illness and addiction!

Should I skip the trite exclamation, "How's that been working for you?" NO individual genes have been found for any mental illness, alcoholism, or addiction. We now know that none exists. The overwhelming amount of DNA isn't organized at all into genes, but occurs in undifferentiated clumps along the paired chromosomes of the genome. These configurations can be radically changed by random crossings of the chromosome strands and other environmental impacts during gestation.

When HGP was completed in 2003, there were no announcements of fabulous genetic discoveries that would soon eliminate all of the usual suspect conditions. Indeed, as I note throughout this memoir (and especially Chapter 9), mental disorders and drug addiction and fatalities are the only things that have grown radically since we mapped the human genome. Despite this disappointing result, it is still commonplace for people to comment about personality, behavior, addiction and mental illness—"it's genetic."

There's One Born Every Minute

But what about the Brain Activity Map Project? "*Despite more than a century of study*, neuroscientists lack a fundamental understanding of how the brain gives rise to the complex thoughts, emotions and behaviors that make us human. Such knowledge would be invaluable for developing clinical innovations to help diagnose and treat brain disorders as wide ranging as depression, stroke and paralysis. *In 2011, neuroscientists and nanoscientists had an idea for revolutionizing our understanding the brain. Now that idea is a national challenge, as President Obama's BRAIN Initiative seeks to decipher the neural code that gives rise to our perceptions and experience*" (emphasis in original).

Greeted with vast enthusiasm by President Obama and scientists and policy advocates, the BRAIN Initiative was (and is still being) promised to spur the "development of next-generation tools for exploring how dynamic patterns of neural activity in the brain control thoughts, feelings and movements." A decade later, have you heard much about these benefits for understanding, say, why 70 percent of Republicans believe Donald Trump won the 2020 election? Or for understanding any aspect of human behavior? Never fear, in 2020, BRAIN announced an award of $4.4 million to Salk Institute neuroscientists in order to gain "a deeper understanding of the link between brain function and behavior."

My Challenge

I am always arguing uphill, so to speak, overcoming assumptions about the nature of addiction by presenting data showing that what people believe is not in fact the case. Nearly always my ideas are short-shrifted, ignored, or even ridiculed.

I live in that space. Sara treated me as a genius, told me to disregard those who minimized or ridiculed my ideas or person. I never lost that protective shield. I can't be deterred—which I think I can safely say now that I am in my midseventies. At some level, I *revel* in popular ridicule and scientific disregard.

America is addicted to its view of addiction as a disease, whereby we return compulsively to a point of view that has failed wherever it has been tried, as shown by the Florida rehabs and sober houses and communities described in Chapter 1, or the opioid death march all around us.

And Americans and addiction experts are congratulating themselves for doing so.

I have described my rejection of this consensus, and how my dissent has slowly seeped into mainstream views, without being fully assimilated, and with my only occasionally being acknowledged. As *Love and Addiction* made clear, it is impossible to think of addictive relationships as actual diseases—for example, how/why would one abstain from love?

Consider Nora Volkow, who has spread the brain disease view of addiction worldwide. Even she now ticks off all the objections to the disease theory of addiction (e.g., most drug users don't become addicted, most people overcome addiction on their own, addiction is heavily linked to people's social status) that I have been detailing for decades. If social status largely determines addiction proneness, if addiction can be reversed in the normal course of life, if supposedly highly addictive substances are used normally by large majorities of people under ordinary circumstances—why are we speaking about these matters as though they are diseases?

In the course of her mea culpa (not quite), Volkow says this about love addiction:

> As discussed by Maia Szalavitz in *Unbroken Brain*, it is in the grip of love—whether romantic love or love for a child—that people may forego other healthy aims, endure hardships, break the law, or otherwise go to the ends of the earth to be with and protect the object of their affection.

I quoted Maia's description of love addiction above. Maia actually, correctly, says that Archie and I in *L&A* "illustrated how *unhealthy* relationships [not love]—whether with drugs or with people—share the same fundamental qualities."

So Volkow, unsurprisingly, isn't able to get the essential psychological difference between love and addiction right: love of a child isn't, in itself, addictive. Destructive love attachments may be.

Since Maia pays tribute to my book in her discussion of love addiction, it might seem that Volkow must be familiar with my name and work. Not. At least that she will ever say—or confront. So don't expect to see the great Peele-Volkow debate any time soon, even as my ideas have stormed her bastion at the National Institute on Drug Abuse.

3

How I Discovered Addiction

This book is about how I became an addiction expert. How did I see what addiction was around me? How did I have the fortitude to deal with the constant impediments I encountered and still encounter—including misunderstandings and doubts from supporters and never-ending attacks from those stuck in the status quo? How have I never swerved from my purpose?

Les Demoiselles d'Avignon is a large oil painting created in 1907 by the Spanish artist Pablo Picasso. In this adaptation of primitivism and abandonment of perspective in favor of a flat, two-dimensional picture plane, Picasso makes a radical departure from traditional European painting. *Les Demoiselles* was revolutionary and controversial and led to widespread anger and disagreement, even amongst the painter's closest associates and friends. At the time of its first exhibition in 1916, the painting was deemed immoral.

— Excerpted from Wikipedia

An addiction exists when a person's attachment to a sensation, an object, or another person is such as to lessen his appreciation of and ability to deal with other things in his environment, or in himself, so that he has become increasingly dependent on that experience as his only source of gratification. A person will be predisposed to addiction to the extent that he cannot establish a meaningful relationship to his environment as a whole, and thus cannot develop a fully elaborated life.

— Stanton Peele and Archie Brodsky,
Love and Addiction, 1975

(As to animal addiction): Monkeys kept in a small cage with an injection apparatus strapped to their backs are deprived of the variety of stimulation their natural environment provides. All they can do is push the lever (injecting the opiate).

— Stanton Peele and Archie Brodsky, 1975,
"A General Theory of Addiction," *Love and*
Addiction (which prompted Rat Park experiments)

Addiction may occur with any potent experience.

— Stanton Peele, "How Can Addiction Occur with Other
than Drug Involvements?" *British Journal of*

"""

Addiction (now called Addiction), 1985

> When I read *The Meaning of Addiction,* I noted how you said that Orthodox Jews who smoked readily gave up their cigarettes on the Sabbath. I knew that. But I never thought what that said about addiction.
>
> — Ethan Nadelmann, founding director,
> Drug Policy Alliance

I saw very early that addiction is not a result of drug use or limited to drugs, that people can recover without abstaining (harm reduction), that people usually recover on their own, and that social and environmental factors are the principal causes and preventive factors in addiction. I published these ideas from the 1970s to the present in popular magazines, professional newsletters, academic journals, books, and then blog posts. I published articles in America's leading journal on alcoholism: one on genetics and another that won the journal's award as the best article of the year. In that piece, "The Limitations of Control-of-Supply Models for Explaining and Treating Drug Addiction," published in *The Journal of Studies on Alcohol and Drugs*, I reviewed the body of cultural and clinical data showing that increased availability or more regular consumption of drugs and alcohol were *not* the equivalent of addiction and alcoholism. In fact, societies where alcohol is regularly and traditionally consumed, like Italy, have *lower* rates of alcoholism.

Rather, it is the style of consumption and the meaning of the substance and its use that determine how it is consumed and how its effects are experienced. In Italy, which displays far fewer alcohol-related harms, alcohol is typically consumed with meals, in multi-generational, gender-mixed groups, and with explicit norms that emphasize that alcohol is *not* to be used as an excuse for misbehavior. When Americans consume opioid painkillers for ailments they are seeking to overcome within normally well-organized and motivated lives, they don't become addicted. Inflating the power and meaning of these substances, demonizing them to give them overwhelming control over the individual, *actually creates the outcomes of addiction and alcoholism that we supposedly detest.*

And, indeed, in what researchers and public health advocates term a "confounding" paradox, despite having "successfully demonized" alcohol and drugs so that their use declined significantly in America through the 2010s, deaths from both substances have achieved "epidemic" proportions.

Although I developed my ideas over decades against intense resistance, the kernels of all of them were part of my and Archie's 1975 mass-marketed best seller, *Love and Addiction*. In *L&A* we said any compelling activity can be addictive if it absorbs a person's consciousness while blocking the possibility for other rewards. As Archie and I wrote:

> Addiction is not a chemical reaction. Addiction is an experience, one which grows out of an individual's routinized response to something that has special meaning for him—something, anything, that he finds so safe and reassuring that he cannot be without it, even as it wreaks havoc on the rest of his life.

I didn't formulate my theory of addiction for career advancement (although I would have welcomed that). I came to it out of conviction and dedication to the truth. For better or worse, my life revolves around finding and expressing meaning.

My story raises five questions: How did I come to this desire for meaning? How was I motivated and able to maintain my vision without any type of institutional support and in the face of overwhelming skepticism and personal attacks? How did I develop my essential insights into addiction, so many of which have become part of the way we see and understand addiction in the twenty-first century? Yet why is it that following these ideas through in all of their implications remains unacceptable popularly and impossible for people in the field? And, finally, why are so many in high places in the addiction field unable, or unwilling, to recognize my seminal role in thinking about addiction, along with my ideas themselves? I have already addressed some of these questions. Let me go on.

Discovering Addiction in My Philly Home

I was never addicted to drugs, like those good middle-class achievers Maia Szalavitz and Marc Lewis, whatever about their upbringings led them into and out of drug addictions in their early (Maia)-late (Marc) twenties.

But I was always fascinated by addiction, by people's being out of control of themselves. I witnessed a neighbor in South Philly (where I lived until age 7) being carried home, drunk, ranting and raving. The man's behavior—his attitude—was in complete contrast with the values I had been taught. I was preoccupied with this spectacle and asked my mother constant questions about it. I saw in his behavior traces of what I observed around me in my home, *sans* the substance use.

When I was twelve, now living in a modest row house in Northeast Philadelphia, I was reading the *Philadelphia Bulletin*. An article described a man with a drinking problem who had returned from rehab, during which time his wife had moved them to a new residence. Seeing all the boxes stacked around the new apartment, he ran out of the house to embark on another bender, disappearing for a week.

I thought, "I know people who act like that, who are overwhelmed by change and challenge. Ted!" That's right, my father, who went ape shit if anything was out of place in our small Philly house. His response was the same as the alcoholic the newspaper described, sans the drinking. I said to myself: "Alcoholism is a way of coping like when my father melts down and screams. Only both his screaming and that guy's drinking make matters worse!"

Whereas, I was to learn, people had developed all kinds of ersatz theories of how alcohol affected alcoholics' brains, yada yada yada, I had just seen into the heart of the matter. Alcoholism was a way of responding to the world for people who regularly relied on that response—couldn't live without it, they thought—in order to deal with otherwise unmanageable life experience, the same way my father relied on his over-the-top emotional reactions.

And Then There Was Love

Remember how Maia Szalavitz, the unloved child, described how she became addicted to heroin: "For me, heroin provided a sense of comfort, safety and love that I couldn't get from other people." Do you see why she was drawn to *Love and Addiction*?

Let me describe how I saw love and addiction in those around me. I was in Penn's General Honors Program with many brilliant kids. When we were sophomores, my Penn roommate "Warren" started dating a high school girl, "Joan." I was a good friend of Warren's. But when he began seeing Joan, he went all in with her. Despite his charm and brilliance, Warren, who was a short nerd, had never had a real girlfriend. He loved the experience.

For her part, Joan, a rebellious teen in her own household, accepted Warren's devotion and control—it was preferable to her home situation. Joan was attractive and smart, a great girlfriend, and Warren welcomed her devotion. Archie and I found it strange that Warren would opt out of his other relationships to spend all of his time with a naive 17-year-old. Warren instead concluded, "Why would I spend time with my friends whenever I have a chance to be with Joan?"

I lived with Warren in several apartments in West Philly, some of which were slums, while we went to Penn. Archie moved into a larger one of them with us after his own roommate got married in our junior year.

(That couple are still married fifty-plus years later.) Archie and I had to find a new third roommate as seniors, however, when Warren and Joan married that summer. Joan, 19, had completed her freshman year at a Philadelphia college, Temple. Warren was 21.

It might have been a true love story, right? Joan completed her sophomore year at Temple while we completed our senior year at Penn. Then Warren, brilliant as he was, got a prestigious fellowship to Berkeley, and Joan transferred there. They moved into a delightful Berkeley apartment. We had plenty of opportunity to visit. After their first year at Berkeley, Joan quit the marriage.

Joan was a good-looking, inquisitive 20-year-old woman who was exposed to Berkeley in the late 1960s. She was sharing the life of a stay-at-home physics grad student. What might happen? Right, and it did. Joan had an affair and left Warren. She was resentful, feeling that she had been dominated by an older(!) man.

I was in graduate school in Michigan when this happened. I said to myself and to Archie, who was living in New York with the roommate who, after replacing Warren in our Penn apartment and was now at Columbia Law School: "I thought that was love. But isn't love a real connection between people that survives shocks and changing life conditions—at least for a substantial period? Joan and Warren were devoted to each other—for barely a couple of years. That connection was a temporary fix for each of their situations. It was an addiction!"

Joan and Warren both remarried. We'll leave those relationships alone. Warren became a distinguished academic. I now sometimes worry whether my own relationship style was clearly better than Warren and Joan's. But I did have an enduring, thirty-year marriage. And there are clearly many worse, more destructive relationships. At one extreme, people abuse and kill their partners, or commit suicide after breakups.

Writer and TV advice columnist E. Jean Carroll described being raped by Donald Trump (whom she didn't know) in Bloomingdale's in her 2019 memoir, *What Do We Need Men For?* Carroll's book reviews her interactions with men throughout her life, all of which carried betrayal, disappointment, and abuse. Brilliant, beautiful, and caring, Carroll makes the case that intimate male-female relationships are inherently fetid. She never had an intimate relationship after her encounter with Trump in the 1990s.

None of the interactions she describes involved love, which she seems not to have known. On the other hand, people obviously have long, happy, satisfying intimate relationships. You and I know some. I thought my brother had one when he committed suicide. Clearly, intimacy and love can be unpacked to find deeper meanings and dysfunctions.

Love is a powerful feeling to which people devote themselves, with good and bad—sometimes the worst—results. Is that a different universe from drugs?

And, Then, There Was Heroin, and Charles Winick

When I was in college, my girlfriend, "Deborah," lived with two male friends who used heroin. I requested that they shoot me up. I then snorted it a few times, once with Deborah, together with another young girlfriend, "Rochelle." We had group sex. (Rochelle went on to become a distinguished professor of Buddhism.)

I didn't get heroin. It made it impossible for me to orgasm—a common effect of narcotics. Why was that a desirable experience? I preferred other available options to the soporific effects of narcosis. In viewing this mystical drug's effects in the context of my life, I concluded it wasn't worth it. Which is what most people conclude when they quit as their lives solidify (as Maia did in her early twenties).

So I have taken heroin, like LSD, as a day-tripper. But I wasn't a candidate for drug addiction, even as everyone believed that heroin was inevitably, inherently addictive.

I Was the Heroin Addict in the Room!

I went to the University of Michigan for graduate school with Don des Jarlais, who became a well-known drug and AIDS researcher. (Don read and commented on an early version of *Love and Addiction*.) Don spoke to his church congregation about drugs. And he brought me in as someone who used heroin.

Does anything show the absurdity of our view of drugs more than parading me, a Ph.D. student, as an example of a heroin user and drug addiction? The visit fell flat. I did come back and lead my own discussion with the group about addiction, beginning with, "Don't you see how heroin isn't even a temptation for a motivated person like me?"

But I was learning that I was the rule, not the exception, just as Maia was the rule for recovery from heroin addiction. And the person I learned that most from was Charles Winick, whom I didn't know personally at the time.

Let me jump to the conclusion of my relationship with Charles. In July of 2015, visiting my friend Larry (with whom I had studied Japanese decades earlier at Stanford) in Idaho, I received a call from Charles's nephew. Charles had died and his nephew asked me to contribute to Charles's memorial service, which I gladly did. Charles's obituary appeared in the *New York Times*. It summarizes what I learned from Charles and what I wrote about his work for his nephew down to (nearly) the last word:

> His views on drug addiction provoked controversy. He said that opiates "are usually harmless, but they are taken under unsatisfactory conditions" (including malnutrition and infection), that most heroin addicts eventually outgrow their addiction, that many addicts with sufficient financial resources can function normally, and that those who cannot should be treated as patients with a chronic disease. [The last clause was the obituary writer's add-on, about which I will say more.]

My connection to Winick tracks back to 1968. While at Michigan, I read a lengthy article in the *Times* about the burning issue of the late sixties, drugs. Of course, the kids I knew smoked marijuana, which everyone did then, yet for which at the time even college kids could get arrested and have their lives ruined. Later, that fate was reserved for inner-city drug users.

Because all illegal drugs were lumped together, the article, published the day after my twenty-second birthday, focused on heroin. Winick was quoted as follows about heroin and other opioids—opiates "are usually harmless, but they are taken under unsatisfactory conditions" that led to malnutrition and infection. Bam! I could say that sentence changed my life, which I later told Charles. Who knew that about heroin? Not I, even though I had taken heroin with two young guys who had jobs and led normal lives.

When I tried to tell people I knew around Michigan about this revelation, they laughed at me. Everyone knew how deadly heroin was! But what did these middle-class people at an elite university actually know about heroin and addiction? Everything they thought they knew—that heroin was instantly and everlastingly addictive—was based on nothingness and myth. And so my fascination with what people thought about drugs and addiction was born. It was one more sign that the subject of addiction and I were meant for each other.

As we wrote *Love and Addiction*, Archie and I read Winick's research, especially the now classic "Maturing Out of Narcotic Addiction." Winick's prescient 1962 research article found that two-thirds to three-quarters of young men known to the Federal Bureau of Narcotics as heroin addicts, who began taking the drugs in their teens and twenties, ceased using heroin by their midthirties. To this day, this paper and the term "maturing out" take my breath away.

Bam! But when I tried telling people that, well, you know, they said heroin inevitably addicted users until they died.

Actually, Winick's most radical research, published the year before "Maturing Out," in 1961, concerned physicians who were discovered pilfering narcotics, drugs that many had ready access to. Winick found that only two of ninety-eight physicians he interviewed who had been to the Lexington Public Health Hospital for addiction treatment turned themselves in because they were using uncontrollably. In fact, "most were useful and effective members of their community" whose drug use had been discovered when their drug records were inspected.

Bam! Highly successful professionals used narcotics regularly without any discernible problems for years, for decades—for their whole lives! That's the story of the pioneer of modern American surgery, William Stewart Halsted, who used cocaine and morphine throughout his distinguished career, a fact that medical historian Howard Markel turned into a 2011 best-selling fable, *An Anatomy of Addiction: Sigmund Freud, William Halsted, and the Miracle Drug Cocaine*. Markel's thesis faces the difficulty described at Amazon: "One (of these addicts) became the father of psychoanalysis; the other of modern surgery." Markel had to work harder fitting Freud into his paradigm, since he gave up cocaine early in his career. Indeed, Markel attributes Freud's later use of free association and discovering the unconscious to his earlier cocaine use. Wasn't that a productive outcome of using drugs?

I went around telling people that narcotics users weren't necessarily disadvantaged, or hurt by their use. Their reactions? Oh, you know.

Later, in *The Meaning of Addiction*, based on the work of Winick and quite a few other researchers, I wrote: "heroin does not appear to differ significantly in the potential range of its use from other types of involvements, and even compulsive users cannot be distinguished from those given to other habitual involvements in the ease with which they desist or shift their patterns of use." Today, Carl Hart makes this point.

At the time, our main point in *Love and Addiction* was this: since no drug or drugs had the special quality of being addictive, and since other behaviors could be equally compulsive and destructive, then, as we wrote, *"why not look at the whole range of things, activities, and even people to which we can and do become addicted? We must, in fact, do this if addiction is to be made a viable concept."*

Which is happening almost a half-century later in the addiction world, as even the official psychiatric manual, *DSM-5*, has opened itself to recognizing "behavioral addictions." Yet Carl, and others, having thrown out the idea of drugs as inherently addictive, can't make the leap to seeing that addiction does exist, but isn't an exclusive function of drug use.

Heroes with Clay Feet

One passage in Winick's maturing-out article really struck me:

> The difference between those who mature out of addiction and those who do not may also mirror the difference between addicts who struggle to abandon addiction and may develop some insight, and those who decide that they are hooked, make no effort to abandon addiction, and give in to what they regard as inevitable.

Here Winick presented the essence of what I believe—that people who were convinced that they were addicts, that they were "hooked," and who gave up on the possibility that they could cease to be addicted became lifelong "addicts." *He knew this in the early 1960s.*

Elsewhere, Winick typically cut to the heart of what addiction was about, which we reprised in *Love and Addiction*:

> The euphoria of the addict is a feeling of temporary well-being induced by the drug's suppression of discomfort or pain. The addict's "high" is a feeling of aloofness from current situations and a postponement of decisions or urgencies. The drug is the decision. It provides a feeling of security and self-sufficiency. It temporarily helps to establish self-confidence and quell any disturbing aggressiveness. The drug itself is so fulfilling that it becomes the center of the user's whole life.

In the case of the inner-city addicts Winick studied, although they found this feeling sublime, in fact it seriously degraded their daily lives. "Addicts seldom achieve vocational success, because their ability to consummate their frequently high aspirations and fantasies is likely to be impaired by self-neglect and their need to engage in self-defeating, self-hurting behavior." Yet Winick's research showed that this wasn't due to the drug, but to the addicted person's severely limited outlook and environment. This was obvious considering the supposedly addicted physicians he studied at Lexington who were virtually all "useful and effective members of their community" (think Halsted and Freud).

But Winick, revolutionary thinker that he was, couldn't get beyond conventional thinking to see that his maturing-out and doctor-"addict" research in fact *disproved* that addiction was a disease, an idea he never relinquished. (See his *Times* obituary above.)

And so, Charles could never make the leap to seeing addiction as a pattern of feeling, thinking, and behavior that extended beyond narcotics—

i.e., that the addiction syndrome wasn't anchored to drugs. This insight was imbedded in Charles's descriptions of inner-city heroin addicts. But even most inner-city heroin users did not display this syndrome, as surveys of such users by social epidemiologists showed.

The Kandels and Addiction

I met Charles at a presentation I made at a seminar run by Denise Kandel at Columbia Medical School. Kandel is a drug epidemiologist who is married to Nobel Prize–winner Eric Kandel. Eric Kandel knows that addiction is a brain disease. He is a professor emeritus of neuroscience and psychiatry at Columbia University, where Carl Hart is currently a professor of psychology and psychiatry. The two shall never meet, or at least debate.

But Eric Kandel did debate Marc Lewis, another anti-disease theorist who pays tribute to my formative role in his thinking. The meeting was described in a 2016 article in *The Chronicle of Higher Education*, "What If Addiction Is Not a Disease?" At the meeting, Kandel lectured Marc as though he were a child, which Marc couldn't handle:

> Before the first morning session was over, it was clear that the accepted wisdom regarding substance abuse and the brain is still largely a matter of debate.
>
> Rhetorical fireworks went off immediately after the conference's inaugural presentation, given by the Nobel Prize-winning neuropsychiatrist Eric Kandel. A professor at Columbia University and director of its Kavli Institute for Brain Science, Kandel described his research on memory disorders, mental illness, and addiction, including studies on mice that show nicotine use can lead to cocaine abuse.
>
> Marc Lewis, a neuroscientist and professor of developmental psychology at Radboud University, in the Netherlands, kicked off the day's first round table by challenging Kandel's implicit contention that addiction is a disease. Lewis's argument, outlined in his 2015 book, *The Biology of Desire: Why Addiction Is Not a Disease*, is that dependence on substances and other behavioral patterns are learned via the "neural circuitry of desire," and do not result in permanent, irreversible changes to the brain.

Kandel then insulted Lewis:

> When Lewis pushed back, arguing that the brain changes all the time, Kandel became exasperated. "I think we need a course in biology before we go any further, to be honest with you," he said.

How arrogant! We can't disagree with Kandel because he's the great scientist. They needed me to explain that real science explains actual human behavior.

When I had presented alongside an NYU neuroscientist almost two decades earlier, he described the behavior of the fabled "crack whore" who will do anything for crack. When I spoke, I described the gambler who spends his family's savings, loses his house and family, and goes to jail.

What is that, I asked? My neuroscientific opponent countered, "That's a behavioral addiction." Of course, that neuroscientist didn't really believe that drug and behavioral syndromes are the same syndromes, because gambling isn't a drug, and they study drugs.

And now, nearly fifty years after I analyzed addiction that way, the establishment is half-way betwixt and between the old view and my view of addiction—as represented by *DSM-5*, which says that gambling is an addiction, but doesn't label any drug that way! I am a go-to source for addictive gambling. Needless to say, however, I make clear that *DSM-5*, and American psychiatry, make no sense in their addiction classification.

Six Questions for Eric Kandel

1. Do most people outgrow addiction? (We know they do.)
2. Have most people in this audience who were addicted to cigarettes quit? (A large majority of ever-smokers will have done so.)
3. Considering that your "studies on mice show nicotine use can lead to cocaine abuse," in what percentage of cases did that happen with humans, say in the 1980s? (A small number of people, often with disadvantaged social backgrounds or divergent life paths, so that we can make no generalizations about the drugs themselves.)
4. If a person destroys their life due to a compulsive habit, is that an addiction? (Yes, as *DSM-5* took the first steps in recognizing.)
5. On what grounds did you decide that it's not an addiction if the compulsive habit doesn't involve a substance? (Per my earlier debate with a neuroscientist, this is an arbitrary American bias that, in my wake, American psychiatry has now resolved in my favor.)
6. Are addictions diagnosed by brain scans? Will they ever be? (No matter what Kandel claims to have discovered in mice—no, never!)

How does AA relate to the brain disease theory?

Although I wasn't at the disease symposium (surprise), the *Chronicle* gave as much space to my views as it did to Marc's or Kandel's. The article *didn't* quote me about brain science, about which the author and I spent hours on the phone. Instead, he used me to discuss AA:

One of the earliest and most compelling critics of AA is Stanton Peele, a psychologist and writer who has been challenging its disease-based model since the mid-70s, when the organization was still an emerging cultural force. Peele argues that AA's methodology, steeped in spiritual rhetoric, is unscientific, predicated on the notion that only by acknowledging their powerlessness over alcohol and accepting a higher power can an addict find salvation. He's also quick to point out, along with other critics of the 12-step model, that traditional treatment programs, which generally rely on it, have a depressingly low success rate.

Peele believes that instead of adapting the disempowering language of disease (which he says is itself stigmatizing), addicts should accept their failings and pursue mindfulness techniques, not to find a cure but to ease anxiety and consider how their history, environmental influences, and personal relationships inform their habits, good and bad. (Well put; my emphasis.)

Everything I say about AA's disease theory is true for the chronic brain-disease theory of addiction. Lewis and others who critique that theory whose work I describe in Chapter 10—Maia Szalavitz, Johann Hari, Bruce Alexander, Sally Satel—would never say bad things about AA. Mention AA, an American icon, and they run for cover. Yet AA has already done seventy-five years of damage in the US that the chronic brain disease model can only catch up to. Here's one of hundreds, thousands of stories that I have received:

Dear Dr. Stanton Peele,
I need your advice.

Let me start off by saying how much I appreciate your research and your dedication to your work in the field of addiction. And my goodness do I wish that you could come to the agency that I work for and give them a training on what you know and have seen in this field. I unfortunately work with people who have very narrow views on recovery. I understand that for them this is what has worked. But that must be the only way?

The 12-step way was my way at first. For several years I was very dedicated and completely abstinent. I "worked a good program." I live in a small town. And if you don't work the program to others' standards, well then, you just aren't in recovery. Same people, same stories, same sadness over and over again. It did work for me in the beginning. I was very tired of my [drug] addiction and the consequences that I had faced as a result.

Here is my truth. In my third year of complete abstinence I went to a concert and had a couple of drinks. I felt like a complete failure. Looking back now, and working in the addiction field myself, I can see clearly how such guilt can derail someone from recovery. I then chose to keep this my secret, which did not feel good. But I knew that if I didn't I would be told that I was in relapse mode and that I would return to my drug of choice soon. We say this about our clients, who are chastised and dehumanized for NOT being in recovery. I returned to my recovery community, continued to participate in the 12-step program, and didn't relate my truth to anyone at the alcohol and drug program where I worked.

The following year I had a couple of drinks at an event. This time I intended to have the drinks. I still felt bad and guilty, because everyone that I work with believes abstinence is the ONLY way to recover. Hell, that is what I thought and had been taught. At this point I was no longer attending the 12-step program. It just felt too dishonest.

I have been in recovery since 2005. I now drink occasionally. I feel like I have a choice and that I can be in recovery and have a drink.

It wasn't until I began to conduct my own research on recovery that I found that there are many paths to recovery. That is when I stumbled on your work, purchased your books, and was so INSPIRED!

I feel proud at times that this is MY life and my recovery, but I know that I will be shunned if I tell my truth. Why? I overcame a serious addiction and I have no desire to live in the dysfunction and chaos that created. I now believe in moderation. I feel that I am a healthy person who is functioning well.

What hurts me the most is having to push 12-step and abstinence onto others for my job. I used to do that very well, but as time goes on I just don't feel that's right. And while our agency is getting a little better at using other, less directive techniques, for the most part, staff here believe that if someone is not abstinent and working a 12-step program, they are failing.

What really angers me is the way that they talk about such people and laugh at them. It has driven me to tears. In the larger world, however, I perceive that most people are not in the 12-step program and have chosen other paths and still live happy, healthy, and productive lives.

How can I make this field better, more realistic? I feel that I need to start speaking my truth. Yet I am afraid. I just want to connect with someone who has a broader idea of recovery.

Thank you for your life's dedication to this work. It has enabled me to truly recover.
—Gordon

"Scott" puts it more simply:

Dr. Peele,
I just wanted to say "thank you."

I just finished your book, *7 Tools to Beat Addiction*, and found it very helpful.

12-step programs have never helped me and would usually push me right back into my bad habits.

I quit smoking cigarettes without any formal intervention, replacement therapy, or counseling, so I knew it was possible.

I am truly inspired by your book and will utilize the tools and training. I'm currently forty-six days (and counting) without abusing illegal drugs.

Keep up your good and very necessary work!
—Scott (February, 2021)

Stories People Tell about Their Addictions

Why would a person be afraid to speak the truth as he encounters it? Do you recall when Drew Barrymore was on the cover of *People* magazine as America's youngest (13-year-old) addict? She reappeared on the cover of *People* after entering rehab and attempting suicide, as recounted in her best seller, *Little Girl Lost*, written at age fourteen.

Now Barrymore is a Hollywood power player, has two daughters to whom she is devoted, and likes wine (Drew founded a winery!). Barrymore now refers to the recovery community as her support, but says that she is not "in recovery," since she "occasionally" drinks wine. Recovery groups and treatment rehabs walk the same fine line in dealing with Barrymore. ("Don't try this at home!") Why would Barrymore never speak out that her 'lifetime disease' was bullshit? Because to do so is to risk all that she has attained if she were to rile the ubiquitous recovery community, in Hollywood and throughout America.

In fact, Barrymore's is the typical story, one that Zach Rhoads (who experienced it) and I tell in our 2019 book, *Outgrowing Addiction*. In his 2014 book on the limitations and failures of AA, *The Sober Truth*, Harvard psychoanalyst Lance Dodes solicited interviews from people who had attended AA. While some reported being helped, a much larger group said they hadn't been. And a considerable number (more than were helped) reported harmful experiences. But Dodes couldn't fully deal with this information.

Other anti-AA books likewise fail to convey the message that AA and its disease theory are actually *at the heart of* American's alcohol and drug problems, rather than *solving* them. In her 2013 book *Her Best-Kept Secret*, Gabrielle Glaser (who is a friend of mine) told about the failures of AA, of whom she was one. Yet in *Secret* and a series of well-placed articles in *The Atlantic* and the harm reduction periodical *Filter*—Glaser claims, against the actual research, that naltrexone and Baclofen are chemical agents that remove the yearning for alcohol and thus solve alcoholism. Anyone who believes this delusion (which I speak more about in Chapter 11) doesn't understand addiction.

The field *has* opened itself to Gordon's (above) and Barrymore's journeys and my messages of self-determination and a broader definition of recovery. But that development is *overwhelmed* by the constant disease bombardment Americans receive. The TV show *Mom*, featuring as a recovering mother and daughter Allison Janney and Anna Faris, is one of a legion. Faris is an appealing actress, writer and advice podcaster. She recounts excessive drinking and drug use in her coming-of-age memoir as an awkward, socially isolated young person, *Unqualified*. But the disease of alcohol and idea of recovery are no part of her story as she grew into an adult social drinker. *That* story you won't see on TV and at the movies.

Mary Karr, author of *The Liar's Club*, is the presiding literary force in presenting AA and recovery as essential to Americans. One of Karr's students, Koren Zailckas, wrote her own alcoholic memoir, *Smashed: Story of a Drunken Girlhood*. While Zailckas gives credit to Karr as the inspiration for youthful memoirists, Zailckas herself gave up her alcoholism without AA after she graduated. Zailckas refuses to call herself an alcoholic, a refusal for which she is now attacked. We simply cannot hear the message that regarding addiction as a disease is *more* than unnecessary. It is the *core* of our addictive culture.

Me, Denise, and Charles

Eric Kandel's wife, Denise Kandel, and Winick are social epidemiologists. They investigate actual patterns of drug use or addiction in different populations. They do so by taking surveys, or by examining public records, or by following the lives of drug users. *In this way, they learn about the actual lives of addicted people.* This research paints a totally different picture from Eric Kandel's inviolable principles of addiction "revealed" by examining brain scans in isolation from people's lived experience—or with mice.

I met Winick after Mary and I had returned from California in 1977 to the New York area. Denise Kandel invited me to speak to a group of drug epidemiologists who met monthly at Columbia's department of psychiatry at the New York State Psychiatric Institute. Mary went with me to the seminar—it was one of those signs she sought, and once in a while got, that I was esteemed as a professional.

Mary was bubbling with excitement when I introduced myself to Winick. She knew how indebted to him I was. After my presentation on how addiction was not a drug phenomenon, but a general pattern of behavior, Charles, a kindly man, said, "I see where you're coming from." But, like Denise Kandel, who isn't a self-effacing personality, Winick was too intellectually modest to think he had light to cast on addiction per se.

Norman Zinberg

I met Harvard psychiatrist Norman Zinberg in several different contexts. I once visited his Cambridge home for a drink, where I met his musical satirist friend, Tom Lehrer. No one's views of addiction were as close to mine as Norman's. Yet he opposed me.

Zinberg had studied heroin users and discovered that they didn't resemble the "man with the golden arm." Unlike Frank Sinatra's character in the film of that name, they didn't experience melodramatic withdrawal when they periodically quit. Nicotine withdrawal is often just as bad, or worse. More shockingly, Zinberg investigated those who went from being addicted to controlled heroin use.

That's a tough story to tell. (Do you believe it?) And, yet, this is the same fluidity that epidemiologists note among problem drinkers, even for those classified as dependent, or alcoholic. Alcohol and drug attachments rise, fall, and disappear depending on where people are in life and with whom they associate—*exactly the opposite of the message of stasis and dissolution the disease theory relentlessly, cruelly drives home.*

Most remarkably, Zinberg understood that group and individual thinking about drugs and addiction (i.e., social learning) not only impacted whether and how people used heroin and other drugs, it *actually determined whether they experienced addiction.* Zinberg noted that hospital patients took narcotics more powerful than heroin without becoming addicted because they didn't see themselves as addicts who would go out to score narcotics on the street after they left the hospital. These findings and insights form the basis for Zinberg's 1984 classic, *Drug, Set, and Setting: The Basis for Controlled Intoxicant Use,* for which he was vilified almost as much as I have been.

Norman observed that people who became addicted to heroin were more likely to believe that the drug was addicting in the first place. He wrote the most radical thing about addiction to appear in a mass-circulation periodical (*The New York Times Magazine*) until I came along. After visiting Vietnam to study rampant heroin use there, Zinberg concluded that soldiers in different units in Vietnam experienced heroin entirely differently. How severely they underwent withdrawal, including not experiencing it at all, was deeply influenced by their and their cohorts' beliefs about the drug.

Howard at Fire Island

Howard Josepher is a famous New York harm reductionist who smokes marijuana and drinks and has done so since he quit heroin in his late twenties (he is now in his eighties). Howard quit heroin at a TC (therapeutic community), which he swears by to this day.

I know Howard and visited him at his fabulous home on Fire Island, a place he had been coming to for decades.

> **Me**: "What did you do about heroin withdrawal when you came here and couldn't score drugs?" (Howard had just described writhing on the floor of his Rikers Island jail cell when he was without drugs for two weeks.)
>
> **Howard**: "I didn't experience that here—I did drink and smoke marijuana, and that got me by."
>
> Which is what he does to this day. Howard might have created FI (Fire Island) therapy, instead of endorsing TCs. People all the time leave off addictions by switching life settings: think of returning Vietnam veterans.

Norman Zinberg's work was a revelation for me; I admired his independence and bravery so much. (Norman never got tenure at Harvard Medical School, even though he was world famous.) I wrote in *Meaning* (which was published in 1985, the year after Zinberg's book) about his one-person campaign, against intense opposition, to explain that controlled use of narcotics was possible and commonplace. In doing so, he regularly contested the world's pharmacologists:

> In their understandable desire to avoid the ambiguities of moral categories of behavior, these investigators seek to restrict the term addiction to the most limited physiological phenomena. Thus they claim that physical dependence is a straightforward measure of addiction. However, this retrenchment is inimical to their purpose of satisfactorily conceptualizing and operationalizing addictive behavior. It is also *irreconcilable with their own observation that the effort to separate psychological habituation and physical dependence is futile, as well as with their forceful objections to the idea that psychic dependence is less inevitable and more susceptible to the elements of set and setting than is physical dependence* [my emphasis].

The italicized sentence is the statement most like my views ever uttered by another figure in the drug addiction field. Zinberg expressed the fundamental insight (albeit in impenetrable language) that the way we, as individuals and a culture, think about something makes it more or less addictive, more so than drugs' chemical effects: "the behavior resulting from the wish for a desired object, whether chemical or human, is not the result of differentiation between a physiological or psychological attachment. . . . Nor does the presence of physical symptoms per se serve to separate these two types of dependence."

But Zinberg wore blinders, too, as did another radical researcher, Lee Robins, who studied returning Vietnam veterans addicted to heroin, most of whom readily quit at home. I noted Robins's blind spots in *The Meaning of Addiction*:

Yet a similar reluctance to acknowledge the consequences of nonaddictive narcotics use is evident even in the writings of the very investigators who have demonstrated that such use occurs. Robins equated the use of illicit drugs with drug abuse, primarily because previous studies had done so, and maintained that among all drugs heroin creates the greatest dependency. She believed this even as she noted that "heroin as used in the streets of the United States does not differ from other drugs in its liability to being used regularly or on a daily basis" and that "heroin is 'worse' than amphetamines or barbiturates only because 'worse' people use it." In this way, controlled use of narcotics—and of all illicit substances—and compulsive use of legal drugs are both disguised, obscuring the personality and social factors that actually distinguish styles of using any kind of drug.

Norman, who was so much on the same page as I was, found me too challenging intellectually and personally. Once, in a well-attended panel discussion at Harvard (Archie was there) involving Zinberg and George Vaillant, the first question from the audience was, "Isn't the main issue what Stanton Peele asks in the title of his book: *How Much Is Too Much?*" Neither of them was prepared to acknowledge me. (Neither ever referred to me in his writing.) And, yet, per the seminar, I was unavoidable.

George Vaillant and Me

Both Zinberg and Vaillant were Harvard psychiatrists. While Zinberg regarded addiction almost identically to how I did, George Vaillant was a champion of AA—he went on to become an AA board member. But his dedication to AA doesn't reflect the depth and breadth of Vaillant's work, which traced how people coped and functioned—sometimes better, sometimes worse—over the course of their lives.* Vaillant came to give intellectual legitimacy to AA and the disease concept in his acclaimed 1983 book, *The Natural History of Alcoholism*. But why "natural history"? *Vaillant found AA and 12-step treatment were "no more effective than the natural course of the disease."*

Although his data analysis showed that most of his alcohol-dependent subjects did drink again after recovery, and that a solid majority recovered *without AA, every single case Vaillant described was of a successful AA member, or someone who didn't join AA, drank again, and died.* I labeled Vaillant's book intellectually dishonest in the *New York Times Book Review*. Vaillant

---

* Although *The Natural History of Alcoholism* is a shipwreck, several of Vaillant's other books are remarkable studies of lives: *Triumphs of Experience, Aging Well* and his original classic, *Adaptation to Life*. Vaillant later engaged in even more farfetched examples of reductionism than he did in *Natural History* in *Spiritual Evolution: A Scientific Defense of Faith*.

was nonetheless lionized; but my views are central to *Natural History's* Wikipedia entry:

> Perhaps the sharpest critic of Vaillant's work was controlled drinking proponent Stanton Peele. In a 1983 review in *The New York Times* (*Book Review*), Peele wrote that "The results of this research do not provide ready support for the disease theory of alcoholism. . . . [For example, Vaillant] finds strong evidence in the inner city group for sociocultural causality in alcoholism." In his book *Diseasing of America* (1989) Peele claimed that "Vaillant emphatically endorses the disease model. . . . However, Vaillant's claims are not supported by his own data."

In fact, I requisitioned Vaillant's data through Harvard Medical School to reanalyze it in *Diseasing*. Vaillant wasn't pleased with me. For years he began his talks deriding my views on controlled drinking. George and I met around the world—for instance, cross-country skiing at a natural recovery work group in Switzerland in 1999 (Mary took a photo of us), or when we shared a cab as joint recipients of lifetime achievement awards at the International Meaning Conference on Addiction in Vancouver in 2006. In person, George was always cordial.

Oddities in Addiction History

In the 1980s ABC flew me to Boston, where I debated Vaillant for hours in a hotel function room (Archie was there) with ABC's medical editor Nancy Snyderman as the moderator. None of it ever aired.

Zinberg, My Role Model, Rejected Me

Although Vaillant was my sworn enemy, I had much more face time—both personally and professionally—with George than Norman. At the same time, while Norman never discussed me and my work, Vaillant spoke of it frequently—only his references to me were always derogatory! But Norman never acknowledged my existence professionally at all. Isn't that sad—for him? The same holds for Kasia Malinowska, head of George Soros's international drug program, as I describe in the next chapter.

Bruce Alexander was my colleague and friend who showed that rats eschewed opiates in a capacious "Rat Park" with other rats, even though they became "addicted" in a small, isolated cage. Bruce, along with Zinberg and Carl Hart (my relationship with whom I discuss in Chapter 10), most understands drugs and addiction the way I do. He organized a conference in Vancouver in the 1980s, a few years before Zinberg died in 1989. When Zinberg spoke after me, he ridiculed my views (he never actually said my name): "Just because I read the newspaper every morning doesn't make me addicted!" I confronted him afterward: "Don't trivialize my ideas with an example like reading the newspaper, Norman." Like Winick, Zinberg simply was incapable of making the intellectual leap that his own work so clearly pointed to.

Nonetheless, as with Wikipedia's entry on Vaillant's book, I have insinuated myself into the core of addiction thinking and history. In an interview, Bruce says he was spurred to do the Rat Park experiments by my writing in *Love and Addiction*. I discuss how I saw this was true in the next section. Googling Bruce Alexander/Rat Park, by far the most cited reference is my book *The Meaning of Addiction*, in which Bruce and I co-authored a chapter: "Adult, Infant, and Animal Addiction."

And here is the first sentence in Zinberg's Wikipedia entry: "Dr. Norman Earl Zinberg was a psychoanalyst and psychiatrist whose research into addiction is seen as a great influence on current clinical models and greatly influenced the work of addiction treatment specialists such as Stanton Peele." Norman can't escape me.

Me and the Michigan Animal Lab

When I returned from South Africa in 1970, after I had gotten my initial contract with Penguin Books in England to write *Love and Addiction*, I moved into a garden apartment complex in Ann Arbor with my graduate school friend, Stan Morse. There, I had a casual liaison with a woman in our complex whose father was a prominent anesthesiologist at the University of Michigan medical school. That indirect linkage was to change the course of my life.

The University of Michigan housed the most extensive laboratory for animal research with drugs in the country. I asked my friend's father for an introduction to the head of Michigan's department of pharmacology, and went to see him to ask permission to see the animal lab. The lab was a sensitive topic because of animal liberation activists, and several such labs had been invaded at other universities.

I was there because one of the most common responses to my theory of addiction was, "Animals become addicted—so how can addiction be psychological and situational?" Even my closest friends and associates—including everyone I told my ideas to around the university—made such objections. That animal addiction was not an analogue for human addiction was apparent to me instantaneously. But I needed to fill in the picture. The pharmacology department chair must have found that I was a serious person, because he allowed me to visit the Michigan animal drug lab. Archie, visiting from New York, came along with me. What a strange pair we must have seemed!

I was later to know the man in charge of the lab, Charles "Bob" Schuster, who became head of the National Institute on Drug Abuse (Nora Volkow's current job), and his wife, Chris Johanson (see footnote in Chapter 1). They were among my biggest mainstream addiction boosters, although that amounted to being nice to me and saying nice things about me to people in the field. While Bob was head of the NIDA, when my family visited DC, he and Chris had Mary, me, and our two older children (Anna wasn't born yet) over for brunch. They had a daughter our children's age, and the kids ran around their large property. Thirty-five years later, Johann Hari (when he was still talking to me) told me that Chris said very nice things about me when he interviewed her about addiction. (Bob was by then dead.)

Back in 1970, at the Michigan animal lab, my and Archie's first contact was James Woods, who was to become a prominent professor of pharmacology. At the time, he was junior faculty and the on-site supervisor of the laboratory. Woods ushered us into his office, where I sat down across from him in my jeans, and Archie stood by the door.

> **Me:** Is it really possible to sort drugs into addictive and non-addictive categories? Don't people have identifiable withdrawal symptoms when they come off of cigarettes and marijuana? (Nicotine, as well as marijuana, was not labeled addictive at that time.)
>
> **Woods:** You could say that's true. But marijuana doesn't cause tolerance. (Note: tolerance is the decreasing observed effect of using a drug as the person adapts to its use. It is thought, like withdrawal, to be a purely biological phenomenon. But neither it nor withdrawal can be understood in such simple, mechanistic terms, as I explained in *Meaning*.)
>
> **Me:** Don't experienced marijuana smokers learn to function better over time when stoned? Isn't that tolerance?
>
> **Woods** (looking bemusedly at me): You could call that tolerance.

Woods seemed impressed with—or is "tolerant of" a better term—24-year-old me. He didn't question my being accompanied by Archie. He let us explore the lab at will. What we learned was that monkeys don't inject themselves with heroin (silly, huh?). They lived in small wire cages wearing an injection apparatus connected to their spines that delivered a drug when they pushed a lever. (This image will never leave my mind.)

And this proved that addiction was a pure, inexorable biological function? It proved the reverse. In an appendix in *Love and Addiction* (where our publisher forced us to put the good stuff) Archie and I wrote:

> Only animals respond to drugs in predictable ways, and only animals (especially encaged animals) respond uniformly to the onset of withdrawal by renewing their dosage of the drug. For a conditioning (learning) theory to explain human addiction, as well as non-addicted drug use, it must take into account the various social and personal reinforcements (i.e., rewards)—ego gratification, social approval, security, consistency with other values people hold—that motivate people in their drug use as in other activities.

Archie and I packed all of these insights into *Love and Addiction*, a book sold at supermarkets. These appendices anticipate almost every debate on addiction current today. We noted that almost no hospital patients continue using narcotics illegally when they finish treatment. They don't do that—even those who relish the narcotic experience—because that is simply not who they are.

In another appendix we anticipate Eric Kandel's and Nora Volkow's claims that addiction affects people's brains so as to deprive them of the ability to choose (i.e., of their free will). Here is the very last paragraph in our appendices as it appeared in *Love and Addiction* in 1975:

> Chemical reactions in the brain can, of course, be observed whenever a psychoactive drug is introduced. The existence of such reactions, and the fact that all psychological processes ultimately take the form of neural and chemical processes, should not be used to beg the questions raised by the impressive array of research, observations, and subjective reports that testify to the variability of human reactions to drugs.

A decade after *Love and Addiction*, I reviewed in *The Meaning of Addiction* how all such biological and "reward" models fail to adequately explain the range of reactions different people have to drugs and how their reactions change—even those who become addicted—as their situations and their lives change and they mature, leave Vietnam, discover vocations, have children, etc. The idea that drugs' effects on the brain deprive people of free will and put them on an inevitable downhill addictive slide is disproven by both a massive range of research data and the most commonplace human experiences—and especially the various shades of sobriety.

This complexity of the lived experience of addiction that we detailed in *Love and Addiction* and that I further explicated in *The Meaning of Addiction* is an essential human truth. Brain chemistry can never explain addiction. Never. There is no brain switch for addiction, only the grada-tions of neural flow that *contribute*, but only partly, to people's subjective experience and willingness to re-engage with a drug experience. Perhaps some people find alcohol or another drug particularly rewarding over time or in a given situation. But that doesn't then mean that they will disregard all of the other rewards in their lives, forever, to continue that experience. *And every piece of evidence and experience, from Drew Barry-more's life to people quitting smoking to Vietnam soldiers returning to the US, tells us that.*

Addiction is as complex as all human behavior. This is proven in daily life by people who quit smoking (and other addictions) because of their children, because of health concerns, because they are tired of being ad-dicted, because their spouses want them to, because they have or develop other values and goals in life. Sometimes the recovery process (most espe-cially with smoking, on average the longest-lived drug addiction at twenty-eight years, compared with sixteen for alcohol and four for cocaine) takes decades—it is a life process, as Archie and Mary and I described in our 1991 book, *The Truth About Addiction and Recovery.*

In a blog post from 2018, Nora Volkow labors under the burden of acknowledging *The Truth About Addiction and Recovery*:

> Some critics also point out, correctly, that a significant percentage of people who do develop addictions eventually recover without medical treatment. It may take years or decades, may arise from simply "aging out" of a disorder that began during youth, or *may result from any number of life changes that help a person replace drug use with other priorities* [my emphasis].

It hurts one's career, ironically, to be so far ahead of one's time, for which I have suffered, *especially* at the hands of those who follow Volkow's lead.

Writing almost forty years later, multivariate dataset analyst Gene Heyman (whom I discuss in Chapter 10) details the factors involved in recovery:

> The correlates of quitting include the absence of additional psychiatric and medi-cal problems, marital status (singles stay addicted longer), economic pressures, fear of judicial sanctions, concern about respect from children and other family members, worries about the many problems that attend regular involvement in illegal activities, more years spent in school, and higher income. Put in more per-sonal terms, *addicts often say that they quit drugs because they wanted to be a better parent, make their own parents proud of them, and not further embarrass their families* [my emphasis].

> ### Summary of My Discovery of the Meaning, Nature, and Sources of Addiction and Recovery
>
> I marvel at my pathway of discovery: family experiences and observations of friends' love lives → reading a Charles Winick quote in the *New York Times* → affair with a neighbor whose father was a prominent anesthesiologist → introduction to head of pharmacology department → day pass to Michigan animal lab (plus guest, Archie) → interaction with head of laboratory to present my views on addiction → observation of harnessed animals on whose behavior addiction theories were based → presenting my theories as an outsider in *Love and Addiction* (and later *The Meaning of Addiction*) → Bruce Alexander's being keyed into my insights in *L&A* and conducting the Rat Park experiments, then writing about "animal addiction" with me in *Meaning* → disputing notions of addiction held by even the most advanced social epidemiologists.
>
> Really, it's an impossible story. When our original British editor objected to my including how I took my first step to the Michigan animal labs by having an affair with a neighbor, my older friend Alta Ann said, "That's just your way of living."

Me and Harold Mulford

Archie and I met Hal Mulford at a 1988 conference of leading anti- and pro-disease figures in alcoholism treatment in San Diego, where we were taken by his unassuming manner and string bow tie. (It *never* seems right to call him "Harold." Forgive me for switching between calling a brilliant theorist "Mulford" and just plain "Hal"—but, in a way, that's the mark of the man.) Taken altogether, Hal was unique. Zinberg and Winick (both of whom focused on the then-big-city drug, heroin) were urban, academically bred Jews, like me. Hal, who was born in 1922, was raised on an Iowa farm and fought in World War II before getting a Ph.D. in sociology at the University of Iowa, where he spent the rest of his career.

Zinberg was a physician, psychiatrist, and psychoanalyst, while Winick was a social psychologist, like me. But I would expand the label of sociologist in Hal's case to "clinical sociologist," because Hal's life work mainly concerned alcoholics. Indeed, he at one point ran a treatment center for alcoholism—not a typical job for a sociologist.

Hal hooked up with Iowa's three-time Democratic governor, one-time elected senator, Harold Hughes. Their connection: Hughes identified himself as an alcoholic and owned and ran treatment rehabs. In his term as a senator, he sponsored the legislation to create the National Institute on Alcohol Abuse and Alcoholism. Hughes was committed to the idea of alcoholism as a disease.

In the 1960s, Hughes hired Mulford to run a private treatment rehab. Which was funny because Mulford strongly objected to the idea of alcoholism as a disease. In its place, Mulford developed the "natural processes model," to which I owe a lot. In Mulford's model, forces are always operating in a person's life driving him or her toward alcoholism, and then, at different points, toward recovery. The recovery forces—as opposed to the alcoholic ones—tend to kick in later in life. But they then tend to dominate, compelling most people sooner or later to leave their alcoholism behind.

How did Hal oppose the disease theory and work for disease-advocate Hughes? Indeed, why was Hal receptive to AA, while his deepest values opposed their "loss-of-control" and "primary disease" model (that is, that alcoholism was a disease—inbred, inexorable, irreversible, and primary—completely independent of who a person is or their life situation)? Both Hughes's ideas and AA's 12 steps fundamentally contradicted Hal's understanding of alcoholism's sources and his prescriptions for addictive behavior.

This discontinuity in Hal's worldview appeared when we were both interviewed in the *Chicago Tribune* in an article titled "Out of Control," where I argued against the disease theory, followed by Hal (here called "Harry"):

> As Stanton Peele, author of *Diseasing of America*, puts it, there is a "discrepancy between understanding addiction within the larger context of a person's life and regarding it as an explanation of that life."
>
> [On the other hand. . .]
>
> Harry Mulford is director of Alcohol Studies at the University of Iowa, and has been involved in alcohol research since the 1960s. He has a deep respect for Alcoholics Anonymous (AA) —"probably the best thing that ever came down the pike for the alcoholics who reach the point where they want some help," he says.

What? Hal implemented his insights when he got a small grant to create Community Alcohol Counselor Offices in Iowa. The system involved hiring a local paraprofessional in each Iowa community to meet with and coordinate services for local alcoholics. The coordinators didn't provide professional addiction treatment—although they could certainly point the client toward AA or other community support groups or therapy. Hal described this process thusly:

> Bob (a coordinator) explains to alcoholics that no one can give them, or sell them, a solution for their problem. They must get it the old fashioned way—work for it.

Any benefit they get from others' efforts to help them is in proportion to the effort they themselves put into the process. To encourage widespread responsibility, Bob does nothing for the alcoholic that the alcoholic cannot assume responsibility for, and he does nothing for the alcoholic that someone else in the community can take responsibility for.

Breathtaking. Hal wrote this in 1988 in "Enhancing the Natural Control of Drinking Behavior: Catching Up with Common Sense."

Why did Hal belie his own understanding to endorse AA? Hal liked community-based programs. AA was the ultimate in an inexpensive, widely available form of community support, and the only group network of its kind at the time. But its ideology became the foundation for the costly, ineffective medical treatment that was to replace Hal's community-resource model. Hal described this denouement:

> The citizens' efforts, being built from the bottom up, were reprogrammed with directives from the top down. The center's operations were soon standardized, "professionalized," and thoroughly bureaucratized. . . . *The new state authority designed its own monitoring system—not for effectiveness, but to police the centers' conformity to the state's [the disease theory's] directives* [my emphasis].

For Mulford, AA's support around not drinking was just one of the panoply of community resources and services the counselor might help a person access—like legal help for a divorce or loan services for financial need. The coordinator was a conduit, an aid, perhaps a shoulder to lean on. And that labor was cheap, even in 1960s terms. These salaries, along with operating costs (mainly local office rental) and a small coordinating state office and brief training program for counselors, made up the entire cost of the program. One such center treated 250 clients for an annual budget of $45,000—the cost (even then) of three to four hospital beds for a month.

By all reports, the Community Alcohol Counselor Program was an overwhelming success—one greatly appreciated by people with drinking problems, their families, and the community. It swam against the trend noted at that 1988 San Diego conference by Robin Room:

> In comparing Scotland and the United States, on the one hand, with developing countries like Mexico and Zambia, on the other hand, in the World Health Organization Community Response Study, we were struck with how much more responsibility Mexicans and Zambians gave to family and friends in dealing with alcohol problems, and how ready Americans and Scots were to cede responsibility for these human problems to official agencies or to professionals. *The provision of treatment, we felt, became a societal alibi for the dismantling of long-standing structures of control of drinking behavior, both formal and informal* [my emphasis].

In this view, the modern spread of treatment actually *depreciated* society's ability to regulate people's drinking. Room, the world's most influential alcohol epidemiologist and one of my greatest bete noires (see my extensive section on this battle in Chapter 11 while referring back to Room's quote here), has since reversed his position in favor of increasing governmental interventions, with results it is hard to find positive, as I detail in Chapter 9.

Hal's community-based alcoholism support system disappeared in the 1970s, when Hughes sponsored legislation that Richard Nixon signed to create the NIAAA* and the era of government-supported hospitalization of alcoholics. As noted, a few such hospital beds each *cost more in a month* than Mulford's counselors' budgets for dealing with entire communities' alcohol problems *for a year*. That's where Iowa and the US remain today.

As I detail in Part II, I too went on to create a private rehab center (albeit a non-disease-oriented one) in Iowa.

Mulford Was Popular—Me, Not So Much

When Hal died in 2012, sociologist Paul Roman wrote a tribute to him in the prestigious international journal *Addiction* (my relationship with which I describe in the Conclusion). Hal had previously published in that journal (in 1994) a piece titled: "What If Alcoholism Had Not Been Invented?: The Dynamics of American Alcohol Mythology." His answer was a mournful marker for his bypassed theoretical insights and practical work in Iowa:

> Local communities nationwide might have taken common-sense actions to facilitate the natural rehabilitation process and provided more benefit to more alcoholics for less cost than treating alccholism. It is expected that Americans will continue to drink and will continue to seek a more harmonious relationship with alcohol. The informal social controls will continue to largely constrain individual appetites for alcohol's pleasures, and most alcoholics will continue to gain control of their excessive drinking in the natural course of events with or without exposure to alcoholism treatment.

Could there be anything about addiction more radical—and ignored in America—than that? *No one* thought more like me about alcoholism than

---

* The first director of the NIAAA, from 1970 to 1975, was Morris Chafetz, whom I knew after his stint at NIAAA. I describe my work with Chafetz in Chapter 11, about my involvement in alcohol research. Chafetz and I agreed that some of those treated for alcoholism could moderate their drinking and that social context was crucial in drinking behavior. Like Mulford, he muddied his own point of view—in Chafetz's case by labeling alcoholism as a "disease requiring treatment."

Hal (as was true for others—Bruce Alexander,* Carl Hart, and Norman Zinberg—with drugs). I was a Jew with foreign-born grandparents who grew up in mid-twentieth-century Philly; Carl is an African American who grew up in the Miami ghetto in the latter part of the century; Hal was born to a mid-American family on an Iowa farm earlier in the century. Ethan Nadelmann once said to me (Hart was a scientific advisor to his Drug Policy Alliance)—"Carl thinks like you." Someone who knew Hal's work once told me, "Your viewpoints shocked me. Then I thought, 'How could two such brilliant people at opposite ends of America think the same way? Maybe they're right.'"

After reading his memorial in *Addiction*, I wrote Roman of my admiration for Hal, and thanked him for his tribute to Hal in the journal. Paul, who periodically sent me complimentary emails about things I had written, in this case accidentally passed along an exchange in which he discussed me with another researcher. The two chortled over my shit-kicking reputation in the field, comparing it unfavorably with Hal's benign demeanor and good reputation. They agreed that I would never be honored like Mulford.

There *are* two big differences between Mulford and me. Hal wanted to eliminate the imperfect terms alcoholism and addiction. I want to perfect them.

And Hal in his demeanor and work never offended people or the status quo. Of course, as beloved as he was, Mulford's ideas and approaches have died with him.

---

* Remarkably, Bruce Alexander grew up in the 30,000-person Morristown/Morris Township community where I raised my three children. Bruce visited me there and in Teaneck, NJ. On his visits, we two geniuses vacuumed and dusted the house. Mary was infinitely hospitable to my guests—Archie, Bruce, (as we shall see in Chapter 11) Nick Heather, and Peter Nathan, director of the Rutgers Center of Alcohol Studies. But she would not be put upon.

4

Risky Troublemaker
A life of adventure, meaning, and conflict

The issue faced by an independent, out-of-the-box thinker like me, one that defeats nearly all such efforts and individuals, is how to make their way in the world, particularly emotionally. I have a unique style and personality that make me suited for such a role. My adventurousness and risk-taking, while courting danger, are a protective cushion most people lack. At the same time, the way I live, have raised my children, and interact with my grandchildren has been an important test of my ideas about avoiding or getting over addiction, as reflected in my book Addiction-Proof Your Child.

I married your father for the wrong reasons—he was fun and exciting.
> — my ex-wife Mary to daughter Anna

The gifts Vicki and I brought for him today say a lot about who Stanton is: there's a book about the rivalry between Bill Russell and Wilt Chamberlain, along with a book about the art world in Manhattan in the mid-twentieth century. And then there's a record album with songs about Ray Kroc, Elvis Presley (whose birthday is the same day as Stanton's), and Sonny Liston.[*] If somebody was going to record a song about Sonny Liston, there's no way we were not going to buy it for Stanton.

Long ago I became accustomed to seeing Stanton reading, watching TV, listening to the radio, and carrying on a conversation, all at the same time. In his thirst for life, Stanton is not the moderate drinker he holds up as a behavioral and cultural ideal. He sucks in life—and shares it with his friends—with his own unique gusto. I know of no more energetic and energizing companion at

---

[*] Sonny Liston was a Philadelphia-based heavyweight champion defeated by Muhammad Ali. A large picture of Liston, wearing a Santa hat, graced the wall over my friend Joel's bed (see Chapter 5). In our freshman year at Penn, Archie and I watched the historic Ali-Liston fight on the Jumbotron screen at Philadelphia's Convention Hall, where, unable to afford the ticket price, we had sneaked in. Among the famous whom Archie and I have met face-to-face on our adventures (each of whom I greeted) are Boston Celtics coach Tom Heinsohn in the lobby of Joe Tecce's restaurant following a playoff loss; Alfred Hitchcock promoting *Frenzy* in the lobby of a Boston theater; and former president Bill Clinton on a small stairway at the Metropolitan Museum.

all levels at once: physically, intellectually, culturally, morally—and I don't know if any such person exists in the world. Stanton has the most well-developed and multi-faceted sense of fun of anyone I know. Traveling with him is an experience that few can withstand, or even survive."

— Archie Brodsky, "Stanton Peele: Sixtieth
Birthday Tribute," January 2006 (see Afterword)

After the market crash in the early 2000s, I also had a very bad year earnings-wise, and Mary reckoned I wasn't being fully adult in our household. "Stanton wears his family obligations lightly," she said. I could defend myself by saying we had a nice house in a nice suburb and substantial savings, and a good family life.

The Kids Are Okay

Without overburnishing our family life, our kids ended up okay. By that, I joke, I mean that none ended up in rehab—or worse. I'm in a field where I know people whose kids have died. That is a tough reality to deal with, and some never escape the burden. I don't add to the weight that they carry. Who knows what led to this result? But I don't think such outcomes are accidents. People must examine and accept their impact on their own and their children's fates.

I consider it a badge of honor that my three kids have survived and flourished. I believe that Mary and I taught them responsibility and self-reliance and the self-respect to care for themselves. It is one of my best claims for myself.

Wonderful people have to confront tragedies. In her autobiography, Cloris Leachman describes her monumental movie (*The Last Picture Show, Young Frankenstein*) and TV (*The Mary Tyler Moore Show, Phyllis*) successes. She had and loved five children. One son died due to a long descent into drugs. Leachman suffered his death. Her best understanding is that she didn't recognize his addiction and gave him money with which to fuel it.

People don't usually kill themselves by accident, and we should do everything we can to prevent that (that's where harm reduction comes in, as described in Chapter 9). But sometimes even well-intentioned, well-equipped, *loving* parents seriously miss the marks with their kids. Everyone loves Joe Biden and considers him a great father. That his son Hunter has had a career of drug and family and love and business missteps isn't something we should pillory Joe for. On the other hand, he's missing something, and he still can't deal with his relationship with his younger, less-favored son. Sorry.

Nonetheless, I accept Mary's point about me. After thirty years, facing a financial rough spot with her youngest child headed to college, she was worn down. Mary, who had an MBA, always worked, nearly always harder than I did—much harder—although ultimately she made less money than I did.

But I still see Mary's point. I am someone who evaluates my life on a day-by-day basis of how much fun I'm having and how well amused I am. And, in the same way that I disregarded the customs of academia and professional life, I disregarded many of the niceties of family life. Mary was sometimes overcome by anxiety when confronted by my actions.

Mary's Sixty-Ninth Birthday Party

In 2017, well after our divorce, I took Mary, now living in North Carolina, out to dinner while she visited New York. Haley, our middle child, in her late thirties, had moved to New Orleans to enter a Ph.D. program in clinical psychology at Tulane. Dana, approaching forty, was a busy e-commerce maven. Anna, nearing thirty, was in Los Angeles conducting a roundtable discussion of cutting-edge comedians she had organized as culture editor for *GQ* magazine.

I arrived at the restaurant shortly after Mary did, before it opened at 5:30. She had a glass of water. I wanted one. Mary said, "They'll be seating us shortly, and you can have one then." I got up, went to a counter with water bottles, and asked if I could have a glass of water. The waitress gave me a glass of water.

We economized at dinner (I paid for dinner, Mary gave the tip) by splitting a salad, an entrée, and a pasta dish. During dinner, I engaged the waiter in conversation, as is my habit. He told us he planned on going to law school. Mary: "My husband went to law school and never bought a textbook; he passed the New Jersey and New York Bars. But he never worked as a lawyer."

"Mary, the guy doesn't want to hear all that."

Mary: "It's true!"

(The author of *Prozac Nation*, Elizabeth Wurtzel, whose privileged life was marked by depression and addiction, and who later in life attended Yale Law School, observed, "I may be the only person who ever went to law school on a lark." Maybe.)

After we ate, Mary announced she had a delicious lemon cookie for dessert that she said we could eat outside. Me: "It's twenty degrees out there!" I insisted, she relented, and we ate the cookie at our table. When we finished, Mary carefully dusted the crumbs off the table, as if to remove any trace of our crime. Once outside, we kissed each other's cheeks goodbye.

> ### Our Wedding Night
>
> In 1975 Mary and I bought a house and lived together in Oakland. In 1976 we decided it was advantageous to get married. We had the ceremony up the coast in Mendocino, wearing sweatshirts, with the justice of the peace's clerk as our witness. We then repaired to the hotel in a nearby cowboy town. The hotel, five stories high, was the tallest building on the main street.
>
> We stayed on the top floor. As I traipsed around nude, Mary said that I should cover up. I pointed out that there was nobody with a vantage point to see into our window. She ran crying into the bathroom, breaking her toe on the marble threshold.
>
> Next morning, Mary explained, "I realized that now I was stuck with you."
>
> A couple of days later, in Las Vegas, we encountered a social work conference being held at our hotel. I asked the organizers if I might speak. They agreed.
>
> My talk went well, except perhaps for one audience member who just clapped too often and laughed too much at my jokes.
>
> My wife.

Mary and I were both after bigger game than cookie crumbs and peeping Toms. And, on those larger topics, Mary was with me hammer and tong, hand and glove, Tristan and Isolde, which I greatly appreciated over our thirty years together. We had a risky lifestyle, often on the brink, even as we lived in middle-class neighborhoods and our three kids had middle-class options and advantages—which Mary insisted on. Those kids are all hard workers and rational risk-takers, bless them! None of them has been hospitalized.

Haley, Anna, and Dana in Chinatown, 2013.

Although we separated in our early-to-mid fifties, neither Mary nor I have have had another long-term partner relationship in this last part of our lives.

Risk Taking and Pleasure Seeking

I have taken risks, a few life-threatening, but more often that have threatened my career and that were potentially marriage-ending ones (which, in fact, ultimately occurred).

Mary recognized the differences between us, and some of the advantages of my approach. She welcomed that our children share my fun and pleasure-seeking. For her part, Mary is capable of great aesthetic pleasure—opera, ballet, art—which I greatly enjoyed sharing with her. (Alta Ann, an older woman, filled this role for me later.)

Meanwhile, I'm glad that our children are all responsible citizens who can work hard and meet their work and other life obligations, a topic Mary and I discussed at her birthday dinner. Me: "I wonder how they became so good at getting jobs and at working hard." That was a joke. Mary played a large role in incubating those traits. But all of our kids also have guts and smarts in seeking jobs and taking work and career risks. I had a lot to do with that. Both Mary and I insisted that the kids shoulder responsibility. Neither of us was a pushover.

And Archie was a constant presence in our children's lives, visiting regularly and spending time with them, leavening out our rough spots as best he could.

Mary insisted we all sit down for dinner every night, at which wine was periodically served to everyone over the age of 13.

Fear Itself

In raising my children, I was preoccupied with allowing them to roam free without fear, the way I have lived myself. Lenore Skenazy is the modern herald against our fear-constrained childrearing. Skenazy started the Free-Range Kids movement, which ripened, with partners, into Let Grow, which strives to make it "easy, normal and legal" for kids to be independent. She and her partners' work in fighting cultural currents is like mine.

Here is Skenazy's origin story:

In 2008, I let my then-9-year-old ride the subway by himself. He'd been asking us—my husband and me—to please take him someplace and let him find his way home. So my husband and I discussed this. Our boy knows how to read a subway map, he speaks the language and we *are* New Yorkers. We're on the subway all the time. That's how it came to be that one sunny Sunday, after lunch at McDonald's, I took him to Bloomingdale's—and left him in the handbag department.

I didn't leave him unprepared, of course! I gave him a map, a MetroCard, quarters for the phone and $20 for emergencies. Bloomingdale's sits on top of a subway station on our local line, and it's always crowded with shoppers. I believed he'd be safe. I believed he could figure out his way. And if he needed to ask someone for directions—which it turns out he did—I even believed the person would not think, "Gee, I was about to go home with my nice, new Bloomingdale's shirt. But now I think I'll abduct this adorable child instead."

Long story short: He got home about forty-five minutes later, ecstatic with independence. I wrote a little column about his adventure and two days later I was on the *Today Show*, NPR, MSNBC and Fox News defending myself as NOT being "America's Worst Mom."

The notion was that I had deliberately put my son in harm's way (possibly to "prove" something) and I was just incredibly lucky that he made it home. One NPR caller asked why I had given my son "one day of fun" even though he would probably end up dead by nightfall.

People really do think that leaving their kids to play outside, or to walk to school or the store, is to place them at imminent risk of their lives, ready at any moment to be kidnapped by strangers cruising the streets looking for victims just like them. In 2021, yet another work was added to the pantheon of books about how American children live in gilded cages: *Hunter, Gather, Parent.*

That never (almost never) happens. Public safety hasn't gotten worse—it's much improved. There were far more murders in New York and other major cities in the 1960s-'70s-'80s-'90s. The New York Police Department recorded 289 murders in 2018, three fewer than the 292 recorded in 2017. That's the lowest number of homicides in nearly seventy years; yet most Americans believe that crime is worsening. .

Parents are riddled with anxiety that their children will be kidnapped. We're steeped in fear as a condition of modern American life. The few legendary stranger kidnapping-killings that occur, starting with Etan Patz, the New York boy who disappeared on his way to school on a crowded New York street in 1979, dominate our thinking. While Trump fear-mongers about roving Latino gangs, Democrats are often equally guilty of using scare tactics, for example, around guns. The push for gun control is accompanied by stories of people being mowed down in a random spray of bullets. Here, for example, is a Democratic congressperson: "We're afraid to send our kids to school or the shopping mall because we're afraid they'll be shot!"

By the definition of The Violence Project—mass shootings involve four or more deaths, not counting the shooter, in a public place among people unrelated to one another—there may be as many as a few hundred deaths (if that many) in America in any given year among 300,000,000-plus people. We should stop these atrocities, including by reasonable gun-control measures that most Americans support. But curtailing your daily life because of them makes no sense. And yet, although I am aware of no mass public shootings in New York City—whose metropolitan area includes 19 million people—in this century, who isn't affected by the 2012 Sandy Hook attack that killed twenty-six people, twenty of them children, or any of a host of other mass killings over the decades?

Etan Patz and Sandy Hook are such overwhelming images that they strike anxiety into any parent's heart. The fear they generate controls all of us. This sense of dread is evident throughout America. It is captured in Barry Glassner's 1990 book, reissued in 2018 after Trump's election, *The Culture of Fear*. Glassner amplifies that Americans are held captive by irrational anxieties, exploited by politicians, leading to results worse than the dreaded outcomes they fantasize, but that almost never occur.

And then came the pandemic.

Raising Non-Addicted Children

I strived, as hard as I could, to harken back to that pre-Patz period in raising our children. Mary sometimes surprised me when she would come over to my side. Once when she let Anna walk to a friend's house at night at age 8, she said to me, "I just read your (1996) pamphlet with Marianne Apostolides, *Don't Panic: A Parent's Guide to Understanding and Preventing Alcohol and Drug Abuse.*[*] The worst things that happen to children—violence, accidents, drug- and alcohol-related deaths—are self-inflicted, not due to dangers they face in the world." Marianne and I wrote the following:

---

[*] This is called a harm-reduction approach to drug education and prevention. I originally published this material in a 1983 pamphlet for CompCare, the 12-step publishing house!

> We're asking you to let your child make mistakes. In practice, you need to judge which experiences your teenager can safely manage. But we as parents have to allow our children to face situations that require them to use self-control and good judgment. In these situations, children will have to consider their options and the consequences of each option. They will make their own decisions—decisions for which they take responsibility. This ability to make good decisions is important, considering that parents can't always be around to protect their children.

All three of my children went through K–12 in the Morris School District—which was 50 percent Black and LatinX, 50 percent white and Asian. With schools more racially segregated nationwide than they have ever been, the Morristown School District is cited as a national model. I wasn't only concerned with my children being open-minded racially (which they are). I wanted them to know how to negotiate urban environments confidently, fearlessly. To live free, to know you can control your life in fundamental ways, to make the things that are important to you come true—to be a mensch, a stand-up person. Those are essential for a life worth living.

"A Bit of a Dick"

Anna does interviews with prominent political and entertainment figures, from a personal angle. She must maintain her poise—and, most important, her values—while penetrating their exteriors. She interviewed the young actor Miles Teller for *Esquire* magazine. His boorishness caused her to label Teller a "bit of a dick." *The New York Times* picked up her piece as an interview that went famously wrong. In 2020, she interviewed, with empathy but firmness, Billy Bush.

Anna and me

In 2007, I published *Addiction-Proof Your Child*, which I dedicated to Anna, not yet twenty. In 2019, I published *Outgrowing Addiction: With Common Sense Instead of "Disease" Therapy*. I wrote the book with Zach Rhoads, a man half my age whose daughter was born the same year the book was published. Zach is a counselor with school kids who act out and their families; he shares my outlook. As a musician, Zach had been addicted to heroin and almost died. He cut back and quit without treatment or AA/NA. He still drinks.

Like Skenazy, we are fighting a cultural trend that has seeped into our consciousness, the very fiber of our beings. And this fear-based outlook has a tremendous impact on young people's—everyone's—mental health and susceptibility to addiction. In case you hadn't noticed, these problems are worsening, even as we constantly admonish people to seek treatment for depression, anxiety, or addiction (see Chapter 9).

Like Skenazy, Zach and I are bucking inexorable cultural trends. Only we include alcohol and drugs in the range of powerful experiences that children must deal with. I imagine a world in which children need to be educated in how to respond to drugs when they take them—as many of them (including my grandkids) already take meds in childhood, and as they explore the worlds of drugs and alcohol from their adolescence on.

My and Zach's thesis in *Addiction-Proof Your Child* and *Outgrowing Addiction* is that children avoid addiction, including other unhealthy and overwhelming involvements aside from drugs, when they have a life purpose, learn responsibility, and are able to find and experience fun and adventure—not due to drug lectures and learning about "the brain disease."

The single thing parents can do to fulfill their children, to guarantee they won't become addicted, is to allow them the freedom, à la Skenazy, to roam and experience their environments, their relationships, their worlds for themselves. Children should also be given positive values about achievement, health, contributing to their families and society, and mindfulness (thinking about their lives).

Here* I do a half-hour video interview with four California boys making a documentary on gaming addiction. Here† Zach and I have a discussion with Robert Schwebel, who in 1998 wrote *Saying No Is Not Enough: Helping Your Kids Make Wise Decisions About Alcohol, Tobacco and Other Drugs*, whose approach is similar to ours.

---

* https://youtu.be/q61v9K578OA

† https://www.youtube.com/watch?v=6h4bJxpwKKU

There is a limit to how popular social commentators will be when they don't demonize drugs as a major danger, even as (per Chapter 9) more and more Americans die due to drug use under our current regimen.

For a Middle-Class Jewish Kid, I Grew Up on the Streets

My life was extreme compared with most people I know in regard to the danger to which I was exposed as a child—as minor as that danger was. I spoke with my cousin Ellis, now in his seventies and a distinguished endocrinologist at UC Irvine, when his daughter was younger. He and his wife wouldn't have thought of letting her walk anywhere on her own in their wealthy beach section of L.A.

I asked Ellis if he remembered when we first attended a baseball game together at Connie Mack Stadium, then the home field of the Philadelphia Phillies. We had to take a bus, then the el (elevated train), and another bus through Kensington, downtrodden then, now a heroin killing field. He said he didn't remember.

"I was nine and you were six."

I walked to Sharswood Elementary School in South Philly, roughly five blocks from my home, starting when I was five, in 1951.

Walking home one day, I saw kids from the Whitman Street gang, whom I knew to attend parochial (Catholic) school, asking kids from Sharswood which side they preferred to win the Civil War (at least they had an interest in history!). If the kid said "The North," they punched him in the face. When they approached me I said, "The South."

When I was 7, in second grade, a transfer kid from a parochial school who was in my class insulted my mother during recess. I insulted his mother. He punched me, I punched him in the stomach, and he doubled over crying. Two "safeties" (student traffic monitors) saw me punch the kid and "reported" me. The same safeties came to take us to our trial, which was in front of a sixth grade teacher and her class—the class my brother Jeffrey was in.

On the way to our hearing, the other kid cried. I didn't. I saw the safeties look at each other. At our hearing, I told my story. I got some penalty, and the other kid didn't. When my mother heard the story at home, she berated my brother for not standing up for me. (Even a braver soul than my brother wouldn't have done so in a kangaroo court like that.)

Several days later the same boy, accompanied by his older brother and some other kids, confronted me on the way home from school. His brother said we had to fight again, since his younger brother had lost our earlier fight. As we wrestled, I got the upper hand again, and the older brother pulled me off the kid.

I saw I could never win. I said, "Look, we're fighting in front of a church. We shouldn't fight here." Walking to the other end of the block, we passed my house. I ran up and knocked on my door. Fortunately, my mother was close by and quickly let me in. The other boy and his brother never bothered me again. Was I a victim of bullying? I wouldn't say that—well, until Richard Solomon, one of the world's leading addiction theorists, Jay Lorsch of the Harvard Business School, and Lou Harris—JFK's and America's most prominent pollster—abused me, as I tell in Part II.

Those sorts of things occurred less frequently after my parents moved us from South Philly to Oxford Circle in the Northeast, to a largely Jewish neighborhood. But we were surrounded by neighborhoods of working-class Irish and Italians. It was mildly dangerous to walk in those neighborhoods, and so, even in Oxford Circle, I had some run-ins. Once on a crowded bus, a couple of kids from a parochial school shouted out as some friends and I chatted energetically, "Look at how the Jews gab, gab gab." Nobody on the bus said anything. We became silent. When I told this story to my daughter Haley's Catholic girlfriend, she apologized. I told her she had nothing to do with it. I'm over it.*

I Don't Look to Institutions for Help

I *never* thought of the police as my friend. In the summer after my senior year in high school, I was visiting my girlfriend Maret, who was babysitting in a development of single homes. Having lost her address, I was walking around looking for the house when two cops grabbed me and pulled me out on the street, where a crowd had gathered. While they held me, another cop ran up and punched me in the stomach.

The cop who hit me came to me in the jail cell to which I was removed. "I found the house you were looking for. Your girlfriend told me who you were."

Sara was outraged. She called the police and they sent out a fat, perfumed cop to "investigate." He said that he had interviewed several bystanders, and they said that *I* had punched the cop!

Using my usual trick of envisioning an absurdist scenario, I said, "Surrounded by cops and neighbors, I punched a policeman?" But I saw instantly that technique meant nothing to the cop.

---

* Another of my cousins, the youngest of the cohort, Richard Fromberg, with whom I became close over the years despite our twelve-year age difference, proofread this manuscript. "I can relate to your growing up in the Northeast stories, and remember similar experiences."

> I turned to my mother: "Sara, this isn't going to get us anywhere." I never expect an institution to support me against its members, staff, and faculty (see my run-ins at Rutgers Law School in Chapter 5).

Institutions *always* protect their members—at least against the likes of me. I go into any institutional interaction expecting to be shot down, if not shackled.

Yet elite institutions are good cover

Nonetheless, when I first walked onto Penn's campus, I felt a serene sense of safety: "No one here will physically assault me for being a Jew! Cops are on their best behavior!" Elite enclaves have advantages. I later moved to Western Powelton Village, then a blighted neighborhood beyond the Penn bubble, with Warren (whose love addiction with Joan I describe in Chapter 3). Of course, when there was no heat in the building in December, we moved out to West Philly with Archie, leaving the African American families in the two floors below us to face the cold.

I have never encountered serious trouble living in or near or negotiating urban neighborhoods, and not in Brooklyn today, where I have drunk in a backroom speakeasy where I was the only white person (everyone was welcoming to me, sharing their booze and telling me to come back). Nonetheless, while that secure sense became second nature to me, I am hyper-vigilant on the street. After all, I did walk apprehensively in the dangerous New York of the 1960-'70s, visiting Archie and our other Penn roommate, then at Columbia Law School. That mindfulness has always been part of my life.

I regarded my Brooklyn girlfriend Eileen as an uber-liberal who would never send her children to an integrated school, come hell or high water. She stands for an entire class of upper-middle-class people who disdain lower socioeconomic white people because *those people* are prejudiced against Black people. But those in Eileen's social niche isolate themselves from *both* disadvantaged groups. Richard Reeves examined the hypocritical biases of the upper 20 percent of Americans in his 2017 book, *Dream Hoarders*. I've seen Reeves speak at the graduate school center of the City University of New York (where I used to meet with Charles Winick). The audience is the very group whose "hoarding" of social resources Reeves analyzes. He predictably pulls his punches in this setting.

Me and the Shoe Store

I've mentioned my father's ratty shoe store in Kensington (where Nora Volkow now goes to understand the social roots of heroin addiction—see Chapter 9). Here's a story that is: (a) unbelievable, (b) potential child abuse, (c) an example of a child encouraged to be preternaturally self-reliant and responsible. Although it was more common for children to be independent in the 1950s, my story is nonetheless extreme compared with others I know in a way that makes my early life unusual.

At age six, I was hanging out at the shoe store when my father realized that he had run out of some stock that he needed. He called the supplier, which was nearby, and came up with the plan that I would take the subway there and bring the box of shoes back in a cab. To do this, he gave me two dollars and two quarters. One quarter was for the subway at the end of our block, which I was to take for two stops. The two dollars were for the cab fare. The remaining quarter was the tip for the driver.

I got off at the correct subway stop (remember, this was way before cell phones) and saw the supplier's building across the street. The people at the wholesalers were ready for me. They brought out the box, called a cab, and put me and the box in it and told the driver where to take me.

By the time I got to the shoe store, the cab's meter read $2.25, so I gave the driver all the money I had, and he took the box out of the cab. My father, waiting, took it into the store.

When I got into the store, Ted asked if I had tipped the driver. I said the fare was $2.25, not $2.00 as he said it would be, so I had to give him all the money I had for the fare. My father yelled (it was more like his ordinary, gruff speaking voice—think of Bernie Sanders when excited): "How'd he get here—by way of Japip?"

And that was all the praise/feedback I got. Of course, without thanking me, my father demonstrated a lot of respect for my abilities, didn't he?

So, you see, I out-Skenazied Skenazy's son—I was actually making a real contribution to my family's well-being at an earlier age. I also sold paper carnations on the street by myself on Mother's Day. One time a guy selling real carnations down the block purchased all of my flowers to eliminate my competition. I was 7. All of this was a test run for my independence and development, as Skenazy's son's trip was. In some ways, I was more like kids who grew up on farms or in the Old West. And I've always identified with that feeling and my ability to deal with any situation.

Basketball

I differ from the Jewish friends I made in Penn's General Honors Program. They were short. I was 6'2". They were nerds. I played street basketball. Not only was I on my varsity high school team in my junior year, but I played on teams in recreational (rec) center leagues around Northeast Philly. As a result, I had experiences like playing before rabid, all-white-male parochial-school crowds, and playing in crowded gyms in front of all-Black crowds against players as tall as 6'9". I played against Fred Carter, Earl Monroe, and others who went on to the National Basketball Association (I scored off Carter).

Those could be intimidating experiences. Later, when I spent a year in South Africa, I made their national team. Yes, I was a Springbok—a South African Olympian. This meant little, since the only international competition available to us was from the neighboring countries of Mozambique and Angola. But I nonetheless played some intense games, like one in Port Elizabeth against a team with two American college players.

We went into an overtime period. Several of our players fouled out, until I was one of four players left on the court. I brought the ball up and passed to a teammate under the basket, who scored. I came down court the next time and made a jump shot from the key. We won. I was mobbed after the game.

In the city outdoor games in Philly rec leagues, physical intimidation was the name of the game. My reaction when someone verbally abused me was to laugh; and when the intimidation was physical, to push back and then to call out to the ref. Both of these mindful types of responses were unusual on those courts. But I saw my daughter Anna do the same thing when she played soccer, decades later. Once she threw a ball inbounds that only traveled a few feet. A nearby parent on the other team guffawed. Anna turned to him: "Go ahead—laugh at a 12-year-old girl if it makes you feel good."

Me and My Grandson

I contribute to the lives of my three grandchildren—more so after my son left his family. They have a heroically dedicated mother, whom I try to support.

I must tread cautiously, while I try to encourage their independence and responsibility, especially with Cassius, the oldest. When Cash was a pre-teen, he and I would go to Central Park or Prospect Park in Brooklyn, or to Park Slope, where I used to live, to roam around. Cash could fish, climb rocks, and walk on the pond ice in the parks.

Once I met Mary with Cassius in Central Park on one of Mary's visits to New York. Before she arrived, Cassius and I discovered that the boat pond had been drained. Cassius quickly jumped in the emptied pond to discover a lot of loose coinage that people had thrown in for luck (bad luck for them!). Other kids soon joined him, and they swapped foreign coins. Cash collected nearly thirty dollars as Mary and I sat at the café next to the pond drinking beers. "He'll never forget this experience," Mary said.

I would pick up Cash from his school in Manhattan—when it was warm enough, we would take the Wall Street ferry to Rockaway Beach. Other times, we went to family swim at the Y in Park Slope and afterward to the bar

Cash with a turtle he caught (and released) in Central Park

next door where Cash threw darts and played pool with the twenty-somethings.

People think this a strange place to go with my grandson, as someone wrote in response to my mentioning it in my *Psychology Today* blog:

This Grandfather Takes a Kid to a Bar?

Author takes grandson to a bar? Either this article is satire, or someone should call child services on this "expert." Disgraceful article. *PT* should be ashamed for publishing it, it's extremely dangerous.

At the bar, the young adult patrons were always kind and attentive to Cash and taught him how to shoot pool. I always left by 9:00 p.m.

Later, before the pandemic, I took Cash on trips, including visiting Zach in Burlington, where he kayaked on Lake Champlain, and to my friend Larry's mountain home in Idaho, where he hiked and fished and we whitewater rafted down the Salmon River (where I fell in, and Larry hauled me out of the river), and to Northern Ireland, where he rode horses and visited my business partner's father's farm and we swam in the cold Irish Sea.

I am so grateful to my daughter-in-law for facilitating these trips (the last, to Northern Ireland when he was 11, took eight days, including two full days of travel). Cash loved our outings, which he called "adventures." He always made friends with a variety of adults. He was always game and cheerful and appreciative. He always helped out. Everyone noted our rapport, that we worked as a team. He was never any trouble.

Cash likewise visited with Mary in North Carolina. Here is Mary's description of Cash's first visit, when he was only 7 (the age at which his father and I drove cross-country), to her condo development.

A Vacation Back to the '50s

Mary: Cassius has been outside for hours, helping neighbors weed, and bringing back their donations of homegrown veggies to share, dinking around looking at butterflies and bees work in the flowers, riding his bike that a neighbor lent him.

Me: Boy, that's what they used to call a neighborhood when I was growing up.

Mary: Ha. Yes, a vacation back to the '50s. He's out there now with the 9-year-old next door. Probably at the tree house near the creek.

Our involvement in our grandchildren's lives became more important when my son separated from his wife while his three kids were ages 3 through 8. All have been diagnosed with one contemporary condition or another (ADHD, oppositional disorder, whatever) and medicated.

Mary feels the way I do about these diagnoses and medications. When Dana, himself a rambunctious boy, was growing up, a counselor suggested to us that we put him on Ritalin. Without looking at each other, Mary and I both shook our heads no. Mary's and my approach with Cassius is to allow him freedom, insist on his being responsible, gently correct him when he fails to meet obligations, and uphold high standards at school and elsewhere.

My colleague Zach Rhoads and other theorists and practitioners say and do what I believe: some kids have difficulty reading, no matter what their IQs. We have methods for helping such children learn to read—which we should use—without ever labeling kids as suffering from dyslexia, ADHD, or any other disease, as we describe in *Outgrowing Addiction*.

When Cash had difficulty concentrating on the reading Mary insisted he do before they could go to the pool, he told her that he had a brain condition that made it hard for him to concentrate. Mary responded: "Everyone has problems, but people develop and change and that's how they have a good life." So could he, she told him.

Mary's perspective here speaks to the value—the belief—Mary and I shared that viewing people's lives as determined by the problems they encountered, defined as brain diseases, trauma, or victimhood of any kind, is a burden that limits, and sometimes hurts, the child. It's not for me to review my ex-wife's life here, but she overcame a lot in terms of her own family and personal background to become a self-determined person who has had a major impact through her environmental work.

My three grandchildren, two boys and a girl, all have the energy that came to me from my father and that I passed along to my son, their father. There are no shrinking violets among the three of them; the same as is true of my own three kids. One woman I knew said, "They're rambunctious, sure—would you rather have three quiet, well-behaved kids?"

No, I wouldn't.

My grandkids playing in Prospect Park

My Life on the Streets of New York

Now in my seventies, I live largely on my own. Although I am wary and always keep my eyes out for danger and problems based on my childhood experiences in Philly, I view New York and its streets as my playground. I ride my bike, go to bars and coffeehouses, smile at people and talk to them, ask about their lives, tell them to behave on the subway—asking younger ones to give up their seats for mothers with small children, for instance—and enter discussions with people at museums and at art movie houses. I view outings in New York like swinging from one interaction to another, making whatever connection I can find. (This all changed with Covid, of course—see Conclusion.)

Leading Museum/Film Discussions

I was at the premiere of a film about a man imprisoned for supposedly knowing about his father's molesting children he tutored, *Capturing the Friedmans*, directed by Andrew Jarecki. After the film, Jarecki and the one son who refused to cop a plea and who himself went to prison led an impromptu group discussion in a corridor outside the screening room. Ed Koch, the former mayor, was standing opposite me. At some point, I simply took charge and asked, "What does the mayor think of the film?" In this case, unlike with the Central Park Five, who he said were guilty even before they were convicted (they were later exonerated), he sided with the falsely accused son.

I engage in complex, technical discussions with people I run into. Once, at the Metropolitan Museum with Archie, I started talking with a woman who was a principal in a large planning firm that had competed with one led by a friend of Archie's for a major development project at Harvard. Archie reviewed the arguments in favor of his friend's firm. The woman vigorously contested Archie, even though her firm had won the contract and was building the project. She never asked how Archie knew so much about this project even though he wasn't a professional planner.

I view New York as a great panorama, laboratory, tableau, and source of untold stories. My favorite TV drama growing up was *The Naked City*, which ended each episode with the intonation: "There are eight million stories in the naked city. This has been one of them." When I started hitchhiking to NYC with my friend Mark Rosenthal, who became a prominent art curator, we spent whole days in the Times Square cafeteria, Hector's, drinking free seltzer and eating complimentary pickles while watching the human procession parade by.

One great partner I had for my New York City pageant later in life was an older woman, Alta Ann Morris, whom I picked up in a movie line. We roamed New York until, after she turned 90, street life became too unwieldy with her—then came the pandemic. Until then, AA's age and WASPy patina allowed us to engage in easy banter with people we met in movies, restaurants, or simply on the street.

Please Resolve this Dispute

On one of our outings, Alta Ann and I visited the Bronx Botanical Garden. We disagreed on the pronunciation of one of the exhibits. In one of the Garden's hothouses, I noticed a woman I had observed earlier, whom I approached, and asked for her read of the word describing one of the plants.

She backed off.

Alta Ann came beside us and in her innocent, squeaky old-lady voice said, "We were just having a disagreement about how to pronounce the word, which was on one of the exhibit signs."

The woman offered her pronunciation. "That's how I learned it in Latin. Why did you ask me?"

"I thought you looked like you were the smartest girl in your parochial school class," I replied.

The woman jerked her head back, as if I had flashed something in front of her face. "That's true," she said. Then she added, "I see that you seek meaning in your interactions." AA nodded vigorously: "He does."

When I told Alta Ann that Mary had accused me of practicing black magic, AA emailed me: "Your quick assessment of that woman, who was of a group and an age to have studied Latin, goes with your Holmesian style and *is* one of your oft-used aids to your passage through daily life." That is what Alta Ann told me after an editor said I should leave out the story of having an affair with a woman whose father got me into the Michigan animal laboratory.

As I did with Mark Rosenthal when we were still in high school, I study people—hopefully surreptitiously—in cafes, in restaurants, walking the street. I notice their pos-

Alta Ann roughing it with a sandwich on the street

tures, their gaits, their facial expressions, their gestures, their builds, their clothing, their companions or family members, how they interact with and talk to one another. These wordless pictures provide endless food, and fun, for me. I detect a lot about people from simply glancing at them. And I *enjoy* thinking. Spending time in, savoring, my mind is my greatest pleasure (as it is for Archie).

So the pandemic isn't so bad for me.

I Seek Meaning

My graduate school classmate Stanley said to me, "Other people when they are together just want to spend time with each other, talking about familiar things, just getting along. You want something valuable to happen."

Guilty. I question people for as long as they'll let me. They often enjoy talking about themselves. Although later, on reflection, they may regret or resent it, as if I've delved into their lives and ferreted out deep secrets. In fact, I have had to curtail these interrogations in recent years.

My rule is, as in therapy: Never use information voluntarily provided to you against a person. And I never would. But people's worries are more existential—that another human being knows such crucial information about them, even though they've told me these things. And that was the case with the manager of my local bar who exiled me.

> **How I Got Kicked Out of My Local Bar**
>
> **Me:** To manager of local bar wearing a Temperance tee-shirt. "Wow, I've never seen a temperance tee-shirt before."
>
> **Manager:** Do you know what Temperance is?
>
> **Me:** Of course. I know your family didn't permit dancing or drinking.
>
> **Manager:** Who told you that?
>
> **Me:** You.
>
> **Manager:** When?
>
> **Me:** A couple of years ago, when we first met.
>
> **Manager:** I don't like you.

On Being Unpopular

Remember Bill White's comment about me: "I think of him as a cross between a bullfighter waving a red cape before the leaders of the addiction field and the Trickster of Native American folklore whose actions puncture and deflate prevailing institutions and ideas."

I have been kicked out of many places for questioning what was being promoted there. I nearly always stand alone in challenging people who are pushing their false views as though they were the truth. That I take that role is what this memoir and my life are about.

It's a short ride from being independent, however, to being ostracized as a renegade. At my sixtieth birthday, Archie said of me:

> Stanton has not hesitated to expose the large blinders worn even by people in his own field, who should know better. As I wrote in a retrospective tribute to *The Meaning of Addiction*, "Peele extends his analytical probing to the point where he undercuts his own allies—which is why, *at a personal level, he hardly has any allies.*" That's an overstatement made for effect, but even when he does have allies, whether in the addiction wars or in the dirt trenches of community and regional environmental preservation, nothing can deter Stanton's seriousness of purpose and his willingness, when necessary, to stand alone [my emphasis].

As Steve Slate, who espouses a freedom model similar to my own on TEDx, said about my role in the field: "We all owe Stanton a debt of gratitude for being willing to be hated for so many years, while standing by what he knew to be the truth." On the other hand, quite a few people—like Gordon in the last chapter—say that I have been their pole star, guiding them out of addiction or giving them the courage to approach addiction differently as a helper, even while working for a 12-step, disease-oriented program.

Let's see where that has gotten me.

The Mayor, Me, and the Commissioner

Let me tell you about the time I ran into the Mayor, gave him an addiction lecture, and he put me in touch with his head of New York's preventive mental health services, impossible as this story is.

New York's mayor, Bill de Blasio, exercised at the Park Slope Y, where I also went. You could tell he was in the house by the phalanx of police and people wearing suits and the official SUVs in front of the building.

The Mayor's daughter had famously entered recovery at age 19. Meanwhile, another best-selling author I know, Gabrielle Glaser (*Her Best-Kept Secret*, about women's drinking), wrote an article about alternative approaches to addiction in the *Times* that mentioned me that appeared one morning when I encountered the Mayor at the Y. I approached de Blasio as he was dismounting his exercise cycle.

"Did you see the article in the *Times* today about different ways of fighting addiction, that don't tell a teenager to declare herself an addict or an alcoholic?"

He said he hadn't.

Some time later, I went up to de Blasio as he waited at the counter at Colson's, the French patisserie across the street from the Y that we both frequented, and engaged him again. This time he countered, "You obviously have some information on the subject. How about if you give me your email and I'll have the person in my administration responsible for these issues contact you?"

And so, early in 2016, Gary Belkin, executive deputy commissioner of the New York City Department of Health and Mental Hygiene, wrote me, "Not sure where you are based [Park Slope at the time, where I ran into the Mayor], but I'm partial to a coffeehouse off Washington Sqare Park. Mornings before work and five-ish after tend to work." Gary and I met for coffee.

Gary was then having to defend the city's Thrive program. Thrive offers peer counseling for people facing substance and mental health issues. It teaches counselors to ask questions rather than to impart opinions or information. The aim is to short-circuit emotional and substance problems before they rise to a clinical level. I *very* much approved of this approach. But Thrive had been attacked by medically-oriented treatment proponents.

Gary asked me to meet with him and several of his staff. Then he called the meeting off. In July of 2017 Gary scheduled a conference call to include Holly Catania (whom I describe below) and Denise Paone (whose work I describe in Chapter 9). Then Gary called that off. Gary and I never met or spoke again. Perhaps the next section explains why that would be.

I'm Not Even Welcome at Open Society Panels

I attended a 2014 panel at George Soros's Open Society Foundations, the progressive international think tank. The occasion was the release of an OSF report by Carl Hart, "Methamphetamine: Fact vs. Fiction."

In his research with meth, people supposedly addicted to meth will take money rather than use the drug. Moreover, Carl points out, meth's chemical structure is virtually identical to the Adderall that is regularly given to children.

Before reviewing his report, seeing me, Carl announced to the audience:

> I just want to acknowledge one of the people who I read as a graduate student and still do read to get some of these ideas. Stanton Peele is in the audience. So I just want people to understand that these ideas are not new. And I'm not the person who invented them. People like Stanton Peele deserve more—most—of the credit [applause].

Carl's book, *High Price*, tells his story of coming up from the Miami inner city, where conditions were equally bad before and after the crack epidemic. These conditions made the epidemic possible—*they* were the problem. Many of his friends ended up dead or imprisoned, while he escaped. Carl avoided heavy drugs like poison en route to becoming an internationally recognized professional. Based on his understanding of their secondary role in people's lives, and recognizing their function, Carl *now* takes drugs, which he began to declare publicly, while chair of Columbia's department of psychology, and in his book, *Drug Use for Grown-Ups*.

Carl, as the subtitle of *High Price* indicates, challenges everything you know about drugs and society. In public, Carl lays out the facts in a detached, ironic way, often shaking his head in exasperation and clucking.

Carl's ideas are like mine and those of Bruce Alexander. (One harm reductionist, Adi Jaffe, called the three of us "radical environmentalists.") Bruce showed that rats living in a capacious space with other rats eschew an opioid mixture they previously were habituated to (see Chapter 3). This is the Rat Park series of experiments, which Bruce says *Love and Addiction* led him to create. For Bruce, like Carl, the environment is the thing.

OSF has never invited me to be on one of their panels, while I've been living in and around New York for forty years. But, buoyed by Carl's introduction, I came to the front of the room as the first commenter after the presentations, and exploded with "Everything that you believe about drugs is wrong"—which Carl regularly announces.

I asked people in this supposedly radical packed house to raise their hands about whether they believed each of the following:

- Most people who take drugs like heroin become addicted.
- Most people who become addicted to heroin and other drugs can't overcome their addictions.
- Treatment is the only way to overcome addiction.
- Drug addiction treatment has proven itself to be effective.
- Anyone can become addicted, and their social conditions have no impact on whether those who use drugs become addicted to them.

Although they had just listened to Carl speak, a majority voted for every drug myth. And so would you, dear reader. This book is dedicated to making both these myths and their power clear, despite their being wrong and dangerous. In that moment, I explained to the group how each of these beliefs was mistaken. They were baffled, by both my content and my whole presentation.

I then did my regular smoking exercise, asking people what the hardest drug to quit is (they shout out in unison "smoking"); asking if any of them had quit (always a majority of those present in drug crowds); then asking, "How many of you joined a support group or used a drug to quit?" As always, only a tiny handful raised their hands. (Sometimes no one does.)

"So you're all telling me that you quit the toughest drug addiction on your own, and yet you believe every piece of crap that comes down the pike about addiction as an irreversible brain disease that must be treated or else you have to join AA/NA?"

There were three other presenters along with Carl on the panel. As I said, OSF would *never* invite me to present. Indeed, some years later, in 2018, I had a connection who wormed me onto a panel at the Rutgers School of Social Work. The primary speakers were the head of OSF's Global Drug Policy Program, Kasia Malinowska, and the man who created the Portuguese drug decriminalization system (including *all* drugs)—Dr. João Goulão.

Kasia had also organized the panel at which Carl spoke that I attended years before, and I met her before the presentation (I knew her assistant, who had worked at Canada's Portland Hotel Service, which I describe visiting in Chapter 7). She brushed me off. During his incomprehensible presentation, I asked Goulão a question. In the Portuguese program, people who are found to be using drugs must attend a panel that directs him or her to some kind of assistance. I asked, "What if they want no help?" Kasia was visibly irritated by me and my question.

After Kasia interviewed Goulão, who had presented chart after chart of technical data, I rose to speak. Kasia conspicuously stepped down from the stage. Sitting in the first row, she worked at her iPhone throughout my presentation.

I began by demonstrating a point that Carl also regularly makes— even counting heroin along with painkillers, "The vast majority of people who use these (opioid) drugs are not addicted."

Here's how I made that point while Kasia buried herself in her email:

"Have any of you had a painkiller?" I asked the audience.

Everyone raised their hands.

"How many of you did so without becoming addicted?" Again, apparently everyone raised their hands.

"But aren't opioids highly addictive? How come no one here became addicted?"

People are often puzzled by my question.

"Isn't that the key to what we're doing here—avoiding addiction? Which you all seem to have done with opioids. So you would seem to know the answer."

After some hesitancy, someone explains: "I had other things to do."

These were the things they wanted or needed to do that ruled out being addicted.

Jacob Sullum, a long-time editor at *Reason*, the vastly popular libertarian magazine and website, my interactions with whom I describe in the Conclusion, has observed me do these routines. Here is how he describes my process.

By asking straightforward, commonsensical questions about drug use and other pleasurable activities, Stanton Peele reveals that what most people think they know about addiction—what they take to be the enlightened, scientific view—is plainly at odds with their own experiences. The vast majority of people can take or leave the same psychoactive substances that supposedly lead inexorably to pharmacological slavery. And even when people develop a strong attachment to those intoxicants, they can and typically do moderate or stop their drug use without formal "treatment." As Peele has patiently [Archie: "not so patiently"] and cogently explained for nearly half a century, addiction is not a chemically triggered disease that hijacks people's brains but a pattern of behavior that makes sense in the context of lives and settings with few other sources of meaning. His approach not only fits the facts better than the disease model of addiction; it replaces that pseudomedical theory's autonomy-negating, coercion-inviting doctrines with a holistic understanding that makes room for individual choice and, ultimately, hope.

So profound. I wonder why Kasia wasn't ready to listen to me? And why has OSF been boycotting me? For one thing, I learned only in 2020, when Ethan Nadelmann finally told me (Ethan, as head of the Drug Policy Alliance, sat on policy groups with Kasia's husband): "Stannin, there's something you need to know about Kasia. Her husband is the foremost AA advocate in Poland." That alone, however, doesn't explain the intense repugnance for me she has displayed over decades.

In that time, have Kasia Malinowska and OSF unnecessarily blinded themselves and hindered their work by doing all they can to ignore me? In other words, would I not be helpful in their quest—in America's quest—to curb the quadrupling of the annual rate of drug deaths over the course of their work this century, a period during which three-quarters of a million Americans have died due to drugs (see Chapter 9)?

For her psychological comfort, Kasia won't listen to my radical point of view, which is the same as Carl's. But I am an unrelenting presence. Carl doesn't aim for the jugular as I do. He lets people slide by.

One of the people on the OSF panel was Holly Catania, a lawyer, who is director of policy and communications for the NYC Department of Health and Mental Hygiene. That's Gary Belkin's organization; Holly was scheduled to be a part of that conference call with Gary in 2017 that never happened. She presented a series of before-and-after pictures used by drug warriors to show the evil effects meth supposedly has on people. Her point: the pictures violated these drug users' privacy—*not* that they presented a distorted view of the effects of drug use. She actually accepted that view as reality.

This distortion was the whole point of convening the highly publicized panel. Carl regularly calls out the pictures that Katania showed this audience to be bullshit: "methamphetamine *alone* will not make you look like one of those grisly 'after' photos in the public service ads."

But he said nothing this time. *No one* in the audience or on the panel said anything about Catania's presentation, *which directly contradicted the purpose of (a) Carl's report, (b) this highly publicized OSF forum on drugs, (c) the entire purpose of the drug policy reform movement.* Bill Piper, a representative of the prestigious Drug Policy Alliance also on the panel, said nothing. Nor did Howard Josepher, a harm reduction pioneer and a friend of mine. Nor did Kasia, the director of the Open Society Foundations' international drug policy program.

I deconstruct this strange tableau of people seeing and hearing no evil in Chapter 9.

I *have* had some continuing involvement with the Drug Policy Alliance, an offshoot of Soros's OSF. Ethan Nadelmann is a longtime friend. At one point, Ethan told me, he tried to get George to read my book, *The Meaning of Addiction*, which Ethan says fundamentally changed his view of addiction and his approach to drugs. But Ethan wouldn't, or couldn't, intervene with Kasia on my behalf. I describe my long, strange trip with Ethan in Chapter 10.

In Part II of this book I describe how, despite these characteristic reactions to me, I have made my way in institutional America, survived and raised a family, while at the same time insinuating my views into mainstream addiction thinking and treatment. My ability to navigate this path was crucial to my life, of course, as well as perhaps, someday, to fundamentally altering American addiction science. If it hasn't already.

Part II

The Journey

Someone might think: "Stanton Peele—who graduated from the University of Pennsylvania, got a Ph.D. from a leading graduate program in social psychology, was among the youngest faculty members ever to teach at Harvard Business School, published a notable book in his twenties, was a member of the New Jersey and New York Bars, won awards in his field, lectures around the world, and was described by the leading alcoholism historian of his era as someone 'familiar to anyone who has worked in any capacity within the modern addictions field'—wants us to believe that he was a deprived professional outsider."*

I do. I am.

I was abandoned by the addiction field.

Meanwhile, my personal successes were matched by my failures.

And sometimes my purpose wavered. But never completely.

---

* As one measure of my (almost) "mainstreamness," I taught at HBS while both Mitt Romney and George W. Bush were students there, and my time at Penn overlapped with Donald Trump's.

5

Powering through School— with the Help of Friends

I didn't approach school like a vassal in servitude to a feudal lord. I didn't accept a subordinate role, even in areas where I felt I had things to learn. Instead, I saw myself as someone who had valuable contributions to make and a destiny to fulfill.

The capacity to shift between serious moral purpose and appreciation of art and other pleasures is our shared sensibility, expressed in emails and letters throughout our lives.

— Archie Brodsky

The summer after graduating from Wilson Junior High School, before entering Northeast High School, "Aaron" (all pseudonyms are placed within quotation marks the first time they appear), who lived about six houses down the block and was a year ahead of me, had a summer job working in the office at Northeast High School.

One day Aaron announced that he had seen the rosters for the gifted classes, and I wasn't on them.

I knew that my not being in the gifted classes at Northeast High School was impossible. I don't doubt my abilities and the recognition of them according to standard performance markers. Aaron was instead expressing a reaction to me—a disbelief in, or resentment of, who I am—that many people, male peers, including my brother and the man who legalized marijuana in America, Ethan Nadelmann, have had.

This is how school worked for me:

- It provided an environment in which I could have a socially accepted, even a valued, role.

- I had skills that allowed me to live a leisurely life while using the system to my advantage.
- It granted me kudos and accolades that would seemingly smooth my way through life after school.
- I always found people in academic settings who liked and were impressed by me and were willing to help me.
- I was always in danger of crashing and burning.

I do have a good education, which took some doing. In addition to funding my Ivy League schooling, my Ph.D., and law school, I had to pass all those classes and tests, write a Ph.D. dissertation, pass the New Jersey and New York Bars, and not piss off too many professors and administrators. That last one was touch and go.

I wasn't a particularly diligent or attentive, and certainly not an obedient, student. I went even further than that—I never backed off when I felt I'd been wronged or when I thought someone in charge was wrong.

But I value the academic ideals of intelligence, achievement, original thinking, honest speaking, valid science, and meaningful productivity. I often defended these values *against* the institutions that supposedly promulgated them (as I was doing at the Open Society panel at the end of Part I).

Jumping to my last stop on the education train ride, I entered law school at age 48. I never bought a law textbook (except for one). I sued the most prominent professor at my law school. I passed the New York Bar examination—regarded as the toughest in the country (John F. Kennedy, Jr., flunked it repeatedly)—in one try, even after showing up in Albany for the bar exam without any identification or a watch.

But I wasn't really good at legal thinking.

Let me review my education before that.

School

I went to Northeast High School in Philly, the school depicted five years after I left it in Frederick Wiseman's documentary, *High School*. I walked there from my home about a mile away. One semester I was late to school every day. At the end of all that, the city of Philadelphia gave me a full scholarship to Penn. But it took some twists for that to happen.

As a child, I was first identified for my math skill. My mother taught me sums before I went to school, at age 5, and I could do rows of addition and subtraction problems very quickly. Later, I was good at geometry, algebra, and trigonometry with little effort.

At age 13, in grade nine, I was part of a junior high school (now called middle school) math program that pushed us a year ahead. Two boys across my crowded block of row houses in Oxford Circle, who were 15, were in the gifted tenth grade geometry class at Northeast High. They showed me a problem that no one in their class could do. I solved it on the spot. They amazed their class by telling them what a 13-year-old kid in junior high had done.

Which was funny, because I wasn't viewed as a nerd math whiz. I was on the basketball team and played basketball in the schoolyard down the street from my home every day after school, usually with "Joel," my closest junior high and high school friend.

When I was in eleventh grade, they took four of us from my advanced math class—Michael Bratman, Steve Pein, Bob Zumoff, and me—and put us into the advanced class ahead of us for trigonometry. It was taught by the head of the school's math department, Dr. Huntsinger, and had only one thin text. I never did look at that book all semester, and didn't do all that well in the tests.

But the night before the citywide trig exam, I studied the book page by page for a couple of hours. A few weeks later, Dr. Huntsinger began our class by saying, "One of our students got the highest mark in the city. He only got one of the thirty-three problems wrong." I knew it was me—I knew which problem I had wrong and figured the right answer after the exam. After class, Ginny Levin, whom I fancied, confronted me with a wry smile and kicked my shin.

In my senior-year physics course, because I never looked at the problems in the textbook, when Mr. Barish gave us one of the text problems on the exam, I solved it my own way. I got the right answer, but Mr. Barish, after coloring in with crayon all of my calculations so I couldn't change anything, wrote on my paper "See me!" He suspected that I had copied the right answer from someone else's paper. In his office, Mr. Barish asked me to show how I solved the problem. He didn't really understand my logic. But he knew from the sheer force of my presentation that he had to give me credit; interactions such as this were to be repeated throughout my academic career.

The person who graduated first in each of Philadelphia's public high schools got a full boat to Penn, called the Mayor's Scholarship, including tuition and an offset against living expenses. I was ranked eighth out of about eight hundred students in my class based on grades. But they calculated your SAT scores into your final class standing, which brought me up to number four.

Michael Bratman, who went on to become head of the philosophy department at Stanford, was first in our class. He was also my nemesis. I considered him to be a rigid academic already, in high school, although we were on the basketball team together.

This is how I (barely) got to go to Penn: Bratman took a scholarship to Haverford instead of the city scholarship he was entitled to. The second in our class entered a special five-year combined college and medical program. Then Bobby Zumoff took the city scholarship designated for our school.

But one of the inner-city high schools in Philly, which had no one accepted at Penn, gave Northeast its scholarship. I got that one. It was kind of like getting a heart transplant from a deprived inner-city kid killed in a gang shooting. And that's how I entered the Ivy League, despite my reputation for not toeing the line.

Or else I wouldn't have gone to college at all directly from high school—which was unheard of where I came from. I applied to and was accepted to some colleges in other cities, but I received no other scholarship offers, and I would never apply to the fallback school in Philadelphia, Temple. My brother attended Temple since it was cheaper, even though he was admitted to Penn, in a pattern that marked his foreshortened life.

Is there a book titled *High School Is Your Template for Life*? It was true for me. Some teachers accepted and helped me. During the semester that I was late every day, my homeroom teacher was a tall, athletic woman gym teacher who shot baskets with me. Our homeroom met in the gymnasium. I came in the back door of the gym before the end of homeroom—which was good enough for her. Other than my lateness, I always treated her with respect and appreciated her forbearance. I'm not an ingrate.

Likewise, my senior-year English teacher, Cy Swartz, just out of college, went out of his way to be supportive, and reviewed my college application essays with me in a coffee shop after school.

My friend "Leon" was a gifted technician, and good in math and such, but a nonstarter in the humanities. He was skinny, a Jewish prince, unhappy and insecure. I never did anything in the shop classes we had to take. But one day each semester, Leon would leave off whatever advanced project he was working on and make me a tie rack or a garden spade. Unlike nearly everyone else in our advanced classes, Leon wasn't intimidated by authority.

Me, Leon, and the Space Program

We had a space program at Northeast High, called Project SPARC, run by Mr. Montgomery. Once we had an extended homeroom that coincided with some space launch. Mr. Montgomery, my and Leon's homeroom teacher, insisted that we listen to the broadcast for the entire period. Instead, Leon and I talked quietly, a sin for which the teacher sent us to the disciplinary vice principal (featured in the Wiseman documentary), Mr. Allen.

Without a trace of being shamed, Leon told Mr. Allen that we didn't feel Mr. Montgomery had the right to tell us how to spend our free period. Mr. Allen agreed!

I established my modus operandi for survival and success early on. I relied on people who liked me, both students and teachers, to whom my insouciance and originality and intelligence were appealing. I followed my own inclinations and did well in learning and testing. That's how I succeeded in high school, through college and graduate and law school. I established my economic survival skills early on, too.

Papa!

I wrote essays for fellow students in high school, one of whom was John Papa, a talented saxophone player. But someone told his teacher. The teacher simply made John write his own paper, for which he got a B. John reckoned that he didn't need to pay me, an issue that can come up, as we will see later, in my sustaining brand of capitalism.

I didn't speak to John after graduation. In my senior year of college, four years later, I was to visit a graduate school in New York. Although a long trip, it was close enough to Penn for me to drive there in a car my parents gave me. I recruited a friend who was also in social psychology to accompany me on the ride. But I was anxious that I didn't have enough money to cover gas and meals for both of us.

To get to New York from Penn, we had to drive along the Roosevelt Boulevard in Northeast Philly. As we got close to my old neighborhood, I saw a panel truck with "Papa Bread" on the side. I shouted, "Papa," and the driver beckoned for me to pull over. John got out, came over to my car, gave me a twenty-dollar bill, then returned to his truck without speaking.

My friend, having heard me shout "Papa," said incredulously, "That wasn't your father!"

Leon, the technician, and John, the musician, had unique skill sets, which I greatly admired, but I wasn't ultimately simpatico with either.

Leon got a job after high school diagnosing Volkswagens at a regional dealership. He did this simply by listening to the car engines when they entered the shop (Leon didn't like to get dirty). He never missed, just as I never saw him miss on a technical task.

Leon was not my best friend in high school. That was "Joel"—whose name I still use in security questions asking about your best childhood friend. But he died of a brain tumor at age 50 in a Hollywood rooming house. Joel lived with his family in a stand-alone home, which was unusual in our neighborhood. I spent my weekends sleeping in the extra bed in his room in a separate wing of his house, listening to Joan Baez and watching late-night movies on television.

Our main daytime activities were playing and watching basketball and other sports and doing creative bits cutting up everyone and everything in school, making tape recordings (Joel's parents gave him every toy) of our raunchy scenarios. But Joel, despite his remarkable skills of impersonation and improvisation, was embarked on a permanent separation from the world of achievement. I would *never* accept such a path for myself.

Although Joel and I shared so much in our alienation from the conventional world, which we lampooned together, his alienation paralyzed and defeated him. Joel didn't become addicted to drugs or alcohol or anything dramatic like that. But his world was as isolated as someone who was addicted. And he wanted me to join him there. However, unlike Joel, even as someone who saw and thought and acted in a way that defied conventional rules and resented the people who maintained them, I needed to engage with and succeed in that world.

Joel is the person with all the pictures on his walls that Archie (who came to know Joel) described at my sixtieth birthday party. Escaping that Oxford Circle bedroom was my *Odyssey*.

My Early Intellectual Connections

Mark Rosenthal is an internationally known modern art curator (his most well-known recent exhibit was the 2015 blockbuster "Diego Rivera and Frida Kahlo in Detroit"). Mark, Joel, and I formed a trio in high school. Joel was incredibly creative—he was a talented graphic artist along with his verbal and athletic brio, while Mark was systematic, practical, organized. And, so, it was perhaps funny that Mark became so distinguished in the art world, while the infinitely creative Joel never produced anything of value—something that still saddens me.

Mark knew New York already in high school. He read the *Village Voice* and introduced us to jazz—we went to the Village Vanguard to see Miles and Mingus. But my favorite place was the Five Spot, where Thelonious Monk regularly played (Mark named his older son Thelonious, called Theo).

Joel was precocious about film. His cultivated aunt got him a subscription to *Cahiers du Cinéma*, in which Andrew Sarris serialized his classic 1968 book, *The American Cinema: Directors and Directions*. Sarris presented the auteur theory—that great films were expressions of the creative visions of their directors—and argued for the greatness of American films and the brilliance of American and Euro-American directors like Hitchcock, Ford, Lubitsch, Welles, et al.—all of whose films I still see regularly.

The American Cinema is a touchstone for my life. It sits by my bed, where I regularly look up films (and their directors) playing at Film Forum (pre-Covid) or on TCM. Although by now I know quite a bit of what's in there, it still delights me to read Sarris's thoughts and writing. Sarris has formed one of the common references for my and Archie's lifetime of intellectual and aesthetic sharing, which, in addition to film, has included folk music and R&B, politics, sports, addiction, our family and personal lives and those of friends, then forensics (psychology and psychiatry and the law), and much more.

As Archie wrote me in 2017 about our shared intellectual life:

> Because the currents of our communication run so deep, I'm most often motivated to respond to you before anyone else, except for timely work or personal matters, sometimes not getting around to other contacts for weeks, months, or ever.
>
> I've thought about what may happen if you predecease me. Losing that communication will leave a hole. It's time that I can and must (if that's how things work out) fill productively. But you also call my attention to things I wouldn't otherwise see, as well as stimulating me to think and write things that otherwise would never come into my head.

We have exchanged letters and emails and visits for all of our nearly sixty years knowing one another (with a few timeouts). Archie has provided me with ballast, insight, perspective, and faith. I've needed that.

College—and Archie

I was admitted, at age 17, to the General Honors Program at Penn, based on my SAT scores. By any other academic criteria, I wouldn't have qualified. The honors program consisted of small, intensive seminars. I met highly intelligent people, some of whom I would know for life.

Penn gave General Honors students our own lounge in which to socialize, out of a recognition that informal intellectual "conversational" exchange is as important to intellectual and personal development as what went on in class. "Yvonne" was one such student from a non-Jewish, Main Line background. The Main Line was an upscale set of suburban communities outside of Philadelphia. It was a very different social milieu from the one in which I was reared. At that time, women weren't allowed in men's dormitories at Penn, and the reverse was certainly forbidden. So Yvonne and I had sex in the Honors lounge.

At our fiftieth reunion (which I didn't attend) Yvonne, who had become a physician, told Archie when he brought up my name that she just went along with having sex with me. But two years after our Honors lounge liaisons, I encountered Yvonne as I was walking to my apartment in Powelton Village, where she also lived. She seemed glad to see me, and we went to my apartment.

I had two girlfriends from Philadelphia while I was at Penn, both of whom I kept up with through graduate school and even after (one of whom, a musician, I remained involved with after her marriage). I wanted to have a soul-sharing relationship, but I couldn't find one until Mary. My primary relationships were with men, in high school, college, and graduate school.

Smart people who did well in high school experience uncertainty and intellectual anxiety when they enter college. My confidence in my ability was unswerving. Although I certainly had many anxious moments in college, I never doubted my brilliance.

Nonetheless, Archie was something else. In high school, Leon and Joel had areas of knowledge and skills that I didn't, that I admired and appreciated. Archie took those skills—and my admiration—to a whole new level. Archie knew things—and, moreover, had an ability to digest information and distill ideas into words—that stunned me.

I have an intellectual disability. I can't remember exact phrases and names. My mother would never permit me to be labeled, however. "Never, ever shortchange yourself" was her mantra. And so, with Mary and Archie (and now my daughter Anna), I sometimes stake out some area I want to discuss, without remembering the names of the people or things involved. Then I turn to them to fill in the blanks. Now I do that reconstruction instantly by Googling phrases and ideas or looking up my previous writings. But my school life and my work have always involved strategies for working around my weaknesses.

> ### On Being Sued in My Sixties, and Getting Archie's Help
>
> Decades later, in my sixties, my rehab partners sued me out of a combination of business and personal reasons, even though we shared a non-disease approach to treating addiction. They wanted out of my advantageous contract, which I had written with Archie's help, since they figured that they had my program, and now they had to do all the work that was bringing in a geyser of money.
>
> They had sued their prior addiction treatment program creators, who ran their own program separately now. Since that group had a successful rehab to fund them, they could afford to fight their and my former partners in court for years. I couldn't do that. Instead, I acted as my own lawyer, with Archie's help, against a high-powered corporate legal firm my partners hired. Readers have to realize that, unquestionably, all of the best courtroom submissions from either side were written by Archie.
>
> At one point I had a meeting with the staff of the program my partners had previously sued. Their group, which I have worked with for decades, promotes a non-disease approach similar to mine, going to the extent of not even believing in addiction. I like their instincts toward self-reliance, but I *do* think addiction is an actual, recognizable syndrome. I just think that, rather than being an independent biological process, it is created by people's thinking and life context. I outlined my multidimensional, cognitive-behavioral model of addiction in *The Meaning of Addiction* in 1985. As of 2020, I was still writing "In Defense of the Concept of Addiction" in *Filter* to get my complex vision across.
>
> Nonetheless, I met with several members of this group to gather their inputs in my court fight. We sat around a table with Archie on speakerphone. When I ultimately negotiated a court-supervised settlement at the federal courthouse with my former partners, Archie participated the same way. I loved the federal judge checking things with Archie—"What does Archie think?"—before moving on to the next point.
>
> In our discussions with my colleagues who had also been in court with my former partners, I would speak until I realized I had said as much as I could, then abruptly stop talking. Archie, at the other end of a purely audio connection, would pick up seamlessly where I left off, taking what I had been discussing to the next level.
>
> After the meeting, the founder and director of the program said to me, "That was the most amazing thing I've ever seen." Clueless, I asked, "What was?"
>
> "The way you interacted with Archie, like an extra part of your brain."

Archie had gone to Central, the academic magnet school for boys in Philly, where he got the Mayor's Scholarship to Penn. But he didn't elect to receive the extra money to live on campus, and instead remained in his parents' home in Philly. Archie was then a socially isolated person. In our junior year he moved in with me and a third roommate, "Warren." After Warren got married (see Chapter 3), we roomed in our senior year with another lifelong friend, "Lewis."

I spent my college years and after trying to learn how to write like Archie. In a class we took together called American Civilization, I would watch Archie sit and squirm nervously during the first half of an exam thinking, or whatever, before he started writing. I, meanwhile, writing from the opening gun, would complete several more pages than Archie. Archie's paper would be returned with an A and a scribbled sentence from the professor extolling his synthesis as the best in the class.

My lifelong writing career since then has been split between working with Archie, as we did on *Love and Addiction* and our 1991 self-help book, *The Truth About Addiction and Recovery*, or else trying to compensate for his missing contribution or to find another writing partner to do so. But, ultimately, I have had to make do with my own writing abilities. I can be funny and evocative, and I do have an abundance of ideas. But I'll never encapsulate as much meaning as succinctly as Archie can.

In 2014 I published *Recover!: An Empowering Program to Help You Stop Thinking Like an Addict* with Ilse Thompson. In 2019 Zach Rhoads and I published *Outgrowing Addiction: With Common Sense Instead of "Disease" Therapy*. (Both comment on working with me in the Afterword.) Neither of those did as well as *L&A* or *Truth*, through no fault of Ilse's or Zach's, both of whom could contribute on-the-ground addiction substance content that Archie couldn't.

However, Archie looked in as my coauthors and I were finishing those books; he is reviewing this book, while also doing the forensic work with psychiatrists through which he supports his household (which includes his talented wife Vicki, who is also working on this book). I need Archie, not only to check the book for style and coherence, but in order accurately to recall my own life.

Archie (right) and me in the 1970s

I am currently working with a number of people in this phase of my professional life, more than I ever have. But Archie is still an impossible act to duplicate. Archie, meanwhile, has made his living by writing for other professionals. He has almost never written in his own voice. Like me, now in his midseventies, he has no pension and hasn't accumulated a nest egg for retirement. He is employed at an hourly rate—which is, essentially, subsistence income.

There is no justice.

Late in my sixties, I was employed by a law firm to critique the treatment of several patients in a well-known rehab chain, for which I wrote several reports. Then I turned the report writing over to Archie, splitting the fee (his share amounting to more than he was usually paid). After I turned in Archie's report, the lawyer told me that his consulting psychiatrist said that this report was the best he had ever read.

When I told this to Archie, he said, "Don't you think I've heard that before?" Archie's family and friends (including me) think he has given his skills away too cheaply. I have tried to compensate in recent years. What does it mean that Archie has played second fiddle (to me and others) his entire professional life? What implications has it had for me and for Archie? Form your own theory. Many others have.

Getting through College

School always worked for me. I can effortlessly synthesize thoughts and information from disparate sources. I never panic in testing situations. And I can write just as quickly as I speak.

After my first two years of special seminar courses in the General Honors program, each semester I took one political science course (I was a poly sci major), one anthropology course (where Penn was a world leader), one statistics or philosophy of science course, one psychology course, and one literature course. I used the same loose-leaf book and binder dividers throughout those last two years at Penn.

In my junior year, I got a 3.8 average (9 A's and one B). In pulling that off, I got three grades changed. When confronted with what I considered an inadequate grade from a graduate assistant—who, let's face it, couldn't be as brilliant as me—I marched into the professor's office and had them read my paper or test. In two cases, one in literature and one in anthropology with a world-famous scholar, Anthony F. C. Wallace, who combined psychology with anthropology, the professors raised my grade.

Bonnie Kind Saves My Career

The professor was not always the savior. There was my social psychology course professor. Despite being a Poly Sci major, I planned on going to grad school in social psychology. Yet I took only one psychology course per semester. In my junior year I took social psychology, which was taught by a rather dour professor, Albert Pepitone. Pepitone had been in on the revolution in social psychology (the best-known example of which is cognitive dissonance), but felt that he had never been given due credit.

At the end of the class, I received my grade by mail in the apartment I shared with Archie: C. This was in the field in which I planned to get a Ph.D.! I instantly called the professor's office, where I got his graduate assistant, Bonnie Kind.

She took one minute to review my course record, then said, "Let me call you back."

After waiting an hour, I was about to go directly to the office to argue my case when the phone rang: "He's changed your grade to a B." (Remember, my ten course grades in my junior year were nine A's and one B.)

"You just spent an hour arguing with him to get him to raise my grade?" I gasped. I just was not used to people sticking up on my behalf. What guts that showed!

Postscript: About a dozen years later, I gave a guest lecture to a class for a teacher I knew at Kean College in New Jersey, where Mary and I lived. Glancing at the campus newspaper, I saw an article about the Dean of Students—Bonnie Kind. I called her office and scheduled a lunch, at which I gave her a copy of *Love and Addiction*. "If it weren't for you," I told her, "this book might never have been written."

Postscript 2: At my sixtieth birthday party at my condo clubhouse in New Jersey after my divorce, Archie gave one of his priceless commemorative speeches (quoted throughout this book and the Afterword) in which he recounted the Bonnie Kind story. "Instead of just thanking her as most undergraduates would have done, Stanton said to her, 'I know you know you didn't have to do this, and it could only be trouble for you. I appreciate and admire your integrity.'"

It was only then, forty years later, that I realized Archie had overheard my phone call with Bonnie.

Bob Bamberg was an English professor whom Archie and I met when he taught in the General Honors program. Bamberg was our first intellectual mentor. We cut our teeth on the ideas and analyses he presented, even though I often disagreed with his socially conservative, pre-1960s slant.

When I was awarded my fellowship, he said, "We (in the English Department) regard your fellowship like one of our own."

Bamberg left Penn to teach at Bates college in Maine. Archie, Mary, and I continued to visit Bamberg there for several years while I was at Harvard Business School. I was building a house down the road from Lewiston, where Bamberg lived in an old house with his family.

At Penn, however, I was closest to a Poly Sci professor, Henry Teune, whom Archie and I had to our apartment for dinner, and at whose apartment with his wife and small daughter we went to watch a late-night Hitchcock movie. It was a tribute to Henry's openness, and to my and Archie's intellectual precocity, that we had such an egalitarian relationship. Henry would take me to the faculty lounge as though it made sense for me to be there in my patched dungarees. He would ask me if I were old enough to drink legally (no, I wasn't 21) and order me a beer.

I did well for myself at Penn, though not as well as Archie. Archie graduated Penn summa cum laude, Phi Beta Kappa, with an award for the best honors thesis in English literature, on D. H. Lawrence's *Women in Love*. He was offered a fellowship to Stanford's graduate program in English, which he chose not to attend. Aspiring to write fiction, he said he didn't want an academic career. I graduated cum laude with the award for the best honors thesis in the social sciences for my *Psychological Aspects of International Conflict*. It came with a $250 award that I used—I needed—to travel to Michigan for graduate school.

As I said, academia was my home ground. I could always succeed there, including getting by financially.

At a Prestigious Graduate School

Provided for by my fellowship, and paying for my gas and first month's rent and deposit with my senior thesis prize money, I trundled off to the University of Michigan's Doctoral Program in Social Psychology in Ann Arbor. I selected the program at Michigan because it combined sociology and psychology, with an emphasis on real-world research. For me, it was the best program in the country. Unfortunately, as one symbol of the problems I was to have at Michigan, the program dissolved before I graduated, so that I got a grandfathered Ph.D. in social psychology from a defunct program.

What remained of social psychology dropped into the psychology department. The reduction of the program into one corner of psychology showed the ever-diminishing perspective in the social sciences, psychology, and psychiatry that I have faced in my lifetime. *It has become the greatest*

academic virtue to shrink the study of human beings to minuscule, artificially iso-
lated islands, no matter how much is lost and how trivial the results. The same
reductionism has prevailed—is even worse—in the addiction field. Reducing human behavior to particular mechanical dynamics not involving how
people think or how they interact within groups and cultures and their actual
situations is now the epitome of the scientific study of humanity.

This reductionism prevails even as no one in the world (including the
brain-disease-fixated director of the National Institute on Drug Abuse)
believes that people in urban Baltimore and rural Appalachia have the
same likelihood of becoming addicted as doctors, politicians, and drug
policy advocates who work with purpose, make good salaries, and teach
their children to believe that the world works for them.

The head of the experimental social psychology program was Bob
Zajonc, whose main scientific contribution was "The Attitudinal Effects
of Mere Exposure," meaning that people mindlessly liked things the more
often they had encountered them. The psych department's version of social
psychology was to run microscopic experiments in which one factor was
manipulated to see if 48 percent of the treated group reacted a certain way,
while only 30 percent of the other (the control) group acted that way. And
that was considered a valid (i.e., statistically significant) result.

Now, decades later, the results of a large number of these experiments
have failed to be replicated. At best, the ideas they developed, like Zajonc's,
were trivial and useless. These researchers may have convinced themselves
that their work was valid and important. But they were actually creating
an arcane body of knowledge whose principal effect was to establish their
reputations and advance themselves in their own remote, artificial world. I
could never, congenitally, be a part of this world.

When I graduated from Penn, I was accepted by a number of graduate
programs with financial support, several of whose faculty called to tell me
they wanted me. I *chose* Michigan because the social psychology program
integrated psychological and broader social perspectives—groups, organizations, and society. It was the promise of such greater engagement that
drew me to Michigan.

Getting through Michigan

Typical of my academic life, I was to find much of value at Michigan, including important emotional and intellectual support, and final disillusionment.
I often skirted the edges of expulsion and permanent exile from the regular,
academic world. But did I really want to be there?

As soon as I got to Michigan I encountered Stanley, a student in the joint social psychology program two years ahead of me. He had attended college at offbeat, engaged Antioch College. I needed an apartment when I arrived in Ann Arbor. Stanley was looking for a roommate and proposed that we live together. He then found his own, single apartment in a small house at the end of a dead-end street overlooking a panoramic view of the campus. Although Stanley, typically, had ignored the plan we agreed on, his pad had a sister apartment above it that I moved into.

I learned from that apartment search that just being near Stanley, with his energy and initiative, was rewarding, although he was erratic and you constantly had to check up on him. But I could harness his skills. Stanley had an encyclopedic knowledge of experimental psychology. He was also tremendously knowledgeable and analytic about history, world cultures, and international politics. And he could relate this knowledge succinctly in well-written English.

I had somehow, instantly found someone at Michigan who was very smart, who looked at things in a broader context than other psychologists, who was also an active researcher. And he was a social misfit.

What a find.

We soon became inseparable, eating dinner together nightly. Whereas I cooked dinner when I lived with Archie, Stanley prepared our meals. Our living together sometimes resulted in complicated romantic entanglements where we slept with the same women, only sometimes in sequence. One woman seemed intent on following my lead in the kind of research I did and life I lived (like me, she later went on to become an activist lawyer). She slept with Stanley without telling me. Stanley, honest to the core, confessed. (We should have had a threesome, but I wasn't up to that.)

All of my relationships with women at Michigan were short-lived. But I met Mary there.

From the start, I was expected to do research and to publish journal articles. But I didn't want to work for a professor. I wasn't in graduate school to pursue other people's thinking and work. The Wilson Fellowship allowed me to be totally independent. But it had a trick clause: it was only for a year. So I had to find funding for my second year in grad school almost as soon as I arrived in Ann Arbor.

Stanley was the man. Here's what we did: The fall I arrived in Ann Arbor, 1967, saw the March on Washington in October. Stanley and I boarded a bus in Chicago and administered questionnaires to the protestors. The questionnaires were lengthy; but it was a long bus ride.

A questionnaire, like all research, has to have a focus, an underlying vision you are exploring about how people think and act. Stanley and I had been discussing whether protestors felt they were in a revolt against America, or that they were making it more like their ideal of what America should be. It turned out to be the latter. (I wonder if that's still true.)

Now that's psychology.

And it so happened that two socially oriented professors at Michigan were doing research in this area, called political roles. One, Dan Katz, who was highly distinguished, was overseas that year. (In the Conclusion I describe my ultimate relationship with Dan Katz in connection with the famed Katz-Newcomb lecture at the University of Michigan.) The other, Herb Kelman (now a professor emeritus of social ethics at Harvard, renowned for his peacemaking efforts in the Middle East), was on campus. Herb agreed to help design the questionnaire and to sponsor our work by getting us a small grant to cover our expenses. The game was on.

In the days before the trip to Chicago to board the buses, we spent late nights at Herb's beautiful home on the Huron River. I let Stanley go over the items in our questionnaire with Herb—I wouldn't usually turn that over to someone, but Stanley was even better at it than I was. The night before we left for Chicago to board our bus of protestors, Herb said, "We're not going to get this done in time." It was 11:30, and I was sitting in the living room talking to Rose, Herb's wife. I said, "You can finish it in another hour—let's go." And they did. I was 21—Stanley was four years older and Herb was 40.

We went to Chicago, rode the buses and gave out the questionnaires, attended the protests, and returned to Chicago to pick up Stanley's car to drive home. Oh, his automatic-transmission Renault caught fire in Indiana, and we had to abandon the car after I threw my coat over the engine to put out the flames. Stanley had AAA road services, so he had his car towed to a repair shop and we got a bus home. A lot of money was wasted there—but that was Stanley.

We proceeded to code all of the protestors' responses and then analyze the data with the statistical programs available at the Institute for Social Research (ISR) at Michigan. We wrote and published two papers, one describing how we conducted research on a live social action, "On Studying a Social Movement" (our original whimsical title, "It's Such a Comfort to Take the Bus," was deemed too offbeat for academia) in the *Public Opinion Quarterly*. The other, with our results, "A Study of Participants in an Anti-Vietnam War Demonstration," was published in the *Journal of Social Issues*. We found that youthful protesters thought of themselves as good citizens, defined by protesting violations of basic American values. Our article won an award from the Society for the Study of Social Issues.

Not bad. Before the year's end, still in my first semester in grad school, still 21, I applied for a federal fellowship to continue funding my education. I needed a faculty spon-

Stan (left) and me in our grad school days

sor, so I went to Herb Kelman with my application. He looked at me quizzically: "You seem to rub some faculty the wrong way, Stanton." This from a man who was faculty sponsor of the Vietnam War resistance movement!

"Herb," I said, "If you don't sign this, I'm out on my ass." I thrust my application in front of him. He signed it, saying, "It's just that you give the impression of not needing anyone's help."

Grad school could be tough for recalcitrant me

When the joint sociology-psychology program I entered dissolved, I opted to grandfather into it, rather than becoming a part of Zajonc's experimental social psychology program. The requirements were vast and difficult. You had to complete a survey research project AND an experiment before they would let you do your Ph.D. dissertation. My experiment was titled, "The Thrill of the Chase: A study of achievement motivation and dating behavior," which I conducted and wrote up and published with Stanley. We identified something we called social achievement motivation, where people selected as potential mates partners who they felt were moderately challenging, but not overly so. Most student-subjects did not follow the addictive style of finding someone they could dominate, or else someone whom they would revere as being far beyond their own level.

In addition to all that, I had to pass a series of tests, rather than one comprehensive Ph.D. exam, since the joint program covered three diverse areas.

These were experimental social psychology, developmental psychology (people changing over their life spans), and social structure (social status and behavior). *These developmental and social perspectives have been critical to how I see human behavior, including addiction and mental illness.* People with exclusively clinical training aren't equipped or inclined to consider these real-world factors.

At the same time that I was studying social psych, I was developing my ideas about addiction—the evolution of which I describe in Chapter 3. Plus, I viewed my time at Michigan as a period to explore myself, movies, and relationships. As a result, I short-shrifted the key classes, called "proseminars," which dealt with the experimental, developmental, and social arenas. The most difficult of these to finesse was experimental social psychology, since it covered specific studies and findings that couldn't necessarily be divined through common sense. You really had to know what the results of a given study were (as unreliable as those results have since often been revealed to be).

The night before the exam, I rushed down to Stanley's apartment to get him to review the course material, which he had studied two years before me. He wasn't home! In a panic, I ran to the campus. As luck would have it, I encountered Stanley just as he was leaving the library. "STANLEY!" I dragged him home, and we spent all night going over each study on the syllabus, with Stanley explaining the result of each and its significance.

Having stayed up all night, I completed the all-day exam, then returned to our shared apartment building. I burst in on Stanley, who was still sleeping. "I aced every question! No one could have done better!" In fact, I got the highest grade, along with Don Des Jarlais, who became a well-known drug and AIDS researcher whom I would run into decades later at conferences around the world.

There was one thing about this exam process I haven't mentioned. Those who were opting to pursue social psychology within the psychology department were instructed to complete both a morning and an afternoon segment of the test, while those of us who were using it as only one-third of the overall comprehensive exam for the passé, integrated program were told to do only the morning part.

Crafty me, seeing that the whole social psych kaboodle was in flux, although I was instructed to only do the morning test since I was staying in the joint program, did both parts. Come to pass, those in the joint program who followed that instruction and only did the morning part were later required to study for and to take an additional exam to replace the afternoon part. Like the afternoon questions would reveal whole new areas of knowledge about those stupid experiments!

But I did one other thing while completing both parts of the test. I wrote a note saying that I thought it was unnecessary to have the two separate parts, that the afternoon demonstrated no greater knowledge, or scientific capacity, than the morning part alone; rather, each session was designed to include topics that represented the research of various faculty members.

Boy, did that get a reaction! Gene Burnstein, a well-respected social psychologist who prided himself on being close to the students (Stan and I had him and his wife over for dinner), told me, "I said in the faculty meeting, 'He's throwing the gauntlet down—let's pick it up and throw him the fuck out of the program!'" But they didn't. Schools were my natural habitat, benign territory for me. I was good enough at schooling that, however many people I irked, I survived. This was bad preparation for the tough life waiting for me outside the student world.

My South African dissertation

Having completed those survey and experimental research projects, and my comprehensive exams, I was now ready to do my dissertation. Here's how people did that in a big academic mill like Michigan. They became part of an ongoing research program and chiseled out some slice of the data that were collected to analyze and write up for themselves. Or, perhaps, they did a study that followed a body of work some professor was engaged in, which the faculty member mapped out for them.

Guess what? I didn't do that. Stanley had decamped for Cape Town, South Africa, where he had landed a visiting faculty job at the university. I had relatives in Johannesburg. So following my first two years in grad school, at age 23, I went to Africa. Stanley had conducted a study of the South African national election, which I then completed with him. Archie ultimately wrote up this research while I was teaching at the Harvard Business School. We published it in the *American Political Science Review* in 1974 as "Ethnic Voting and Political Change in South Africa."

We showed that South Africa was the ultimate in identity politics. The ruling National Party, which consecrated apartheid, stood for Afrikaner (Dutch descendant) pride and identity. The opposition party, the United Party, and the left Progressive Party were both rooted in the minority English-speaking community. We asked respondents what language they spoke at home as a child, and what language they used at home now. The only way Afrikaans-born South Africans would switch political parties, no matter how liberal their political ideology, was if they had actually become English-speaking South Africans.

We were keying into people's identities, how they saw themselves, and how this affected crucial parts of their lives and behavior. We wrote another paper based on research Stanley did, "Coloured Power or Coloured Bourgeoisie," based on the so-called Coloured (mixed-race) population in Cape Town, where Stanley lived and worked. Some theories hold that it is relatively better-off groups like the Cape Coloureds* in South Africa that lead revolutions. We found instead that, aspiring to be accepted, they were often more conservative than white voters. This same analysis applies to many Latinx voters (like Cuban Americans) in the US today. They "reject this designation (as a minority, people of color). They prefer to see themselves as a group integrating into the American mainstream." In my concluding chapter, I describe how my work on political identity ties into my work on addiction.

Aftermath: Law School

I entered law school in 1994, when I was 48 years old, with three children. I didn't really want to be a lawyer, if that meant leaving psychology. But I felt that law school would give me better intellectual breadth and operating skills politically, as well as for understanding the situation of drug users, many of whom I would come to represent in family court. I was living in Morristown, New Jersey. It was convenient, and cheap, for me to go to Rutgers night law school in Newark. Ethan Nadelmann (then at Princeton's school of government, he was to become my most longstanding professional associate in the drug and addiction field—see Chapter 10) wrote me a recommendation which included the line: "I wish I could be there to see Stanton confront professors not used to being challenged when he finds they are off track." I had him remove that sentence, although it proved prescient.

Guess what: I found a younger student, a serious, smart, but slightly offbeat former Catholic schoolgirl who lived near me in Morris County and with whom I carpooled. Since I never bought a textbook, "Regina" reviewed for me the assigned cases in our two classes during our half-hour commute to school four nights a week. I actually can't absorb lectures

---

* I know that the term used now is "people of color." But the name used for this mixed-race group in South Africa, even today, is "Cape Coloureds."

or read uninteresting legal material. I have always relied on people like Regina who can digest and clearly present information. I can then tap directly into their minds.

I wasn't as brilliant at law as I was at psychology. I didn't instantly see all facets of a case and tune into the true center of the legal issues. But, as my mother made me realize, you don't have to be—can't be—good at everything. Regina, my colleague, was an excellent legal scholar, which compensated for my mediocrity in legal analysis.

Tapping Into People's Minds

I can enter other people's minds—not to take control of them (that's impossible), but to use what they know.

Once, at Anna Peele's apartment, we played Trivial Pursuit. Anna and her husband, Alex, were one team. Two friends of Alex's formed another. I was paired with "Lynne," the younger sister of one of the friends. She was open and personable, but she had had a lifetime of psychological problems and her thinking was opaque and jumbled.

I soon realized that the clues and answers in this updated version of the game were about contemporary cultural matters I knew nothing about. I said, "The names in the questions are like mysterious bugs buzzing around my ears." The woman said, "Welcome to my world."

But she *did* know the facts in the trivia questions; she just couldn't package that information into answers. So I asked her for her reactions to the questions, then sorted through the bits she provided to get the correct answers.

We won. Afterward, Anna—who isn't given to praising me—said, "Everyone was impressed with how you worked with Lynne, Dad."

But Regina got benefits from our partnership, too. Together, we entered the law school negotiation and trial competitions. We won the negotiation competition and went to the regional finals, where we also did well. We came in second in the trial competition, because the woman judge objected to Regina's (quite sensible) approach of speaking in a motherly way to a child witness (played by young Anna—who was great) during questioning.

Still, a first and a second for competitions that included both day and night students—not bad! (When I told Ethan I had won the negotiation competition, he responded, "You mean they let you enter that with regular students?")

There was one more competition the next year, our last, where you argued an appeal-style brief before a panel of faculty judges. I made the finals in the competition, based on an initial argument and written brief. But my brief was lame, and I was in last place among the eight final contestants. I argued against the first-place brief writer, a top day student. I beat him badly, so he didn't make the final four. But my brief was so weak that, even combined with my superlative oral arguments, I also didn't make the finals.

Based on our successes, Regina was invited to join an elite honors society of law students and got a clerkship with a local judge. She was, as always, utterly capable and loved. The judge she worked for threw a party when Regina passed the bar exam. The judge practically cried when she described how effective Regina had been as her clerk (since she realized she'd never have another clerk like her). Regina went on to head a prominent medical organization's legal department.

I didn't get invited into anything, despite my demonstrated skills at negotiating, trial work, and courtroom persuasion.

Attending classes, I became annoyed by our ego-bloated constitutional law professor, Gary Francione. Francione was an animal rights activist, and I thought he took his arguments on animals beyond reason—we don't display that level of regard for some human beings! I had heard that he had made a special deal with the Rutgers Medical School never to investigate their animal research in return for certain favors from Rutgers. I sued in state court via the open public records act to see the medical school's files concerning negotiations with Francione. Francione had to hire an attorney while he seethed in the back of the court as I argued my case.

It was hopeless on my part, due to the combination of my rudimentary courtroom skills and the baked-in institutional resistance to my cause. I never saw Francione again, but I imagine he might hate me to this day. (It so happens that one of my online addiction coaches worked closely with Francione for years on animal rights—I never told her about my set-to with him, but she might read it here.)

I took the NJ and NY bar exams in the fall of 1997, after graduating law school that spring and studying with Regina over the summer at a bar prep course we took. I had to take the New York Bar exam in Albany, hundreds of miles away. I drove hours to Albany, stayed at a fleabag hotel, and was up all night from the heat (the place didn't have air conditioning) and anxiety—including my realization that I had brought no ID, not even my driver's license. I also had no watch. The next day, I somehow wormed my way into the test site, a vast hall which I quickly realized had no clock. The woman at the desk next to me pulled out five wristwatches and carefully placed them on her desktop.

I turned to her: "Could you lend me one of your watches? If your other watches fail, I promise I will instantly return it to you." After the exam, I drove to New Jersey to complete the next two of the three days of exams—first stopping at home to pick up my ID. I stayed with my friend, Rutgers law and philosophy professor Doug Husak (with whom I wrote an article while at law school on Supreme Court drug-testing decisions), who lent me his watch.

The first day in Jersey I took the multi-state, computer-scored, non-essay part of the bar examination required by both NY and NJ. I powered through the first half of the test in the morning, then returned after a leisurely bathroom break, turned the next page in the exam booklet, and realized that the questions were many times as long and complex as the first part! I finished in a frenzy. In the afternoon, I marveled again at how easy the initial part of the exam was, powered through it, then took a walk around the grounds of the hotel where the exam was administered. When I came back—same thing.

When I described my day to Mary, she said, "You don't know that you intentionally bring things to an emergency, red-lights-screeching level before you trouble yourself to concentrate and take them seriously?" (I *did* love *Man On Wire*, the documentary about Philippe Petit's walking on a wire across the towers of the World Trade Center; Mary hated it.)

The next day after the multiple choice, I did the New Jersey essay exams covering the major areas of law. Unlike the New York exam, which had trick questions about special areas of New York law to keep too many people from passing, New Jersey stuck to the basics.

I passed both bars, New York and New Jersey, first try. Privileged? Lucky? Gifted? Crafty?

My Act in Court

In family court hearings, I never made legal arguments to the judge, or really even factual ones. The judge knew the law better than I did, and usually had already decided where he or she was heading. I instead explored where the judge was willing to go with the case by asking questions. Everyone noted my peculiar courtroom style.

A publicly assigned client of mine lost custody of her children because she had left them unattended in a shelter all night in order to be with her boyfriend. The state was seeking to permanently revoke her parental rights. The attorney general's office sent a senior lawyer from Trenton, along with the county's prosecutor for the state, to prosecute the case. The state also provided a lawyer for the children, who sat with the prosecutors. Thus I sat alone competing with three seasoned lawyers.

The prosecutors presented as a witness the woman who managed the shelter. When I cross-examined, I asked if she thought the mother was bonded to her two small daughters—which I knew she was. The witness—a caring professional—agreed that she was. I asked, "Is it bad for a child to be deprived of a bonded relationship with a parent?" Looking shaken, the woman agreed that it was. I asked, "What are the consequences of breaking such a bond?" The woman hesitantly described the kind of heartbreaking damage that could result. "Yet you want to do that to these children?" The woman, with anguish in her voice, said, "I really had to wrestle with myself to testify today."

"Your honor," I suggested after she left the stand. "Would you interview the two children in your chambers?" The attorney representing the children jumped up and said that it would be traumatic for the children to be subjected to cross-examination by the prosecutors and me. I said, "How about if the prosecutors and I absent ourselves so that you and the judge can question the children yourselves." What could she do but agree? I knew that a semi-retired older judge who was a grandfather would *never* deprive the small girls of their mother. Which he didn't. The AG's office *never* lost cases to terminate parental rights. But I beat the State. And I believe that was a good thing in this case.

I also testified in major cases around the country, usually as an expert for the prosecution. I was an expert witness for the federal prosecutor in Jackson, Mississippi, in a death-penalty trial of a man who had killed his coke dealer and the dealer's girlfriend. Before the trial began, I was questioned for hours during voir dire (examination of my expert credentials with the jury not present) by a woman attorney who specialized in defending such cases. The attorney was well informed of my views on addiction. She was making the argument that the man's addiction made it impossible for him to exercise judgment (as Nora Volkow, the director of the National Institute on Drug Abuse, argues). At one point she prodded me, "Do you mean that my mother, who quit smoking twelve years ago, doesn't wake up every morning thinking about cigarettes?" I responded, "And if she decided she wanted one, would she kill somebody to get it?" The attorney stamped her foot and pirouetted away from me.

The judge declared me an expert: "Dr. Peele is listed as an adviser on substance disorders in the volume (then *DSM-IV*) we are using as a reference. How can I ignore one of the professionals who wrote that document?

However, I want to caution the defense and Dr. Peele that, as entertaining as this questioning has been, I won't tolerate any theatrics in front of the jury." After the hearing, I asked the federal prosecutor why he didn't jump in to object to the attorney's hectoring me. He answered, "Why? You were doing fine."

The defendant was convicted of first-degree murder—life without parole—but one juror refused to vote for the death penalty, which was fine by me.

I could have been a wondrous courtroom attorney.

6

My Blessed Life and Fall From Grace

A brief recap and look ahead: My life so far, if not privileged, was fortunate. Life at home with my father was tough, but I tried not to let it hinder me. My mother loved me and thought I was a genius. I got a full-boat scholarship to an Ivy League college and was part of a hands-on program for the best students there. I did well enough to win a prestigious fellowship to grad school. I had Archie and Stanley to get me through those institutions, along with faculty members who took a shine to me.

In the following few years, my life seemed even more blessed. I traveled to South Africa and readily found a job and girlfriends. While there, I contacted Penguin Books to write Love *and* Addiction *and conducted the research for my Ph.D. dissertation. I then returned to Michigan to complete my dissertation, got a faculty position at the Harvard Business School, and completed* L&A, *a book that jump-started a revolution in the addiction field.*

Yet all of this success, taken together, resulted in my fall from grace. I entered several decades where I struggled to make a living, although I continued to write books, get media attention, and even win awards. I was singled out and vilified in an organized campaign against the idea of harm reduction in alcoholism—called "controlled drinking." Later, Mary divorced me, after thirty years together, and I entered an emotional tailspin.

I have been recapturing my groove in my seventies, re-emerging as a force in the great addiction war and drug epidemic, as we will see. This memoir is part of that project.

Everybody's in show biz, it doesn't matter who you are
And those who are successful, be always on your guard
Success walks hand in hand with failure, along Hollywood Boulevard
— Ray Davies (The Kinks), "Celluloid Heroes"

South Africa

After my second year at Michigan, I got the idea to travel to Kenya, to see how psychological principles could be used in developing nations. I arrived just when the reform political leader Tom Mboya (one of whose lieutenants was Barack Obama, Sr.), to whom I had an introduction, was assassinated. So instead, I proceeded to South Africa. I had a cousin, Rose, a decade-and-a-half older than me, who lived in Johannesburg. Meanwhile, my graduate school friend, Stanley, was a visiting lecturer at the University of Cape Town.

And that's how I spent mid-year-1969 to mid-year-1970. It was a time out from my American life. South Africa had no television and no rock-and-roll radio stations out of a fear that outside influences might topple the white apartheid government. It took days for European and American newspapers to reach South Africa, and even then access to them was limited. I had fallen off the end of the known world.

I began my stint in South Africa by living with "Aunt" Rose in the living room of her apartment in Hillbrow, a dense, inner-city neighborhood in Johannesburg regarded as South Africa's Greenwich Village. Good news: I quickly got a job working at the National Institute for Personnel Research, or NIPR, where I met two of my South African girlfriends.

My job involved survey design and data analysis, which I had been trained to conduct at Michigan, and included consulting with businesses around South Africa, which tied forward to the Harvard Business School. Seeing Black Africans in these work settings was sobering. One well-meaning supervisor told me how dangerous it was for workers to return to their African townships with their pay, and that a number of workers would disappear over the year. I felt a constant state of unease. I couldn't come to grips with my aunt's treating her maid like an indentured servant.

My first South African girlfriend was part of the Afrikaner, or Dutch-descended, population. Indeed, she was a late arrival to that group—her father was a Dutch engineer who moved to South Africa as an adult. He was well-connected to the ruling Afrikaans elite, and I sometimes dined with them on his estate. Bemused by American me, they were willing to speak English, rather than Afrikaans, because I wasn't a South African English-speaker, whom they resented if they couldn't speak their language. On the other hand, he told me that, as a Jew, I should be classified as Asian in South Africa's complex racial categories.

"Frieda" was a tall, robust blond woman, like me in her early twenties, who lived with her parents. Although intelligent, she was disconnected from the world as I knew it. Her father balanced his feelings about me between admiring that I would have only one glass of Scotch at dinner and resenting that I was having sex with his daughter. In her midtwenties, Frieda couldn't spend the night with me.

Not being a patient young man, I took up with another woman at the NIPR, a Jewish woman a few years older than me named "Rachel." Rachel was smaller, also attractive, less earthy, and more intellectual. She understood the South African system and avoided challenging it until she left the country, eventually ending up in New York, where she became a successful psychotherapist. How resourceful! Indeed, when she first moved to New York years after I had returned, Mary and I had her to our home in Morristown. When I run into her around New York every decade or so, she fails to recognize me.

After living with Rose, I moved in, simply as a roommate, with two women in a suburban house on Johannesburg's rim. My roommates liked me because, unlike other candidates for the position, I didn't expect them to look after me. Such independence was rare in the 1970s, but Sara had prepared me well. And we *did* have a maid who drew me a bath and made my breakfast daily. My female roommates, one Danish and one English, partied a lot.

I met "Joy" at a group singalong. She was an English-speaking South African. Joy was the only one of the women with whom I was to continue my affair when I returned to the States. She pitched in to help Archie and me move to Boston, renting a truck to pick up some of my and Archie's stuff in Philly and New York. She was indefatigable and able. A software analyst, she had skills that crossed the ocean. Joy asked me if I wanted her to stay. As adaptable—and as committed to me—as she was, she had a South African outlook that would always grate on me.

While I was working in South Africa at its government research and consulting agency, I also conducted research with Stanley. He was nine hundred miles south in Cape Town, on the cusp between the Indian and Atlantic Oceans, in the shadow of Table Mountain. So beautiful, so wafted by sea breezes—heavenly. We exchanged visits, and he got to know my girlfriends and my aunt Rose. I also joined a leading sports club to play on their basketball team and even became a Springbok—the name given to members of all of South Africa's national teams. I played basketball around South Africa and nearby countries. What can I say—when you're young, life can be good in ways it never will be again.

> ### You're Not in the US Anymore
>
> I also taught some classes at the University of the Witwatersrand, where I met a psychologist who was running an experiment on the chemical versus the cognitive effects of alcohol, a topic I was deeply interested in. It involved drinking various combinations of vodka and water.
>
> Later (in 1973), Alan Marlatt was to conduct his famous "think-drink" study. Here's a preview: active alcoholics were given heavily flavored drinks that did or didn't contain alcohol—subjects couldn't tell which. They drank more when they believed the drink was alcoholic, whether or not it actually contained alcohol. The real alcohol content had no effect on their behavior. This study, of course, undercut the idea that alcoholics lose control of their drinking when they taste any amount of alcohol. I discuss my relationship with Alan, and the impact of his work on my theories of addiction, in Chapter 11.
>
> The South African experiment that I participated in, to which I drove, wasn't so subtle. And I wasn't an alcoholic, or really an experienced spirits drinker. My drink, in a full-size kitchen glass, appeared by taste to contain mostly vodka. I protested throughout the experiment while consuming the drink, but the two experimental assistants insisted that I finish it. When I was done answering the protocol questions, I unsteadily walked over to Rachel's nearby NIPR office, where I was sick.
>
> I later asked to speak to the psychologist experimenter. He laid a trip on me about being a bad scientist to try to stop the experiment midstream as I did, and now to complain about the study. I was outraged, but the university had no ethics body to which to report the experimenter. This was South Africa.

I understand powerlessness, the futility of objecting to being mistreated, the privileges of those in powerful positions and my impotence against them. I always hated those feelings, which I am hypersensitive toward, and I have never given into them. My life is a struggle against them, with mixed results.

I returned to America after a year in Africa, going by ship to the UK with Stanley and having a shipboard romance with a young Rhodesian woman with whom I traveled in Europe, including staying with Dan Katz in Denmark. I re-engaged at Michigan and began my work on addiction.

Getting Hired at Harvard

When I returned to the States in the fall, I first stayed in a New York apartment Archie was sharing with our third Penn roommate, Lewis, who was starting his first job as a lawyer. It was subsistence living. For myself in Michigan, I lived with Stanley in a new apartment development. I was no longer on a fellowship. I went to Bill Gamson, a politically radical sociologist who was charged with finding funding for social psych students completing their degrees. But he had no help to offer me. Stanley, as usual, to the rescue: "The Ford Foundation gives a fellowship so that people can complete their Ph.D. in ten semesters—you qualify."

Did I mention that Stanley was very, very helpful in navigating university life?

I got the Ford Foundation ten-term fellowship and set about analyzing the data we had collected in South Africa at the University of Michigan's ISR—the world-famous Institute for Social Research. But I was also researching and writing *Love and Addiction*. You will recall from Chapter 3 that Archie and I were processing the marital breakup of our old roommate, Warren, when he was in grad school at Berkeley. Later came my and Archie's epic visit to the animal labs at Michigan. I was always all about addiction, no matter what else I was involved in.

On the side, in order to make some spending money, I taught at a Michigan community college. Soon after I returned to Michigan, I began the chore of finding a job at a university after I completed my Ph.D. But the department's most prominent social psychologists, Bob Zajonc and Gene Burnstein, wouldn't help me. Zajonc, as I said, was known for highlighting the effects of mere exposure. Burnstein, as I described, thought they should kick me out of Michigan for my extracurricular comments on the comprehensive social psychology exam.

As for Zajonc's feelings about me, let me tell this story.

Cool It, Bob

In the previous chapter I describe the experiment I conducted at Michigan about partner selection. The experimental group at the Institute for Social Research, headed by Zajonc, had a video recording machine. Stanley and I used it to show videos of women who had been rated at different degrees of attractiveness. Subjects then picked one of the women to date. The experiment was an off-kilter variation of achievement motivation, where those with high achievement motivation took on middle-range risks in selecting tasks. I wanted to know if people (in this case men) with high social achievement motivation picked women in the middle range of challenge. My thinking was cutting across the grain, as usual. Achievement and affiliation were considered opposing motivations.

[In motivation theory, low achievement motivation is demonstrated either by taking no risks at all or by taking impossible risks, so that you won't be blamed for failing. In my love-addiction theory, people welcomed addictive attachments when they sought certainty and low risk in their relationships. Or else they pursued impossible dreams, like fixating on a distant figure, which accomplished the same goal. The controlling form of addiction showed the ugly side of men who dominated and abused women, and women who allowed that sort of control, even when it was distressing and interfered with their lives, and sometimes led to assaults and murder, cases of which we described in *Love and Addiction*. Such "lovers" preferred certainty to safety and personal fulfillment.]

I had met Mary through a roommate of hers whom I had dated—they were undergrads two years younger than me. Impressed by her verve and intelligence, I hired her to recruit subjects for the experiment on the Michigan quad. She was so energetic and reliable in that job that I hired her to run the experiment. Mary would schedule the subjects and show them the video, and they would select a woman to date (they didn't really meet the women). She collected background information on the subjects and had them take a personality test so that we could analyze which men selected which women. Finally, she would debrief them (gently explain the experiment).

What a capable person! I am drawn, above all, to competent, productive people. And I had never met a woman as capable overall as Mary. But Mary had some difficulty operating the reel-to-reel video machine. One day I came to the lab to find Zajonc berating Mary for threading the videotape incorrectly. I said, "Cool it, Bob. Mary's doing a great job. You purchased this machine with research money, but Stanley and I are the only people at ISR who have ever used it for research. So cut her, and us, a break."

When we became involved later, Mary told me she was impressed with my sangfroid in not being intimidated by authority. That's a true thing to like about me.

But being at loggerheads with Zajonc and Burnstein meant I would get no help from them in finding an academic job. They were obligated to find jobs for their own and other students who toed the line and who wanted to be experimental social psychologists. My attitude, my defining myself as an independent agent, came at a cost. It always has.

So Stanley and I went to the library to review the catalogues of universities in parts of the country where I was willing to live. We identified social psychologists at those universities whom Stanley figured Dan Katz, my Ph.D. supervisor, would know. Dan, who did the kind of socially relevant research I wanted, had become my faculty adviser after Herb Kelman left Michigan for Harvard. He was also at the absolute top of the academic hierarchy.

Dan had written the first comprehensive volume on organizational psychology, titled *The Social Psychology of Organizations*. I could relate to that material. One of Dan's old colleagues, Stanley figured out, was at the Harvard Business School. Dan wrote him on my behalf, and I was summoned to Boston for an interview. I got the job. Me at the Harvard Business School. Kind of unlikely, don't you think?

Did I mention how useful Stanley was . . . yes, I believe I did.

At Michigan I wasn't actually an organizational psychology student, although I was familiar with the field. Organizational behavior was what the Harvard Business School job was. One organizational psych student told me, "We heard someone not in our program was hired at Harvard Business School, and a lot of people are pissed off." I mentioned that to Dan. He peered over his glasses and said, "We needn't worry about that, Stanton."

Betwixt Two Worlds: High Flying and Subsistence

I was looking for university jobs while, in my early twenties, living a threadbare existence. I taught two courses at Schoolcraft Community College, about thirty miles from Ann Arbor, for $250 a course. That worked out to $40 a week for food and expenses, including the $150 monthly rent I split with Stanley.

A woman who lived in Ann Arbor taught full-time at Schoolcraft, and I was able to get a ride with her the afternoons when I taught my two classes. She was a compulsive talker. As we rode, I didn't say a word while she talked nonstop. I learned all about her musician husband who couldn't earn a dime.

One time I had five dollars on me (gas in those days was thirty-one cents a gallon) and I offered to fill her tank. But she told me that she didn't need gas. Another time, she said, "I need gas for my car now. You can pay for it this time." I looked at her and said, "I don't have any money."

During one commute I said, "I won't be riding with you later this week."

"Where will you be?"

I hesitated; "I'm going to Boston to be interviewed at the Harvard Business School."

I was dating Charlotte Kasl, who was divorced from a social psychology faculty member, and to whom I was introduced by Ernie Harburg. Ernie was an older, offbeat social psychologist, and a friend, with interests similar to mine. His work was mind-body stuff. For instance, Ernie found that attitudes toward alcohol and guilt predicted hangovers better than did the amount a person drank. Brilliant. We created and published a psychological measure of sensible drinking based on this work. But while I was at Mathematica, which I describe in the next chapter, we could never get funding for that research. In Chapter 11, I speak about my lifelong project of nurturing sensible, healthy drinking as a cultural norm.

Ernie was the son of Yip Harburg, who wrote the lyrics to "Over the Rainbow" and other popular songs. Ernie was president of the Yip Harburg Foundation. When I moved to New York, where Ernie commuted from Ann Arbor, Ernie charged the meals we had to Yip's foundation. I always got a kick out of telling male servers, who may or may not have been gay, "The guy who wrote 'Somewhere Over the Rainbow' is buying this meal," and watching them react.

Charlotte slept at my and Stanley's place the night before I flew to my Harvard interview. In the morning, while trimming my hair, she jabbed her finger on the scissors, and yelled in pain. "Shhh," I hushed her, worried about Stanley sleeping in the next room. She was doubly angry with me.

This was in 1970, twenty years before Charlotte wrote a best seller about sex and addiction. Charlotte had been a music major. I would painstakingly explain my ideas about love and addiction to her (remember, I was writing drafts of *Love and Addiction* as a grad student). I actually was to see Charlotte in subsequent years. She had me come to Ohio University in Athens, Ohio, when she was still teaching music, to speak.

But I hadn't heard from Charlotte for years when Ernie Harburg called me excitedly, saying, "Charlotte just published a book with the same title as yours!" Not quite. Charlotte's book was *Women, Sex, and Addiction*. She had become an ardent feminist, in a way that might have led to her neglecting mentioning any influence I had had on her.

Charlotte discovered that some people quit drinking without AA. She subsequently came up with 16 steps, supplementing the 12 steps with more modern thinking. Charlotte was touted for grafting feminist ideas onto AA—thus updating without challenging the 12 steps. The highly regarded alcoholism historian and AA advocate, Bill White, interviewed a list of seminal theorists in the addiction field. He eventually got to me in 2015. But Charlotte made his list years before I did.

My Years at Harvard Business School

So I got the job at Harvard Business School in Boston. Archie also moved to Boston—where he still lives, with his wife, Vicki, nearly a half-century later. I arrived at HBS, age 25, younger than my average student, having never seen a case study—on which HBS was based—being taught, let alone teaching one. Standing in front of eighty hard-charging B-school students was not a task for the faint-hearted, especially since I really didn't know anything about American business, along with not knowing how to teach the case method. I learned, however. That was no mean feat, and I had some anxious times.

Death at the Harvard Business School

Two years before I made the trip, another Michigan social psychology graduate, Stuart Kanter, who had also been a psychology student at Penn as an undergraduate, had preceded me at HBS. But he couldn't get a grip on the HBS culture. As told in the 1973 book, *The Gospel According to the Harvard Business School*, under terrific stress from the students, he shot himself in his office.

Success walks hand in hand with failure on Hollywood Boulevard. And Kanter's path is one I possibly could have followed. No one at Michigan or Harvard ever discussed my predecessor's story with me to prepare me for the HBS culture. I was on my own.

And I did have difficulty grasping how to guide a large class in case discussions using the Socratic method HBS teachers favored. This required questioning the students in a structured way that led to the class reaching a consensus conclusion. I had participated in discussion groups and seminars in Penn's General Honors Program and in grad school in Michigan. But HBS classes were wilder and more elemental.

You had to let people say what they wished. In front of antagonistic recovery groups (which I presented to for years), this was a living hell. (Watch the 1987 video of me on *Oprah*.) Yet sometimes, when well done, allowing people to express their feelings, even negative ones, and having other people respond, sometimes on your side, can lead to remarkable experiences. I learned to float with and shape audience reactions. This was to become my signature high-wire style on the addiction lecture circuit, sometimes driving groups to distraction and rebellion. My workshops were an adventure, not an "aren't-we-recovering-people-all-wonderful" self-congratulation like all the others.

Obviously, I was happier when the group was on my side. One such group in Nova Scotia invited Archie and me to present a workshop built on *Love and Addiction*. After one session, Archie told me, "You have a gift for this." But they loved Archie, too—as did my HBS classes when Archie guest lectured on *Love and Addiction* and other topics.

My style still surprises people. I have often been told by conference organizers during breaks to stop calling on people in the audience. But I want to know what people are thinking.

People come up to me after sessions and say, "You're brave."

Although my provocative approach with groups relies on the skills I learned at Harvard Business School, I never fit into the HBS culture. That proved especially true with two senior faculty members, Jay Lorsch and Tony Athos.

We had teaching meetings for the instructors of the first-year mandatory courses on organizational behavior. A different faculty member led each week's discussion. Jay Lorsch was a piece of work. Another junior faculty member told me he was stricken to overhear Jay belittling his research to others in a hallway "in—forget stentorian tones—hog-calling tones." While I was presenting at one meeting, Jay continued talking to another senior faculty member. I said, "Jay, do you mind not talking while I'm speaking?" Jay hit the roof. "I know you have daddy problems, but don't take them out on me," he screamed at me. This was Jay's application of Freud at work.

Within a couple of days, each of the other four junior faculty members who witnessed Jay's outburst sidled up to me. "Someone finally told Jay off—good for you," they each said. None, of course, said anything publicly.

But it was Tony Athos who killed me at HBS. Tony was the most popular instructor among the organizational faculty. He taught an elective second-year interpersonal behavior course that recruited the third of the students who were drawn to psychology. But Tony's approach to the subject was highly structured, HBS style. At a personal level, Tony had a confessional style that was very different from hard-charging Jay's. Occasionally we had lunch together.

Given the poor ratings the first-year behavior course received, the administration begged Tony to lead the first-year teaching group. He took several members of that teaching group to a conference for organizational behavior instructors. I called Tony and asked why I wasn't included. After I learned the case-teaching ropes, I had the highest teaching rating for the first-year course the year before, my second year at HBS. So I thought I should be included.

Tony listened silently. Early one morning not long after, Tony's secretary summoned me to his office. I thought he was consulting with me about planning the course. Instead, he quickly told me he was dropping me from the teaching group.

I was doomed at HBS.

I Am Persistent and Won't Be Deterred

But I wasn't lying fallow at HBS while I was pissing people off and not getting promoted. I finished my dissertation and, as I mentioned, Archie, Stanley, and I published its results on South Africans' ethnic voting patterns in the *American Political Science Review.*

And all along Archie and I were writing *Love and Addiction.* We worked in and around Boston, writing and revising in our apartments, then in the office of a consulting firm for small businesses that I created with a bright HBS student. Archie and my secretary—whom I stole from the school—were my staff. We ended up mainly a writing operation. That enterprise only lasted a year or so, after which I secured a small office for Archie between my office and the bathroom at the Business School.

I began writing *Love and Addiction* when I was 24, and it was published when I was 29. Even earlier, in South Africa, I had outlined my ideas about addictive relationships in a university literary magazine, ideas explained in Part I and throughout this book. I sent the article to Penguin Books in the UK and, en route home from South Africa, met an editor there who was interested in the book, leading to a publishing contract and an advance. I began working seriously on *L&A* at Michigan while analyzing my dissertation data. It was during that year that I explored the Michigan animal lab, explained love addiction to Charlotte Kasl, and was invited to see one of the world's leading psychologists back at Penn, Richard Solomon.

Being Bullied by One of the World's Leading Psychologists

At Michigan, I read in my University of Pennsylvania alumni magazine that Penn's most distinguished psychologist, Richard Solomon, was developing the opponent-process model of emotion. Solomon said that any powerful experience created a kickback in the nervous system, like a visual afterimage or like withdrawal from a drug. He included love in his model.

I wrote Solomon about my theory of love addiction, sending him my South African article. He wrote me back and asked me to visit him at Penn when I passed through Philadelphia.

When I arrived at his office in my jeans, Solomon was prepared to devote any amount of time (which turned out to be the better part of an hour) to humiliating me. He had his secretary make copies of the typed chapters of my book that I had brought, while he derided me for not knowing the selective

> references on human addiction that he featured. He pushed articles at me: "Have you read these?"
>
> In this exchange between a distinguished member of the National Academy of Sciences and me, a 24-year-old grad student, I had the broader grasp of human addiction research. I knew the literature on the natural life course of addiction and maturing out. That research showed that people had highly variable reactions to drugs, were not usually likely to become addicted, and most of those who did showed a marked tendency to recover on their own.
>
> By contrast, the opponent-process model described an invariant neurologic response undergone by all organisms, let alone all people. And it was a one-track process. My theory of addiction included that people—obviously—differed greatly in how they interpreted and behaved while "being in love." Only a few incurred great personal costs, were hurt and humiliated by their "love" relationships, and yet couldn't quit. As I was later to write about such people, "Love Is the Hardest Addiction to Quit," which became one of my most viral *Psychology Today* blogposts.

While my interaction with Solomon was challenging, I was also amused by how he treated me. His reaction typifies how experts have always dealt with me and my ideas. But I knew what I knew: my model was more scientifically valid and clinically relevant than Solomon's. As we wrote in *Love and Addiction*:

> Solomon's "opponent-process" theory is a creative demonstration that addiction is not a special reaction to a drug, but a primary and universal form of motivation. The theory, however, does not really explain the psychology of addiction. In its abstractness it doesn't explore the cultural and personality factors—the when, where, and why—in addiction. What accounts for the differences in human consciousness that enable some people to act on the basis of a larger and more varied set of motivations, while others have their entire lives determined by the mechanistic effects of the opponent process? After all, not everyone becomes mired down in a once positive experience, from love or drugs, which has gone sour. Thus, this model doesn't deal with what sets some drug users apart from other drug users, some lovers from other lovers—i.e., the addicted person from the person who is not addicted.

Forming a Relationship in Boston

When I arrived in Boston, I thought it would be a good idea to buy a house, which I proceeded to do with a small down payment my father lent me (as reassured and persuaded to do so by my lawyer friend, Archie's roommate). The house was in Medford, down the street from Tufts University. I ended up living there with four Tufts students, which turned out to be a bad idea.

To get out of that house, I moved into an apartment in North Cambridge with "Eunice," a tall, stately, reserved woman who was working at the Business School. Truth be told, I still think of Eunice. We had an active and imaginative sex life. Meanwhile, I inspired her to return to college to finish her undergraduate degree, after which (with our relationship over) she got an MBA and became a senior officer at a major firm. I actually called Eunice, now married and mother of an adult child, after my divorce from Mary—she wasn't receptive, despite all I had done for her! (That's a joke.)

The searcher

It might seem that I was leading a successful, contented life teaching at Harvard and living with Eunice. But it didn't really fit me. I was always wanting more—I still am. I have never rested. I might have married Eunice, as I might have married Frieda in South Africa or brought Joy to the US, all of whom would have been dedicated and able partners. But none of those partnerships would have worked.

Eunice watched me complete my dissertation, mornings and weekends, while I was at Harvard. "You are always pursuing a goal," she observed. When we met, Eunice had been largely purposeless. Although very able, she was resigned to working as a very able administrative secretary. Then, building on her own great practical intelligence, she became highly successful. That's my niche, finding people in lost corners who have great ability and encouraging them to move ahead—while helping me.

So why didn't I stay with Eunice? She was incredibly capable, and I relied on her for dealing with a range of life matters. But her greatest gifts were practical, not along intellectual and aesthetic lines, which are a strong part of my constellation, and which were Mary's strong suits. I know—if you're going to insist on everything, you get nothing. And what do I have now? And who are you going to find who has everything? Questions to ponder for eternity.

What a good friend can do for you

Of course, I had Archie to help me think these things through. I did marry Mary, and we had raised three children together over thirty years before divorcing. Some years after my divorce, I visited my old buddy, Larry. Having met Larry studying Japanese one summer at Stanford while I was at Michigan, I kept in touch and visited him when he returned to live in his home state of Idaho.

Once, I was sitting in a circle of a dozen of Larry's friends after a hike:

> ### "You Had a Better Relationship with Mary"
>
> The group started talking about people's divorces. I told the assembled hikers and friends of Larry's how after my divorce I had lamented not marrying Eunice. Listening to me, Archie had said, "I saw you argue with Mary and with Eunice. You and Mary were on the same wavelength, even when you were fighting. You weren't with Eunice." I told the hikers, "After that, I never had that regretful thought again."
>
> There was silence in the group. Then one woman said, "That's a good friend."

Have I mentioned, Archie is helpful? In fact, it might seem that many of my closest, most trusting relationships have been with men—Joel, Stanley, Larry, Archie. But I have always been intensely drawn to women. As for Archie, I have asked him for help with nearly all of my life problems and issues, practical and emotional both. Some old friends think I have relied too much on Archie. But when I meet new friends, they admire—are sometimes overwhelmed—by the depth and range of our communication.

> ### Disclosure
>
> When Archie read this, he commented, "Funny that my comparison of your relationships with Eunice and Mary was about how you argued with each of them."

Through our time together, Archie helped me negotiate every contract I ever entered into, and assisted me in getting out of several. We worked together to create my contract with my partners in my residential addiction treatment program. At one point, my rehab partner requested a small change in the contract, which I agreed to without checking with Archie, a move that cost us a lot of money—I'm an idiot! I have tried not to repeat that mistake. Then, Archie fought alongside me when my partners sued me to get out of paying me at all.

My Life with Mary

On one trip back to Ann Arbor to complete my Ph.D., I encountered some difficulty with my computer printout. At the time, all data analysis programs were run through an office in the basement of the Institute for Social Research by a data processing group. A tall, somewhat nerdy, but attractive, very smart woman named "Ruth" headed that group.

She and I discussed my computer output problem. I'm not especially good with computers. But I figured out that, by happenstance for my sequence of instructions, the page-turning instruction came in a bad spot and my program malfunctioned. Ruth denied that was possible. I said, "It's obvious that's the only explanation for this error." I was confident. I was right.

Ruth's intelligence and thoughtfulness drew us together. We spent the night in her apartment. As a "date," I'm interesting. I am sexually energetic and creative. I am always thinking, if you go for that sort of thing. And I am an engaged person. But I lose focus rapidly.

If I note that some women liked me in this period, it's because I've been forced to confront the decline in my appeal after my divorce in my midfifties, and especially later, after my sixties. Older women are looking for different things. For one thing, they expect you to be financially secure, and perhaps more emotionally contained. It's been a hard adjustment for me.

Ruth and I enjoyed our affair. But when Ruth drove me to the airport after one visit when I stayed with her in Ann Arbor, she insisted on stopping for gas before dropping me off, even though I reckoned that she had ample fuel to return to the station afterward. I missed my plane. Ruth came to visit me in New York, where I was staying at Archie's apartment, but really, we were over. To deal with me, you have to tolerate a degree of uncertainty and risk.

The next time I returned to Ann Arbor, Ruth was away. I called Mary, who, you will recall, had managed my experiment at ISR a few years earlier, but who refused to become involved with me then. Nonetheless, this time we did spend the night in Ruth's apartment, where Ruth let me stay while she was gone. Somehow my and Mary's time had come. We shared basic values of achievement and engagement. Mary, like me, was highly literate, if somewhat less practical in institutional America. And either I had calmed down somewhat or Mary was at a more open point in her life.

Mary was just graduating from Michigan after taking some time off. She was headed to San Francisco to live with her cousin. I visited Mary in California, having broken up with Eunice. We were able to maintain a strong bicoastal relationship for six months through mail and weekly phone calls, and then Mary moved to Boston to be with me.

We lived together briefly in the Newton home of "Helen," the widow of the lead violinist in the Boston Symphony and Boston Pops orchestras. Helen then got Mary a job working with the state arts council. Mary soon got her own apartment.

When Mary, characteristically, took the initiative to conceive a plan for the Council, the director told her: "You're a clerk and you'll always be one here." Prompted by that putdown, after working at the Council for a year or two, she enrolled in the Boston University Business School. I helped to get Mary admitted there through connections I had from Harvard. Along with her

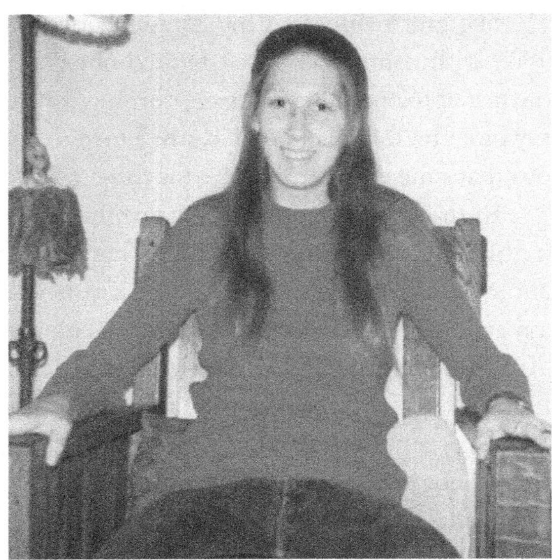

Mary in her Boston apartment

parents, I helped pay for Mary's graduate education. Her MBA was one example of the fruitful, cooperative, and mutually supportive relationship we had over the succeeding decades.

I came to live in Helen's attic apartment when I moved out of my apartment with Eunice. I placed an ad in the local shopping newspaper saying a Harvard instructor was seeking a room in a home. Helen answered. It was a good living arrangement—cheap, in a nice near-in suburban home. Things still seemed to be dropping magically into my lap.

People were puzzled by my arrangement with my landlady. We had good rapport, and she greeted my women visitors—including Mary, when she lived there with me briefly after she first moved to Boston—warmly. However, in the year or so I lived there, both of her children moved home. (I'm glad that I was such a unifying force for her family!) Let's just say that my days with Helen were then numbered, and I moved to an apartment with a city planner friend, before moving to California with Mary after leaving Harvard in 1975.

Completing *Love and Addiction*

As I said, I had been researching *Love and Addiction* when I returned to Michigan to finish my dissertation. I continued working on it at Harvard while living with Eunice in 1972. I completed my Ph.D. in 1973, with Mary as my partner. As for *L&A*, I completed that as my stint at Harvard was coming to an end.

Archie was there every step of that odyssey, along with Mary, who joined us for most of the arduous journey. I mean, who knew how to write a book, let alone a best seller? I just had a lot of good ideas. We began writing it for the Penguin editor in England, with whom we couldn't settle on a final manuscript, then rewrote it for a small American publisher, Taplinger, who wanted us to make it more popular.

The writing and revision took more than four years. Our process wasn't the academic professional approach that usually went into a psychology text. Nonetheless, the range and depth of my references to the scientific literature exceed those of any other popular book in the addiction field, even more than those of "scientists" like Carl Hart and Marc Lewis. And my penetration of this literature was greater than anyone else's, such as Maia Szalavitz's.

Archie's, Mary's, and my combined effort in producing *Love and Addiction* was more like a sixties commune. Creating *L&A* sealed our triumvirate. Moreover, it was my personal rocket ship into the future. It launched me into a universe of national and international debates on the nature of addiction and alcoholism and their treatment, debates that have intensified right into the present, which the rest of this book documents.

I describe the promise and ultimate impact of *L&A* in Chapter 1. *Love and Addiction* didn't make me famous or rich when it was published. And it had an odd public face. It was excerpted in *Cosmopolitan* and *Self*, "women's" magazines. I was interviewed by touchy-feely Phil Donahue in 1975 and 1976, when the hardback and paperback editions were released, as well as on *Good Morning America* and other popular television shows.

In that pre-Internet, pre-streaming, pre-cable era, television was mainly limited to shows on the major network channels. But there were also local and syndicated interview

Mary and me in our early days

shows, along with the networks' *Today* and *Good Morning America* programs. Local news shows came on around 5:00 p.m., before the early-evening national network news broadcasts. These local shows also conducted interviews on flashy topics. Daytimes, the networks—and in major cities like New York, a few non-network stations—aired local talk shows. I appeared on dozens of these, including sharing a waiting room once with Henry Fonda! He was extremely friendly and chatty.

But I didn't intend *L&A* to be a self-help book about addictive love relationships. I was about redefining addiction. As Archie and I described the fundamental addiction template: "Addiction is not a chemical reaction—addiction is an experience, one which grows out of an individual's routinized subjective response to something that has special meaning for him—something, anything, that he finds so safe and reassuring that he cannot be without it." The *Whole Earth Catalogue* was one of the few places to label *L&A* as an entirely new road map to the world of addiction. My title for Chapter 3, "A General Theory of Addiction," was meant to call to mind Einstein's revolutionary theory of relativity. Bruce Alexander, who created the Rat Park experiments, later told me, "When *Love and Addiction* came out in 1975, it opened my eyes completely."

Re-envisioning the meaning of addiction wasn't a topic people were ready for. Medical professionals considered such revisionism a foolhardy, bizarre idea, like questioning whether we had landed on the moon. The psychiatrist sister of a friend of ours sniffed, "We already know what addiction is." I have often reflected on her comment amidst the growing crescendo of doubt that we initiated over the standard addiction concept. However, because *L&A* fit no obvious niche, being neither a love guide (like the subsequent best sellers *Women Who Love Too Much*, 1985, and *Codependent No More*, 1986) nor a medical text, our hardback sales were disappointing. They weren't enough to rescue the fading fortunes of the specialty house, Taplinger,

Pensive me at Harvard

and its owner, Terry Taplinger, who had picked up the American publishing rights from Penguin and then took over publication when we broke with Penguin.

Nonetheless, *Love and Addiction* made my life. People came to regard it, in Maia Szalavitz's words in her 2016 best seller, *Unbroken Brain: A Revolutionary New Way of Understanding Addiction*, published more than thirty years later, as groundbreaking. Or, as Tom Horvath, president and founder of SMART Recovery, claimed: "The modern understanding of addiction and recovery begins with *Love and Addiction*." Meanwhile, in its Signet mass-market paperback edition, *L&A* grew in sales and reputation. Signet was an imprint of a major publisher, New American Library (NAL), and *L&A* became an NAL "Best of the Backlist" book. As such, it sold many more copies in the 1980s and 1990s than it did when it first had been published. I made more national media appearances in the 1980s and 1990s on *Oprah* and other shows than I did in the '70s.

Out in the Cold

Love and Addiction was published after Harvard's decision not to promote me. I was still not 30 years old. Having spent four years teaching at a business school, my never-too-secure connection to the academic psychology community was severed. There was nothing more Stanley or Dan Katz could do for me.

I was out in the cold on my own. Well, with Mary and Archie. Eventually, decades later, Mary would divorce me. Meanwhile, Archie and I had made a vow in college to strike into the heart of the intellectual world. Other than working through me, Archie hasn't done that yet. And whether or not I have done so is the subject of this book.

Together, Archie and I bridged literature and psychology in our chapter, "'Love' as an Addiction." We used the contrast between the two couples in D. H. Lawrence's *Women in Love*, as interpreted by Archie in his senior thesis (judged the best in Penn's English department when we graduated), as a key illustrative example in *Love and Addiction*. For Archie, Gerald and Gudrun, contrasted with the more secure Rupert and Ursula, embodied an addictive connection:

> Gerald Crich is a fictional example of someone who lacks a well-developed core being, a secure sense of himself. A person feeling this inner emptiness must fill it. In relationships, this can only be done by subsuming someone else's being within yourself, or else by allowing someone to subsume you. Often two people simultaneously engulf and are engulfed by each other. The result is a full-fledged

addiction, where each partner draws the other back at any sign of a loosening of the bonds that hold them together.

Archie was awarded a fellowship to Stanford's graduate program in English, which he rejected. Archie didn't want to be a graduate student. Instead, he vowed to strike out on his own as a writer. He wrote columns briefly for *Rolling Stone*, where he was recruited by rock critic and editor Greil Marcus based on a manuscript he sent in about rhythm and blues, another shared passion of ours. For the most part, however, he has worked as an amanuensis for a series of psychologists and psychiatrists, never earning enough to retire.

And, yet, many of our friends would say, he has ended up with a more gratifying home and personal life than I have. At his sixtieth birthday party, I watched as people from the corners of his writing, personal, and political-activist (including in the National Writers Union and as an advocate for midwives and home birth) lives showered him with appreciation and love, a near-universal sentiment from men and women, as his partner, Vicki, looked lovingly on. He is a fortunate and gifted man.

7

Making a Living
While entering, and being banned from, the addiction field

I feel like I'm married to a riverboat gambler.

— Mary Arnold

My greatest success in life has been to survive, to raise three kids and send them to college, to live in pleasant surroundings, and not to have to go to work every morning, but to invent myself each day.

— Stanton Peele

A Latter-Day Suburban Beatnik, Well-Married

Watching *The Making of Apocalypse Now* with our Morristown film group, when Francis Ford Coppola's wife, Eleanor, described the chaos they encountered in Cambodia: "I always thought Francis would make things work." Mary exclaimed: "That's the way I feel about Stanton!"

And so, not yet 30, I was turned out of Harvard, never to hold another academic position—or any job—for as long as a year. Mary and I moved to California and bought a house in Oakland with the paperback advance money from *Love and Addiction*. We received the equivalent today of $500,000, which Archie and I had to split with the hardback publisher, Taplinger.

Mary diligently went to work utilizing her MBA. Meanwhile, I was an outcast in the addiction world, due to the combination of my denying the scientific validity of the medical-biological definition of addiction and my repudiation of AA and its disease theory as the salvation for the addiction problems on which America had increasingly become focused. And, yet, I maintained and developed my addiction brand and held a toehold in the field.

We moved back East from California to create a family in New Jersey, where we raised all three of our kids. After they graduated high school, all five of us eventually moved separately to New York, until Mary decamped for North Carolina and Haley moved to New Orleans to get a Ph.D. in counseling psychology at Tulane University. Although she is the only one of my children to get training like my own, I think I see aspects of myself in Anna's celebrity interviews, and even Dana's overseeing e-commerce software system development.

Mary's belief in and support of me included her innermost understanding of my work and my mission, even as she chafed at my not earning a secure income during some of those years. Archie: "Her commitment went beyond simply a spouse's loyalty—it reflected a shared worldview and values that made your marriage work amid uncertainty and some conflict."

Tom Horvath was the long-time President of SMART Recovery, a major support-group that differs from AA by encouraging self-empowerment. SMART uses cognitive behavior therapy (CBT) and Albert Ellis's Rational Emotive Therapy (RET) techniques. Tom has helped me throughout my career. I put him on the board of the residential rehab that I partnered in. Tom once told me, "Stanton, the thing that people most often ask me about you is, 'How does he make a living?'"

My son, Dana, who now makes many times the money I do as a high-end e-commerce engineer: "Dad, you write well and speak well, you have an endless stream of ideas—you should have made big money."

Anna: "When you and mom went to college, it cost a nickel. And when I went to NYU (which cost a fortune), that was the one time in your life that you were making big money in your rehab." (As I describe in the next chapter, that's only partly true.)

Marc Lewis, a neuroscientist who has had two best sellers in which he argues that addiction isn't a disease, and who has graciously acknowledged my seminal work: "Stanton, you had your time with *Love and Addiction* (1975), *The Meaning of Addiction* (1985), and *Diseasing of America* (1989). The last opened my eyes when I read it. It's time for others to be in the spotlight."

My quick answers to Tom, Dana, Anna, and Marc:

"Tom, I've made money a hundred different ways, sometimes quite a lot—including the treatment program on which you served on the board."

"Dana, making millions isn't even a secondary goal for me. I'm all about winning in the idea marketplace."

"Anna, we did put your sister and brother through college—and Dana went to Penn. That cost plenty."

"Marc, this isn't a seasonal sport for me, I'm shooting for all-time recognition."

At 75, I'm still functioning and supporting myself in Brooklyn—among the most expensive real estate markets in the US. Most important, I am still pissing people off, almost universally. Witness the fervid assaults I now receive from Gabor Maté's fans for questioning the value he places on dragging people back into the worst traumas of their lives as "therapy." Meanwhile, I am persona non grata among my drug policy reform colleagues, who—with good intentions—give people substitute opioids and say that they're treating addiction (which I discuss in Chapter 9).

Leaving Harvard for California

Two monumental things in my life happened in the spring of 1975—I wasn't promoted at Harvard Business School, and *Love and Addiction* was published. But *L&A* made almost no immediate difference in my life at the time (other than providing the cash to buy a home in Oakland). The hardback publisher, Taplinger, was just too small, and the book didn't fit in the self-help category. Nor was it packaged as a serious idea book, which it has since become.

Mary had a lifelong dream of moving to California, to the Bay Area, which we then did. There, she set out to find a job with her MBA. I had to figure out where I was going without a university position, now that I had no possibility of being an academic psychologist. The answer turned out to be teaching weekend extension courses at the University of California for $250. Mary got a job with Potlatch, a Fortune 500 company that made paper-based containers and boxes. Despite her MBA, as a woman she got a fairly minimal salary. But we were happy she had landed any job at all after searching for one for months in the San Francisco Bay area.

Here are the three main take-aways from our move to California:

1. *Mary never stopped working on our behalf.* Mary felt obligated for having spurred our relocation, for my support for her while she earned her MBA, and for my having the cash to buy a house. Per family code, inherited from her Texan father and Romanian mother, she was driven to want to contribute to our well-being. There may have been someone in America who would have been more dedicated to our household and helping me, but I can't think of any.

2. *Economically, we worked as a unit.* I can make money work—in small time, penny-pinching ways, and in larger ways, like buying that house. Mary's Texan father owned and managed a few cabs in Michigan. He and Mary's brothers fixed everything in their converted farmhouse. Her mother kept things going at home and later went to college to became a home-ec teacher.

  Mary's family code was self-reliance ("I never saw a repairman in our house"). She knew how to make do—to cook, to sew, not to rely on shopping as a form of entertainment. After the sizable down payment I made with my book money, our monthly survival nut was a few hundred dollars. But we were okay in the Bay Area even as Mary was making peanuts and I next to nothing.

3. L&A *didn't revolutionize the world the way Mary and I knew it should have.* At the time and for years after, it seemed our view that *L&A* revolutionized the addiction field was limited to Mary, me, and Archie. Now, however, people often tell me that *L&A* changed their thinking about addiction. Somehow, seemingly, I revolutionized the field in a way that has surfaced only recently—although even now without fully appreciating the meaning of this revolution (see Part III).

Meeting a Big Fan

Mary was sent to work at the Potlatch box manufacturing plant in Louisville, Kentucky, where I visited her from Oakland. Mary went to the YMCA in Louisville, where I joined her one night. The young man behind the counter knew Mary. She introduced me as her husband, even though we had different last names.

While he worked, he was reading a heavily underlined copy of *L&A*. I casually said to him, "I wrote that book." He looked at me incredulously. Mary: "No, it's true—my husband wrote that. He's Stanton Peele."

But here's the strange thing. Having the author in front of him, despite all the passages he had underlined that obviously meant so much to him, he was tongue-tied and didn't have a single comment or question for me.

God Save Me from My Admirers

Actually, my greatest disillusionments have come at the hands of "fans," rather than detractors.

One man contacted me from Britain to be his mentor as he began a coaching practice. He was in recovery, and thus abstained, which already made us a bad match. But, worse, he had a young son for whom his fervent desire was that the boy should never drink or take a drug his entire life. I hope readers of this memoir understand that doubling down on a supposed genetic legacy of addiction sets a child up for an unnecessary lifelong addict identity, as well as *increasing the likelihood* that the child will misuse substances (as I describe in Chapter 2).

That naive man seeking a mentor could perhaps be excused for misconceiving my values and views. More bitter to me was my being contacted by a *New York Times* features writer, Ian Urbina, who wanted me to serve as an expert for an article on the American Psychiatric Association's diagnostic manual, *DSM-5*, which was released in 2013. His slant was—since *DSM-5* classified substance use disorders (SUDs) as "mild," "moderate," and "severe"—that people with mild problems would inflate the numbers of those being diagnosed, to wit, "Addiction Diagnoses May Rise Under Guideline Changes." (See the Conclusion for the experts who *did* comment.)

I *do* believe DSM missed the boat on addiction by classifying *a* single non-drug activity as addictive, gambling (which I described in *Reason* and *Psychology Today*). However, as I also pointed out, DSM's model is consistent with harm reduction, since it doesn't classify use of any drug (e.g., heroin), or any level of use, as a disorder. Instead, a disorder diagnosis requires that a condition causes problems. DSM offers two overriding criteria for any diagnosis—*impairment and distress*. If drug use—or anything else—doesn't impair and distress a person, there is no disorder.

I have always realized that people throw around terms like alcoholism. They also call all drug use, even moderate use, addiction. (Which Carl Hart points out in *Drug Use for Grown-Ups*.) But *DSM*, if taken seriously, actually *opposes* those misconceptions.

And my main concern, as I discuss in Part III, is how our thinking about and dealing with addiction has led to vast seas of it in the US, so Urbina was missing the crux of my material. Urbina claimed that he had read my work. But he had some big-color splotch on his pallet labeled "Stanton Peele opposes current American addiction treatment," and that was all that he saw.

What I'm Really About

Such off-the-mark reactions to my work are typical. I regularly meet professionals who claim my work influenced them or that my books were crucial in their development, but who can't cite even one of my ideas. *People don't deal in specific ideas, but rather in larger images and reputations. I am the out-of-bounds rebel who thought love is addictive and who opposes the disease theory. Okay. That's a start.*

In fact, *Love and Addiction* has six major themes that both constituted our purpose in writing it and have outlined the future of addiction theorizing, continuing to the present.

1. It laid out a general theory of addiction that went beyond the boundaries of heroin—then considered the be-all and end-all of addiction. My definition incorporated cigarettes, cocaine, and marijuana—none of which were then defined, or thought of, as addictive—as well as shopping, gambling, and love relationships. This definition was experiential. It said that addiction stemmed from any powerful involvement that consumed a person's life and absorbed their identity with negative consequences.

2. *L&A* analyzed *how* relationships could be as extremely addictive as drugs—more so—including leading people to murder and to suicide rather than endure being separated from a love object. People often responded at a gut level to this insight. When I lecture, I say, "If love were a drug, it would be banned."

3. As a definition of love, I proposed the criteria that a relationship be open, supportive, and constructive. The "open" part represented an alternative,1960s-70s sensibility that some people still pursue today. In any case, relationships can be seen either to limit, even destroy people, at one extreme, or to enhance their capabilities and expand their horizons—which I called love.

4. *Love and Addiction* was a social commentary that observed how modern life forced primary couples into such tightly knit social and economic units that they shut out the community, even the extended family. The weight this placed on the nuclear unit, when it succeeded, severely limited people's emotional connections to others. And, increasingly, people have failed to achieve such a primary connection, leading to epidemic loneliness and the single lifestyle as a major modern alternative to marriage and intimacy. This narrowing of emotional focus and loss of intimacy and community, pioneered in the US and spreading worldwide, has untold radical consequences for what it means to be a human being. In 2020, conservative writer David Brooks created a major stir with his article, "The Nuclear Family Was a Mistake."

5. *L&A* proposed a radical reconception of addiction with the following meanings: addiction is not an on-or-off biological switch,

but rather a clinical, experiential scale along which people gravitate both in the short and long term. Addiction, like all human activity, is sensitive to immediate environmental conditions and the larger state of people's lives. This means that people can, and commonly do, leave addictions behind when they mature or their lives achieve sufficient stability. It means that the most important single determinant cause of addiction is social and economic inequality and deprivation. *Recognizing addiction in this way makes clear that our cultural and individual conceptions of addiction are crucial determinants of its incidence, prevalence, and persistence.*

6. The purpose of *Love and Addiction*—of my whole addiction project—is to remove addiction from the pharmacological and medical realms. Addiction occurs for the whole human being in a social and cultural context. This perspective leads directly to the ideas of harm reduction, recovery as a typical natural outcome, social and economic remediation of addiction and that *drugs are not special, exclusive engines of addiction. There is no list of addictive things. Addiction is a part of ordinary human experience.*

My Life-Sustaining Helper

After we returned east from California in 1977, Mary delivered a hand-written note at the *New York Times* addressed to John Leonard, then chief book review editor, extolling *L&A* and pleading with him to give the book its due. Years later, while we were in Paris, Mary went around to book-stores copying the names of publishers whom she wrote about publishing a French edition of *L&A*. These were both quixotic enter-prises—that's not the way to accom-plish those tasks. On the other hand, how could I ever hope to have some-one who identified with and devoted herself more to my life purpose? Such devotion makes me

Mary and me

think of the B-side of the Motown group Martha and the Vandellas' hit single, "Heat Wave." That song was titled "A Love Like Yours Don't Come Knocking Everyday."

> ### "You Don't Laugh at My Jokes Like That"
>
> I was invited to give a community lecture on addiction at the Smithsonian Institution in Washington, DC. Several of my Washington friends attended with their wives. Mary, in the audience, responded to every provocative comment I made. Afterward, I heard one friend say to his wife, "You never laugh at my jokes like that." On the other hand, they're still married.

Me and the Addiction World

In California I taught weekend courses around the state through the extension system of the University of California, where I encountered nothing but grief and hatred from the recovering people seeking certification as substance abuse counselors. Considering anything beyond the disease theory, not accepting it totally, was incomprehensible to them. They simply wouldn't hear it. The great University of California fielded course after course that rehashed the 12-step mantras of higher power, abstinence, and AA into the 1970s and beyond. A disgrace.

I was addressing people, at Berkeley and thereafter, who felt they owed their lives to AA, who had never taken a psychology course, and who had never heard of or imagined another way of thinking about addiction than the AA/disease way. I explained that people learned to rely on a substance or other involvement as their emotional mainstay in the face of unmet emotional needs and social and other problems. They couldn't care less about the evidence in favor of or the value of my approach. To them, I was Satan, which they regularly told me. Today, Gabor Maté's "trauma-is-everything" army plays that role in my life. (See Chapter 1 for a choice example.)

At the same time, unknown to me, *Love and Addiction* was percolating out there. Alan Marlatt later told me he had picked up the book and instantly realized that it changed the addiction field. It influenced his work on relapse prevention, in which he included gambling as well as smoking, alcohol, and drugs. Relapse prevention was built on Marlatt's research showing that loss of control in alcoholism was a myth (review in Chapter 11) and that one could put the stops on any behavioral cascade, whether a mindless descent into smoking, heroin, alcohol, binge-eating, or gambling. All followed similar patterns. Alan wrote strong blurbs for my books starting with *The Meaning of Addiction* in 1985. When I visited his office at the University of Washington, I noticed that he kept *Meaning* in a small bookcase next to his desk. I discuss Alan's work and views of me, along with other leading alcoholism researchers, in Chapter 11.

Despite Alan's early endorsements, I was to remain an off-brand addiction theorist. Unlike Alan, I was never a part of the academic club. I was the devil to the 12-step club and the allied treatment industry, which I was to dissect in *Diseasing of America* in 1989. I did find support occasionally in the grass roots. For instance, living in Oakland, I was invited to speak to the Haight-Ashbury Free Clinic drug counselors, among whom I had many fans. But I didn't know how to build such appreciation into an ongoing operation, and nothing more came of these occasional glimmers of recognition.

Incidentally, the Free Clinic was co-founded and run by a physician, David Smith, whom I came to know later through Dan Barmettler's national conferences (organized by his Institute for Integral Development). Naturally, these conferences were almost exclusively 12-step and AA-oriented. Smith was a 12-step and disease reactionary, but he did have me come to San Francisco to speak after I moved back east. Altogether, however, my time in California was a lost period, where I explored the city with some Bay Area outsiders—not destructive people, but people outside of the mainstream, while Mary worked at her corporate job.

Leaving California and Starting a Family in New Jersey

And so, having written a book that many addiction opinion leaders were later to view as revolutionary and groundbreaking, I was for all intents and purposes a nonentity in California. Mary and I lived in a pleasant house close to downtown Oakland and a short bus ride from San Francisco. Meanwhile, I was footloose and fancy free in the Bay Area—which became doubly true when Potlatch sent Mary to Louisville to work at a factory where they manufactured boxes. We visited back and forth between Kentucky and Oakland; we had an open marriage.

We enjoyed our stay in California. But I was adrift as I turned 30. Then Potlatch transferred Mary to New Jersey, to sell cardboard packaging to businesses. At first we maintained bicoastal residences, with me traveling back and forth from Oakland to New York.

Mary got pregnant with a child conceived at Santa Cruz at one of those aggravating weekend courses I taught for the University of California. So I sold the Oakland home and set up a household with Mary.

Mary with Dana, our firstborn

In New Jersey, I continued to do largely nothing, other than having two children born at home in Teaneck—first Dana, then Haley.* We had the help of a cooperative doctor and Mary's mother, Marie, another remarkable woman. Our third child, Anna, was born after we moved to Morristown.

Dana was born in our first home in Teaneck in 1978, with next-door neighbor Shelley Gutin, wife of an exercise physiology professor at Columbia Teachers College, shooting a video. Dana was born breech, and Mary calmly told me to take our doctor, Steve Jaffe, into the next room to keep him occupied while his nurse midwife spread olive oil on Mary's vulva lips to facilitate Dana's emergence eight hours later.

That woman has guts.

We moved to a larger home in Teaneck before Haley was born. Meanwhile, I taught courses at the Pratt Institute department of planning, which happened to be headed by Art Zabarkes, who had lived two blocks down from me when I was growing up in Philadelphia. We played basketball in the schoolyard near our homes. When Mary and I moved to a bigger house, I had a Pratt student fix up the attic. The student then moved into one part of the attic, the other part of which was my retreat.

---

* A 2021 movie, Kornel Mundruczo's *Pieces of a Woman* (Mundruczó is a man), which depicts a home birth in the most lurid, fear-inducing light, thus resembling standard media presentations of drug use, requires debunking. Home births with medical backup for low-risk women are safer than standard hospital births in terms of having fewer medical interventions (e.g., inductions, cesareans, episiotomies) and better infant outcomes (fewer severe lacerations or low Apgar scores). Six well-controlled studies found that home births lead to no maternal deaths. Archie, despite not having children, was for some years president of Massachusetts Friends of Midwives and a nationally prominent advocate for midwifery and out-of-hospital birth.

On the day Mary gave birth to Haley in 1980, when mother-in-law Marie had already arrived, I took Dana on a day trip to keep him out of Mary's hair. Mary almost immediately entered labor. As she was giving birth, the bed collapsed. Mary knocked on the door to the attic and asked our tenant if he could put the bed back together, which he quickly did. Steve Jaffe arrived shortly and Haley was born.

When I got home with Dana, the doctor had left and all was peaceful. Marie served a lasagna Mary had previously made. The woman who had agreed to take pictures, Karen Yucht, whose husband was a therapist, arrived too late for the birth, but joined Dana, Marie, Mary, and me for the dinner Mary had made.

Wow—Mary, frontier woman!

Living in Suburbia, with Oprah and Canada Thrown In

Meanwhile, *Love and Addiction*, published in 1975, hadn't made back its sizable paperback advance. Of course, I had already spent my share of that money on our homes. But, beginning in the 1980s, sales grew steadily as best sellers like *Women Who Love Too Much*, then *Codependent No More*, popularized the idea that love can be addictive. New American Library, the major trade publisher that had picked up the paperback rights, designated *L&A* as one of its "Best of the Backlist" books. It was reprinted many times, and was reissued with a new Authors' Preface in 1991. In the 1980s, Archie and I started receiving royalty checks again. I appeared on *Oprah* three times.

Earlier, I was contacted by the provincial director of the Addiction Research Foundation (ARF) in Calgary, Alberta. I was invited to give the keynote address to the annual ARF conference, which was to be held in Alberta in the summer of 1978.

This was the first time anyone in the addiction field had reached out to say that my work and ideas were important. It was finally some justification of my genius and the existence to which I subjected Mary, who believed so deeply in me. While in Alberta, we took a side trip to Banff in the Canadian Rockies. Sitting in a hot-spring-fed pool under a starlit sky was like a reward from God for us.

I had by now distilled the essential material from *Love and Addiction* into a message to addiction workers. At the conference, I described how people became addicted to an experience—whether produced by drugs, alcohol, love, or food—as their source of satisfaction in life. But the involvement had a destructive impact on their lives, which is what made it an addiction.

I defined addictions by the following criteria:

1. *Absorbs* consciousness, feelings (any experience capable of this could be addictive)

2. *Elicits* predictable, immediate response (drugs do this well, but not only drugs)

3. *Provides* essential feelings (e.g., control, pain relief, self-worth, security)

4. *Produces* feelings temporarily, only during the experience

5. *Degrades* functioning, options, and satisfactions (impairs, per DSM)

6. *Hurts* self-respect (distresses, per DSM):

> The narrowing of focus due to the experience, together with its ability temporarily to relieve negative feelings about self and the world, makes the addictive experience increasingly central in, and essential to, the person's functioning. But people often gradually move beyond this sequence as their lives progress.

It was a compact speech that people could relate to, causing them to go, "ah-ha."

And it was a decidedly non-disease model of addiction, one steeped in people's lived experience. By speaking of addiction to an experience (which is now called "process addiction"), I bypassed people's addiction-disease defenses and got them to reflect on addiction in normal human terms.

The speech in Alberta worked well, after which a recovering-AA local journalist gave a rebuttal. His response, per usual, was hostile and dismissive: "You're not in recovery, so how can you possibly know about addiction?" As I rose to respond, a man handed me a note: "Please don't respond in kind."

My Response

I turned to the man: "Of all the people with drinking problems you know, how many of them ended up going to AA at some point? Would one in ten be a reasonable answer in your own personal experience?" (This figure is one that emerges from epidemiological research, like NESARC.) He nodded, "That sounds about right."

"And of all those you've encountered in your life in AA, how many remained and succeeded in the program? Is one in ten fair?" A famous survey by AA itself found that only 5 percent of attendees remained as long as a year. This man agreed that it is a small group.

"So," I said, "let's do the math. One-tenth of one-tenth is one in a hundred people who benefit from AA. And what do you think happens to the other ninety-nine of that hundred? Their drinking gets worse and worse until they die, right? Recovering people are told, believe, and broadcast to others that a person with a drinking problem who doesn't attend AA will end up either in prison, an institution, or a grave. So tell me, why is the treatment world failing ninety-nine out of one hundred people so badly?"

"Now about that AA mantra," I continued. "First, it isn't true. Most people with a drinking problem who don't enter AA will recover on their own. Second, *accepting* AA's mantra is in fact harmful. It discourages people from summoning their own resources in order to create a recovery that is true for them. Somehow—or is it simply common sense—a large majority of people manage to do so anyhow. This single reality, recovery without treatment (which Nora Volkow, director of the National Institute on Drug Abuse, acknowledges—see Chapter 9—without understanding its meaning), is the greatest deflation of the disease theory.

"Of course, not all of those ninety-nine people who reject AA succeed, for sure. So let me ask you another question. AA has been the dominant approach to alcoholism and addiction, and you and others feel that it is the only tool we have to fight these things, correct? What would you recommend to the other ninety-nine people in one hundred with addictive problems who don't follow the AA path? And what should the great nation of Canada devote its addiction-fighting resources to? Should they force those other ninety-nine out of one hundred to go to AA and to stick with it, even though they dislike and reject it?

"Finally, with AA as the all-purpose alcohol and drug addiction dogma for the last thirty to forty years, how are we doing? Have alcohol and drug problems declined or remained the same? Most people think that they've increased. But you're happy with the situation and don't want to listen to what I say." Turning fully toward him, I asked, "Is that right?"

At a meeting of addiction professionals in Canada I got a rousing response. But my ideas couldn't penetrate the standard wisdom that has held the US in lock step in the 1970s until today, supplemented by brain-disease and trauma determinism. People like my commentator and Gabor Maté *dominate* this world, and AA, brain-disease and trauma true believers (think Donald Trump supporters) push their experiences as universal truths. Those who recover naturally—even famous ones, like Drew Barrymore and Lindsay Lohan (see Chapter 9)—don't tell their stories. They fear offending the recovery and trauma communities, and being accused of denial. So we never get to the truth.

Mary in the Audience

My ability to present publicly, to speak logically and articulately but at the same time draw out audiences in active interactions, and the confidence I demonstrate in engaging their experiences and thinking never failed to impress Mary, as it did at the Smithsonian and when she saw me teach at Harvard. (I should disclose that I was so nervous doing my first international keynote address in Calgary that I called Archie from a payphone before going on.)

I Debate a World-Class Disease Figure

Years later, I was invited by a cable TV program to debate Judith Rapoport, a distinguished Harvard Medical School professor, director of the National Institute of Mental Health's Institute for Child Psychiatry, and author of the 1989 best seller, *The Boy Who Couldn't Stop Washing*. Her argument: obsessive-compulsive disorder (OCD) is a widespread neurological disease, genetically caused, which has millions of sufferers who often don't recognize their condition. Rapoport single-handedly added OCD to the mental disease map.

[Other mental illnesses that became prominent in the late twentieth century were attention-deficit and bipolar disorders. Meanwhile, people doubled down on recognizing, diagnosing, and treating depression, while extending autism by identifying a spectrum of less serious, but nonetheless diagnosable, manifestations of the "disease." This modern revolution has led to an epidemic of mental illness, one now being cemented and built up by the pandemic. As I point out in Chapter 9, we are one fucked-up nation, uniquely so in the modern world, but rapidly gathering other nations under our mental illness umbrella. I'll just say here that people are happier and progress better in life the less likely they are to identify themselves with negative traits.]

Rapoport had no idea who I was and disregarded me as we sat waiting for the cameras to roll. On camera, she presented her views confidently and well. After we both spoke, the program took calls from viewers. A woman caller said, "I'm really worried about my daughter. She insists that all of her dresses be in order, hung up just so in her closet. It reminds me that when I was her age, I would spend hours arranging my shoes precisely under my bed."

Rapoport instantly responded that both behaviors were classic indicators of a brain-based obsessive-compulsive disorder that her daughter had genetically inherited.

I then asked the woman, "Do you still spend hours lining up your shoes under your bed?"

> "No," she laughed. "Who has time for that, with my family and my job?"
>
> "If your parents had consulted with Dr. Rapoport when you were a kid, she would have diagnosed you with the lifelong disease of OCD, for which she would have prescribed antidepressants. You know, you might still be lining your shoes up—in which case you might have no husband and child. And that's what she's recommending that you do to your daughter now."

In the limo home to Teaneck that the network provided, Mary smiled, "I was almost worried when I heard her credentials and watched her opening comments." But Mary had an unshakable confidence in me that was as much as I needed to sustain me in an almost ubiquitously hostile (more like completely dismissive) addiction world. To quote Jackie Wilson, "Ooh, just a kiss, just a smile, hold my hand, baby, just once in a while. That's all I need, that's all I need, and I'll be satisfied."

National and International Lecturer

Following the ARF conference in Calgary, I began giving workshops and lectures around the country. An important part of this activity was my involvement with a group that presented national conferences on addiction to recovery (12-step-based) audiences. One organizer was Gary Seidler, of U. S. Journal Training, who was in the publications department of the Addiction Research Foundation when I wrote for them. ARF is now the Centre for Addiction and Mental Health—CAMH. Looking ahead, neither this national conference organization nor CAMH would *ever* invite me to speak today.

But in 1978, the year I appeared at Canada's national conference, I rewrote the essence of *L&A* in a popular journal ARF published, *Addictions*. "The Addiction Experience" explained how people became addicted to an experience depending on who they were and where they were in life. I emphasized how American soldiers addicted in Vietnam—even the sizable proportion of them who tried drugs, including narcotics, stateside—almost universally gave up these addictions at home. Extracted from the uncertainty, loss of control, and lack of positive options they faced in the Asian war zone, these men no longer needed to rely on the soporific effects of narcotics.

"Experience" was immediately picked up by the University of Montreal and translated into French, a document that has now spread around the world. The next year I licensed this piece for standalone publication by the Hazelden Foundation in Minnesota, famous as the center of the AA, 12-step treatment universe. The editor-in-chief told me it was the best thing she had ever read for illuminating her own addiction. In 1988, Hazelden stopped publishing the pamphlet, after eight years of consistently high sales. The new editor-in-chief, Linda Peterson, wrote me that she took this step because, "Unfortunately, we have heard much criticism from our customers who are not in agreement with your stand on the disease concept." (Both the English and French versions are now available at my website and Amazon.)

Nonetheless, I began a period, starting in 1978, when I traveled around the country to speak to national addiction conferences. Sticking to the "addictive experience" model, I got good responses. Still, as the only non-AA speaker at the conferences, I was often the target of hostile responses. Psychologists who explored what was called "controlled drinking" and other AA bêtes noirs lived in a separate, protected academic world. It's true that I enjoyed being out there, living on the edge. But it was equally true that I was a non-invitee in the safe haven of academia. *They* weren't out there beating their heads against the AA behemoth and its diehard supporters. Rather, I was their stalking horse.

These *U.S. Journal* (and similar) conferences continue around the US. They are updated versions of 12-step recovery where harm reduction is unspoken. Rather, the same old bromides are melded together with trauma, spirituality, and imagined and proposed biological concepts and pathways to explain love (cf. best-selling author Helen Fisher) and every other addiction. And I am more anathema than ever. (Although, on the eve of the pandemic, I was invited to participate in a series of trauma and addiction conferences across Canada, including Vancouver. When these were cancelled, we began working on video conferences.)

Over my career, I toured the world speaking—more so than I spoke in the United States. I was frequently invited to Canada after Calgary—in Ottawa to an elite group of military human resource leaders, in New Brunswick province to their regional addiction group, in Toronto for the International Harm Reduction Association conference and separately to the Addiction Research Foundation headquarters, in Montreal to the world conference of therapeutic communities and the Canadian Psychological Association, in Quebec to the Francophone provincial addiction group, and in Nova Scotia (with Archie) to a provincial group for which *Love and Addiction* was a central text.

I have spoken many times in Vancouver, including to the British Columbia Centre for Addictions Research and the BC Psychological Association (this was when I had my infamous meeting with Gabor Maté in 2015, which I described in Part I). In 2011 I was invited to present by Liz Evans, the founder of the Portland Hotel Society (PHS), which ran the

Insite drug injection site in Vancouver—the only one in North America. Liz had seen me speak at Harm Reduction International in Liverpool the previous year. She was inherently opposed to the disease theory; PHS, by providing housing, work, and social connection for a homeless and mentally ill population, embodied my "life process program." Gabor Maté had made his reputation as the medical director of PHS, on whose *extremely* traumatized population he based his general view that all addiction is due to trauma in his 2008 best seller, *In the Realm of Hungry Ghosts*.

Liz, in many ways a very strong person, wasn't able to be strong in defending my views. She didn't have the means to contest trauma theory as a variety of the disease theory. That was a rocky trip.*

Mary went on some of these earlier trips, including Australia, the UK, and Europe—like my speech in front of the Queen of the Netherlands in Amsterdam (the queen had no idea what I was talking about and dished out the normal disease nonsense). After Mary and I separated, Anna sometimes accompanied me as an international companion—for example, when I spoke to the French national addiction counselors' organization in Paris. I have lectured many times in Australia in Sydney, Brisbane (where I gave the keynote address at an Australian national conference), and Melbourne (where a lecture series was named for me at Deakin University); in continental Europe in Budapest, Helsinki, Copenhagen, Florence, Turin, and Rome; and all around the British Isles in Dublin, Galway, Glasgow, Edinburgh, London, Liverpool, Bath, and Bournemouth.

Stanton speaking at Durham Castle, UK, 1996

The Sobells' Massacre

In 1982, a major event occurred around what we now call harm reduction (HR), or an improvement in a person's drinking, drug use, or other unhealthy habits without abstaining.

Among those with destructive drinking habits, for example, some quit drinking entirely. But most don't. In fact, epidemiological research

---

* Liz, her partner, and senior staff stepped down as the heads of PHS in 2014 due to financial questions being raised. I met one of these staff, who had become Kasia Malinowka's assistant, at Carl Hart's Open Society Foundations talk at the end of Chapter 4. I had just published *Recover! Stop Thinking of Yourself as an Addict*, with Ilse Thompson. When Kasia ignored me, this woman greeted me warmly.

consistently has shown that, as they matured, a majority of people with alcohol dependence have reduced their heavy drinking but continued to drink.

This message was simply impermissible in the alcoholism field in the 1980s. À la AA and the disease theory, abstinence was the sine qua non of treatment. And I was one of a small group of harm reduction proponents before HR's time. Being before your time, my specialty, is not a sound career strategy. Conflict around this issue seriously impeded the fields of alcoholism and addiction for several decades; it damaged, for a time it seemed irreparably, my life and my career.

Early in the 1970s, a husband-and-wife Ph.D. student team had used behavioral techniques to teach twenty alcoholics at the Patton State VA Hospital in Southern California to moderate their drinking—called controlled drinking (CD). The students, Mark and Linda Sobell, reported that the controlled-drinking-trained patients did far better after one and two years than twenty comparable patients who underwent the standard 12-step abstinence program at the hospital.

Obviously, cutting down drinking was advice some physicians gave their patients and some people practiced on their own, with varying success. Today, a primary care provider telling a problem drinker to cut back is a technique called a "brief intervention." As such, it has been validated as a highly effective, easy-to-administer therapy for people who are part of a health care system.

But, in the 1970s-1980s, exploring drinking moderation in such a bold experiment, as the Sobells did, was 'in your face' of the traditional American alcoholism movement. And, as sure as the rain will fall, the forces of AA and America's temperance tradition rained down on the Sobells and all who would dare to support them. It was a typhoon, a tsunami, a bloodbath. And I was in the middle of it.

The attack on the Sobells' research came from a 12-step and abstinence advocate named Mary Pendery, Ph.D., who worked as an alcoholism counselor at Patton State. Pendery, who pursued the Sobells and their research for the better part of the 1970s, finally picked up a good head of steam when she enlisted a UCLA psychology professor, Irving Maltzman, in her crusade, as well as the head of UCLA's psychiatry department, L. Jolyon West.

Together, the three authored an article attacking the Sobells' research in the highly prestigious journal *Science* in 1982. The ARF (where the Sobells now worked) then commissioned its own review of the Sobells' research by a panel of independent investigators. First and foremost, the ARF reviewers noted, the *Science* article didn't examine the AA and abstinence comparison group from the original study. Without this essential comparison, the ARF committee observed, no sense could be made from examining the group given CD treatment: the *Science* paper was merely a one-sided tract that highlighted relapses observed among those who were trained to moderate their drinking. But did they do better or worse than the "abstainers"?

For instance, Pendery and her co-authors found that four of the CD group had died in the decade following treatment. In 1983, the most prestigious American television news magazine, CBS's *60 Minutes*, filmed Harry Reasoner walking alongside the grave of one CD subject. But the Sobells also examined California state records and found that six of the abstinence-trained subjects had died in that period. Pendery et al. presented no data to contradict the Sobells' basic finding: at two years the twenty controlled-drinking subjects functioned far better, abstaining or drinking moderately an average eight out of nine days, while the twenty patients who had been trained to abstain functioned well only four out of nine days.

The Sobells were able to defend themselves in their professional lives, and they went on to become tenured faculty at the Nova Southeastern University in Florida. But the Sobells and their CD allies were not similarly protected from vilification by the 12-step industrial complex. One rehab director (at Rhode Island's prominent Edgehill Newport Center) wrote a journal article damning a "gang of eight" CD supporters, which featured Alan Marlatt of the University of Washington, Bill Miller of the University of New Mexico, and myself.

And so something had been discovered that was twice as good as the prevailing approach in limiting alcoholic relapses—and it was crushed. The treatment industry thus maintained the fantasy that abstinence was the only useful strategy for dealing with alcoholism and that reducing drinking as a viable approach had been completely refuted. Pendery et al.'s *Science* article held that it was even immoral to try to help people control their drinking—an irrational, disabling prejudice that continued beyond the end of the twentieth century and has impeded the harm-reduction movement into the present.

America's temperance-AA-abstinence monomania has permanently warped the American response to drugs and alcohol, as I examine in Chapter 9.

Nonetheless, in the present, with the advent of motivational interviewing and brief interventions, harm reduction and relapse prevention, large swaths of forward-looking practitioners and nearly all researchers in the field have lost the abstinence fixation that has straight-jacketed treatment options in this country. Maia Szalavitz, author of *Unbroken Brain* and perhaps the most visible addiction writer in America, speaks about drinking wine now and thus being disqualified by AA as "sober" (see Chapter 10). Nonetheless, there remain many 12-step clinicians, probably still a strong majority, who impose the all-or-none model on the people they treat. And most Americans still accept that model.

However, as treatment is practiced around the world, a different vision has arisen from the ashes of AA. Here is one of many examples (this study is Taiwanese) of the acceptance of non-abstinence outcomes:

> Once presumed unsuitable for dependent drinkers, the evidence is stacking up that brief advice after screening can lead even these drinkers to cut back. This study of heavy drinking hospital patients provides one of the most convincing demonstrations yet that brief intervention can work in this setting, and the drinking reductions were particularly steep among dependent patients.

I have written in a 12-step-oriented periodical, *The Fix*, no less, as well as in *Psychology Today* and *Huffington Post*, that America's abstinence fixation continued as long as it did (and mostly still does) in at least some degree due to Pendery et al. and the journal *Science*. This has been to the detriment of many souls, including the deaths of hundreds of thousands of IV drug users, by ruling out needle exchange and harm reduction. As Ethan Nadelmann put it:

> Where the 12-step thing has the most to own up to is its role in impeding harm reduction interventions to stem the spread of HIV/AIDS. Why was it that Australia and England and the Netherlands were able to stop the spread, and keep the number for injecting drug users under 5 to 10 percent, and the US was not? It's that notion—that abstinence is the only permissible approach, that we are not going to "enable" a junkie by giving him a clean needle. There has to be a kind of owning up to that role in hundreds of thousands of people dying unnecessarily.

And Then There Was Me

It's impossible to recreate the paranoia, the purges, the witch-hunting, that occurred in the addiction field in the 1980s in the wake of the controlled-drinking conflict. I wrote two pieces in the immediate aftermath of that 1982 dispute—one for the American Psychological Association's flagship publication, *American Psychologist*, and one for the popular magazine, *Psychology Today*. My article in *AP*, "The Cultural Context of Psychological Approaches to Alcoholism," was an academic piece that placed the controversy, as the title says, in its cultural and historical context. I was joined in this venue (to his everlasting credit) by Alan Marlatt, whose piece was titled "The Controlled-Drinking Controversy: A Commentary."

My article in *PT*, "Through a Glass Darkly," had the elaborate subtitle: "Can some alcoholics learn to drink in moderation? The answer, at least in this country, may be more political than scientific." It appeared in the first issue of the magazine after it was purchased by the American Psychological Association. And it created a firestorm.

My academic *American Psychologist* piece, published in 1984, pointed out about CD therapy that there was no longer any "alcoholism center in the United States using the technique as official policy." Really at that point, I was among only a few people in America publicly supporting it. Other academics famed for taking behavioral moderate-drinking approaches (like Bill Miller, always a cautious man, as I describe in Chapter 11) strictly limited it to "problem" drinkers—not "real" alcoholics. I alone (in the US) reported that the technique now known as harm reduction was effective across the range of addiction and alcoholism problems.

And I suffered for it. The Edgehill Newport Center director, John Wallace, authored an article titled "Can Stanton Peele's Opinions Be Taken Seriously?" (Guess what his answer was.) My *Psychology Today* piece, published in 1983, in which I concluded that the *Science* article "reflects political forces and prejudice in America that forbid a reasonable discussion of the issues," got me into even more trouble.

At this point I might interject, "Why me?" I had no academic or institutional position. I didn't do controlled drinking research. I was just an addiction theorist and therapist, a scholar and writer in the addiction field, a commentator on America's preoccupation with addiction and alcoholism as irreversible diseases. But that was enough for me to be buried in the shitstorm that ensued. Indeed, strangely, I (along with Mary) may have been the main victim, unprotected as I was.

I had been invited to give the keynote address at the Texas Commission on Alcoholism's well-known summer school in 1983, held on the campus of the University of Texas in Austin. This state-funded institution instantly rescinded my invitation after the *PT* article appeared. I threatened to sue the Commission, and my talk was reinstated. But even I didn't have the guts to go up against the AA-abstinence juggernaut in Texas. Instead, I gave a keynote speech about Romeo and Juliet's addictive love and resulting joint suicide. (My later *PT* blogpost on the subject has had several hundred thousand visits.)

Despite my reinstatement in Texas, I was blacklisted then, and for another decade or more, throughout the addiction and alcoholism fields. And, so, when Mary left her corporate job after Anna's birth, I had to get survey research jobs to support my family. On the other side, Mary Pendery moved to a VA hospital in Wyoming in 1994. There she reconnected with an alcoholism patient she had known while he was being treated at the San Diego VA. The man arrived extremely intoxicated for a visit with Pendery. He shot Pendery dead and then killed himself.

This whole tragic, dysfunctional, so-American string of events has changed little about American thinking, and nothing in its addiction journalism. I describe in Chapter 2 how Ronan Farrow and *Today* in 2017, in a program about the supposed genetics of addiction, vilified me as a benighted defender of misguided medical beliefs (exactly opposite of who I am) since I deny that addiction is inherited. My response: the three women presented as transgenerational victims of their genetic addiction weren't able to avoid their supposed fates *despite* the unanimous acceptance of the medical-genetic view of addiction that has prevailed throughout their lives. What good has it done?

The *New York Times* took on Farrow's reporting in 2020: "He delivers narratives that are irresistibly cinematic—with unmistakable heroes and villains—and often omits the complicating facts and inconvenient details that may make them less dramatic. At times, he does not always follow the typical journalistic imperatives of corroboration and rigorous disclosure, or he suggests conspiracies that are tantalizing but he cannot prove." Perfect for him. But in a world where he flourishes, my already off-center career was completely derailed.

Mary Carries Our Load

Mary had worked steadily from 1975 for Potlatch, the cardboard packaging manufacturer. Then Potlatch went under. Seeing this coming, Mary got a job at that reliable old giant, AT&T, in New York. In 1982, AT&T was broken up, and Mary went to work for a surviving division (eventually Verizon) in Basking Ridge, New Jersey. The company paid for our family's move to Morristown. Dana and Haley, born (at home) in Teaneck in 1978 and 1980, along with Anna, born in 1988 in Morristown, all attended public school K–12 in Morristown.

Mary continued working with AT&T and its successors. When she became pregnant with Anna in 1987, however, she quit. Typically, she arranged to do piecework at home, often tedious numbers-checking stuff. She never wavered in her industriousness and support of the family.

Truth be told, it tugged at Mary's heart to return to work after giving birth to our first two children. And we both would agree they lost something with home care, then day care, under my supervision in those early years. Still, our older kids are successful, competent, and have intimate relationships of their own. Dana, now divorced, has been the only one to have children. Those three grandkids are regular presences in our lives.

Meanwhile, I had to support my own brood in the 1980s–90s after I was exiled from the addiction lecture circuit and mainstream academic circles. I awoke every morning thinking about money. I began consulting with doctors who had fallen into the clutches of their impaired physicians' programs after having been discovered using drugs at work, or who were reported for heavy drinking by their wives, or had a DUI, and had been forced by their medical boards to enter rehabs, which were always 12-step-based.

Doctors cooperated in order to keep their licenses. But a number of them regretted signing an agreement in which they swore to abstain from alcohol or to attend AA meetings for years. A few of these recalcitrants chose to challenge their agreements by arguing either that they were not diagnosed properly or that the state medical board's compelling them to swear to a higher power violated the First Amendment's guarantee against forced religious worship. Coerced AA treatment had indeed been ruled unconstitutional by several appeals courts when it came to traffic and criminal courts forcing atheists or other non-Christians into AA on the basis of a DUI or to gain parole. I often wrote about this, including in my 2000 book with Charles Bufé and Archie, *Resisting 12-Step Coercion.* SMART Recovery and my Life Process Program offer those with DUIs an alternative to AA. As I regularly point out, if 12-step treatment is so great, why does America's private and public alcoholism treatment industry require constant reprovisioning by coerced treatment?

Doctors, often high-end specialists, had enough money to pursue this fight. I usually ended up brokering an agreement with the board to allow the doctors to select their own therapy providers, a psychologist or a psychiatrist who addressed underlying issues the physician had, such as anxiety or depression or stress due to work or a divorce, while monitoring their performance and substance use. I would get $5,000-10,000 for this work.

I Failed Arguing Before the Federal Second Circuit Court of Appeals

In the US, the federal and state courts are separate. The top of the federal system is the Supreme Court. At the bottom are district courts. Between the two are the federal appeals courts.

I had a client who was an operator in a subway track-switching tower for the Metropolitan Transit Authority (MTA). She was a small woman who, having had a beer at lunch, tested >.02 BAL at a random test she underwent when she got back to work. This exceeded the restrictive federal requirement for sobriety for transportation workers. (Douglas Husak, a law professor, and I wrote in 1998 about how this standard was established by the Supreme Court through scare tactics.)

The woman dutifully went to a rehab specified by the MTA employee assistance program (EAP). Both the rehab and EAP were run by diehard 12-steppers. She objected to submitting to a "higher power," which she found antithetical to her Jewish beliefs. Although she got through rehab, the woman then had to attend weekly meetings with her EAP counselor. She repeatedly refused to concede that she was alcoholic and was powerless over alcohol based on her having had one beer at lunch. She felt like she was attending a brainwashing camp. Each week, the counselor then sent her for urine testing. This process was a useless, demeaning, constant part of the woman's life, an example of the stranglehold AA and the 12 steps have on America to this day, as I detailed in *Filter*.

The EAP could require her to do these interviews and tests for six years. That's where she was headed when she engaged me. Eventually I argued her case before a three-judge panel in the Second Circuit in New York. I had to be specially qualified to argue before a circuit court; my old law school partner vouched for me as part of that elite application process. For my court appearance, I had to write a brief according to notoriously stringent federal standards, making three bound copies. What a pain in the ass! My argument was based on an inherent right a person had to control her identity, and not to be forced to call herself—think of herself as—an alcoholic based on someone else's cockamamie ideas.

I knew from the start that the judges would assume that the woman was an alcoholic trying to get out from under treatment. I could see as I argued that I wasn't penetrating the judges' minds. I halted my legal argument and asked: "Do any of you or your relatives take the subway? Because you know, since returning from rehab, the plaintiff still works for the MTA. She is switching the subways that you and your loved ones ride." The judges turned with alarm to the MTA lawyer, who affirmed my statement. Even the MTA knew she wasn't an alcoholic!

I was making a creative, novel—if essential—legal argument. The word, the concept, "identity" doesn't appear in the Constitution. We lost. I was working pro bono (for free). If I could have brought Archie in, I might have made constitutional law history with untold implications for sexual self-identification. Ah well, you can't be great at everything.

Working in Corporate America—ME!

Although I had ways of making money, significant money sometimes, Mary had continued to work for Verizon until she gave birth to Anna when she was 40 and I was 42 (Anna was born ten and eight years after our older children). Anna changed everything.

Mary continued to work, although not full time. Some time later she converted her environmental activism to working for non-profits. Of course, Mary approached her work for non-profits like a high-powered corporate job; it just paid less.

> ### The Hardest Worker I've Ever Seen
>
> Mary volunteered at the Morris County Soil Conservation Commission, a government group. The head of the agency said to Mary, "You're the hardest worker I've ever seen."
>
> The Commission advertised for a new employee. I instructed Mary, "You have to tell them that if they don't hire you for that job, you'll stop volunteering, and they'll end up with a net loss of labor."
>
> She got the job—at less than half her corporate salary.

I started working in the New York intellectual technocracy bubble. I began writing survey reports for Lou Harris & Associates. Lou Harris had become famous as John F. Kennedy's pollster, which he parlayed into making "Lou Harris" the best-known survey research brand in the US. Harris staff would FedEx over a bunch of computer output to our home. I would have Mary go over the tables, drawing boxes around significant results, and then I would quickly write a narrative report based on the data. I would bill Harris $5,000 for that.

I dealt exclusively with Harris's operational commander—a funny, very smart Englishman named Humphrey Taylor, with whom I had good rapport. Except Humphrey soon realized, after I wrote several emergency reports, that I was making tens of thousands of dollars without having to show up in the office to do other Harris work. Humphrey was a partner in the business—that was his money I was collecting.

Humphrey called me in to New York from Morristown to tell me that I needed to become a full-time employee, for which he offered me a $65,000 salary. I duly reported the offer to Mary, who said, "You're not going to pour your life's blood out on the sidewalks of New York for that." (Harris was located on Fifth Avenue, in Rockefeller Center, directly across from St. Patrick's Cathedral. My office window opened on Fifth Avenue, where

I often could hear protestors—gay marriage supporters, pro-choice—protesting outside.)

When I called Humphrey to relay what Mary had said, Humphrey—who was not easily discomfited—asked, "What does Mary feel it would take for you to pour your life's blood out on the sidewalks of New York?" I dutifully asked Mary, and she said "ten thousand more—$75,000." (This was 1988. The last full-time job I had, at Harvard Business School, had a starting salary in 1971 of $12,500 for nine months.) I relayed the figure to Humphrey and he said, "Done." I then had Mary call Humphrey and work out my employment contract.

I had a major success at Harris—an important one for the company's profitability. It was called Health Care Outlook. We did several surveys a year of different types of health care companies. I analyzed these survey results with a health economist from the Institute of the Future in Palo Alto, a transplanted Scotsman named Ian Morrison. Ian was very smart, a bit unconventional, and we got along famously. Our job involved getting drug and insurance companies to subscribe to our service for $30,000 a year, which added up to a tidy figure when you got twenty-five to thirty major companies to buy in.

I was well-suited for this entrepreneurial sort of job. I could do the sales end—that was easy, because we gathered solid information and offered something useful for companies. Then I could design and conduct the surveys. Ian and I followed by traveling to the sites of the individual companies to present our results in a cogent and useful way. This was before PowerPoint, so we used projected transparencies, which Ian and I wrote together to create a storyline.

What fun!

Ian and I presented well together—joking, trading points back and forth, and involving clients—usually a room of twenty or so top corporate people. Ian stayed at my house in New Jersey when he visited Harris. He was a great favorite with my kids and Mary. But Ian could do nothing to keep me at Harris, as much as Humphrey liked me. After all, he was himself a corporate creation. And my independent ways soon ran me afoul of the old man, Lou Harris, himself. When Humphrey asked me to conduct a survey for the American Institute of Architects, I busily set about creating a questionnaire, sampling AIA respondents, collecting and analyzing the data, and writing up the findings.

I could do all of those technical things, and I got along well with my corresponding professionals at AIA, including giving a well-received talk at AIA headquarters in DC. I didn't realize at the time that such accolades wouldn't secure my job. Lou was used to being the focus of attention. When we walked together from Rockefeller Center to the 1988 AIA conference meeting in Manhattan, a speech before thousands that only Lou Harris could give, Lou told me, "You gave me a pig's ear, and I turned it into a silk purse." Lou added the Harris slant to his keynote address: "Ever since mankind emerged from caves, architects have been designing places for them to live, . . ." yadayada. This narrative was Harris bullshit that said nothing about the data.

I was a goner at Harris. Mary told me I had to get a new job. Looking around at comparable survey research firms in the area, I came up with Mathematica, an organization that competed for high-powered government projects—like assessing the impact of using debit cards, rather than food stamps, for programs providing food for low-income families. Humphrey came through for me by telling the head of surveys there, George Carcagno, "If it were up to me, Stanton would still be working at Harris."

To summarize: I had gotten a job when Mary insisted, and I lasted less than a year despite being quite good at the work.

Working at Harris put me in an influential milieu in American research on health care, which was my specialty there. I became part of a study with researchers at Harvard Medical School to measure patient satisfaction with their hospital stays. A consultant on the Harvard side was Paul Cleary, an extremely nice man and capable researcher who went on to become a prominent public health and AIDS researcher at Yale University. It so happens that he had done his Ph.D. work in sociology at the University of Wisconsin with Howard Leventhal. Leventhal brilliantly (with Paul) showed that smoking was not a straightforward function of maintaining nicotine blood levels, but rather entailed any number of subjective and environmental factors.

Leventhal (whom I have never met) wrote a generous recommendation for my book, *The Meaning of Addiction*. His later work, "Smoking Prevention: Towards a Process Approach," is a model for what addiction research and treatment should seek, say, and do:

> [Smoking prevention programs] focus on external, perceptible, and remote threats, e.g., smoking is seen as evil, a response to peer pressure, and a long term threat to health, and ignore discourse about proximal, subjective feelings respecting the changing sexual urges and feelings of social anxiety that accompany adolescence. The socialization of these affects is left to the peer group. It is suggested that future programs intensify their focus on motivation for resisting smoking based upon a revised view of the adolescents' objectives in self-definition, and combine this with the best of the current skills approach.

Both of these analyses of smoking by Leventhal—one about maintaining addiction, the other about its prevalence and reduction—say what I think. Addiction can never be understood biologically; it entails all aspects of being human; its most important component is its tie-in to people's identities.

We did that hospital study under the auspices of The Commonwealth Fund, an influential health research foundation whose work I discuss in reference to America's addiction epidemic in Chapter 9. At Harris, I couldn't avoid the bad taste of American business values and disrespect for employees, starting at the top with the old man himself. It pervaded the organization, the corporate world. Once, Humphrey, I and the head of the Commonwealth Fund's health care research group visited some corporate office. Humphrey couldn't find a file folder he had misplaced. The Commonwealth guy nonchalantly picked up my briefcase and rifled through it. As you may have gleaned, on my own, I would never have accepted such treatment. Although, considering Mary, I turned the other cheek that time, my recalcitrance was evident, and, despite the profit center I had helped create in Health Care Outlook, Harris replaced me.

Yet, after Harris, I went on to earn what many people (certainly my parents) would regard as a small fortune. I became solidly middle class, perhaps a bit more, for a decade and a half.

8

Big Money Entrepreneur
Marketing my brand to Exxon, alcohol producers, and a rehab

Mary, tiring of her role of supporting the family and of my not using my saleable skills, insisted that I go to work for Harris surveys. She was sympathetic to the duress of my working under the constraints of the Harris system, and Lou Harris himself. But after I was fired by Harris, she sent me directly to my next job at a high-end research organization.

When I was fired there, I went on to become mini-rich—or rich enough— surfing corporate America. This work involved the judicious use of my addiction "brand," raising existential issues about drugs and alcohol and my involvement in the field.

Fired Again—Perhaps I'm Not an Employee Type

So George Carcagno, head of the survey division, hired me at Mathematica, a firm that conducted research for the government. Here are examples of its projects:

- Evaluation of adolescent pregnancy prevention approaches
- Role of social networks among low-income fathers
- Looking at head-start classrooms
- Linking to employment activities for prerelease inmates
- Competency-based education: Outcomes of community college IT programs

I was surprised that working for Harris, which was a seat-of the-pants operation led by a small group of quick-witted researchers, allowed me to be hired at a respected research organization like Mathematica. Mathematica wanted me to expand their business to commercial clients like the big drug and insurance companies with which I worked at Harris. I was given a year to perform that mission.

I succeeded at Mathematica, after a fashion. Prudential was the insurance carrier for the AARP. I got Prudential to hire me, through Mathematica, to do their AARP health insurance market research. A quick synopsis of working for AARP-Prudential as an employee at Mathematica: (a) I commuted an hour each way daily from Morristown to Princeton, (b) my AARP work made a lot of money for Mathematica, (c) I never got along in the bureaucratic Mathematica environment, (d) I lasted less than a year there, too, (e) but when Mathematica fired me, AARP-Prudential went with me as an independent contractor and I made a ton more money by cutting out Mathematica.

At Louis Harris, I was responsible for the whole gamut of a project, from dealing with the client, to designing the survey, to making sure it was run properly by those who conducted the actual phone calls, to analyzing the results, to writing a report and presenting the results to the company or organization that hired us.

Mathematica was structured—there was a cadre of people who were responsible for supervising the survey part of the operation within the survey department, which was housed in an entirely separate building in the techno-industrial complex outside of Princeton where Mathematica lived. "Carla" was assigned as my liaison with the survey center.

But I preferred doing it myself, as I had at Harris, and controlling the whole process.

AARP had asked especially that we check out a group (called a cell in a research design) of much older single women, essentially widows, to understand their insurance needs. But that was a hard group of people to reach and get to respond to an elaborate health insurance survey.

The survey center struggled to get respondents for that cell. Every morning I asked Carla how it was going—I had a lot riding on satisfying the AARP and, through them, my employers at Mathematica. She fended me off. One day I went into her office to read the survey completion output from the night before. Carla found out and came to my office door, screaming. I gently shut the door in her face. George called me into his office within the hour and, soon after, Carla charged in.

Carla proceeded to berate me for half an hour. "Everyone hates Stanton," she finally blurted out. I said nothing. After that outburst, George interrupted Carla: "If I were Stanton, I'd be getting very angry at you." George looked at me for a reaction. "Stanton, is there anything you want to say?"

"Yes, I wanted to know when Carla thought we were going to finish interviewing that group of widowed women." That's my Olympian disdain (my old friend Joel's term) that some people hate—Carla was an annoyance in my pursuit of my life and place in history. Carla: "We're almost done with that."

The next morning I learned, to my astonishment, that Carla had left on vacation. I immediately rushed over to the survey center. A group of interviewers were sitting around a table being trained to conduct a new study. I asked the director of the survey center, "Have we finished the AARP survey?" "Not yet," he said. I said, "Everyone here is going to make calls and we're going to finish the insurance survey before noon."

Which they did. Of course, I wasn't allowed to do that. George called me into his office. "What makes you think that you can go over to the survey center and tell them which calls to make?" I answered, "Well, you're paying me big bucks (even more than I got at Harris), so I thought you wanted me to demonstrate executive capabilities." George: "Among other things that are wrong with that is the cost of that special cell of older women respondents. We're hardly making a profit on this study."

I went back to my office, called the Prudential vice president I was working with, and asked for $5,000 more. He agreed. I went back to George's office and told him what I had done. This was something I had also done with Humphrey Taylor at Harris, after which he would jump up from his chair, come around to the other side of his desk, and vigorously shake my hand.

George instead said, "I don't want to upset Prudential." George fired me shortly after that, saying I wasn't earning my wages. Once again, I failed to reach the one-year mark in my employment. I joked: "I demonstrate strong executive capacity—I act decisively and make things happen. But you usually have to hold a job for at least a year before they make you president."

I proved that I could get a corporate job. I just couldn't keep one for a year.

While I was at Mathematica in 1989, I had other fish to fry:

1. I wrote an article for *The Atlantic* contesting the supposed discovery of a gene for alcoholism. (I describe in the Conclusion regularly writing for popular publications, including on genetics.)

2. I appeared on *Oprah* and contested the entire audience on the disease theory. The junior staff at Mathematica set up a TV to watch the show. (Ethan Nadelmann first saw me on this episode of *Oprah*, as I describe in Chapter 10.)

3. My boss, George Carcagno, went to the national conference for survey researchers and met Don Cahalan at the bar. Cahalan was the emeritus researcher who applied national survey techniques to alcohol problems in the late 1960s, leading to the formation of the fabled Berkeley Alcohol Research Group. Mary and I had visited Don and his wife at his home in the Berkeley Hills.

Don praised me to the sky to George. When one of ARG's surveys showed a downtrend in drinking, I asked Don, "Could that be due to more marijuana use?" Don: "I never thought of that." (See Chapter 11 for Cahalan's monumental research accomplishments with Robin Room.) George couldn't make sense of how I, a minuscule and annoying figure at Mathematica, could be held in such high professional esteem—meanwhile, he saw people screaming at me on *Oprah*.

When I was at Harris, NBC's science editor, Robert Bazell, interviewed me about the disease theory of alcoholism for NBC's *Nightly News* in the Harris offices. (NBC was, like Harris, headquartered at Rockefeller Center.) Lou Harris reveled in national media exposure, as I describe in the previous chapter. I can only imagine his reaction while Bazell and his crew were filming me in the Harris conference room. This was shortly before Lou fired me.

These incidents with my various corporate employers bespeak my anomalous position in the world. I'm a skilled, if minor (and unassimilable) figure in the corporate universe. But, in other regards, I'm a world figure who was interviewed by *NBC Nightly News* and appeared on *Oprah* to argue about the nature of alcoholism. Other times I had to ask George for time off included participating in a think tank on addiction at Harvard, traveling to Melbourne for a speech named after me(!), and testifying in a criminal trial in the Eastern District of Virginia, outside Washington, DC, of a prominent AA member who drove drunk and killed a woman. The federal prosecutor used me as a witness to dispute the man's defense that he was an alcoholic who couldn't help getting drunk, getting into his car, and driving once he had a drink. My testimony was about the choices the man made throughout this "progression." Then there was the time that I had to exit a meeting in DC with government funders to conduct a radio interview with Denny Mc-Clain on a recovery radio show he hosted between prison stints.*

All of this contributed to my not lasting a year at Mathematica, the same fate I had at Harris.

---

* McClain was a former Detroit Tigers pitcher. In 1968, he was the last major league pitcher to win thirty games. He subsequently was imprisoned for drug deals and financial shenanigans.

Working in the Health Care World

Mary was my biggest backer throughout my working at Mathematica, then my leaving it. Mary (who had worked in sales at AT&T/Verizon and for a Fortune 500 package-manufacturing company): "You got them one major new customer in less than a year. It involved a business they were never in before. George and Mathematica don't know what's going on in the business world. You've done as much as—more than—they could have hoped for."

After firing me, George came back to me when it came time to do the next AARP insurance survey. He gave me $5,000 for designing, conducting, analyzing, and presenting its results to AARP and Prudential. But then it occurred to me (or was it Mary?) that I was the essential ingredient in this equation—Prudential wanted me, they didn't care about Mathematica. So I stole the project from them. George—who was a nice enough bloke but also a typical example of corporate, privileged America—was pissed at me for taking the business to support my three kids instead of accepting $5,000 from him for doing the work for Mathematica.

I found a company to do the surveys that I designed and did all the rest myself (analysis, report, and presentations). I was a health care research consultant for AARP insurance! That was a strange trip, one that had taken a little more than two years, from doing stray gigs in my study in Morristown, to becoming research director on health care at Louis Harris, to working for Mathematica, to becoming AARP's chief health insurance market researcher. And so my family and I entered an unusually prosperous period. The Prudential surveys I did on my own were very lucrative. By making myself the contractor, I got to keep the entire profit margin for the study, which was for me a tremendous amount of money.

It is my nature to want my work to be meaningful. After doing a standard survey report for Prudential, I made a list of ten takeaways that could be used to sell their insurance, devise new products, and find new markets. I liked doing that kind of thinking. My contact, a VP at Prudential, liked my doing that: "We love that you try to bring everything home for us. Half of your ten recommendations are undoable, even illegal. Two or three are things we've thought of, maybe even tried or are trying. And each year you give us two or three new ideas that we process and act on. That more than makes up for what we pay you to do those surveys."

We started doing technical insurance studies that proposed products and fractionalized out which kinds of customers would respond to them (called conjoint analysis). I would come into Prudential's AARP corporate head-quarters outside of Philadelphia to be a part of corporate planning meetings.

I brought in a small boutique market research firm to do those analyses. I became friendly with the analytic guy, and Mary and I exchanged dinners with him and his wife. "Ron" and I developed a good working relationship, as I had had with Ian Morrison while I was at Harris. I appreciated Ian's and Ron's brilliance—Ian's expertise on health care, Ron's technical analytic skills.

They in turn enjoyed what I could do. As occurred with the woman who headed computing services at Michigan, there were times when I picked up on anomalies in Ron's programs that he missed—which tends to impress technical people. Plus Ron and I would go down the Delaware River near his house on inner tubes with his son and Anna.

After I was divorced, I reconnected with Ron. He had gotten divorced and remarried. His new wife was quite beautiful and sharp, and highly strung. I visited them only once, when she insistently queried me about dealing with her adult son from a previous marriage. Well-educated, he was unable to become engaged in life and was drinking excessively. Each time she asked me for advice, I turned to Ron for his ideas. Who else? He was smart, knew her son, and had a good relationship with his own son—who had a strong partner relationship and good job.

My approach is to tie therapy into people's ongoing lives—by searching out their own resources for ongoing insight and support to help them deal with their issues. Ron's answers were sensible, straightforward, and practical. Instead of telling her the "right" answers, I shunted her questions back to her and Ron. In fact, his wife became enraged as I persistently involved Ron, *her husband*. Although Ron and I had a fun visit, swimming in the woods near his semi-rural home, Ron told me that I wasn't welcome to come back. "She's really angry," he told me as I left.

This story exemplifies the way people see therapists as providing the right, true answers (or doctors providing medications, or AA offering mantras) in order for people to solve problems or "get better." Ron's wife, of course, had already seen many professionals over decades; she had received an infinite amount of "right" answers. My approach was simply to find positive personal and family patterns and resources that she could use and maintain.

I regretted this bad experience with Ron. AARP had shifted its insurance provider to a company other than Prudential. When my involvement at Prudential ended, I entered another fallow period that contributed to my divorce, and continued after it. Working with Ron as we had done in the past would have been a real boon to my life.

Ron's marital life, like my own, had been his undoing, each in its own way.

Dispensing Harm Reduction Advice from a Surgeon's Chair, with Benefits

I do work in natural settings with people if I feel I can be helpful. Let me tell you about my dental surgery.

I had several baby teeth that never grew out. In my midforties, these started to decay. I went to a high-end dental surgeon. On my first visit, the surgeon asked about my views on his son, who had gone to rehab in Florida around his heroin use. After the program, his son moved into a halfway house. This is the practice I describe in the Prologue, where young people never left the community where they were treated. At the halfway house, his son continued to smoke marijuana and to drink. The surgeon told me that the rehab staff insisted his son had relapsed and shouldn't go home. The surgeon was unsure about their advice.

Me: "Marijuana and alcohol ain't heroin. There are people who manage their heroin use, and those who don't. There are people who manage their marijuana and alcohol use. Some people can do the latter, and not the former. You should look for signs that your son is in that group. You can permit him to move home. But be clear on the standards you expect him to meet, such as going to school or working, being reliable, and so on." (That was harm reduction therapy; see Chapter 9.)

I spent perhaps a half hour in the dental chair discussing this with him.

Some years later I had to return to replace another of my baby teeth.

Surgeon: "You saved my family. I let my son come home, did what you said, and things worked out."

I began worrying about how much I was paying the surgeon to replace my tooth after I had given him such valuable free professional advice. I wrote him a letter about it. He wrote back: "Stanton, I don't usually pay professionals for advice when they're sitting in a chair in my office. However, I gave you a professional discount, which you may not have been aware of. (True: the bill was so enormous I missed the discount.) And I'm doing likewise for this implant."

Postscript: Anna needed her wisdom teeth removed. As Anna and I left the office, the dental surgeon's assistant notified me that he was giving me a professional discount for that service. By now, I figured the guy and I were okay.

Before my AARP sinecure evaporated, I had one last flirtation with normality. Prudential Insurance's national research headquarters were down the highway from me in New Jersey. Based on my work with Prudential's AARP branch, I began consulting with the main research division on physician satisfaction surveys. Then the Harvard Ph.D./M.D. in charge of Prudential's market research, customer satisfaction, and tracking treatment outcomes asked me to head their survey department. Tracking patient outcomes en masse depending on their treatment would have been something valuable, and that I liked doing.

When I hesitated, he said, "You don't have to come in every day. You don't have to dress up when you do come in. But you will have to give up all of your other professional activities." I never seriously considered taking the job (I never even asked what the salary was). If I had, I might have become a normal person—at least outwardly—and Mary and I probably wouldn't have gotten divorced. But I wouldn't have been Stanton Peele.

Mary never wavered in her support of my decision, even though my taking the job would have lifted a great burden of anxiety from her shoulders.

When Mary said, "I feel like I'm married to a riverboat gambler," she said it without bitterness or accusation.

That lady's got guts.

But, we will see, as I learned, her patience and support weren't infinite. Mary's disillusionment was cumulative. As long as she threw in her lot with me, for decades, she understood and supported me when I didn't fit the corporate mold. But she eventually rejected the way of life I chose. As a practical woman, she would say, "Stanton has two licenses (after I became a lawyer in addition to being a psychologist) to print money!"

She was right, of course—if you go for that sort of thing.

Writing Books in My Spare Time

As I was working with Louis Harris, Mathematica, and Prudential, and going to law school at night, I was writing two books. The first was *Diseasing of America*, published in 1989, about how we are convinced, even coerced, into converting our emotional problems, including addiction, into diseases from which the treatment industry profits. And, in 1991, Simon & Schuster published *The Truth About Addiction and Recovery*, which I wrote with Archie and to which Mary contributed. *Truth* is a self-help book that reviews the problems with the disease model, then tackles, in separate chapters, alcoholism, drug use and addiction, smoking, overeating and obesity, addiction to gambling and other activities, and love and sex addiction.

The first chapter of *Truth* is titled, "Why it doesn't make sense to call addiction a disease" (which is available online). It includes a chart distinguishing the disease approach from my Life Process Program. (Carol Tavris used the chart in her introductory textbook.)

Here is a later version of the chart that contrasts the underlying view of the world presented by the brain disease and AA models with that of my life process or developmental approach. This is from my 2019 book with Zach Rhoads, *Outgrowing Addiction: With Common Sense Instead of "Disease" Therapy*. Most essentially, even though disease models claim to be value free, they are riddled with cultural and moral assumptions that make them useless.

Ways of Conceiving Addiction: The Disease Models (AA and Brain Disease) versus the Developmental Model

	Disease	**Developmental**
Nature	All-or-nothing disease state	Extreme end of continuum of normal behavior
Cause	Drugs, biology, genes, trauma	Problems in coping, unmanageable situations and lives
Objects	Some drugs and alcohol	Range of engulfing experiences
Course	Irreversible, life-long; kept at bay by AA groups or meds	Usually reduces or disappears over life course w/o treatment
Agency	Can't be controlled; individual is powerless	People exercise choice, display agency, are empowered
Treatment	Spiritual, group support (AA); drug treatment (MAT)	Natural development; focus on purpose, life resources, skills training, motivational enhancement
Community	Restricted to fellow addicts	Larger community connections
Identity	"I am an alcoholic/addict"	"I am a person with the same needs & capacities as everybody"
Outcomes	Either abstinence/meds, or else self-destruction/death	Positive outcomes from abstinence to normal use to reduced harms
Parenting	Convey disease heritage	Employ sound parenting skills
Value model	Value-free (brain disease) or disguised moralism (AA)	Pro-social values: engagement, purpose, social contribution

But that was only the first part of *Truth*. The rest of the book was devoted to outlining the Life Process Program (or LPP), a combination of cognitive behavioral techniques with information gleaned from the majority of people who outgrow their addictions. That was an ambitious work, written with Archie and with Mary (who contributed research, drawings, and tables of self-help techniques). What a cottage industry I ran while supporting my family and going to law school!

Don't cry for me, Argentina. I still had plenty of time to go to the mall at night to play Pac Man, then wander over to my friend Tom's bookstore and man the cash register for him. Tom and I rode our bikes in the dark down the steep roadways in Jockey Hollow Park after the store closed. In the summer, I swam in the abandoned Morristown reservoir with John Passacantando, my neighbor (and son-in-law of Bill Moyers), who later headed Greenpeace. I played basketball and biked with another neighbor, a former college athlete, Stu Levitt (see Afterword for quote from Stu).

But changing the map of addiction was, is, my purpose. *Truth* was to have a long life (it still sells), but it wasn't a best seller. Years later, the academic entrepreneur and writer, John Norcross, told me that he and his colleagues—who kept the field current on best-selling books about addiction—thought *Truth* would become a classic. But when they did surveys on the leading self-help works in the field (a primary example of which was John Norcross's book with James Prochaska and Carlo DiClemente about the stages of change, *Changing for Good*),* ours didn't produce enough of a blip for them to keep listing it. Nonetheless, *Truth* was a lead-in to many profitable dealings over my life, especially the treatment program I was to create.

Several years later, in 1997, *Oprah*'s producers contacted me to appear on their show around the drunk-driving arrest of the Ukrainian Olympic champion figure skater Oksana Baiul. I had appeared on *Oprah* several times many years earlier. I was called this time because Baiul said she

---

* Prochaska and DiCelemente's *stages of change* claims that addicted/recovered people rotate through a set series of stages, from precontemplation to maintenance and possible relapse. I note instead that the model may useful in work with a particular person. But taking the stages as a universal set of principles offers, according to a critical analysis of the data, "the feeling that one has gained insight into something important and technical and scientifically valid, yet which accords with common sense understandings. . . . [Instead] the model amounts to a broad guide to what (not) to do with patients at different stages of change. If it truly gets to the heart of the change process, then interventions built on the model ought to improve on those that are not. It is at this crunch point, when it actively engages with change through treatment, that *research support is almost entirely lacking* (my emphasis). That is true not just of drug and alcohol problems and of smoking, but of therapy for psychological problems in general."

wasn't an alcoholic, and I might have provided support for her to reject that label. But I had contracted to represent a criminal defendant in court that day (I was a lawyer by then). I couldn't travel to Chicago, even though Oprah's show regularly turned the books of authors who appeared on it, like James Frey's *A Million Little Pieces*, into best sellers. I regretted turning that appearance down. But I was honor-bound to my client, crook though he be, for the pittance he was paying me. Even my honorable wife, Mary, suggested that I ditch him. I couldn't.

The Exxon *Valdez*

In 1993, while I was conducting insurance market research with AARP and Prudential, I became involved in a case that made headlines worldwide—the Exxon *Valdez*. The *Valdez* ran aground in 1989 in Prince William Sound, Alaska, spilling hundreds of thousands of barrels of crude oil. Lawyers for Exxon contacted me around the role of Joseph Hazelwood, captain of the *Valdez*, who had previously been in alcoholism rehab and who had been drinking that evening. He was below deck when the *Valdez* collided with a reef.

Let me jump to the verdict in re Hazelwood—he was acquitted of criminal charges related to drunkenness, since witnesses provided reliable testimony that he was sober that evening. As a result, Hazelwood never lost his pilot's license. But he couldn't be employed again as a ship's captain—he was a national laughingstock. Example: a David Letterman "Top Ten" list of Hazelwood excuses included, "I was just trying to scrape some ice off the reef for my margarita." People's lives come and go.

I wasn't involved in the criminal trial. But Exxon was sued separately for its negligence, which included its employment and supervision of Hazelwood. Among the things I was known for, à la *Diseasing of America*, was labeling the recovery-rehab narrative—disease → treatment → recovery —ineffectual and false. Jumping to the end of that trial, in 1994, a jury awarded the plaintiffs $287 million in compensatory damages and $5 billion in punitive damages. On various appeals the punitive part was reduced to around a billion dollars.

I'm glad Exxon had to pay for the clean-up, damages, and penalties. Why shouldn't they?

Nonetheless, I worked (with Archie) for Exxon's attorneys on the issue of whether a person formerly in alcoholism treatment, as Hazelwood had been, could function responsibly in spite of having some drinks. I didn't testify at the trial because I had discussed Hazelwood in *Diseasing of America*, and my mixed comments there could have been used against me in court. So I was restricted to a behind-the-scenes, incognito consulting role. As I had done in arraying potential Prudential insurance products, I suggested themes and arguments for Exxon's attorneys to use. Archie and I compiled scientific evidence relevant to Hazelwood's treatment and drinking—all of which were reality-based and in which I believed.

I made a great deal of money working as an alcoholism consultant for Exxon's counsel. When you're fighting over billions of dollars, whatever I might charge didn't amount to pocket change. I wasn't involved in any of the appeals or settlement discussions leading to the final billion-dollar resolution, since these further proceedings didn't hinge on alcohol issues. Nonetheless, with what I did earn, I built a separate wing of our house in Morristown for my office.

Alcohol Consulting

I challenge what we believe about addiction and behavior in relation to alcohol, and drugs, and cigarettes, and love, and shopping. I receive no salary to do that. So how do I make a living with my unpopular views, my attacks on cultural shibboleths? I'm usually picked up by advocates requesting arguments opposing popular views, as Exxon did in the case of Hazelwood's alcoholism treatment.

As an example of this process of trying to tell the truth on my own, with no funding, in 1993 I published an article in the flagship journal of the American Public Health Association about the benefits of moderate drinking. Written as dispassionate science, the article, "The Conflict Between Public Health Goals and the Temperance Mentality," showed that cultural prejudices prevented us from considering alcohol's benefits due to the moralistic temperance model I discuss in Chapter 11. My stance got me noticed by industry groups. Beginning about the same time as the *Valdez*, from the middle through the end of the 1990s, I began to consult with the beverage alcohol industry.

The best things about working with the alcohol producers were their conferences. Archie worked with me and often joined me at these fiestas. I took Mary to the more scrumptious of these, like a California conference for foodies that included a fabulous "peanut cruise" on San Francisco Bay. Another such extended trip was a pleasure conference in Perugia, Italy, a center of the chocolate industry. Mary really enjoyed those outings with their amazing food, wine, and settings. She was part small-town girl from the Midwest and part international connoisseur and bon vivant who reveled in, without demanding, these portholes to the high life. And, so did I, like the time I got to watch a Rockies baseball game with Colorado's governor from the Coors box at Denver's Coors Stadium. Yes, Coors (or Killian's Irish, which I prefer) beer was on draught. No one got drunk.

What Dwight Heath and I know

One person I often met at such gatherings was Dwight Heath, a long-time alcohol anthropologist at Brown University, whose career traces back to his famous 1958 study of the Camba Indians in Bolivia. In 2010, Malcolm Gladwell described Dwight's 1950s research in a piece in *The New Yorker* titled, "How much people drink may matter less than how they drink it."

Dwight and his wife Anna had traveled to a remote region of Bolivia to live among the Camba. When they returned to Dwight's graduate studies at Yale, home at the time of the Center of Alcohol Studies, Dwight by chance encountered E. M. Jellinek on campus. Jellinek had invented the modern disease theory of alcoholism. He and Mark Keller, the first editor of the Center's journal, asked Dwight to explain his tan in the middle of a New Haven winter. After Dwight told them his story, they excitedly asked him to describe how the Camba drank for the *Journal of Studies on Alcohol*, which he did exactly three decades before I won the Keller Award from the same journal.

Here was how the Camba drank: Every weekend and holiday the Heaths went to a party where guests sat in a circle drinking a strong local rum from Saturday night until Monday morning, when they went to work. People regularly passed out at the party, awoke and started drinking again. The Heaths brought samples of the rum back to New Haven, which turned out to be 180 proof (90 percent pure alcohol). Yale laboratory scientists said the brew was impossible for humans to drink—and so Dwight drank a jar for them.

Although the Camba had weekly benders with laboratory-proof alcohol, Heath told Gladwell, "There was no social pathology—none. No arguments, no disputes, no sexual aggression, no verbal aggression. There was pleasant conversation or silence. The drinking didn't interfere with work. And there was no alcoholism." That is, people never drank during the week or drank alone. In other words, drinking a lot of alcohol or taking a lot of a drug doesn't addict you to it. This radical idea is one I have always embraced, as I expressed in *The Meaning of Addiction* and my 1987 Keller-award winning article. (Mark Keller watched one of my presentations and approached me afterward. "Finally," he said, "someone who really knows what addiction is.")

Gladwell also explores the classic book *Drunken Comportment* (1969), by Craig MacAndrew and Robert Edgerton, a sociologist and an anthropologist. *Comportment* examined how people in different cultures follow accepted cultural rules when drinking, even when drunk. For example, no matter how drunk people got, including orgies, they refrained from sexual relations that would be considered incestuous in their culture, even when cultural outsiders couldn't comprehend what qualified a given relationship as incest.

Gladwell summarized Heath's and *Drunken Comportment*'s indelible findings from worlds other than America: "The content of the rules matters less than the fact of the rule, the existence of a drinking regimen that both encourages and constrains alcohol's use." We drink like we are taught to, including intoxicated behavior and alcoholism. This social learning takes place in America at large, or in our own specific cultural and social niches.

Gladwell's point about alcohol is every bit as true in the case of other drugs. As Carl Hart notes, the difference between the drug Adderall, which we give to children, and street meth is simply the packaging of the drug, the image it has, and why and how it is used. The same is true with the largely benign use of powerful medical painkillers. The fundamental insight that cultural customs around drugs and alcohol are crucial to how they are consumed and the consequences of their consumption has colossal implications. Drug panics appear, surge and decline, it often seems randomly, along with vast shifts in our perception of the dangers of alcohol. I deal with these issues in Part III, about our modern views of opioids, alcohol, and addiction. All of these are manifestations of the ways that substances tap into society's—America's—fears and our conceptions of personal autonomy.

As for Dwight Heath, the unique human, I followed Dwight's lead in Quebec, San Francisco, New York, and other places where we met. For example, while we were in DC working for an alcohol producers' organization, I stayed at a nearby bed and breakfast Dwight discovered. The wife of the owner was Dominican, and she told me Dwight spoke Spanish with a perfect Dominican accent. When I asked Dwight how he came to speak Spanish with a Dominican accent, he looked at me bemusedly, "Why would I speak to her with a Mexican or a Spanish accent?" In other words, Dwight spoke whatever dialect of Spanish a conversation required.

Dwight grew up in Lowell, Massachusetts, the son of a government auto mechanic. At one point a high school counselor called Dwight to his office and asked why he hadn't applied to any colleges. Dwight felt that his family couldn't afford college. The counselor informed Dwight of things called scholarships. Dwight applied to one university, Harvard, where he was admitted with a scholarship. In this and every other way, Dwight made up his life. He drew tattoos on women's chests after they had radical mastectomies. He had his own organic apple orchard. Everything Dwight did and thought was original and unique.

Dwight and I got along famously. We each created ourselves—no one did what either of us did before we did it. Mary loved Dwight. She referred to him as "a ghost," likening him to the shaman in Carlos Castaneda's work. But when Dwight invited us to stay with him and his wife, Mary became ill and we couldn't go to the home described by Gladwell, "not far from the Brown University campus, in Providence, in a house filled with hundreds of African statues and sculptures, with books and papers piled high on tables."

This was at the end of our marriage. A couple of years later, however, I drove Anna to be interviewed for admission to Brown (she ultimately went to NYU). I hadn't thought to schedule ahead to see Dwight. But as we drove through town, a car window rolled down. Dwight beckoned for us to follow him, and we had lunch and wine at his home.[*] He told me to pick out one of the African artifacts stacked all around. Anna selected a spear, but Dwight suggested we pick something smaller. I took a metal bracelet that now sits on the window ledge next to my bed in my Brooklyn apartment.

Is alcohol bad?

How was working for alcohol producers in keeping with my values? One way to approach that question is to ask whether alcohol is beneficial, or healthy. I wrote a piece for *Pacific Standard* that was one of its ten most popular for that year, entitled "The Truth We Won't Admit: Drinking Is Healthy."

Why would I write that? There is actually no debate that people who drink live longer than people who abstain (as I discuss in Chapter 11). This statement is true, even at the same time that drinking a lot—particularly in binges—is unhealthy. I added as a caveat in my *Pacific Standard* piece, "Drinking ten drinks Friday and Saturday nights does not convey the benefits of two or three drinks daily, even though your weekly

---

[*] Anna wasn't 21. In fact, she was still a teenager. Dwight has written extensively about Spain, where the drinking age is 16, but even that liberal boundary is ignored. I took Anna to Portugal and Spain, to France and Italy, and Mary and I took her to Cannes and the Mediterranean; in all these places, she was served wine as a teenager.

totals would be the same: Frequent, heavy binge drinking is unhealthy." Of course, this defies the Camba's drinking. Yet more important than the amount consumed for healthy use of a substance is its integration into a culture, which is pegged to its cultural meaning. And, as *Drunken Comportment* showed, this meaning is often indecipherable to those outside the culture.

> ### Impacting Views of Alcohol, Drugs and Addiction
>
> *Visions of Addiction* (the title of my 1987 edited volume of differing views of what addiction is), as well as of drugs and alcohol and their effects, are deeply baked into the culture's and individuals' thinking. Yet these visions are critical to how people use and are affected by substances. My and Zach Rhoads's 2019 book, *Outgrowing Addiction*, includes as an appendix, written with Dr. Noriko Martinez, a child and family therapist and Loyola University professor, a manual for assessing these mind maps. Surfacing people's views of the elements of addiction (for example, asking people whether they feel drugs can change the course of people's lives or whether people control their own destinies; asking whether they see addiction as limited to drugs) allows parents to be mindful of their own visions of and what they communicate to children about drugs, alcohol, and addiction. My 2014 book with Ilse Thompson, *Recover!*, uses mindfulness exercises that Ilse wrote to access and impact how people with potential addictive problems see and are influenced by their images of drugs, alcohol, and other powerful experiences. Zach Rhoads has written similar exercises for our Life Process Program.

The debate is over why drinkers as a rule live longer. One attempted refutation of the evidence that drinking is healthy is that unhealthy people, or problem drinkers, fill the abstinence ranks, leaving only healthy drinkers. But every epidemiological study worth its salt filters out such for-cause abstainers, with the same results. The next counterargument is that drinkers live longer because of other healthy habits that accompany drinking—employment, sociability, marriage, integration in a community, and personal habits like eating well and exercising. Tim Stockwell, an alcohol researcher at the University of Victoria (British Columbia), makes this case in "Moderate Alcohol Use in Older Years: A Sign or Cause of Good Health?"

I'll accept Stockwell's counterargument, even though research continues to show that alcohol reduces overall mortality, as well as lowering the risk of dementia. I wanted the alcohol industry to put forward this positive image of drinking in a context of health and overall well-being. I believed that they should market alcohol, not as a symbol of sexual prowess and attractiveness, but as an accompaniment to a full, healthy social, family, and community life. Every village in Italy has, across the town square from the church, a café to which people repair after the service to have lunch and wine with their families among their neighbors and friends. Consider Allaman Allamani's description of the role of wine in Italian life in Chapter 11. This is true for Greece, Spain, France, Italy, etc.

Human beings have grown up alongside alcohol. Beverage alcohol has been found at the site of every original center of civilization, as established by Patrick McGovern, University of Pennsylvania archeologist. International surveys show that the more alcohol a society consumes, the fewer alcohol-related problems and alcohol-related deaths (including cirrhosis) it has. These societies, such as those in Southern Europe, integrate drinking with a positive community life. And alcohol consumed in tune with community rituals conveys benefits even when consumption is heavy and irregular, as it did for the Camba. (I return in more detail to these debates with anti-alcohol public health figures in Chapter 11.)

Obviously, people other than the Camba and Southern Europeans have figured that out. Here is Eric Asimov recommending good wines for the pandemic lockdown in the *New York Times*:

> A good wine can also inspire thoughtful contemplation and introspection, which perhaps now more than ever is in short supply. And it can lead to caring conversations as well, to listening as well as talking, to shared bonds, to new memories and more humane ways of thinking. I'm not saying good wine is a panacea. It's up to people to find solutions. But wine has the power to bring people together as surely as a great meal. . . . [in] reflection on values, joy, sorrow, and shared humanity.

Living the good life

Tim Stockwell had me lecture at the British Columbia Centre for Addiction. I made fun of some of Tim's thinking, including his rejection of the term "addiction," despite its being emblazoned in his Center's name. The packed auditorium was enthusiastic. Afterward Tim, his co-director at the Center, the Center's medical director, and I went out for dinner. We spoke about how our parents' style differed from our own. We nurture our children consciously while our parents were more hands off. None of us would raise our kids the way we were raised. But we wondered if kids are the better off for it.

> ### Tim Stockwell's "Trauma"
>
> Both Tim's father, Brian Stockwell, and grandfather had been directors of the Reuters news service: "Brian Stockwell gave his life's work at Reuters, as did his father before him." When Tim graduated university, his father looked at him and mused, "I don't suppose you could manage Reuters." Without waiting for an answer, he turned away. "I don't suppose so."[*]

Tim survived this parenting slight to get a Ph.D., become a leading alcohol researcher, and have a happy family of his own. Thank God!

Meanwhile, the four of us—the socially privileged, educated elite—imbibed alcohol, ate delicious food, and had stimulating conversation. In fact, better-educated, higher-earning adults are *far more likely to consume alcohol*, and to do so moderately, than those without these advantages. Who wouldn't choose this Italianate lifestyle? I once attended a lecture by an anti-alcohol pediatrician. We spoke briefly afterward. Although she had just told us about the dangers of alcohol for adults and children, she had just returned from her own wedding, held on a hillside in Tuscany, Italy. Even the teens present had wine.

In the next chapter I review two studies: *The World Happiness Report* (2019), which announced the shocking decline in happiness for Americans in recent decades, especially for the young, among whom we have seen "the rapid rise of adolescent depression, suicidal ideation, and self-harm," and a Commonwealth Fund report (2020) that found Americans have the shortest life spans and highest suicide rate among wealthy nations.

My whole life goal has been to reverse these trends. Despite Tim's personal enjoyment of alcohol, he is a charter member of a group of WHO alcohol epidemiologists I describe in Chapter 11 whose mission is to condemn alcohol, thus removing drinking from positive social contexts and driving it into isolated, guilty societal corners. Demonizing alcohol is futile, wrongheaded, and counterproductive. I haven't been invited to speak again at Tim's Center and to comparable epidemiological and research groups for over a decade, despite having made a number of remarkable (and well-regarded) appearances at them.

My lack of appeal to alcohol producers

At the same time that I was rejected by alcohol epidemiologists, I tried for several years to work through the alcohol producers themselves to get out healthy drinking messages. I began my alcohol consulting with the Wine

---

[*] I sent Tim an email offering him an opportunity to review what I have written about him, but never heard back.

Institute (TWI), then headed by John DeLuca, former deputy mayor of San Francisco. Archie and I wrote and spoke about alcohol and culture for TWI and the useful models for sensible drinking that wine cultures offer.

In 1997, Marcus Grant, representing an organization formed by a group of alcohol beverage producers, the International Center for Alcohol Policies, known as ICAP, contacted me to organize a conference around alcohol and pleasure. Grant had been chief assistant to the progenitor of alcohol and addiction research in the UK, Griffith Edwards (whose review of my book, *The Meaning of Addiction*, I discuss in the Conclusion). Marcus went on to work for the World Health Organization in Europe for a decade before founding ICAP.

ICAP represented the alcohol industry in the public health world. Unfortunately, despite some quite good work, over the nearly two decades that Grant headed ICAP, public health interests became entirely hostile to commercial alcohol interests. When Marcus originally contacted me, this permanent division wasn't yet clear. I organized a conference called "Permission for Pleasure" in New York in 1998, inviting a range of luminaries in the field. It would be impossible to get such speakers to a conference sponsored by alcohol manufacturers today.

For the conference Archie and I surveyed the benefits of moderate drinking and I explored the meaning and promotion of pleasure in alcohol consumption. I spent another year editing a volume, which was titled *Alcohol and Pleasure* (1999). Along with my and Archie's contributions, the conference and the volume included a roster of important researchers, like Tim Stockwell(!), Alan Marlatt, Dwight Heath, Carlos Camargo, Jr. (of Harvard Medical School), John Orley (the World Health Organization), Barbara Leigh (University of Washington), and many others, including Latin American, Asian, and African speakers. The conference considered the value of moderate drinking, the cultural concomitants to such drinking, and the core questions: "Is drinking pleasurable?" and "Is pleasure in and of itself healthy and to be valued?" (Yes to both.)

But the fault lines in the field are so deep that this work was never taken seriously. In 2002 I participated in one last ICAP alcohol conference, in Dublin. Bittersweetly, Mary accompanied me to Ireland just after we decided to separate. And that was the end of both my marriage and my work with the alcohol producers. I had become more insistent in presenting my community- and family-based social-drinking model—embodied by Spanish, Greek and Italian cafes. But producers didn't want to rock the boat. You see, they're doing fine as things are.

People will continue to consume alcohol. Indeed, they are drinking more. And, it turns out, "even in time of pandemic, both men and women are holding the worst of their imbibing to a comparative minimum." People are fundamentally health-seeking organisms, when encouraged and given the chance.

I encourage this search for enjoyment and the good life, as great a challenge as that is today, along with people's belief that they deserve and can attain them while being their own best guardians of their health. I find the continuing campaign by public health forces against these ideas and beliefs, and to demonize alcohol, to be a fight against humanity.

Quitting Smoking

In the mid-2000s I was approached by an attorney for cigarette manufacturers to work on their defense cases. I told him that I would never testify in a trial in defense of cigarette manufacturers against people who got lung cancer or emphysema from smoking. But I was willing to contest—I wanted to do so—the idea that people who were addicted to cigarettes found it impossible to quit, which is what anti-tobacco lawyers got experts to swear to.

My expert reports contested what had, erroneously, become conventional wisdom about smoking during my lifetime. In fact, in 1975 we were the first to declare in *Love and Addiction* that smoking was addictive, arguing that it did crucially change people's mood and that withdrawal from it (as well as coffee) was every bit as severe as the narcotic withdrawal experience. Let me say it again—smoking and coffee are addictive in exactly the same sense as heroin and painkillers may be. There is no qualitatively different type of addiction that appears with heroin.

So, with smoking, I argue the complex reality that, yes, tobacco and nicotine are addictive in exactly the way heroin and other opioids are; and, no, although it may be difficult to do so, this doesn't mean that people cannot quit smoking without medical aids. Amply marketed, these now include along with various nicotine replacement products the antidepressant bupropion and varenicline, which "can help reduce cravings," "reduce withdrawal," and "block nicotine brain receptors," according to the Mayo Clinic. *In fact, to this day, despite the plethora of products on the market, people overwhelmingly still quit on their own—as I regularly prove by questioning audiences.*

____

* As I have described, I ask audiences experienced with drug addiction and alcoholism which is the hardest drug to quit, to which they reply in unison, "nicotine/smoking." They then reveal that virtually all of the large number of them who have quit smoking did so without chemical aids.

> ### A Remarkable Truth Lost in the Fog of History
>
> The Surgeon General and Department of Health and Human Services (DHHS) only got around to officially recognizing tobacco as addictive in their 1988 report, *Nicotine Addiction*—thirteen years after *Love and Addiction* said so. The 1964 *Surgeon General's Report* (SGR) that said smoking caused cancer *didn't* say that it was addictive. In fact, it declared that smoking *wasn't addictive, but habituating.*
>
> When I detail this history at harm reduction conferences, the audiences shout out, "That's because tobacco companies fund the researchers, who are in their pockets."
>
> I shake my head sadly. "You're all such *comme-il-faut* socialists. The researchers saying this were the *most* anti-tobacco force in America. After all, they declared smoking was cancer-causing in the 1964 SGR. But they, like you, danced around with nonsensical ways of thinking about addiction. Only these change from generation to generation. For them nicotine wasn't narcotics, so it wasn't really addictive. For you, it's all something about brain chemistry and receptors."

When the label "addictive" was finally applied to smoking, it was used to explain why people couldn't quit, even though *everyone* knows people who have done so (like my Uncle Ozzie and my wife, Mary). Just ask everyone you know who has smoked. It *is* true, as I point out in Chapter 2, that smoking is the longest-lived drug addiction, lasting far longer on average than alcoholism and addiction to illicit drugs. Nonetheless, *people typically quit, and do so on their own.*

Another remarkable DHHS smoking document was published in 2002, titled *Those Who Continue to Smoke.* The bottom line: "Surprisingly, none of the papers suggest that the population of smokers who remains [addicted] is more addicted, more resistant to cessation messages, less likely to attempt cessation, or increasingly composed of those with limited self-control or poor mental health."

That's right—anyone can quit smoking, no matter how dependent they are, or how long they have been addicted, *or how bad they seemingly were at quitting up until then.*

Two more amazing findings about smoking and addiction. The 2002 volume found an accelerating trend—"there has been a decline rather than an increase over the last two decades in the fraction of smokers smoking twenty-five or more cigarettes per day, and the mean number of cigarettes smoked per day as reported by smokers has declined." Addicted smokers today smoke less! In other words, even addicted people regulate their behavior in line with social rules and changing values. *How people are addicted to cigarettes has changed before our eyes.*

The last amazing thing? Gene Heyman, at Boston College, found that the probability of quitting all drug addictions, the same as with smoking, remains the same no matter how long the person has been addicted. Being addicted is not a life sentence, even when it seems as though you are a hard-core addict. This is one more nail in the coffin of the destructive way we are taught to think of addiction (as, among many others, *New York Times* columnist David Brooks declares publicly, see Chapter 10)—that it is an inescapable trap, if not for everyone, then for a cadre of "true" addicts.

I wrote reports, in response to the experts retained by the lawyers for those suing tobacco companies, showing that their "scientific" theories of addiction to smoking were wrong, based on the simple evidence of people's actual behavior. I reviewed the data about people's lifetime smoking against idealized brain schematics and graphs purporting to show how people were irreversibly addicted to nicotine. And, in fact, when I reviewed the cases, I found that the smokers who developed cancer had nearly always quit—some near the end of their lives, but usually somewhere in the course of them.

For example, a man who had begun smoking in his early teens continued for fifty years until he had a heart attack in his sixties. When he awoke in the hospital, he asked his daughter for a cigarette. She said, "Daddy, if you smoke I'll never speak to you again." So he quit.

What theory explains his quitting? Nora Volkow may chew this one over; he quit for love, with no prior preparation or other assistance. It's as simple as life: people quit when they feel that smoking or another addiction hurts or prevents something they care about more.

But I was no more popular with tobacco companies than I am anywhere else. They didn't want to give in to the reality of addiction to smoking even with my bottom line: "Yes it's addictive—people still can quit, and do so all the time."

I Was in the Rehab Business

Soon after failing to sufficiently impress the tobacco companies, in 2008, I was contacted by a married couple who were running a non-disease addiction rehab center. They needed me to replace their current program provider, whom (I later learned) they were suing. (This was the group that I later visited to devise legal strategies, with Archie's disembodied voice patched in.)

Archie and I negotiated a partnership contract with their legal team, and I adapted my Life Process Program (LPP) from my book with Archie and Mary, *The Truth About Addiction and Recovery*, into an eight-week residential treatment program. LPP focuses on root causes and practical life solutions for addiction, as well as on values, purpose, and meaning—a condensed course in maturing out. I trained and supervised a group of non-recovering counselors.

Under my direction, the program received state licensing and qualified to receive insurance payments. We were in the clover! Then, in 2011, my partners said that we should renegotiate our agreement, which they decided was too favorable to me. I expressed a willingness to renegotiate, but I wasn't going to accede to the kinds of demands they were making. My partners sued me. Archie and I spent a year and a half combating their team of lawyers in federal court in Iowa. We finally reached a court-mediated settlement in 2012.

Going against a team of high-priced attorneys was stressful. The settlement was thus a relief. Of course, I couldn't have carried out the legal battle to completion without Archie. After all was done, however, Archie and I couldn't help but rue what our lives would have been like if we continued to have a share in that oil well.

Live Till I Die

I have shown that I will always resurface. After being rejected by academia and the addiction field, I found ways to get by, selling my skills in corporate jobs, then finding corporate gold veins to mine. Anna: "You're like a cockroach, Dad—you'll always survive." An academic couple who wandered into one of the recovery conferences at which I spoke regularly for a time: "You're an idea merchant." Will Godfrey, editor for my latter-day-addiction-blogging self: "I know you can come up with an infinite supply of new ideas." Mary: "If I had your brains, I'd win the Nobel Prize" (I'm working on it!). Although there were dry times, my mind is a never-ceasing generative engine. My skill set and alertness and options are always there for me.

I Picked Up Some Loose Coins Here

There was the bed-and-breakfast Dwight found near the International Center for Alcohol Policies, where he spoke Dominican-dialect Spanish with the owner's wife. The owner of the B&B, "Bernie," also owned a small consulting firm. But Bernie was having trouble managing his well-educated staff. He asked me if I could consult with them.

> I agreed to spend five days working with the group for $10,000. I first interviewed the staff. It seemed that the group, led by Bernie, was crossing wires in their communications and decision making. Mary suggested that I come up with a set of internal regulations called "Rules of Engagement." I then had a day-long group meet, which Bernie joined in the afternoon. The group and I created a list of ten organizational rules.
>
> The first rule was: "A person must always participate in any decisions that affect his or her work." The last contracted workday was for me to outline a path to find Bernie's successor. But when he told the group what I was to do, they rebelled, saying that Bernie's unilateral decision to have me do that job violated their first rule. When Bernie told me that, I laughed and told him just to mail me my final payment of $2,000. It was Bernie's turn to laugh, "Not for doing nothing, my friend."
>
> That New Year's Eve, as I was hanging around my wing and Mary was elsewhere in the house, I got a call from Bernie, who was doing year-end accounts. "I was looking on the wall where we framed our 'Rules of Engagement.' I thought how much value we got from you. So I'm just going to send you the remaining $2,000." I shouted to Mary, "We made $2,000 tonight!" As you know, Mary liked that sort of thing.

It seems that I will always come up with needed cash. (Remember the $20 John Papa gave me en route to Stony Brook?) Thus have I lived a comfortable middle-class existence, albeit always on the edge. We went out to dinner, took package tours to Europe, and sent our kids to college.

Beyond that, I made a small fortune working for alcohol producers, Exxon, the addiction rehab industry, and cigarette manufacturers. I valued these enterprises because, through them, I was able to present essential truths about addiction, sometimes to the discomfort of my clients or partners. And I established a lifestyle that avoided wasting years of being an employee and time like that I spent driving between Ann Arbor and Schoolcraft College in Livonia, or my attic rooms in a home in Newton and Harvard Business School, or going to New York to work at Harris, or between Morristown and Princeton to work at Mathematica, or, later, traveling around New Jersey to senior care homes.

That wasn't to be my life. My chosen role was to fight against misinformation and myths about drugs, alcohol and addiction, and ultimately to understand human motivation and improve lives by placing psychology in a social context.

◆

So I didn't end up financially set for life. With the abundant money I did make for fifteen years, aside from buying a place for Anna in the West Village, the part of Manhattan least corrupted by towers in the sky, I tried to enjoy my life. You know the Frank Sinatra song, "Live Till I Die"? Maybe it was running through my mind when I said my childhood bedtime prayer (which otherwise made no sense): "I want to live until I die."

And I will never, ever give up my purpose. This is how I enter old age in Brooklyn on a pretty thin economic and social thread. But I am nothing daunted, as I tell in Part III of this memoir, "Here, Now and Then."

And I still fight my fight.

Part III

Here, Now and Then

I have laid out a map for theory and practice in addiction for fifty years. My views on addiction—and mental health—are distant from the American consensus, including the drug policy reform movement.

Mental health indicators in the United States are abysmal—the worst in the world. Yet Americans, convinced of their exceptionalism, don't question their thinking and carry on with more of the same.

In my mid-70s, I continue to hold unpopular views and get into trouble. I must fight between bitterness and generativity. But I seem to have a sustainable life and career—and my views are influencing more people and policies.

On balance, however, the US can't escape its disease perspective on addiction as part of modern America's medicalization of life. Even drug reform movement efforts, embodied by Ethan Nadelmann, intended to liberate us from our temperance mentality often reinforce it.

A whole new wave of anti-disease theorists and writers likewise, shrinking from the abyss, end up largely reinforcing—and certainly not containing—our headlong rush to the diseasification of human experience, drug use, and mental problems.

Our conventional view of addiction—aided and abetted by science—does nothing so much as convince people of their vulnerability. It is one more element in a pervasive sense of loss of control that is the major contributor to drug and alcohol addiction, along with a host of other maladies of our age. We feel we must warn people against the dangers of the substances our society has banned, or attempted to curtail, but cannot eradicate. This book argues that our best hope is to convey these dangers realistically, by rationally pointing out the costs of excess and, more importantly, by convincing people of the benefits of health and positive life experiences. *Otherwise, the idea of addiction can only become another burden to the psyche* [my emphasis].

— Stanton Peele, *The Meaning of Addiction* (1985)

9

The Remedy for Addiction Is Empowerment, Engagement, and Purpose

We instead double down on medical control, disease pigeonholes, and hopelessness

Americans believe that we have the most advanced mental health system in the world based on disease treatments and medications. They feel we can always rely on these standbys to solve our mental health problems.

In the drug arena this takes the form of MAT (medication-assisted treatment), which is embraced across the board, from the National Institute on Drug Abuse to the leading drug policy reform groups—all of which regard drug misuse and addiction as a disease.

Meanwhile, the US is at the bottom of the world's mental health and drug-deaths heap—and getting worse—according to both international comparisons and internal American data.

Most professionals, even my closest friends and allies, find my rejection of our dismal, futile disease-treatment consensus counterproductive.

You are preoccupied with refuting the disease theory, ignoring everything else. You know everyone who reads your diatribes against MAT thinks you've gone off the deep end and discounts your views.

— Ethan Nadelmann, founding director of the Drug Policy Alliance

Although the brain disease model of addiction is perceived by many as received knowledge it is not supported by research or logic. . . . The relevant research shows most of those who meet the American Psychiatric Association's criteria for addiction quit using illegal drugs by about age 30, that they usually quit without professional help, and that the correlates of quitting include legal concerns, economic pressures, and the desire for respect, particularly from family members.

— Gene Heyman, quantitative addiction researcher, Boston College

We're Sick

America isn't a happy or well-adjusted society. Our kids, especially, are showing the stresses of a distorted life structure. But, for the most part, well-off people and opinion leaders are shielded from the worst mental health and addiction outcomes. As a result, we accept and endure our current dystopia.

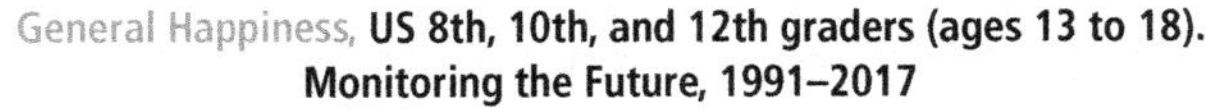

General Happiness, **US 8th, 10th, and 12th graders (ages 13 to 18).**
Monitoring the Future, 1991–2017

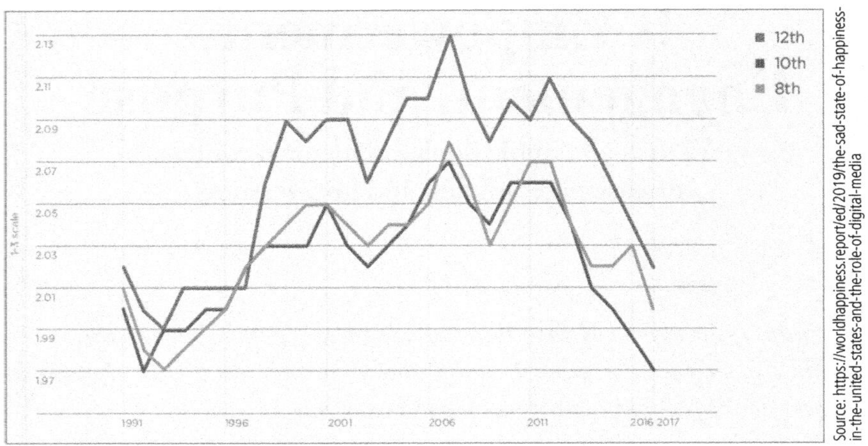

The *World Happiness Report* of 2019 ended with Jeffrey Sachs's "Addiction and Unhappiness in America." Sachs is the director of the Center for Sustainable Development of Columbia University. He finds that "the US is in the midst of epidemics of several addictions, both of substances and behaviors." Another chapter in the volume, by Jean Twenge, author of *iGen*—"The Sad State of Happiness in the United States and the Role of Digital Media"—noted the decline in American happiness overall, but especially "the rapid rise of adolescent depression, suicidal ideation, and self-harm after 2010, and a marked decline in subjective well-being." Twenge provides the above table from the *Monitoring the Future Study* of secondary school students.

The Global Burden of Disease study ranked losses due to both disability and death associated with drugs for 196 nations, including both wealthy and impoverished countries, war-torn nations and those that produce coca and opium. The United States was second overall in Disability-Adjusted Life Years (DALYs) lost for all forms of drug use combined. The US scored first for cocaine DALY losses, second for those from amphetamines, and third for those from opioids. Finally, as described by Sachs, the US ranks fifth in the world in DALYs from anxiety disorders and eleventh in the world from depressive disorders. Across all mental disorders, the US ranks fourth in the world in disability-adjusted life years lost.

Treat, Treat, Treat

In reaction to our deepening downward spiral with drugs and addiction, virtually every addiction expert in the US responds to these data by saying, "We of course need far more treatment." Sachs (an economist) naturally includes in his recommendations for conquering our multiple addiction epidemics "a rapid scale up of publicly financed mental health services for addiction, anxiety and mood disorders." Or, typically, I received this mass mailing: "Addiction Is on the Rise—Here's How We Reverse the Trend. The National Addiction Center recently reported that an estimated twenty-one million Americans have at least one addiction, yet only 10 percent receive treatment. One of the most common reasons an addict doesn't seek help is because of the stigma that surrounds addiction."

Who could be against this obvious solution for addictions and mental disorders—remove addiction stigma so that people can flood into treatment?

If this were the answer, we'd be home free. Because America is also an unquestioned world leader in psychiatric and medical care for addictions and mood disorders.

Which causes which?

A ridiculous question, isn't it? Treatment is good; we always seek more.

In 2020, the Commonwealth Fund published the results of its international study of American health care in comparison with ten other economically advanced countries. These were the top two findings:

- The US spends more on health care than any other high-income country but has the lowest life expectancy.
- The US has the highest suicide rate among wealthy nations.

In response to several high-profile suicides in 2018, there was a national hue and cry for more mental health care. But the US is already a world leader in attending to mental health and various forms of mental health treatment.

As Benedict Carey reported in the *New York Times*, "Defying Prevention Efforts, Suicide Rates are Climbing Across the Nation": "Suicide rates rose steadily in nearly every state from 1999 to 2016, increasing 25 percent nationally." Twice as many Americans kill themselves as are murdered.

Carey discusses what he regards as a "morbid puzzle":

> The rise in suicide rates has coincided over the past two decades with a vast increase in the number of Americans given a diagnosis of depression or anxiety, and treated with medication. . . . More than fifteen million Americans have been on the drugs for more than five years, *a rate that has more than tripled since 2000* [my emphasis].

We have an epidemic of treatment, of mental disorders and suicide, of premature death, of addiction in general, of societal discontent and individual unhappiness, and of drug deaths in particular.

These trends do *not* comprise a paradox. Our worship of Volkow and her colleagues' neuroscientific approach to addiction and mental health, which supposes that people's lived experience can be separated from their mental health outcomes and addictions, is, instead, a *major cause* of these current epidemics.

The CDC's 2018 suicide report, titled "More than a Mental Health Concern" notes that more than half of suicides don't involve a known mental disorder. The report lists these among its top suicide-prevention efforts by states and communities:

- Identify and support people at risk of suicide.
- Teach coping and problem-solving skills to help people meet challenges with their relationships, jobs, health, or other concerns.
- Promote safe and supportive environments.
- *Offer activities that bring people together so they feel connected and not alone* (my emphasis).

However, when asked whether the data showing antidepressant treatment and suicides rising rapidly alongside one another are discouraging, Thomas Insel, the former director of the National Institute of Mental Health (quoted by Carey), responded:

> I don't think so. I think the increase in demand for the services is so huge that the expansion of treatment thus far is simply insufficient to make a dent in what is a huge social change.

This means: "We're not medicating nearly enough people." Insel doesn't mention creating greater social connectedness and teaching coping and problem-solving skills to help people meet challenges, the recommendations at the top of the CDC list. As commonsensical as everyone knows these measures to be, they are increasingly short-shrifted.

We Can't Treat Our Way Out of Addiction (and Lord Knows We've Tried)

I have argued for many decades that we will never treat our way out of addiction and that the American treatment mania is dysfunctional. In 1985,

I wrote in the *Journal of Substance Abuse Treatment*, "What Treatment for Addiction Can Do and What It Can't; What Treatment for Addiction Should Do and What It Shouldn't":

> I disagree radically with the point of view sometimes expressed on the pages of this journal that we need more treatment for addiction. We already have too much addiction treatment. We search for innovative new ways to recruit clients for an expanding treatment network—such as the widespread reliance on mandatory referrals from employee assistance programs and from the courts. . . . While more and more people are in treatment, our addiction problems as a society worsen all the time. . . .
>
> In the case of drug abuse and addiction, even more [than with alcohol] a stark increase in both treatment and abuse has occurred over the past half century. Therapy for addiction has not been able to, it cannot, reduce substance abuse in our society. The best hope for eliminating addiction is to enhance each individual's personal and situational resources; the single best means yet discovered for accomplishing this is for a person to grow up.

When it comes to treatment (which I have provided and do provide in a residential setting and online), I conclude that it can succeed only to the extent that it:

- enhances self-esteem and esteem-gathering opportunities,
- enhances the skills that enable people to control their situations and directs people to more manageable environments,
- enhances interpersonal skills and helps people become involved in more fruitful relationships,
- enhances work habits and encourages people to find manageable tasks and satisfying endeavors, and
- increases people's tolerance for imperfection and discomfort while removing them from painful circumstances inimical to life.

Instead of doing these things, I wrote, treatment in the US worsens addiction:

> Addiction treatment is preoccupied with the nature of the substance or involvement rather than with the person's relationship to self, others, and the world. Addiction treatment shares with most therapy an overemphasis on the experience of therapy itself rather than on the person's life structure.

We're the US—Follow Us!

Reviewing the state of American drug use and addiction and mental health:

- The 2019 *World Happiness Report* found that over the last decade Americans' contentment, particularly young people's, has declined markedly.

- The 2017 *Global Burden of Disease Report* found that, out of 196 nations, the US was number two in quality-life-years (DALYs) lost to drugs (#1 for cocaine, #2 for amphetamines, #3 for opioids).
- *Global Burden* found the US ranked fourth overall in mental disorders DALYs lost, fifth in anxiety DALYs, and eleventh in depressive disorders DALYs out of 196 nations.
- A 2020 Commonwealth Fund report found that, compared with ten other wealthy nations, the US spent by far the most on health care, but that Americans had the shortest life spans—and the highest suicide rate.

So, our logic is, let's hold up the United States as a model worldwide. In fact, in his brilliant work, "Crazy Like Us: The Globalization of the American Psyche" (2010), Ethan Watters shows how the US spreads not only its pharmaceutical and psychiatric treatments, *but even how we think about ourselves and mental illness.* Former *New England Journal of Medicine* co-editor Marcia Angell has analyzed an epidemic of mental illness in America since the 1990s. While this claim has been debated, even those who disagree with Angell accept that "more young people are reporting mental distress."

Volkow acceded to the command of NIDA in 2003. It is during her regime that drug deaths in America have spiraled up. In 2014, the prestigious British journal *Nature* broadcast to the world that it should follow the lead of Volkow:

> *Europe should look to the United States and to inspirational figures such Nora Volkow,* head of the US National Institute on Drug Abuse in Bethesda, Maryland, who regularly testifies on the science of addiction to the US Congress to justify the institute's research budget.* Volkow—a neuroscientist born in Mexico, a country blighted by drug wars—has the scientific clarity of vision, and the relentless patience, to be able to argue for the promise of research effectively year in, year out. *Such wisdom also exists in Europe, but politicians too frequently ignore it* [my emphases].

My One-Person Campaign Against the Brain Disease Theory

It has been my effort, covering six decades (see Chapter 3), to show that Volkow's brain disease thinking is exactly the opposite of what we should be thinking and doing. As I wrote in *The Meaning of Addiction*, a concept of addiction that serves to convince people of their vulnerability to loss of control in the face of dangerous substances "can only become another burden to the psyche."

---

* The NIDA's 2020 FY budget is $1.3 billion, which comprises 85 percent of the world's funded research on addiction—a percentage that has held since the agency was created in 1974.

Volkow's predecessor, Alan Leshner, authored a landmark article in the seminal journal *Science* in 1997: "Addiction is a Brain Disease, and It Matters." Shortly after that article appeared, I received a rare invitation (it came from iconoclastic psychologist Scott Lilienfeld) to speak at a prestigious medical school, Emory, in Atlanta. I told a group of addiction researchers there that I wanted to change the title of my remarks to "Alan Leshner Is Full of It." They were unreceptive.

I have likewise been dogging Volkow. One of my first blogposts for *Psychology Today* was my satirical "Open Letter to Nora Volkow: We Can Never Reduce Alcoholism and Addiction to Biology":

Dearest Nora (and Thanks for the Passover Card)

These differences [in addictive behavior] can never be resolved at the neurological level. Indeed, believing that drug use patterns are biological inevitabilities actually influences the person's susceptibility to addiction. (I know, Nora, this is a real Escher brain twister!) Individual and cultural interpretations of drug experiences demonstrably overwhelm other considerations. Drinking within countries and cultures is remarkably consistent—and differs monumentally from drinking in others. . . .

Humans regard their own experience as inviolable truth. They believe that what happens in their minds is the way God and nature intended people to be. This is why addicts and alcoholics are positive that these substances have special effects. That is why people are convinced the way people drink around them is the way drinking affects all humans. The human mind is simply not good at transcending personal experience to imagine other ways of being—as most notably evidenced in their views about God, substances, and addiction. . . .

This is why your effort to formulate addiction in the laboratory will never capture the truths of addiction. Yet the limits of individual experience are also what has convinced you and your colleagues that your experiments showing how cocaine impacts the brain "prove" how and why cocaine is addictive. Generalizing from your limited perspective to universal truth is actually a psychological dysfunction, just the way AA members' beliefs about their alcohol use contribute to their alcoholism.

In 2008, I was quite isolated in my opposition to the dominant brain disease meme.

Things were not much better when I wrote my 2014 book with Ilse Thompson, *Recover!* Nor are they in 2020, even as psychedelic drug therapies are widely recognized for their potential. In *Recover!*, I introduced the concept of *neuromeme*, here described by Patrick Smith in a 2020 *Double Blind Magazine* article.

> The term neuromeme was first coined by psychologist Stanton Peele, as a response to the trend in addiction treatment for an over-reliance on neurology to explain addictive behaviors. In his book *Recover!*, Peele states: "As a culture, we increasingly seek explanations for our behavior in neurochemicals and brain activation, as though that were the total answer." The most insidious side-effect of the neuromeme, according to Peele, is "the idea that we have no control over whether and how the addictive process starts and, once it's occurred, whether or not we quit."

Smith brilliantly explains about emerging psychedelic therapies, "Why Psychedelic Trips Are So Much More than a Series of Neurological Mechanisms." I believe that, while intense mental and emotional experiences *can* be valuable, even critical, tools for positive change, they aren't magical potions. They allow people to rearrange their perceptions in ways that make sense for them and that they may carry into their daily lives. When I was invited in 2016 to the Global Ibogaine Conference in Tepoztlan, Mexico, to lay out my common-sense thinking about how drug and other experiences can spur personal reorientations, some welcomed my views; others deeply resented them.

Those who explain the benefits of psychedelic drugs purely in terms of references to how they impact this or that part of the brain (with no evidence that this happens more or less to people who have more or less successful trips) are reflecting the broader cultural neuromeme revolutions, led by Volkow. I wrote a response to *Nature*'s urging the world to follow Volkow's lead: "Why We Need to Stop Nora Volkow from Taking Over the World," summarized here:

> Volkow holds worldwide sway with her approach, which focuses exclusively on neuroscience and the brain, an approach that is increasingly seen to be the key to eliminating addiction. "Groundbreaking discoveries about the brain have revolutionized our understanding of drug addiction, enabling us to respond effectively to the problem," trumpets the White House website, beneath a video of Volkow proselytizing her theory.
>
> Yet there are no diagnoses or treatments based on neuroscientific research pegged to the brain scans so avidly pursued and enthusiastically presented by Volkow and her school. We are told to be patient because the brave new scientific paradigm must mature before it produces real-life applications. Instead, the neuroscientific "revolution" is creating a mass of bystanders and victims of their own disease—even as study after study shows that most addicts outgrow their habits.

Volkow has pulled off a remarkable coup in the field of addiction. She has built an international reputation—and mission—by persuading us that we can't do what we have been doing for centuries: resolve addictions through our values, purposes and life experiences. Studies following addicts and alcoholics over the course of their lives show this to be a regular occurrence. People who have quit smoking or left behind a drug habit or outgrown a youthful drinking problem know this. By denying this naturally occurring phenomenon so as to fit drug use, drinking and many other human activities into an institutionalized, medical framework, Volkow and her expanding neuroscience legions are effectively reducing natural recovery—along with help that contributes to the natural processes that lead to recovery—while prolonging otherwise-transient addictive behavior. And they are glorying in this achievement.

Ironies in the Brain Disease Theory's Dominance in America: I: Volkow Backtracking

Volkow can be observed backtracking radically in her approach to drug addictions and harms. According to her NIDA blog in 2019, "Addressing the Socioeconomic Complexities of Addiction—Lessons from the Kensington Neighborhood in Philadelphia," she visited that neighborhood for the first time in September 2019 (remember that my father had his shoe store in Kensington). She discovered, two decades into her directorship, the following:

> *Philadelphia's rate of overdose deaths skyrocketed this past decade,* tripling the city's number of homicide deaths and greatly exceeding the peak number of deaths from AIDS in 1994. . . . It was humbling not only to see the challenges facing a city with a longstanding opioid problem but also to see the engagement and dedication of people on the ground attempting to help, as well as the struggles of those battling their own drug addiction amidst extremely hard socioeconomic challenges. . . .
>
> Whenever I ask people on the front lines of America's drug crisis what more we can do to support and help their work, they remind me how essential it is to address the basic needs of individuals with addiction, such as stable and safe housing, food, basic medical care, and an opportunity for employment [my emphasis].

I have been on the board of Above and Beyond, an inner-city Chicago community harm-reduction program that emphasizes the pillars of community and family, education and employment, housing and health, which Volkow trumpeted here, in 2019. (See comment in Afterword from the executive director of the organization.) Would she have achieved her momentous new realization earlier if she had paid more attention to my writing and thinking?

Irony II: Drug Policy Reform Advocates Are All In for the Disease Theory

The second irony is how the drug policy reform movement, once seen as a radical way to rethink the nature of drug use and addiction and our relationship to drugs, has gone whole-hog brain disease, even more so now, it seems, than Volkow. In Chapter 1, I described how the 2019 International Drug Policy Reform Conference conducted a panel on overdose deaths that emphasized how these struck in *everyone's* back yard. A reformer's article in America's most prominent business magazine, *Forbes*, said the panel showed that American medicine was going wrong by not fully accepting that addiction is the same type of disease as diabetes and heart disease.

In fact, the drug policy reform movement has become completely invested in MAT, or medication-assisted treatment—which is claimed to be the one effective way to deal with addiction. I wasn't at the 2019 conference, although I had spoken at a previous one in 2015. Much earlier, in 1994, the conference's organizer, the Drug Policy Alliance (then the Drug Policy Foundation, DPF) presented me with its lifetime achievement award.

In 1996, I participated at the DPF conference in a plenary debate with a leading psychiatric treatment proponent, Robert Millman,[*] on the role of treatment in addiction and drug policy reform. Here is what I argued at DPA twenty-five years ago:

> The conception is that shifting from coercive drug policies to treatment will radically transform the American drug use and treatment scene. I disagree: expanding the treatment system will (1) expand what is already largely coercive treatment serving as an adjunct to the criminal justice system, (2) refuse to acknowledge nonharmful use and force mainly nonproblem users into treatment, (3) serve to divert social resources from the worst-off street users who are the main symbols of the drug epidemic, (4) have an overall negative impact on outcomes for drug users in the United States.

Ignoring my little jeremiad (which Ethan arranged), the Drug Policy Alliance of today refuses to confront the disease theory. At the same time, it rails against coercive treatment, which is entirely rooted in the "disease" of addiction.

---

[*] Millman was the Saul Steinberg Professor of Psychiatry and Public Health at Weill Cornell Medical College, where he was the Director of the Drug and Alcohol Abuse Treatment and Research Service at New York-Presbyterian Hospital.

The US Isn't Brain-Diseasified Enough Yet!

The United States government and media have been embarked on a quarter-century campaign to convince what must seem to them a massively ignorant population. NIDA director Leshner's 1997 announcement in *Science* that addiction is a brain disease was far from the start. Before Leshner, Americans had been bombarded for decades with high-profile media telling them how mental illness and addiction are diseases. Richard Restak's 1980s reductive best sellers, *The Brain* (1984) and *The Mind* (1988), were both turned into multi-part PBS series named for the books. In 1998 PBS featured a series by famed journalist Bill Moyers, *Moyers on Addiction: Close to Home.** Moyers touted brain disease theory *and* worshipped AA—a commonplace non sequitur. The last show in the series featured a group of inner-city men who had kept clean for the latter part of their lives due to their AA meetings.

In 2007, HBO launched a heavily promoted multi-part series, *Addiction*, in collaboration with Volkow and NIDA. And, just to make sure people didn't forget by the next decade, in 2018 the highly-regarded PBS science program, *Nova*, did another brain-disease-primer series called *Addiction* to explain the opioids crisis. It is critical to understanding Americans' view of addiction that both the HBO and Nova series created secondary school curricula that are used across the nation to teach kids that addiction is a brain disease. When I spoke at schools, I confronted kids who had been taught the brain disease model as fundamental science, as though it was Newtonian physics. (I no longer speak in high schools.)

The American government doesn't stop at television and education programs, however. Distressed that Americans had not been sufficiently inundated with the disease message, in 2016 the US Surgeon General, Vivek Murthy, issued a special expert addiction report. Murthy instructed Americans in alarmist terms that "Addressing the addiction crisis in

---

* I was a consultant on the series (I was brought in by Maia Szalavitz), but Moyers ostentatiously ignored me. Quite separately, Mary and I were friendly with Moyers's daughter, who lived across the road from us in Morris Township, and her then husband, John Passacatando. The family member who prompted Bill's focus on addiction was his son, William Cope Moyers, who has written about his addiction history in his 2006 book, *Broken: My Story of Addiction and Redemption*. William became a spokesman for the 12-step treatment program, Hazelden. In 2017, William contacted me to discuss addiction, when I told him that I knew his sister. We still correspond from time to time—I asked him for a blurb for this book!

As told in Chapter 7, the publication arm of Hazelden put out my pamphlet, *The Addiction Experience*, in 1980. The editor said that it resonated with her personal experience more than anything she had ever read. Hazelden, however, discontinued publication of the pamphlet in 1988, after eight years of high sales. A new editor, Linda Peterson, wrote me, "Unfortunately, we have heard much criticism from our customers who are *not in agreement with your stand on the disease concept*" (my emphasis).

America will require seeing addiction as a chronic illness. Addiction has been a challenge for a long time, but we finally have the opportunity and the tools to address it."* (I critique Murthy's inaccuracies and irrelevance at https://www.psychologytoday.com/us/blog/addiction-in-society/201703/the-solution-the-opioid-crisis.)

Donald Trump redid the Obama administration's addiction disease initiative by appointing a special commission of his own on Combating Addiction and the Opioid Crisis, headed by Chris Christie. The Commission followed Christie's lead in designating addiction as a disease toward which much more treatment must be directed. And Joe Biden? As a Senator, Biden proposed "Recognizing Addiction as a Disease" as American law. An important initial step for his administration was to reappoint Murthy as Surgeon General.

This is something that Republicans and Democrats can agree on!

Lastly, we can address directly the *Forbes*/drug reformist contention I review in Chapter 1—that American medicine itself doesn't take addiction's disease nature seriously enough, like diabetes and heart disease. For some time, the leading medical organization dealing with addiction has been the American Society of Addiction Medicine (ASAM). I debated its founder, G. Douglas Talbott, on *Hannity and Colmes*.

For years ASAM was not recognized as an official medical organization by the American Medical Association. That was remedied in 2016 when the American Board of Medical Specialties designated addiction medicine as a subspecialty, creating the American Board of Addiction Medicine. According to the *New York Times*, this official medical body had resolved the question of whether addiction is a "physical disease, one that needs continuing medical treatment in much the same way as, say, diabetes or epilepsy. Increasingly, the medical establishment is putting its weight behind the physical diagnosis."

Thus, it seems unnecessary that drug reformers and *Forbes* worry that addiction isn't being regarded enough like heart disease. After all, American media, the government drug abuse agency (NIDA), the Surgeon General, both Republican and Democratic administrations, and the American medical establishment have all gone as far as it is possible to go in this direction.

---

* In 2020, Murthy (who was Surgeon General from 2014 to 2017, and was appointed again by Joe Biden in 2021) wrote *Together: The Healing Power of Human Connection*, thus joining his predecessor as SG, Joycelyn Elders (with whom I shared a podium in 2019 at the Cato Institute), and me in understanding the fundamental role of human connection and community in fighting addiction. He joins Johann Hari, Bruce Alexander, and me in this viewpoint.

My Views Aren't Welcome among "Radical" Drug Reformers

The International Drug Policy Reform Conference was organized by the Drug Policy Alliance (DPA), with whose founder, Ethan Nadelmann, I have a long relationship (see Chapter 10). DPA, along with every drug policy reform group, has pushed two policies in the face of the current epidemic of drug deaths—reducing opioid painkiller prescriptions and medication-assisted treatment. In November 2017, The New School held a Town Hall meeting, calling it a "Celebration," touting "New Solutions for The Opioid Crisis," at which the leading New York harm reductionists discussed the progress in the field. Here is a graph from the presentation by Denise Paone of the NYC Department of Health and Mental Hygiene.[*]

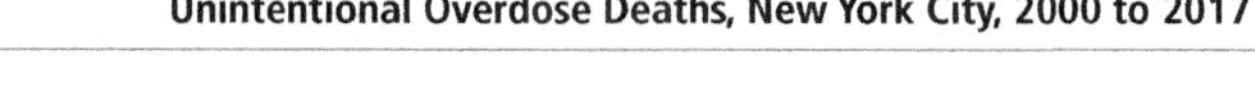

Unintentional Overdose Deaths, New York City, 2000 to 2017

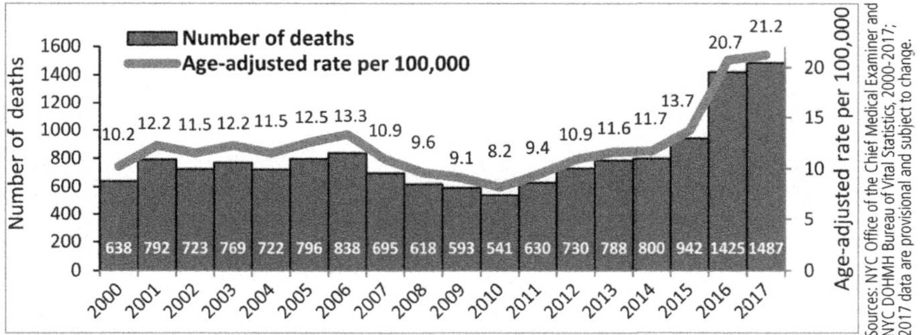

This is the drug crisis in the US as experienced in NYC. Presentation after presentation showed that this increase in drug deaths was continuing in New York through 2017 (nationally, 2017 set an all-time American record of more than 70,000 drug-related deaths).

What were we celebrating? Paone listed the steps New York was taking to reduce deaths:

1. Expanding naloxone (Narcan) distribution (naloxone is a rapid reversal drug that is nearly universally successful with opioid overdoses)

2. Rapid response in targeted communities to drug poisoning events

3. Health care provider education campaign to reduce prescribed opioids

---

[*] I can trace my life and times through Denise Paone. I taught a course at Columbia University Teachers College when I first arrived in New York in the late 1970s (my next-door neighbor was a professor there). Denise was my student. I was let go in favor of hiring a full-time faculty member, and Denise organized a petition on my behalf. Meanwhile, Denise was to conference with me (along with Holly Catania, whose role in the 2014 Carl Hart meth conference I describe in Chapter 4) on a phone call with Commissioner Gary Belkin scheduled in 2017. That call never happened.

4. Expanding access to buprenorphine (this is medication-assisted treatment, MAT, which administers safe opioids to habitual opioid users)

So why were deaths still rising? No one presenting or in the audience seemed to find this anomaly troubling. Andrew Tatarsky (a colleague for decades who praised my work in Chapter 1), who was directing the event, didn't call on me when I raised my hand to ask this question.

Nationally, the Drug-Deaths Surge Data Are the Same

The data are staggering. From 1999 to 2017, the rate of annual drug deaths increased by a rate of 350 percent per year. *More than 700,000 people died in that time.* In 2018, finally, there was a tick back of *4 percent* in drug deaths in the US.

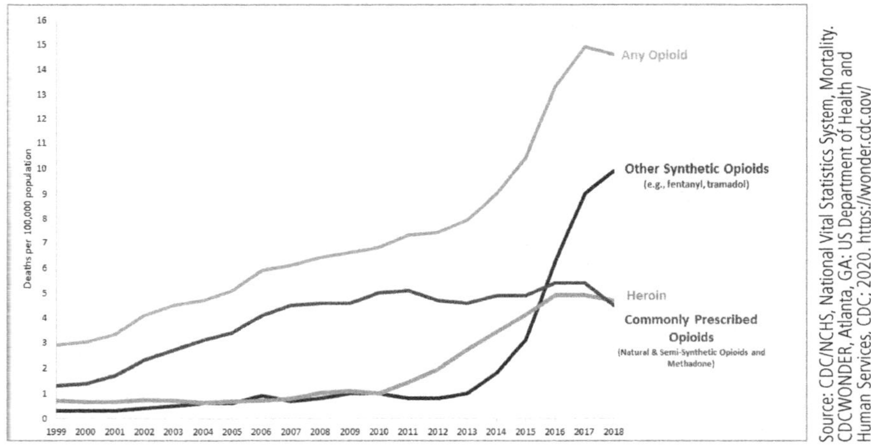

Overdose Death Rates Involving Opioids, by Type, United States, 1999–2018

Pre- and post-pandemic, drug deaths continue to accelerate

Why had the death rate risen so precipitously since the late 1990s, and why—given the national alarm bells over such deaths, so that all of the steps Paone identified in New York were reflected nationwide—was the drop in deaths so minuscule?

The standard answer to the first question is "drug manufacturers' greed and perfidy." *But painkiller prescriptions dropped 25 percent in the peak period of growing drug deaths in the US from 2012 to 2017.* I often face audiences who continue to insist that pharmaceutical supplies are the cause of the continuing upsurge in drug deaths, even as deaths grow while prescribed medications decline. Moreover, there has been an upsurge in non-opioid deaths due to cocaine and methamphetamines, nonprescribed medications (and also benzodiazepines).

And, why, given the range of steps taken—some obviously beneficial, like rapid-response teams and broad availability of naloxone (Narcan) instant reversal—did deaths drop by only 4 percent in 2018? In particular, why such limited benefits when MAT opioid substitution programs have been widely deployed, in New York and nationwide?

Under controlled conditions, MAT programs have been shown to reduce deaths significantly in limited populations. *Yet, when deployed across states, the benefits of MAT have been mixed to nonexistent to negative.* One reason for this is that large percentages of people drop out from MAT (methadone and buprenorphine) programs. After leaving such programs, convinced that they are addicts with no other choice, they return to street drugs, with often-disastrous results.

The 2018 CDC drug-deaths report noted: "For fourteen states and the District of Columbia, the drug overdose rate was lower in 2018 than 2017." But eighteen states showed an increase in drug deaths between 2017 and 2018, despite active MAT Programs. Missouri is an example:

> Over the last several years, Missouri has received $65 million in federal grants to address the opioid crisis, (researcher Rachel) Winograd says, and she has helped the state decide where and how to spend that money. They've focused on expanding access to medication-assisted treatment, and "saturating our communities with naloxone—the opiate overdose antidote."
>
> "The fact that the numbers didn't go down and that people were dying at an even higher rate—it was devastating," Winograd says.

Beginning in 2019, the small drop in drug deaths reversed itself with a fury never before seen. "More than 87,000 Americans died of drug overdoses over the 12-month period that ended in September 2020 . . . eclipsing the toll from any year since the epidemic began in the 1990s." *This represents an increase of 20,000 yearly deaths over 2018.*

The source problem

The fact that opioid drug deaths are ever-increasing is due primarily to drug-mixing and contaminated drugs. *Restricting opioid availability through prescriptions makes such mixing and resort to unregulated drugs more likely.* This is because it forces more people to find their own sources of painkillers they want or need. And, so, an AMA report issued in late 2020 about rising drug deaths made a recommendation that would amaze most people—including policy experts: "*Remove existing barriers for patients with pain to obtain necessary medications. This includes removing arbitrary dose, quantity and refill restrictions on controlled substances*" (my emphasis). That is, make painkillers *more* accessible through legitimate prescriptions.

Among other problems in regard to regulating painkillers, and to providing substitutes for opioids such as methadone, buprenorphine, and suboxone for street drug users in response to drug deaths, is that the drugs causing such deaths aren't limited to opioids. There has also been a steep rise in lethal cocaine and methamphetamine use. *And our response to these is the same.* In New York, for example, in 2020, "NY Governor's Office Points to Stimulant Addiction Meds as Deaths Rise":

> In response to increasing numbers of cocaine- and methamphetamine-related deaths in New York, Governor Andrew Cuomo's administration has issued guidance on the pharmaceutical options available to prescribers looking to support use management for patients with stimulant use disorders. Stimulant-involved deaths, often occurring when drugs are mixed with or adulterated by fentanyl, are rising fast—exemplified by the doubling of New York City's cocaine-related fatality rates from 2014 to 2018. In response, the state's Office of Addiction Services and Supports (OASAS) is advising service providers on pharmacological treatments that clinicians may consider, though stopping short of a full-out recommendation given the medication's *lack of regulatory authorization.* (My emphasis: *Cuomo is recommending drugs that haven't passed clinical tests required for approved use.*)

OASAS, New York state's drug and alcohol treatment agency (need I mention that, after nearly forty-five years living in the New York region, OASAS has *never* had me speak), is calling for the use of unapproved pharmaceutical agents to treat cocaine addiction—something that would be quite shocking in other contexts.

Why is this happening?

The reliance on medications (MAT) doubles down on the message that addiction is a disease that can be cured medically. As I observed in *Filter Magazine*, in likening adherence to the disease theory to climate change denial:

> Convincing us that addiction is inevitable and inescapable—in the face of ubiquitous evidence that it is culturally and cognitively inculcated and very escapable—is a self-fulfilling prophecy.

Nora Volkow is struggling to come to grips with these realities

The director of the NIDA, Nora Volkow, is now questioning her own disease views. In another NIDA blogpost (aside from the December 2019 one cited above), Volkow acknowledged critiques of the disease theory by essentially saying they are true, but then *offering reductive biomedical explanations for them.* She is defensive, but self-assured. The blogpost is titled "What Does It Mean When We Call Addiction a Brain Disorder?"

- "Medications cannot take the place of an individual's willpower" [an argument Volkow previously disparaged, as described in *The Lancet*].
- "Viewing addiction this way minimizes its important social and environmental causes."
- "Addiction is not fundamentally different from other experiences that redirect our basic motivational systems" [like falling in love].

Volkow applies her argument against a learning model of addiction to her awareness that most people don't get addicted to "addictive" drugs. She is sure this can, and will, be explained genetically:

What the brain disorder model, within the larger biopsychosocial framework, captures better than other models—such as those that focus on addiction as a learned behavior—is the crucial dimension of interindividual biological variability that makes some people more susceptible than others to this hijacking. Many people try drugs but most do not start to use compulsively or develop an addiction. Studies are identifying gene variants that confer resilience or risk for addiction, as well as environmental factors in early life that affect that risk. This knowledge will enable development of precisely targeted prevention and treatment strategies, just as it is making possible the larger domain of personalized medicine.

After fifty years of futile biogenetic theorizing about addiction, Volkow assures us, once again, that the true genetic source and treatment of addiction are just around the corner. But please note her subsequent sad-faced October 2019 blogpost in which Volkow acknowledges the downward addiction spiral in Kensington, Philadelphia, due to the depths of inner-city despair. When *will* that gene be discovered?

Volkow also notes the most fundamental challenge of all:

Some critics also point out, correctly, that a significant percentage of people who do develop addictions eventually recover without medical treatment [see my article in *Reason*]. It may take years or decades, may arise from simply aging out of a disorder that began during youth, or may result from any number of life changes that help a person replace drug use with other priorities.

This is *the single, consistent finding most difficult for Volkow et al. to explain away*. So, she punts: "We still do not understand all the factors that make some people better able to recover than others or the neurobiological mechanisms that support recovery—these are important areas for research." Oh, yes, we do understand. Per Charles Winick, writing in 1962 that addicts who fail to "mature out" are those "who decide that they are 'hooked,' make no effort to abandon addiction, and give in to what they regard as inevitable."

Volkow further notes that persistent paradox: *"when people recover from addiction on their own, it is often because effective treatment has not been readily available or affordable, or the individual has not sought it out"* (my emphasis). She assumes that this means many more would get better if only such treatment were readily available and utilized. Yet, in a study of longer-term recovery from smoking addiction at Harvard's Center for Global Control of Tobacco, researchers discovered that not only did nicotine replacement therapy, which had been shown effective in clinical trials, not improve results, but that,

> One subgroup, heavy smokers who used replacement products without counseling, was twice as likely to relapse as heavy smokers who did not use them. "Our study shows that what happens in the real world is very different from what happens in clinical trials," said Hillel R. Alpert of Harvard, a co-author of the study. "We were hoping for a very different story," said Dr. Gregory N. Connolly, director of Harvard's Center for Global Tobacco Control and a co-author of the study. "We invested millions in such treatment."

Recovery without treatment is part of the natural course of addiction. It entails mobilizing resources and motivation for which treatment cannot substitute and which treatment, at best, can only facilitate. Archie and I explained this truth in 1991 in The Truth About Addiction and Recovery, *and it forms the basis for the Life Process Program. Volkow is still flailing in her effort to figure it out—or to explain it away.*

The Critical Factor in Harm Reduction Treatment

In response to our latest drug death spiral, DPA organized a webcast in late 2020: "Effective Harm Reduction Responses to the Worsening Overdose Crisis Caused By COVID-19." The expert panel doubled down on current HR policies. One panel member did discuss the approach of *providing drug users with pure drugs (called, for instance, heroin maintenance) or offering them safe (supervised) consumption sites.* No deaths have ever been reported in European and Canadian maintenance and consumption sites. *Unfortunately, although frequently discussed, no such effective programs exist here. They are anathema in the US.* (As I discuss in Chapter 7, Liz Evans invited me to speak at the Insite supervised drug site in Vancouver.)

Medication-assisted treatments like Suboxone and methadone can prevent deaths, relative to unregulated street use of drugs. They may also serve as a psychological and practical bridge to improve drug users' lives. For example, clean-needle programs have been shown not only to eliminate HIV and other infections. They also often help users to regulate or desist problematic drug use. Methadone and Suboxone (MAT) are generally not used this way, however, but are seen as permanent treatment adjuncts. *Harm reduction succeeds instead when it allows people to learn that they can modify their use of drugs in beneficial ways and thus assert greater control of their lives.*

Critical factoids about the American drug deaths epidemic
The 2018 CDC report on drug deaths* noted that the state with the highest drug death rate is West Virginia, which has led the nation in drug deaths since 2014. West Virginia is the poorest state in the US, followed by Maryland, which has the most troubled city in the country, Baltimore. In 2018, West Virginia's public health commissioner, Rahul Gupta, examined every single drug death in the state over the previous year—"all 887 of them." He found a "depressing pattern of vulnerability":

> If you're a male between the ages of 35 to 54, with less than a high school education, you're single and you've worked in a blue-collar industry, you pretty much are at a very, very high risk of overdosing.

So, while drug policy advocates and their well-off neighbors should of course exercise mindfulness in their use of opioid painkillers (as my questioning of them reveals that they invariably do), that is not where the drug death crisis takes place. The CDC's 2018 report of "overdose" deaths made one further critical point: From 2012 through 2018, the rate of drug overdose deaths involving cocaine more than tripled and the rate for deaths involving psychostimulants (drugs such as methamphetamine) increased nearly five-fold. In other words, *the drug deaths crisis is not related to specific substances (i.e., opioids); it is related to specific groups of people.*

The drug deaths epidemic includes not only poor white rural Americans, but also inner-city drug users: "The Opioid Crisis Is Surging in Black, Urban Communities." According to the Office of the Medical Examiner in Washington, D.C., overall opioid overdose deaths among Black men between the ages of 40 and 69 increased 245 percent from 2014 to 2017. Volkow has suddenly acquired the insight, after seventeen years in her job, that she reported in 2019 in her endearingly titled "Nora's Blog": "Whenever I ask people on the front lines of America's drug crisis what more we can do to support and help their work, *they remind me how essential it is to address the basic needs of individuals with addiction, such as stable*

---

* Per my description of the myth of drug overdoses, the CDC titles its report "drug overdoses," but the HMTL file is labeled "drug-poisoning."

and safe housing, food, basic medical care, and an opportunity for employment" (my emphasis).

No One Believes Me (or Carl)

No one makes the above point more regularly and forcefully (aside from me) than Carl Hart. But our views are rejected in the very venues where Carl is worshipped. I note this paradox when I attend his lectures or other symposia like the harm reduction "celebration" I described in New York in 2017 or the 2019 DPA conference described in *Forbes*. This rejection is doubly strange since I speak to groups of people seeking new models of addiction, often libertarian or British or Irish, that are primed—have invited me—to question our assumptions about addiction. Consider the titles of recent conferences and workshops I participated in: "Is It the Drugs? Rethinking conventional views of substance use, abuse, and addiction"; "Addiction, Nature or Nurture: Where does it come from and what can be done?"; "Changing the Conversation on Addiction." And *these audiences reject my and Carl's views.*

I enjoy seeing Carl Hart speak, as he did at the "radical" Open Society Foundations (where, as I describe in Chapter 4, I interjected myself, enumerating myths that large majorities of the audience believed) or at a public interview with Carl conducted by former *New York Times* columnist John Tierney and sponsored by the libertarian magazine *Reason*. In these settings, the audiences recoil from any movement away from the standard line—that opioids are addictive and anyone who takes them regularly becomes addicted no matter who or where they are, why or how they use the drugs. After the *Reason* talk, where Carl said that 80 to 90 percent of users of illicit drugs, including heroin, don't have problems and that withdrawal from narcotics is like a bad case of flu, a man deeply disturbed by Carl's remarks confronted me, insisting, "What he said isn't true!" I told him he was speaking to the wrong person. More remarkably, interviewer Tierney, a libertarian friend of mine, told me later that *he* didn't accept Carl's key points.

I have a theory

At this point in my presentations, I stop and say, "I have a theory—would you like to hear it?"

> People's primary concern is getting along with, and having the approval of, their cohorts. *Reducing deaths of people not present* (remember, in the audiences I speak to, people have all taken opioids—virtually none has had a problem), who live in separate communities is an unreality that has no meaning compared with what everybody around them believes.

Sad to say, people's deaths in provinces they don't visit mean nothing to these audiences. Meetings where harm reduction advocates swap reassuring bromides and congratulate one another for their great policies while drug deaths soar are the standard way human beings operate. The process is notable in this instance because drug policy reform advocates claim so much more for themselves.

What's my problem?

Well, aside from my personality.

We can start with my debate with Doug Talbott on the old Hannity & Colmes show (Colmes is long gone, while Hannity is Trump's best friend) that I described earlier. Liberal Alan Colmes begins by reading James Milam's quote: "Stanton Peele is a liar. He's in total denial of science and has been completely shut out of the scientific community." (You can get a feel for my situation and my reactions by tuning into https://youtu.be/4gRldtP827s.)

In terms of people's actual experience of addiction, we have a colossal recovery industry, fueled by people who swear their lives were saved by and depend on knowing they have a disease. (William Moyers is one of them.) There have been thousands of addiction memoirs, many by extremely well-known people, that offer this narrative to Americans. When people's stories diverge from the 12-step template, they either avoid telling them or soft-pedal their narratives. I show how this regularly occurs in the recovery narratives of Drew Barrymore (who was declared a lifetime addict at age 13), Lindsay Lohan (who was seen as an incorrigible alcoholic through her twenties), and Robert Downey, Jr. (the epitome of the recidivist drug addict into his thirties). None became 12-step stalwarts.

Zach Rhoads and I have created a podcast strictly for the purpose of changing the American recovery narrative. We discuss Barrymore, who founded a winery and is forced to say that she's "not in recovery" since she drinks wine. Lohan owns and manages a series of Mediterranean clubs. Both have had substantial professional success and built solid family structures—Barrymore with her daughters, Lohan with her mother and siblings.

A group of six recovery books were reviewed as a genre in the *Times* in 2020. These included: *Will: A Memoir*; *Stray*; *Strung Out: One Last Hit and Other Lies that Nearly Killed Me*; *In Pain: A Bioethicist's Personal Struggle with Opioids*; *We Are the Luckiest: The Surprising Magic of a Sober Life*; and *Blossoms and Bones: Drawing a Life Back Together*. In addition to these six books, the *Times* published a separate article about Ben Affleck on its home page detailing his "getting sober (again)."

None of these twenty-first-century contemporary personal addiction tales fits the traditional recovery story mold. Nonetheless, reflecting AA's recovery categories, the discussions of the books in the *Times* were divided into the 12-step headlines: "Hitting Bottom," "Getting Clean," "Making Amends."

Stray, by Stephanie Danler, recounts her "heavy drinking, cocaine, and sedative use." Her father was a "recovering alcoholic, opiate- and crystal methedrine addict" while her mother "was a lifelong alcoholic." With all of this, this "recovery" book is about how Danler didn't become addicted! Instead, she was able to "steer clear of an addictive spiral without rehab."

So, too, did Laura McKowen, author of *We Are the Luckiest*. Although she says that she left her "4-year-old daughter alone in a hotel room overnight because I was blackout drunk," McKowen nonetheless "kicked her substance abuse habit in part by using an approach that she calls the 'pregnancy principle,' and attempting to clean her body—and psyche—of impurities, as she did when she was an expectant mother."

In my online Life Process Program (LPP), we avoid 12-step concepts of "recovery," "sobriety," and certainly "disease." We avoid labeling people "addicted." Instead, we focus on people's larger values and positive life experiences and roles they have fulfilled. Parenthood is the number one candidate in this personal value/role inventory.

Affleck, although he calls himself an alcoholic, tells this story:

> People with compulsive behavior, and I am one, have this kind of basic discomfort all the time that they're trying to make go away. You're trying to make yourself feel better with eating or drinking or sex or gambling or shopping or whatever. But that ends up making your life worse. Then you do more of it to make that discomfort go away. Then the real pain starts. It becomes a vicious cycle you can't break. That's at least what happened to me.
>
> I drank relatively normally for a long time. What happened was that I started drinking more and more when my marriage was falling apart. This was 2015, 2016. My drinking, of course, created more marital problems.

That's the description of addiction and recovery I use in LPP and that Archie and I first developed in *Love and Addiction*. The addiction cycle Affleck describes is one that most people have experienced in some form. Addiction traces back to general and specific experiences, feelings, and life problems (such as marital ones); it is a self-feeding experiential process, so that the addictive behavior that is sought for relief worsens the problems that the behavior is then further used to remedy. And recovery involves addressing these issues and creating a holistic, healthy—or at least manageable—life, as McKowen and Affleck (who also cites his kids) did.

Here is how Travis Rieder prevailed over an addictive drug, as told in *In Pain: A Bioethicist's Personal Struggle with Opioids*:

> Rather than a recovery story, Mr. Rieder said that his story of his brain "floating in a vat of opioids for months" is one of heading off addiction before it fully forms. With the support of family "that I desperately wanted to come back from the brink for," he said in an interview, he never went back on medication, despite the pain of withdrawal, so he "didn't teach my brain that opioids are the only things worth valuing."

Rieder's narrative is the same as the well-connected members of my audiences who take opioids but don't become addicted. Indeed, so far, out of six books reviewed about "Recovery," none describes actually becoming addicted to a substance!

Memoirist Kim Krans *does* label herself "addicted." Her *Blossoms and Bones: Drawing a Life Back Together* is about her food addiction. Krans's "hitting bottom" was "in a fancy Manhattan hotel room with . . . another decimated minibar." But it wasn't the booze that was decimated, only those overpriced snacks they stock. (Has that ever happened for any readers?)

Krans "got clean" by living in an ashram for six months while writing her book.

> I literally drew myself back together, one day and one page at a time. Each morning after meditation I would sit with the "feeling" of addiction and allow it to guide my pen across the page. What began as incoherent scribbles of fear and doubt soon became a heroine's journey through the underworld of addiction.

Krans's technique, which we use in LPP and which Ilse Thompson and I elaborate in *Recover!*, is called "mindfulness." Of course, Krans's recovery from food addiction didn't lead to "sobriety" in its 12-step meaning of abstinence. Rather, she had to create a new relationship with food. That non-abstinent approach is called "harm reduction." In LPP, harm reduction is built around an overall improved lifestyle, rather than focusing solely on the substance or addiction. And, as I have reviewed with government national alcoholism surveys, *this is most often done without abstaining, even in the case of alcohol.*

The Abstinence Fixation

Recognizing that addiction isn't limited to drugs, but includes work, food, sex and love, shopping, and other potentially consuming experiences, *instantly* dispels the abstinence shibboleth in American addictionology. You can abstain from drugs (depending on which drugs) and alcohol if you want to, and if you think that it's easiest or best for you. That's up to you. But you can't abstain from food, and mainly not from sex and love and other essential human experiences that can turn addictive. Moreover, making abstinence a fundamental plank of American addiction treatment and theory is a sign of our mistaken conception of addiction and our inability to get a handle on it (which we shall see around my discussion of harm reduction).

My favorite case example of the need for abstinence in recovery, or not, is the great Irish actor Richard Harris: "At the height of his stardom in the 1960s and early 1970s Harris was almost as well known for his hellraiser lifestyle and heavy drinking as he was for his acting career. *He was a longtime alcoholic until he became a teetotaler in 1981, although he did resume drinking Guinness a decade later.* He gave up drugs after almost dying from a cocaine overdose in 1978" (my emphasis).

This story is so ho-hum you might not notice it: "A senior citizen/ grandfather stopped acting like a wild man? That's news?" But armed by Nora Volkow with knowledge of the genetic brain disease theory, the story is incomprehensible.

I have avoided thus far the most gruesome-sounding of the reviewed books: *Strung Out: One Last Hit and Other Lies that Nearly Killed Me*, by Erin Khar.

Hitting Bottom

Ms. Khar began dabbling with heroin at 13. She indulged on and off for the next 15 years, at times stealing from her parents and pawning her possessions to help pay for heroin or crack cocaine. "The lower I got, the more I craved getting lower," she writes. "I wanted to abandon all my senses and remember nothing. I wanted to get so low that I'd forget my name and my body. I no longer wanted to exist."

That's horrendous! Khar's recovery, however, occupies one sentence in the *Times* review:

Getting Clean

At 28, after learning she was pregnant with her son Atticus, through the 12-step approach; with help from Kundalini yoga and Judaism.

Does this mean that she "became sober" instantly on learning she was pregnant? Khar's is the only book reviewed to mention the 12 steps, which she combines with Judaism and yoga. Another, very prominent case combining yoga and Eastern thinking with the 12-steps involves another Jew, Robert Downey, Jr. (Downey's father was half Jewish; he was married in a synagogue to Susan Levin in 2005.) In 2008 Downey declared he quit drugs when he married, and that the basis for his sobriety was "family, therapy, meditation, twelve-step recovery programs, yoga, and the practice of Wing Chun kung fu." This was after years of "rehabs that didn't work, followed by jails that did not impress" (Downey married Levin in his late thirties).

After his seemingly never-ending drug problems involving valium, cocaine, heroin, alcohol, marijuana, meth, etc., and several prison sentences, Downey described the process through which he recovered on *Oprah*.

> [After his last arrest in April 2001, when he knew he would likely be facing another stint in prison or *another form of incarceration such as court-ordered rehab*] I said, "You know what? I don't think I can continue doing this." And I reached out for help, and I ran with it. *It's not that difficult to overcome these seemingly ghastly problems . . . what's hard is to decide to do it* (as told to Oprah in 2004, my emphases).

I Met Robert Downey Jr.'s Family

I describe how my uncle Ozzie quit smoking after twenty-five years in Chapter 11. Ozzie's last name is Levin, like Downey's in-laws. Ozzie and Downey's wife are both Jewish. As a group, Jews don't relate easily to the 12 steps. Jewish beliefs don't focus on turning one's will over to God and powerlessness. Rather, as a group, they focus on family, achievement, and community. When I traveled to Southern California for Ozzie's grandson's bar mitzvah, I found myself in a hotel breakfast line with Susan Levin's father. Downey's father-in-law told me that his son-in-law was a good family man.

I quoted above Nora Volkow's belated discovery that recovery must *"address the basic needs of individuals with addiction, such as stable and safe housing, food, basic medical care, and an opportunity for employment"* (my emphasis). What Volkow's summary of critical factors omits is family and community.

America will always be suffused with recovery tales. But *these recent ones are very different from the old Temperance tale and the standard recovery story of hitting bottom, being powerless, finding God, and becoming a 12-stepper forever.* These twenty-first-century recovery tales instead:

- Don't focus on the substance or object of addiction and abstinence.
- Don't deify AA/NA, even when the worst drug addictions are involved.
- Focus instead on personal values, life meaning, purpose, and family.
- Resolve with reoriented lives built around new, non-addict identities.

Final note

These were all privileged, well-educated people with substantial life resources. This dichotomy between those who avoid addiction or who recover and those who do not is expressed today by the declining life spans caused by "deaths of despair." These are the lives of people in inner-city Baltimore, Kensington (Philadelphia), or rural West Virginia and New England who don't do yoga, write books, or have all the money in the world (like Affleck and Downey). These are the people, as Nora Volkow seemingly has just discovered, who often die prematurely.

New York Times columnist Nicholas Kristof and his wife, Sheryl WuDunn, wrote a 2020 book *Tightrope*, about the working class and farm families Kristof grew up among in Oregon, many of whose lives ended badly: Working-class men and women like them increasingly are dying "deaths of despair"—from drugs, alcohol, and suicide. Life expectancy in the United States, for the first time in a century, has declined for whites. Yet Kristof himself extols the disease theory!

The people Kristof describes don't recover by writing books and giving addiction lectures like the *Times* authors; Nic Sheff and his father, David Sheff, author of *Beautiful Boy*; William Cope Moyers, son of Bill Moyers; or US Representative Madeleine Dean and her son Harry Cunnane, who wrote *Under Our Roof* (2021) about Harry overcoming his opioid addiction at the Caron Foundation rehab, where he is now "resource director." As Above and Beyond attempts to do in inner-city Chicago, or as Liz Evans did with addicted and mentally ill people in Vancouver (Chapter 7), or as Alan Marlatt and others have done (see Chapter 11) with wet housing (residences for fringe members of society who are alcoholic), we need to assist people to have lives worth living and to gain self-respect. When we fantasize instead that addiction is a medical problem that can be cured with a drug, we make it impossible to fathom the meaning of addiction and to assist recovery.

Deaths That Don't Count

So some deaths get more attention than others. Ethan Nadelmann declared that "Where the 12-step thing has the most to own up to is its role in impeding harm reduction interventions to stem the spread of HIV/AIDS. Why was it that Australia and England and the Netherlands were able to stop the spread, and keep the number for injecting drug users under 5 to 10 percent, and the US was not? It's that notion—that abstinence is the only permissible approach, that we are not going to 'enable' a junkie by giving him a clean needle. *There has to be a kind of owning up to that role in hundreds of thousands of people dying unnecessarily*" (my emphasis).

There has been no owning up. Whereas gay AIDS-epidemic activism was spawned by ACT UP, a well-heeled grass roots movement, and embodied in *Angels in America*, a perennial hit play and HBO series, nothing equivalent arose when AIDS's target population shifted to minorities. Who would speak for them?

After AIDS began as a gay male problem, by 1993 most of its victims were people of color. In 1994, as the HIV/AIDS epidemic grew in New Jersey (where I lived), Christine Todd Whitman became governor and appointed a Governor's Advisory Council on AIDS. She selected David Troast, a loyal Republican, to head the council.

In 1996, Troast told the *New York Times* that "he was initially opposed to needle exchange programs, but was persuaded after visiting a similar program in the Bronx and by recent studies showing that easier access to clean needles slows the spread of the virus that causes AIDS." So the council—comprising religious and community leaders, health care professionals, social service providers, state legislators, and administration officials—voted in support of needle exchange.

Whitman ignored her Advisory Council and nixed support for needle exchanges. More than this, New Jersey actively stamped out the distribution of clean needles, using decoy addicts to arrest needle activists, thus killing all organized needle exchange efforts in the state. Her aggressive anti-needle-exchange campaign made New Jersey the foremost front in the nation's fierce political battle against clean needles.

The Centers for Disease Control and Prevention, the National Institutes of Health, and the Surgeon General released studies concluding that needle exchanges significantly decreased the spread of HIV without increasing drug use. Governor Whitman, exactly as Donald Trump did after her, made up her own science, however, dismissing this research as "dubious, at best."

Troast projected that 650 lives a year would be saved by reducing the transmission of the HIV virus, which causes AIDS, among the state's estimated 200,000 IV drug users. Whitman vetoed this life-saving policy in 1996. Only in 2007 did New Jersey become the last state in the US to adopt a needle exchange program. Multiplying Troast's estimate of 650 lost lives a year by the 12-year delay in implementing needle exchange in New Jersey yields a total of about 7,500 deaths (this does not include transmission to children—New Jersey was also a leader in pediatric HIV/AIDS cases).

Whitman has never indicated any regrets about this delay and its consequences. Nor did it hurt her career in the least. Seemingly, these Black or drug-user lives mattered little to New Jerseyans of the era. Not only was she re-elected, but she remains a revered model of "moderation" in the Republican Party, as against Donald Trump's rabid anti-scientism. Whitman is regularly called on to fill this role on MSNBC, the liberal answer to Fox News. Indeed, Whitman was a featured speaker at the 2020 Democratic National Convention! *"I've never seen such an orchestrated war on the environment or science," she said.* Scientific irrationality caused by hating drugs and ignoring the poor and disadvantaged are crimes for which one never has to apologize.

Even the Groups Sympathetic to Me or My Views Pussyfoot Around Them

I have repeatedly noted here Volkow's sudden recognition that people's actual lives are crucial to their achieving recovery, and that residents in inner cities and elsewhere with high drug-death rates require housing, health care, and job and educational opportunities that give their lives purpose. For several years, I served an advisory role to the board of the inner-city Chicago treatment program, Above and Beyond (A&B).

In the fall of 2018, after participating in the Rutgers Social Work School symposium on opioid addiction with Kasia Malinowksa and Portuguese drug policy innovator João Goulão that I describe in Chapter 4, I flew in a three-piece suit to the annual fund raiser A&B was holding in a downtown Chicago hotel, attended by the city's glitterati. Nothing in my usual life looks like any of this. As I describe in the Conclusion, I live in an alcove studio apartment in a perhaps-transitioning-up Brooklyn neighborhood.

At its gala, A&B showed a video describing their approach as non–12-step and harm reduction—you don't keep many participants in a program in a deprived area with homeless people or those in public housing if you insist categorically on permanent abstinence. I supported Above & Beyond because they use a four pillars approach of education and work (purpose), home, health, family and community.

And then A&B hired and promoted as their keynote speaker Ryan Leaf, *a staunch 12-step, powerlessness advocate for the Hazelden/Betty Ford Foundation.*

Leaf is a good-looking white former college football star who played four seasons in the NFL but who ultimately didn't succeed there. He then developed a major painkiller problem. As well as having been a football star, college graduate, and professional athlete, he came from a supportive, intact middle-class family. Taken all together, although he had been addicted to drugs, he had nothing else in common with A&B's inner-city, largely African American, often-homeless underclass population. This is a group whose traumas are ever-present in their lives.

Leaf showed up the night before the gala and breezed by the A&B building in the morning, where he had his breakfast without talking to any staff or clients. He likewise took no questions and disappeared instantly after his talk with his $8,000 fee. Leaf is totally committed to the 12 steps and abstinence—he described a fellow recovered patient who drank again and soon died. That's like declaring death sentences for most of the A&B population. If Leaf had digested anything about A&B's harm reduction approach, he would have seen its opposition to his basic worldview, and he would have despised it.

Thus, this audience of Chicago's powerful and connected (including Mayor Rahm Emanuel) left the annual conference of a harm reduction, non–12-step program with no idea that there was anything importantly different about Above and Beyond from AA's disease and recovery modus operandi. Sometime after the "show," I tried to make this point to the board, unsuccessfully. They answered, "People loved him, and we made hundreds of thousands of dollars!" Later, one board member wrote me: "*Stanton, one more time, Leaf never in any way represented what the A&B Center is philosophically, clinically, or in our attachment to the community that we serve.*"

Exactly. They used their platform to present someone whose social milieu, commitment to the disease theory, and basic values were antithetical to their own—and this was a non-issue for them.

I had one more interaction with the board in which I conducted a mini-workshop to establish A&B's values foundation. I suggested keywords like "authentic," "collaborative," "empowering," "community," "non-disease," "harm reduction." Nothing came of it. Despite its staff's and board's dedication to our non-disease approach, A&B couldn't identify clearly its own distinct set of values, and how we differed from the disease brand, 12 steps, and AA.

But maybe I still had an effect
I resigned. (See the Afterword for A&B's executive director's view of me.) In 2020, A&B had Johann Hari speak at their (virtual) gala. Johann received millions of hits for his TED talk, "Everything You Think You Know

About Addiction Is Wrong" (a line that I often use). But at least Johann understands what Above and Beyond does. So when the CEO asked me to announce Johann's talk, "Redefining Recovery," a subject I have written about and discussed with the Above and Beyond board, I titled my post, "Is Johann Hari Having a Plagiarism Relapse?" As you will see in the next chapter, Johann has had a problem borrowing material without acknowledgement, including from me.

My Radical Idea of Addiction Persists and Constantly Re-Emerges

Both Jeffrey Sachs and Jean Twenge decisively locate the source of our addiction epidemics in the 2019 *World Happiness Report*—digital addiction. It itself comprises our worst addiction epidemic. Per Sachs:

> Consider the article in this year's report by Prof. Jean Twenge on the rapid rise of adolescent depression, suicidal ideation, and self-harm after 2010, and a marked decline in happiness, apparently due in part to the astoundingly large amount of time that young people are spending on digital media: smartphones, videogames, computers, and the like.
>
> It's plausible to describe a significant fraction of adolescents as addicted to screen time, and that is certainly how many young people themselves describe it. They regard their own heavy use of smartphones and other screens as a major problem to overcome, with 54% saying that they spend too much time on their devices. The numbers cited by Twenge are indeed startling: "By 2017, the average 12th grader (17–18 years old) spent more than 6 hours a day of leisure time on just three digital media activities (internet, social media, and texting)."

Sachs then sets about defining addiction: "An addiction, generally speaking, is a behavior like substance use, excessive gambling, or excessive use of digital media, which individuals pursue compulsively in the face of adverse consequences known to the individual." He reviews the entire waterfront of addiction theories, including the opponent-process model. This is Richard Solomon's nonsensical model that I discuss in Chapter 6: an intense, pleasurable experience produces an opposite brain reaction, like a visual afterimage, in this case going from pleasure to pain—ergo addiction. But how does this account for the US's being awash in addictions in 2020? Why would opponent-process rear its ugly head now; had Americans been having unusually large amounts of pleasure in previous years?

As I have noted, *DSM-5 explicitly rejected sex and video games as addictive because, it claimed, there aren't sufficient biological markers to show that this is the case.* For instance, the *DSM-5* addiction group argued, sex doesn't produce the same brain waves it claims addictive drugs demonstrate (although no drugs are designated as "addictive" in *DSM-5*). The *International Classification of Diseases*, 11th edition (*ICD-11*), on the other hand, *does* recognize gaming addiction.

How do the two leading diagnostic manuals worldwide arrive at such opposite conclusions? What criteria is each using to make this designation? *DSM*'s reductive thinking is that gaming can't be classified as addictive because it doesn't influence "addictive brain waves." (Sounds like a *Flash Gordon* episode, doesn't it?) The criteria I outline in Chapter 7 instead demonstrate that digital media *can* fulfill the definition of addiction:

Do digital media meet the criteria for addiction?

- Absorb consciousness, feelings
- Create immediate, predictable sensations
- Provide an artificial sense of control, self-esteem
- Depreciate life options (impair)
- Worsen sense of self (distress)

Twenge argues that young people, sequestered in their rooms (even before COVID) attached to digital media, have lost touch with the worlds and people outside of their four walls. In Chapter 4, I spoke of the exaggerated fear that dominates American home life. Twenge describes parents welcoming their children being riveted to their iPhones, posting on various social media. *This way they are safe from the dangers they would find outside the home.* What the children are missing is *actual* experience and connection. The motivation to seek predictable sensations, rewards, and feelings, listed among the criteria for addiction, arises, above all, from exactly this fear. The greatest antidote to addiction, as Zach and I showed in *Outgrowing Addiction*, is unencumbered experience. Such experience sometimes leads to failure, even pain. But the capacity to face and learn from negative outcomes is the sine qua non of the self-agency that is the opposite of addiction.

Drug Policy Reform Gone Wrong

As I have noted, drug policy reform has gone in the wrong direction, and is increasingly doing so. When I met Ethan Nadelmann in 1989, there were a few radical drug policy reformers ("drug legalizers") out there. Over the next thirty years Ethan changed that reality by bringing drug policy reform out in the open, so that even elected officials now talk about the once-impossible dream that drug-taking would no longer be a crime. Yet, at the same time, in key ways, the end product of the reform movement has become as reactionary as what it replaced.

How Drug Policy Reform Meanings Changed from 1990 to 2020

Old Drug Policy Reform	New Drug Policy Reform
Anti–supply side	Blame Big Pharma
Consumer-driven pain relief	Cut painkiller prescriptions
Anti–drug scare	Fentanyl!
Improve society and lives	More medical treatment

A Fundamentally New Way of Thinking

There are five concepts you need to know in order to understand the history and current status of drugs and addiction. In many ways, these concepts have been broadly accepted, but in a current form that belies and undermines their revolutionary impacts. Here they are, followed by popular reform movement reads on each of them, then my interpretations.

Harm reduction

Drug reformers: Dealing with drugs, drug problems, and addiction without requiring users to abstain.

My read: Concentrating on the person's ability to manage their life regardless of their drug use profile.

The medical approach to addiction

Reformers: Medical approaches are objective, humane ways of treating people with drug problems.

My read: The disease view, embedded in American thinking since temperance times, teaches people that addiction, and thus drug use, is beyond the individual's and the community's ability to control—*this current policy reform meme is exact opposite of the message drug policy reform should be conveying.*

MAT

Reformers: Medication-assisted treatment is a modern miracle that cures addiction, favored by Nora Volkow and NIDA, Ethan Nadelmann and DPA, and drug courts nationwide.

My read: MAT is the latest magical elixir for addiction, a false solution that obviates the need to create an equitable society and fulfilled people who are contented with their lives and who believe that they can manage their worlds.

Evidence-based treatment

Reformers: MAT has been demonstrated to be effective.

My read: Recall the shocked discovery by Harvard's Center for Global Control of Tobacco, which spent millions on nicotine-replacement therapy drugs (NRT), that these drugs, "proven" effective in the laboratory, led to *more* relapses among dependent smokers who quit. In the same way, people receiving medical narcotics (e.g., methadone, Suboxone) under tightly controlled clinical conditions are less likely than those taking street drugs to die. Such clinical stabilization and supervision can allow for real change and growth *if clinicians understand and practice what it really takes to overcome/outgrow addiction—home, purpose, health, family/community.*

However, (a) the tightly controlled parameters of MAT studies are impossible to maintain over time for people in the real world, (b) this becomes especially clear when people discontinue their "medicine" and become *more* prone to relapse, and (c) the exclusive belief in and reliance on such elixirs makes addiction and death ultimately more likely.

Stigma

Reformers: Addiction has been stigmatized as a moral failing; people instead need to freely admit that they have an irreversible biological disease.

My read: We have taken a long-time American trope, born in temperance and elevated by AA, that people's addictive behaviors define who they are, which was once a moral statement, and reified it into a scientific bias. AA's mantra, "I am an alcoholic/addict," has become the modern brain disease catechism, including Gabor Maté and other supposed addiction concept and drug policy reformers.

This belief isn't true, and it's destructive.

We need to think about drugs and addiction in a fundamentally new way. Nora Volkow can't do that. Drug reformers can't do that. Americans haven't been able to do that.

I try to do it.

Conclusion

As I describe with regard to my role models in addiction in Chapter 3, and return to in the next chapter, no one fully believes what I believe about drugs and addiction. I *have* said—apropos of Maia Szalavitz, Carl Hart, Marc Lewis, and Johann Hari—that there is a movement away from the disease theory of addiction. But none of these pioneering theorists fully grasps what is true of addiction.

Likewise, with the advent of harm reduction and drug policy reform groups, and yet the growing epidemic of drug deaths, you might expect more people in the field to be following my lead. That hasn't happened. The disease—the demonic—view of drugs as being capable of taking possession of a person is baked into American thinking. And, as I discuss in the following chapters, while this vision arose and is most potent in the US, the World Health Organization and the temperance nations that dominate its drugs and alcohol perspective and approach are busily spreading it worldwide. *Ironically, at the same time as there are leading-edge signs of a reversal of disease thinking in America, it is now being spread to cultures where it doesn't naturally occur.*

I discuss in the next chapter how our most radical addiction theorists and researchers, the ones with whom I am most identified, are carried along by America's deep cultural currents surrounding drugs and addiction.

10

Revolutionary Addiction Thinkers and Me

**Few think about addiction like me;
no one confronts the field like me.**

In this chapter and the next, I review my relationships with, and the thinking of, people who are associated with new and different views of addiction, including alcoholism. They include every major revisionist addiction thinker. All of them fail to make some essential leap. While Maia Szalavitz and Marc Lewis, who were drug-addicted, were protected from complete immersion in the disease theory by their Jewish mindsets, they retain elements of the disease theory in their reductive biological thinking; while Bruce Alexander, Ethan Nadelmann, and Johann Hari find disease thinking wrong, for various reasons (agreeable personalities, craving public attention, political expedience) they don't make a cause célèbre of it; while (in the next chapter) Bill Miller, Jim Orford, and Nick Heather—brilliant WASPs—understand that alcoholic drinking behavior follows the same rules as all human behavior, they humbly avoid making universalistic proclamations about addiction. The same is true for the neuropsychologist Carl Hart, who investigates drug use, and whose views I deal with in this chapter (and who is not a WASP).

"I think alone."—Stanton Peele (Nod to George Thorogood, "I Drink Alone")

The Rev (in Doonesbury comics): "This crop of young people is amazing in their new and independent way of thinking."

Doonesbury: "Do you really think so? Aren't they just displaying a new kind of groupthink?"

The Rev (thought balloon): "Where's the inquisition when you need it?"

I Think Differently; I Work Alone

My theories and thinking are actively opposed, in lesser or greater degree, by *virtually all* of even the most *advanced* thinkers about addiction—at least in terms of my personal style in clearly laying out how wrongheaded our approaches are.

I have identified in earlier chapters a number of addiction theorists and researchers who share my way of thinking to some extent, but who either rejected me or discounted my views. Norman Zinberg and Charles Winick couldn't see addiction beyond drugs (Zinberg) or other than in disease terms (Winick). Sociologist Harold Mulford and anthropologist Dwight Heath, although they liked me and my thinking, didn't think in terms of alcoholism (Heath) or disliked the concept (Mulford)—they were content simply to relay their vision of how people naturally relate to alcohol (with which I agree). But they didn't buck prevailing visions of treatment in America.

These differences persist. As I describe in the last chapter, with the advent of harm reduction and drug policy reform groups, you might expect a lot more people in the field to be following my lead. But nothing could be farther from the truth. The disease—the demonic—view of drugs as being capable of taking possession of a person is deep-baked into American society. So much so that groups that view themselves as progressive, even radical, buy into exactly the same drug and addiction myths as our forebears.

Remember how I ended Part I, by describing the panel run by George Soros's Open Society Foundations (OSF) built on Carl Hart's radical report on methamphetamines, the subtitle for which was "Lessons Learned from the Crack Hysteria." At this panel, Holly Catania, Director of Policy and Communications for New York's Department of Health and Mental Hygiene's Bureau of Alcohol and Drugs, showed before and-after-pictures about the effects of meth, in which the "after" pictures depicted the wrecked faces of meth addicts—presumed to be the unavoidable, inevitable effect of regular use of the drug. This before-and-after schema is *the same one used by temperance proponents to show the ravages of alcohol.*

Catania's point: it was ethically wrong to show the pictures of the wreckage of these meth addicts' lives. She didn't question that this, indeed, was what happened to meth users. *Catania was selling the drug-addict myth from the heights of radical drug reformers' New York summit, OSF. Not one individual present in this packed house, including Kasia Malinowska, Director of OSF's Global Drug Program, or Carl Hart himself, the "truth teller" who explicitly rejects the meth-addict myth*—"There are severe consequences to people for exaggerating the effects of drugs"—*uttered a peep.*

Why would no one in the audience for—and no participant in—the Open Society Foundations panel on "meth myths" object to a panelist presenting a primal drug myth herself? This groupthink occurred in 2014, in the midst of New York City's and the US's drug-death spiral.

The audience. As a rule, audiences are trained not to think actively, but to accept. And, as I pointed out with my questioning following the panel, this audience overwhelmingly *believed* all the primal drug myths. Yet this audience was in a house of radical reform, OSF, to listen to a radical drug researcher, Carl Hart, explain the myths of meth. They would never perceive a discordant element or question it if they did.

Carl Hart, author of the OSF "Meth Myths" report and chief presenter, was not alert to drug myths being propagated by the panel itself. Perhaps Holly Catania's showing the ravaged faces of meth users as inescapable truth simply escaped him (even as Carl uses these before-and-after images as an *example* of a meth myth). At another level, Carl doesn't have tools with which to turn that situation into a teachable moment—certainly without offending Holly and Kasia.

Kasia Malinowska is the director of global drug policy for OSF, which funded Hart's meth-myths report and organized the panel. It was one of OSF's largest-ever events. Malinowska's role is to challenge policies biased against drugs and users. Her concern isn't to question whether "expert" information is unsupported or wrongheaded, even as Carl Hart's 2014 report began:

> The rise in methamphetamine use has provoked a barrage of misinformation and reckless policies, such as mandatory minimum sentences, increased penalties for minor offenders and major restrictions against certain medicines.
>
> This new report, *Methamphetamine: Fact vs. Fiction and Lessons from the Crack Hysteria,* reveals the extreme stigmatization of users and dangerous policy responses that are reminiscent of the crack hysteria in the 1980s and 1990s, which led to grossly misguided laws that accelerated mass incarceration in the United States.

Two other participants in the OSF panel who said nothing about Catania's lurid presentation were Bill Piper, national policy director for DPA, and Howard Josepher, founder of a model harm reduction program in New York that has DPA's strong backing. (I describe visiting Howard's Fire Island home in Chapter 3, "How I Discovered Addiction.") To this day, when I relate the OSF scenario to Ethan, he wrinkles his nose and pretends it didn't happen, or that he doesn't understand what I'm getting at. I think I can best state his objection as: "Stannin, why do you always want to make such a fuss?"

Fundamentally, as I discuss in Chapter 9, we have accelerated our hysteria around the drugs mentioned—meth, cocaine, opioids, including synthetic opioids like fentanyl—while becoming a world leader in problems, and deaths, associated with them. That lethality is the natural result of our demonization of drugs.

The March of the Unradical Revisionist Addiction Theorists

Maia Szalavitz is the author of *Unbroken Brain*, the largest best seller yet to "question" the truths of addiction. Maia entered my life as a producer of Bill Moyers's 1998 PBS series: *Addiction: Close to the Family*. Moyers's son William, who became head of media relations for Hazelden, had a long string of relapses, on which he based his 2006 best seller, *Broken*. Moyers wrote another book about his recovery in 2013, when he appeared with his father and Susan Cheevers at the legendary 92nd St. YMHA (Young Men's Hebrew Assocation—now YM-YWHA). Meanwhile, Andrew Zimmern devoted a tribute segment to AA, William Moyers, and Hazelden in his 2020 MSNBC series, *What's Eating America*. The special also had a breathless scene looking at brain scans with yet another researcher claiming (two decades after the older Moyers made the same claim) we were on the verge of finding the source of addiction in the brain.

In the meantime, the younger Moyers now sends me enquiring emails about recent developments in addiction. Perhaps William somewhere fathoms the fundamental question: *Why, if he, his father before him, and best sellers like Andrew Zimmern are spot on and the popular, agreed-on approaches they swear by are so successful, does addiction continue to spiral out of control, which is their favorite topic?* This self-refuting idiocy is the American addiction albatross.

Maia's burden

"Ginger" wrote on my Facebook page, partly facetiously:

> You know I love ya and deeply respect your work and character. But you are a *curmudgeon*! People like Maia Szalavitz and Johann Hari are only saying what you've been saying all along. They're just more pleasant about it.

Maia has come into her own as an addiction theorist in her middle age. In doing so, she has come closer to my point of view, which she sometimes doffs her cap toward. But we remain apart on key issues, as her interview with Zach makes clear.

Maia, who is twenty years younger than me, went to a Hazelden-like program and got over her addiction to heroin and cocaine, formed while she was a student at Columbia University in her early twenties. She returned to Brooklyn College, became what she calls a "neuroscience journalist," co-authored books with prominent scientists, and established herself as a regular contributor to *Time*, *Vice*, and a host of popular journals and addiction periodicals. Maia always, naturally, was interested in addiction, and tuned into *Love and Addiction* from the start. Like all of us, she wanted to be loved. Love relationships and relationship addictions were a central issue for her, and to her becoming addicted to drugs.

Emotionally, ideologically, Maia is deeply committed to a select few things—she *hates* tough love and boot camp programs for kids. I admire her commitment in this arena (it was the basis of her first book in 2006, *Help at Any Cost*). She was early in on childhood trauma with best sellers with child psychiatrist Bruce Perry. But on many questions she is half in/half out. She adhered to the 12 steps for a while, then started critiquing them, saying AA and NA could discourage the exploration of other methods. Maia quit drugs—although she has returned to white wine. She now recognizes (sort of) that her recovery was a natural personal development.

Maia believes her brain is unbroken. But she feels that it is seriously damaged. She thinks that some emotional short circuit in her brain caused her to have an emotional disorder, and that psychiatric drugs resolved that disorder and thus "cured" her addiction. This narrative is central to her larger perspective—there is some brain-based solution to her and other people's problems that will be discovered. But this narrative runs counter to other views she holds and things she knows about addiction and recovery. And her outlook undercuts her image, her claim, to be a myth-buster.

Here are five myths Szalavitz was credited with dispelling in *Unbroken Brain:*

- There is an "addictive personality" which all people with addiction share.
- Once an addict, always an addict.
- Addiction is an "equal opportunity" disease.
- Babies can be "born addicted" to drugs.
- Addicts have "hijacked brains" and are powerless over their behavior and unable to learn until they stop taking drugs.

You will recognize that I've been combating such myths virtually my whole life. For instance, I provide this list in my 1989 book, *Diseasing of America:*

- Alcoholics inherit their alcoholism and thus are born as alcoholics.
- Alcoholism always grows worse without treatment, so that alcoholics can never cut back or quit on their own.
- Alcoholism as a disease can strike any individual—it is an "equal-opportunity destroyer"—and respects no social, religious, ethnic or sexual bounds.
- Treatment based on AA principles is the only effective treatment for alcoholism—in the words of one proponent, a modern medical "miracle"—without which no one can hope to arrest a drinking problem.
- Those who reject the AA approach for their drinking problems, or observers who contradict any of the contentions about alcoholism listed here, are practicing a special denial that means death for alcoholics.

Notice the almost identical wording of some of the myths Szalavitz attacked almost thirty years after I did ("equal opportunity," for instance). I had chapters on natural recovery and infant and animal addiction in my 1985 book, *The Meaning of Addiction*. Forty years before Maia's noting the myth that "babies can be born addicted" to drugs, Archie and I had written in *Love and Addiction* that addiction was meaningful only with respect to adult human beings (see Chapter 3).

Recently, Maia's following on my path is more instantaneous. For example, her piece on natural recovery—"Most People with Addiction Simply Grow Out of It: Why Is this Widely Denied?" was published in November 2014. Aside from the fact that I'd been publishing popular pieces on natural recovery since 1983, my natural recovery article for the very popular *Reason* website, "Government Says You Can't Overcome Addiction, Contrary to What Government Research Shows," appeared in February 2014. Maia published, "It's Time to Reclaim the Word 'Recovery'" in December 2014; my piece for *Reason*, "The Hijacking of Sobriety by the Recovery Movement," was published in May 2014.

Why, after all, is Maia famous for challenging these misconceptions thirty to forty years after I did? For one thing, that she did so thirty or forty years later was good timing. For another, she's not in your face.

Unbroken Brain is split at its core. Maia recounts going to rehab but also says in the *New York Times* that treatment isn't necessary: "Addiction doesn't last a lifetime: In fact, most people recover, often on their own." But she was rescued by treatment, and she's still being treated, if not for addiction, then for her mental state:

My own nearly 30-year recovery started with traditional rehab and abstinence, which I practiced for 13 years. Now, however, it includes *medical use of anti-depressants*, exercise, strong relationships, deep commitment to my work and moderate use of some legal substances (my emphasis).

Maia is appealingly human. She is also highly privileged (which she realizes): her father was a chemist (I believe that pleasing him impels her "scientism").

Maia returned to college when she left rehab, never to use her "addict" drugs again. She has resumed her privileged position in society after a detour. Maia believes she inherited her anxieties and depression genetically—she's a *neuroscience* journalist, not a psychological one. She doesn't ferret out psychological and social causes of her, or society's, problems. These are outside her ken, but who cares?

Which leads Szalavitz to love medications, for her and society: "Many of those who recover do it through professional treatment with medications like methadone or buprenorphine, not through abstinence." This is Maia's version of the current concept of harm reduction. She is undeterred by our society's bad, and worsening, performance in avoiding drug deaths, suicide, and depression, despite her, and our, full-throttle embrace of psychiatric and addiction medicine.

Believing the Unbelievable Believably

I hope I don't seem to resent or dislike Maia—she's a very nice person. And more power to her for the views she expresses—especially when she describes how *Love and Addiction* was a breakthrough. But persistent differences appear in how Maia and I view addiction. At the same time, I believe she has been acutely aware of my views.

Maia's skill is in couching things benignly, in offending as few people as possible or, if she does say provocative things, backtracking rapidly. In my radical "Why Liberals Love the Disease Theory of Addiction, by a Liberal Who Hates It" in *Pacific Standard* magazine, I confronted drug policy advocates' favorite point: that minorities are unfairly penalized for "crimes" involving drugs for which middle-class people are excused. Which is true, and which drug policy reform has taken steps to remedy—somewhat.

But middle-class and advantaged people do better at resisting addiction—like the members of my audience who in overwhelming numbers put their painkillers back in their medicine cabinets. And, in the uncommon cases where they succumb to addiction, they do far better at recovering (like Nic Sheff, William Moyers, Drew Barrymore, Jamie Lee Curtis, Robert

Downey, Jr., Harry Cunnane). Advantaged people have more to regain when they recover, more to lose if they don't, and more resources to get there. Underlying these visible assets is something more difficult to convey: middle-class people believe that their efforts will be rewarded, and so they persist in their efforts to recover and succeed in life. This is called self-efficacy, or personal agency. Like Maia, they value and pursue achievement.

Let's face it—few people are as industrious and optimistic as Maia was to write steadily for decades in order to establish herself as America's premier reformist addiction specialist. I certainly admire her for it. Her "bougie" values are not perfect guiderails in life, as she herself demonstrated; but they *are* helpful for people to get ahead and to escape addiction.

As I tried to word this advantage in my article:

> The tendency for liberals to endorse the disease theory of addiction has strong wellsprings. You see, there's a trap that the privileged and enlightened find very hard to escape: We are frightened to say that people in our country who are disadvantaged economically, socially, or, alas, racially, are more likely to become addicted. That would mean that they are different from us in a bad way. Much safer is to play up that drugs are bad, that drugs trap unfortunate people, and that these people have diseases against which they are powerless.

Here's how Szalavitz finesses the same point: "Addiction rates are higher in poor people—not because they are less moral or have greater access to drugs (hear, hear!), but because they are more likely to experience childhood trauma, chronic stress, high school dropout, mental illness and unemployment, all of which raise the odds of getting and staying hooked." After discarding the chaff—poor and Black people are less moral and have more access to drugs—Maia lists a group of external factors to explain their addiction-proneness. This list, while true, skirts the psychological and sociocultural meaning and causes of addiction. Disadvantaged people's lives are spiraling out of control, as described by economists Anne Case and Angus Deaton in *Deaths of Despair and the Future of Capitalism*, in ways that fundamentally affect their feelings about themselves and their view of the world. Maia doesn't, can't, deal with these essential elements of despair.

The AA Behemoth

AA looms over the addiction field in the US. No other major disease critic or policy reformer aside from me dares to take it on. But Maia did confront the 12 steps' onerous influence in 2017, some forty years after I did, by writing, "After 75 Years of Alcoholics Anonymous, It's Time to Admit We Have a Problem":

For much of the past 50 years or so, *voicing any serious skepticism toward Alcoholics Anonymous or any other 12-step program was sacrilege*—the equivalent, in polite company, of questioning the virtue of American mothers or the patriotism of our troops. If your problem was drink, AA was the answer; if drugs, Narcotics Anonymous. And if those programs didn't work, it was your fault: You weren't "working the steps." The only alternative, as the 12-step slogan has it, was "jails, institutions, or death" [my emphasis].

Of course, I have for decades been one of few addiction specialists willing to publicly question AA, with results for my career described in Chapter 7. Maia has never gone that route, but takes a middling, ambivalent, position. In the strangest manifestation of Maia's split personality around addiction, her stressing the need to overcome AA's hegemony is far from the only thing she has written on that topic. Indeed (and this is indecipherable), it was not the only thing she published about AA in *Pacific Standard*. Try to make sense of these two headlines.

After 75 Years of Alcoholics Anonymous, It's Time to Admit We
Have a Problem: Challenging the 12-Step Hegemony.

Maia Szalavitz, Feb. 10, 2014

What I've Finally Concluded About 12-Step Programs
After 25 Years Writing About Drugs and Addiction

Alcoholics Anonymous and the rest remain the biggest and most polarizing force in the addiction community. I quit heroin and cocaine using the steps and have covered addiction as a journalist—and I'd argue that the *picture is decidedly mixed* [my emphasis].

Maia Szalavitz, Sept. 24, 2014.

And, so, Maia decries the impact of AA and the 12 steps on addiction in America—sort of. Szalavitz noted that the 12 steps have formed the basis for 90 percent of US treatment programs in a period when American drug and alcohol deaths (and suicides) have turned sharply upward. I'm not accusing Szalavitz of plagiarizing my work. She has her own point of view. But she has followed my breadcrumb trail and, like Pat Boone's remake of Little Richard's "Tutti Frutti," turned it into white bread digestible by middle America.

Marc Lewis

I've dined with Marc from Brooklyn to Belfast (including wine) and I've presented with him in Belfast (I'm *never* invited to speak in New York). We talk about how formidable our wives of Romanian descent are (in my case, was). Marc has been gracious in noting my pioneering role, telling me that my *Diseasing of America* (which appeared in 1989, more than a decade after I began my revisionism) changed his view of addiction, indeed the whole field's, and the course of his work.

Marc has become perhaps the best-regarded academic to contest the disease view of addiction—he made this radical statement in *Scientific American*: "Why the Disease Definition of Addiction Does Far More Harm than Good." *Scientific American* would *never* publish anything by me—I've tried. I give great credit to Marc because he confronts existing misconceptions of addiction, and the power players who purvey them—up to a point (he won't take on AA, for example).

But I question how Marc differs from those he critiques. I can't say something to Marc about addiction without his objecting. While Marc does recognize that the disease theory has the practical consequence of diverting resources from studying and intervening in areas of life that really matter, he finds saying anything psychological or societal about addiction uncomfortable. Yet those analyses are central to all of my work and to understanding addiction. As indicated by the title of his first best seller, *Memoirs of an Addicted Brain: A Neuroscientist Examines His Former Life on Drugs*, Lewis relies on his status as a neuroscientist to establish credibility. He has no explanation for why he escaped addiction, when he quit after being found unconscious in a bathroom, a bit older (age thirty) than some, other than seeing it as being due to his natural brain development. In this way, Marc's view of addiction and recovery is as reductive as the disease theory is.

And, as this might predict, Marc is wedded (as is Maia) to Gabor Maté's "all addiction is due to childhood trauma." Since neither he nor Maia can penetrate their own experience, they both fall back onto the all-purpose explanation for addiction: trauma (although Maia says that she wasn't mistreated). Marc had a rough, albeit middle-class, upbringing by rejective parents. I admire his and Maia's overcoming their childhood hardships. But their recoveries were not random, despite their lack of insight into them.

Gene Heyman and John Davies

Some disease critics reject the idea of addiction altogether. Two noteworthy examples are Gene Heyman in his book *Addiction Is a Disorder of Choice* (2009) and John Davies in his *The Myth of Addiction* (1992).

Heyman is an American statistical epidemiologist who analyzes government data sets. He shows that people quit addictions regularly over their addict careers, including late bloomers as well as early remitters—"each year a constant proportion of those still addicted remitted, independent of the number of years since the onset of dependence." This is a breathtaking finding. As Winick did in 1962 in his "Maturing Out of Narcotic Addiction," Heyman traces people's jettisoning of addiction to the growth of other involvements in their lives that their addiction negates. Unfortunately, as we shall see, Heyman (like Sally Satel) ranks prison high among such negating factors—ergo, let's imprison drug users.

It is true that most, but not all, people have more to lose as they mature and thus are willing and able to discard their addictions. I focus on this development of a full life palette as a therapeutic approach in my 1991 book (with Archie and Mary), *The Truth About Addiction and Recovery*, and in my online Life Process Program. Opportunity, education, social and family support, and other "pillars of recovery" are critical determinants of whether or not people or whole communities are able to escape or reduce addiction. But neither Heyman nor Davies focuses on these improvable aspects of individual and social lives.

Davies was a social psychologist like me. Davies, now deceased, was British. (I met him in both the US and Britain. I have never met Heyman.) He shows that drugs per se don't cause negative consequences for people, even as people often attribute these consequences to drugs. Davies thus debunks the supposed power of drugs to capture people's lives, as I did in my work from *Love and Addiction* and *The Meaning of Addiction*. Davies (1997) recognized this agreement:

> Addiction is still seen as something that happens to people, almost without regard to their own motives or intentions, rather than as a subtle dialectic between an external pharmacology and an internal pharmacology which is underlain . . . by such entities as desires, wishes, motives, beliefs and so forth. A number of notable works which do not fit this mold have come to light over the last couple of decades, but the fact that they can be easily recalled (e.g., Heather and Robertson, Peele, Orford) is an indicant of the relative rarity of these acts of nonconformity. [The others Davies names are all British.]

Both Davies and Heyman are nonreductionists, a necessary corrective in thinking about addiction: per Heyman, "the word 'compulsive' identifies patterns of behavior, and all behavior has a biological basis, including voluntary actions." That is, there is nothing special about addictive behavior that makes it biological in nature.

My problem with both Heyman's "choice" and Davies's "myth" formulations is that people *do* become addicted, most for a specified, shorter or longer, period of time. But some continue their addictions for extended periods. And some people kill themselves pursuing their addictions, despite ample negative experiences. (As I have noted, youthful, naïve, unexpected overdoses are not the rule in drug deaths; these instead are most often the result of hollowed out lives and the long-term physical and spiritual deterioration that shadows such lives, as represented by deaths of despair.) *Fatal outcomes are not common*, even as their gross number mounts; harm reduction treatment makes such fatalities less likely still.

But what is operating to cause such persistent self-destructiveness when it occurs?

Davies and Heyman have no insight into the nature of this aspect of addiction. They don't recognize the existential despair of these worst-case scenarios. This cycle of disability and distress is central to my model of the self-feeding nature of addiction as described in *Love and Addiction*.

> When a person does something in response to his anxiety that he doesn't respect (like getting drunk or overeating), his disgust with himself causes his anxiety to increase. As a result, and now also faced by a bleaker objective situation, he is even more needful of the reassurance the addictive experience offers him. This is the cycle of addiction. Eventually, the addict depends totally on the addiction for his gratifications in life, and nothing else can interest him. He has given up hope of managing his existence; forgetfulness is the one aim he is capable of pursuing wholeheartedly.

In the worst cases, a few addicted people lose any sense of their own humanity and become the person capable only of pursuing an addiction. One such person was Terry McGovern.

Terry: My Daughter's Life-and-Death Struggle with Alcoholism

Terry is a memoir written by US Senator and presidential candidate George McGovern. Raised in a solid, loving family, Terry McGovern would seem to have had zero adverse childhood events. But she was a vulnerable girl, became involved with drugs, and then drank alcoholically. After leaving a treatment program at age 45, living in a halfway house in Madison, Wisconsin, with the chance of reuniting with her husband and daughters, she bought and drank a bottle of liquor and froze to death overnight on the street.

Her father said of Terry: "*She knew what it meant to love other people. But she fell short of loving herself*" (my emphasis).

On top of failing to deal with this psychological and existential distress and dysfunction, Heyman *adds* to it with his punitive approach. If the negative consequences of addictions drive people to change, why not tip the scale by punishing addicted people, including imprisoning them? This is simply unforgivable, inhumane, and ultimately unworkable. Punishment—which Terry McGovern experienced throughout her life—didn't, couldn't, save her. Addiction became something more than a pluses-versus-minuses choice for McGovern.

Johann Hari

Johann has been able to take the same insights that I have—that addiction, depression, and anxiety grow out of people's personal experiences, and are best handled by community and connection—and turn them into best sellers. He converts complex academic issues into personal story telling, including his own treatment with antidepressants as a gay boy in a working-class family, in his best sellers, *Chasing the Scream: The First and Last Days of the War on Drugs* (2015) and *Lost Connections: Uncovering the Real Causes of Depression—and the Unexpected Solutions* (2018). Johann is very good at what he does. He is a genius for transcending the assaults on his identity in his youth and his resulting depression by gaining a larger picture of addiction and emotional disorders. Added to that is his ability to relate to people through his writing and presentations.

But, then, Johann aims to please, an urge he has turned into an art form. He'll please his audience, in person or writing, no matter what, until any meaning or urgency for change is lost. Worse, Johann has sometimes displayed serious ethical shortcomings. As Johann's Wikipedia entry describes that: "In 2011 Hari resigned as a columnist at *The Independent* after being accused of plagiarism, and of making pejorative edits to the Wikipedia pages of journalists who had criticized his conduct." Hari admitted to these mishaps, such as using material from other writers without acknowledging the sources, and apologized.

I admire that Johann didn't blame his misdemeanors on drugs or his mental disorders or on his having been abused. But I *am* concerned with Johann's value choices in my dealings with him.

Johann summarizes his views in his multi-million-viewed TED talks and *Huffington Post* articles this way: "*Everything you think you know about addiction is wrong.* What causes heroin addiction? Everyone asked this question would say that it's heroin." He then cites Gabor Maté and Bruce Alexander in noting that opioids themselves don't cause addiction, that people ("your grandmother") receiving very strong opioids in a hospital don't become addicted and rats in the rich Rat Park environment reject opioids.

It was a blow after my decades of lonely labor to discover my point of view so widely propagated without reference to me. In his lectures and writing he goes on to assert that love is the solution for addiction. Johann has told me that he was deeply affected by *Love and Addiction*, in which Archie and I describe love and addiction as opposing experiences. Johann did write a blurb for my paperback edition of *Recover!*, for which I thank him. But he has never cited me or my work. This is true even now that we know each other. After he interviewed me for hours in my Park Slope apartment, Johann *still* doesn't reference me. But he has picked up several of my techniques, like asking his TED audience (which is trending toward 20 million views) how they respond to using narcotics.

I last saw Johann when he presented at the Open Society Foundations in New York in 2019. He introduced me from the podium, as Carl Hart does. Only he said, "Stanton Peele developed the idea of process addictions. He's a formative figure in the field, although we disagree on every issue." We actually agree on virtually every issue. Only Johann needs to establish his distance from me.

Where Johann and I differ is in our moral approach to our lives and to ideas, however. This became apparent around a court case where Johann's and my relationship went badly off track.

The Eldred case

In July 2017, I got an email from an attorney asking me to sign on to a brief in support of Julie Eldred, who had been returned to prison for violating her probation by using drugs, based on the argument that *she had a chronic, relapsing brain disease.*

The facts: "After Julie Eldred was granted probation for stealing jewelry to buy drugs, she got busy fulfilling the judge's conditions. She began an intensive all-day outpatient treatment program. She even went an extra step and started daily doses of Suboxone, a medication that can quell opiate cravings. Then she relapsed and snorted her drug of choice—fentanyl." (Yes, some people prefer fentanyl.) So, please note that:

1. Eldred was receiving a double dose of the disease theory, through her treatment program (IOP) and taking a prescribed a substitute opioid, Suboxone, based on the belief that she had a disease and required one such drug to quit another.

2. She returned to her preferred drug, fentanyl.

3. Eldred was briefly jailed for violating the conditions of her probation, but was soon released to . . . re-enter an IOP and MAT.

First, let me be clear, I believe no human beings should be imprisoned, *or threatened with prison*, for using drugs, whether they can be said to be addicted, take the drugs for pleasure, or *anything in between*. (Although, it should be noted, Eldred was imprisoned for theft.) If people dislike the impact of their drug use on their lives, they should have ready access to help about how best to address their concerns, including using the drugs safely, reducing use, quitting, or finding some substitute drug. I would advise exactly the same for someone in a "love" relationship that impaired or distressed or deeply hurt them (including suffering abuse).

But when the question is framed as "Should Julie Eldred be jailed for her drug use?" outright opposition to imprisoning drug users gets translated (as it was by Eldred's earnest attorney) into "my client has a disease that should be treated"—as though the only way to free Eldred is by claiming she has a medical disease. *This response exacerbates the underlying problem our society has in dealing with drugs.*

Thus Maia Szalavitz, whom some identify as an opponent of the disease theory, and who is *known for her hatred of coerced treatment,* endorsed the argument *that Eldred should be treated* and not imprisoned *since she had the disease of addiction.*

Eldred's attorney contacted me on the recommendation of Johann Hari. Johann, who had just written a best seller and spoke around the world discounting the disease model of addiction, was endorsing a legal argument *that would have enshrined in the law the disease theory that we both deeply oppose.* Johann recruited me to sign on to it; he was incensed—and publicly vilified me—when I refused. *Somehow, in Johann's universe, I ended up the villain for opposing the disease theory.*

Johann argues that although we know that it's nonsense to call homosexuality a disease, in past decades it was a useful tactic to argue for this position in place of criminalizing gay relationships. But you can't negotiate truth and science on the grounds of legal convenience. For instance, what about people whose sexuality is plastic and changeable, such as those who say they are bisexual, omnisexual, or nonbinary? Worldwide culture is now embracing greater sexual openness between men. Meanwhile, some women choose a same-sex partner out of sexual politics and the rejection of male dominance. Should these people be jailed because they choose a same-sex relationship?

Translated into drug use and addiction, if someone's drug use isn't compulsive, but is obviously a choice they make, do *they* deserve to be imprisoned? Ethical compromises like Johann Hari's always fail in the end. *We need instead to eliminate whole hog the idea that drug use for any reason is a chargeable offense.*

Sally Satel

Sally is extremely brilliant; and extremely circumscribed. No radical theorist knows as much about brain science, writes so clearly, and is so bold in denouncing ridiculous biological explanations as she does in *Brainwashed: The Seductive Appeal of Mindless Neuroscience* (with Scott Lilienfeld, 2013).

Sally has referred well-placed addiction therapy clients and their families to me—indicating her trust in me. She has written nice blurbs for my books. She has also exchanged more emails with me during my later life than any other professional colleague, in the form of: "Can you believe what they said?" The "they" is most often Nora Volkow. Sally would *never* say such things in public.

Sally would also *never* cite my radical views in her own writing. (Sally declined to write a blurb for this memoir.)

Sally is limited by her proper, paint-within-the-lines persona. For example, she was interviewed before a large in-person and video audience at the American Enterprise Institute (where she is a fellow), along with co-author Scott Lilienfeld, by *New York Times* columnist David Brooks. At one point, Brooks said (with obtuse self-assurance), "Of course, addicts can never recover." Sally honestly (to her good credit) responded, "That's not true." She then let the matter drop.

Had I been there, I would have stopped the proceedings: "David, why would a scientifically well-informed person like you believe such a wrong thing, given the cascades of data showing that the opposite is true?" I would then turn to the audience and ask them what they thought the toughest addiction to quit is, then run them through my "How many of you have quit smoking" exercise. Then I would return to Brooks and say, "Isn't it remarkable how persistent such myths are, *even when they contradict people's, including your own, personal experience?*"

Do you see why Brooks would *never* interview me, or why I wouldn't be invited to speak at AEI? Here is an exchange Sally had with Carl Hart in 2018 at the Howard Center's annual conference in Burlington, Vermont. (No transcript or video was released. Zach Rhoads was present and reconstructed the event for me.)

Carl (standing and addressing the audience): "Heroin is not the problem. I'm the chair of psychology at Columbia. Sometimes I need to go to functions with boring-ass people, and I'll do a little heroin and it makes me feel more calm and social and less bored. And it helps me sleep at night. I wake up wide-eyed and bushy-tailed the next day, ready to take care of my responsibilities."

Sally (seated on the panel): "Did you say heroin?"

Carl: "Yes."

Sally: "I don't think you should go around announcing that."

Carl (shrugging, annoyed): "I'm fifty years old, man; it's time that I'm allowed to be honest about my drug use. I'll say it again: drugs are not the problem."

Sally is saying that it's naughty and wrong to take drugs, so don't let people know that responsible—nay, distinguished—people use drugs. (This was essentially Sally's review of Carl's book, *Drug Use for Grown-Ups*, in the *Wall Street Journal*.) It's no wonder we don't know there are more such people than we imagine. But, worse, like Gene Heyman, Sally has forcefully taken the position that it is good to arrest drug users so that they can be coerced into treatment (see her 1999 book, *Drug Treatment: The Case for Coercion*). This has proven a sore point, as we will see around the Eldred case.

Carl Hart

Carl Hart is a one-person experiment. He emerged from the Miami ghetto, purposeful and intent and motivated not to use drugs, to the heights of academia (the first African American tenured science professor at Columbia, chair of the psychology department). Carl's remarkable journey is the first part of his best-selling memoir, *High Price*. He goes on to question our fundamental beliefs about drugs—that they cause people to misbehave, that they are inherently destructive and addictive. His views are captured in his quote: "Drugs are not the problem." His research shows that habituated meth users can readily switch off or change their drug use when given alternative rewards—which turn out to be rather small amounts of money. Carl's experience within the Miami community shows that drugs aren't the primary determinants of social environments—the continued poverty of inner cities like Miami persisted after the crack epidemic passed.

Carl's experiments with meth users are part of a well-established type of research that used to be called "behavioral pharmacology," where drug use is tested under different environmental conditions and with varied reward options. Charles Schuster did this kind of research at the University of Michigan animal labs Archie and I visited. So did Bruce Alexander, who created the "Rat Park" environment where rats refused a morphine solution in a large enclosure with wood chips and Ferris wheels and (most important of all) rats of the opposite gender.

I wrote a review of the cocaine animal-"addiction" literature (with Rich DeGrandpre) in 1998. Contrary to the image of rats stimulating their brains until they die, rodents and other mammals readily switch off from cocaine (like Carl's meth users) when offered appealing alternative rewards—which, for rats, include highly sweetened water. To summarize, rats would rather drink sufficiently sweetened solutions and have sex than take cocaine or opioids (remember how, in Chapter 3, I was baffled by the allure of heroin when I was unable to have an orgasm). Making use of this finding that addicted human beings will take money in place of drugs and alcohol, behavioral therapists have successfully used monetary rewards to wean people off drugs. But controlling people's lives in this way isn't a humane policy or lasting remedy. Neither does punishing people for drug use/addiction by imprisoning them.

Carl disdains drug policy reformers whose basic concern is psychedelics, while disparaging (often under the label "addictive") heroin, meth, and other drugs more commonly used by people of color and the poor. Carl accuses these middle-class druggies of "psychedelic exceptionalism"—a variety of white privilege—expressed in their regarding *their* drugs as okay while inner-city drugs are "bad." Nonetheless, Carl is highly sought after by drug policy reformers, and often speaks at their forums, occasionally with me. Reformers are tickled to find such an esteemed minority academic with his brilliant, iconoclastic view of drugs. But he's *too* iconoclastic even for them. Certainly for Sally Satel, as her reaction to him on the Vermont panel shows.

Carl is a skilled researcher and an excellent writer. But I often wonder about reactions of faculty, parents, and alumni at Columbia to someone who calmly reveals that he uses heroin. And this has materialized with the 2020 publication of his book, *Drug Use for Grown-Ups*, in which Carl continues his argument that drugs are a normal, largely positive part of life. For this reason, Carl dislikes the use of the term "harm reduction" as the primary way to approach drug use, a central point in my work as well.

What is most odd about my and Carl's relationship is that he has looked to me for signals on how to survive playing the renegade role in the addiction field. Carl wrote me: "I rarely read what others have to say about addiction. Frankly, I find most of this crap too boring, thoughtless, and cowardly. The exact opposite is true of your writing. Thank you for being a role model for me." Look to me as a role model? I, who have nothing? This from someone who holds a professorship at a major Ivy League institution, has written a contemporary best seller, and is seen as a beacon by people looking for new views on drugs?

But I *do* know how to get in trouble while seeming to be able to survive. The following is one strange tale from the blogpost that prompted that email from Carl in the last paragraph.

Escorted by Security from a National AA Board Meeting

Some ambitious member of AA's national board invited me to attend their annual meeting at a New York hotel. When I left my New Jersey house to attend, Mary asked, "*Where* are you going?" The man seemed well-meaning; he wanted to lift the blinkers from my eyes about what they did at AA. And I'll go anywhere.

During dessert we listened to three stories by recovering alcoholics. Each was supposed to talk ten minutes, but went on far longer. Two were verging-on-middle-aged men who had gone bad with alcohol after never having drunk it while growing up at home. The other speaker was a young tattooed woman who had descended into drugs. She had been homeless and lived in a cemetery for a time. *Her* story was the most interesting. At the hour-and-three-quarters point I leaned over to my host: "Are you as bored out of your skull as I am?"

I then went up to the head of AA's board, a distinguished Rockefeller University professor, and asked him, "Do you serve your children alcohol?" Surprised, he answered, "Yes." Me: "Don't you think that it would be valuable to explain to people here that you inoculate your children with that experience so that they won't end up like those two men did?" He smiled politely, "I don't think so." (How was that for scientific integrity and courage?) I then approached the woman who edited the legendary *AA Grapevine*, and asked if I could write an article about teaching young people to drink at home.

Soon after, my host whispered. "We're having security escort you out."

While praising me, Carl himself would never have such an interaction about AA. He couldn't even call out Holly Catania for making a fundamental attibution error (that pictured users deteriorated because they took meth) at a public symposium meant to dispel such myths! Nonetheless, with the publication of *Grown-Ups*, Carl now experiences the onslaught of disbelief that I have for decades. The review in the *New York Times* of his book is instantly, in its opening paragaph, disoriented and upset with Carl's announcement that he uses narcotics:

> It doesn't take long to get to what is perhaps the boldest and most controversial statement in Carl Hart's new book, "Drug Use for Grown-Ups: Chasing Liberty in the Land of Fear." In the prologue, he writes, "I am now entering my fifth year as a regular heroin user." In all honesty, I don't know how to feel about this admission. It's not easy to square all that I've learned about this drug with the image I also hold of Hart: a tenured professor of psychology at Columbia University, an experienced neuroscientist, a father.

As typical reactions like this indicate—like all the revisionist drug theorists I have described—Carl has little impact on drug policy and views about addiction. Such views have a life of their own in America. Meanwhile, Carl's ideas place him most decidedly in the non-disease camp. But Carl doesn't take on addiction per se ("he declares 'unapologetically' that his book is not about addiction"). He sees addiction as one of the bougie frames that psychedelic exceptionalists and other elitists apply to poor people's drug use. Of course, that is exactly why he should *want* to broaden, and deepen, our conceptions of addiction.

Carl isn't inclined to imagine addiction beyond drugs. Without a theory of addiction, Carl is thrown back on saying "some people become addicted due to social causes and emotional problems," and leaves it at that. His views on childrearing and addiction boil down to "tell them the truth about drugs."

Thus came my and Carl's breakup. Sally Satel, Marc Lewis, Nick Heather, Carl, and I, along with several other prominent addiction theorists, were on an Internet list, organized out of Britain, called Addiction Theory Network (ATN). The purpose of the list, as far as I and a number of others were concerned, was to attack the theoretical basis and dominance of the disease theory. Then, seemingly out of the blue, Carl and another list member named Pat O'Hare (who originated Harm Reduction International* and who has had me come to Liverpool to speak) attacked members of the list as ivory-tower academics with a masturbatory preoccupation with the disease theory. Instead, they should address inequality and the war on drugs.

---

* At the risk of sharing too much, in 1994, at the International Harm Reduction Conference, organized by what was then named the Addiction Research Foundation in Toronto, I was invited by Robin Room (then ARF's research director) as a featured speaker on the addiction concept. At a social event, I stripped down to my swim trunks and danced a few numbers (*not* slow dances) with Ethan. Pat O'Hare's wife took a photo of us, which Pat digs up and sends me every decade or so.

In exchanges on the list, Carl came out macho, telling people what he might do to them in a back alley. Watching all of this, Marc Lewis wrote me about Carl's attitude toward the other list members, which might fairly be called insulting. He asked me to say something on the list about it, while he laid low! Once again, how do I occupy this position of interposing myself between two professors and best-selling authors? People see me as their stalking horse for fighting battles around addiction. The situation reminded me of my role in the 1980s when, with no institutional armor to protect me, I became the go-to person in America for defending harm reduction—as a result of which I was personally and professionally ostracized.

It all struck me as so ludicrous and offensive that I publicized the dispute on Facebook, pissing everyone off, so that the list managers, Nick Heather and another old friend, Derek Heim, kicked me off the list.

Fair enough.

A month or two later I got an email from Carl—which I have still never had the guts to open!

But, a year later, I got an email from Carl asking me to call him, which I did. Carl was upset because he had always looked up to and sought communion with me and here I had attacked him. He was hurt! I apologized.

After my apology, we resumed being distant buddies. Carl wrote a blurb for my 2019 book with Zach Rhoads, *Outgrowing Addiction: With Common Sense Instead of "Disease" Therapy*. In fact, Marc Lewis, Sally Satel, and Nick Heather also wrote very nice blurbs on my and Zach's behalf— thank goodness they're all such forgiving people! Indeed, eventually Nick and Derek invited me to return to the list if I could behave myself. I asked them to hold the invitation in abeyance. Archie's response: "Perfect! Especially abeyance. You're right not to get back on, since you would likely re-offend everyone by being you."

Oh, when Zach interviewed Carl about his book, Carl described how he found direction for his views by reading my work in grad school in the 1990s, and how he appreciates the stress and conflict I have experienced throughout my career, as Carl now does. He even told Zach he appreciates Zach's support of me in the face of this ongoing opprobrium. As I told Zach, Carl's concern was touching!

Nick Heather on the Value of Attacking the Disease Theory

Nick Heather has long been an influential presence in my professional life. I will deal with his research on alcohol in the next chapter. However, he did write a response to Carl that I'll repeat here (with his permission) because of its admirably cogent and measured tone:

> Carl,
>
> I admire your work but to say that arguing about whether addiction is a disease is masturbation is silly and, frankly, offensive—at least to me. The understanding of addiction as a disease has very practical consequences:
>
> 1. It ensures that society's main response to the problem of addiction is the invention and promotion of yet more poisonous psychoactive substances to shove down people's throats. . . .When you call something a disease, this entitles you to do virtually anything you like to people who are labeled as having that disease, and all in the name of science.
> 2. The disease understanding deeply affects how people with problems of addiction understand their own predicament and what they should do about it. It destroys their confidence that they can recover, either on their own or with the help of friends and loved ones, which the evidence clearly shows they can. Of course, Stanton Peele, Gene Heyman and others have been eloquently making this point for many years.
> 3. The brain disease model now swallows up nearly all the world's funding for research on addiction and leaves paltry amounts for research on prevention and talking treatments. We desperately need to persuade policy-makers and politicians that there is an alternative to seeing addiction as a biological disease. This point is increasingly being made by people in the field. . . .
>
> As for the war on drugs, this is something I have passionately argued against for far longer than you have (over 50 years). But why should that prevent me from arguing against something that is strongly related to the war on drugs and may be, in the long run, equally important for social justice and the humane response to people's misfortunes and unhappiness?
>
> Keep up the good work and very best wishes,
>
> Nick
> Nick Heather Ph.D., Emeritus Professor of Alcohol & Other Drug Studies, Faculty of Health & Life Sciences, Northumbria University

The Failures of Ethan Nadelmann

Of all the figures I have known around addiction, the one I was closest to and spent the most time with, the one with whom I shared the most intimacy and contact between our families, the one I slept with the most (in separate beds) in the US and abroad, was Ethan Nadelmann.

Let me go back: I met Ethan in 1989 when he was still at Princeton University's Woodrow Wilson School of Public Policy and I was at Mathematica in nearby Plainsboro. I was sitting in my office when Ethan called. He told me he had read and admired my book, *The Meaning of Addiction,* and wanted to get together. We did—thus beginning a long, sometimes contentious relationship, and also a deep friendship, spanning the thirty-plus years since then. Before the pandemic, we hugged and kissed whenever we'd meet.

By strange happenstance, I was appearing on *Oprah* that week. Ethan thus saw me on television before ever meeting me. For the last several de-

Ethan in Central Park

cades, I have had to listen to Ethan say, "Stannin, you were clearly smarter than everybody on *Oprah* (the audience was stocked with AA buffs). But you pissed off everyone." Ethan was becoming nationally known for his drug legalization and harm reduction ideas. For Ethan, not appealing to an audience is a cardinal sin.

For a dozen years or so, Ethan and I got together every few months for long dinners in New York, where he moved after he left Princeton to head his Soros-funded drug reform group. Our connection covered every area of our lives. When Ethan contacted me in Princeton, his marriage was in trouble. I became his de facto therapist. Ethan found my help invaluable, which he told people—especially people who were wary of me— for decades. "Stanton didn't tell me what I should do. He only asked me questions."

Our families got together. Ethan knew my two older kids, and my younger daughter and Ethan's daughter were the same age. One momentous summer day Mary and I went to the beach with Ethan and his then-girlfriend. Ethan's girlfriend's aunt was the legendary cognitive therapist Albert Ellis's life partner. After the beach we went to their apartment above the Ellis Institute in Manhattan. I questioned Ellis late into the night about his pioneering work in cognitive behavioral therapy.*

---

* Ellis had written in praise of *Love and Addiction*, as had Ivan Illich, whose *Deschooling Society* Archie and I admired. I had visited Illich in Cuernavaca, where I stayed with the co-director of Illich's institute, Everett Reimer, whose son was a friend of mine at Michigan.

While Ethan was at Princeton, he received a grant from the Smart Family Foundation to convene a group of alcohol, drug, and addiction professionals to develop drug policy. He invited me to join. We met in Princeton in 1990 and 1991. Very academic, the group—sometimes twenty to thirty people—spun its wheels floating ideas about drug use and policy around a large table where we all sat. No book or other product came out of it. What Ethan was *really* doing was mulling over ideas in preparation for launching his own drug policy reform organization. (Thanks to Ethan for providing this and other information and dates.)

In 1994, with funding from George Soros, Ethan created The Lindesmith Center. * Ethan had an uncanny ability to appeal to radical thinkers and funders. In 2000 Ethan stepped up his real-world profile when he combined Lindesmith with the Drug Policy Foundation, another Soros group, into the Drug Policy Alliance. DPA gained strength, size, and influence, making it and Ethan critical players in American drug policy reform. Today, a strong majority of Americans favor legalizing marijuana, which is occurring in states around the country. Ethan was a central player in this historic movement. In a larger way, the Ethan-led DPA opened the US to the idea that drug policy wasn't a given—that Americans could, and should, evaluate and revise how we deal with drugs.

Ethan organized seminars at Lindesmith throughout the 1990s. He told me that I was—by far—the person who presented most often at these. In 1994, the year Ethan created The Lindesmith Center, he got the Drug Policy Foundation to present me its annual Career Achievement Award for Scholarship, worth $5,000. I became friendly with a young woman intern at The Lindesmith Center, Marianne Apostolides (now an award-winning Canadian writer). In 1996 she got a $5,000 grant for me to update for Lindesmith a pamphlet I had written originally for CompCare (like Hazelden, a Minneapolis disease-oriented publisher). This work concerned parents' and their kids' communications about drugs—*Don't Panic: A Parent's Guide to Understanding and Preventing Drug and Alcohol Abuse.*

Ethan also made me a senior fellow at Lindesmith, which gave me some official status. But, in general, Ethan kept me at arm's length with his organizations, especially the DPA. That early grant for the pamphlet and the Lindesmith award, along with funding for my debate about treatment

---

* Alfred Lindesmith was an Indiana sociologist, largely unacknowledged other than by Ethan (he died in 1991), who both presented a cognitive theory of addiction and argued for drug policy reform. Indeed, in the 1930s, Harry Anslinger, Johann's bête noir in *Chasing the Scream*, had Lindesmith investigated for being a drug addict!

in Washington, D.C., in 1996 (which I describe in Chapter 9), were the last money I ever received from an Ethan-led organization.

Ethan wrote a letter of recommendation for my application to Rutgers Law School in 1993. It included a line where Ethan gleefully imagined how I would deal with a law professor who said something ridiculous or if the school tried to stifle me—both of which happened, as I describe in Chapter 5. I asked Ethan to omit previewing my disruptiveness in his recommendation. In retrospect, Ethan's picture of me was of a guided missile against any organization I joined, which amused him—but not when it came to any organization he headed.

So, despite my frequent appearance at Lindesmith seminars, my writing for Lindesmith, and my winning an Ethan-sponsored award for my brilliance, Ethan, as CEO, was wary of me in the extreme. Nonetheless, through the 1990s and even into the early 2000s, Ethan and I remained intimates. I stayed at his apartment, shared his birthday dinners with him and his girlfriend and a few other New Yorkers, traveled to Canada and Australia with him, stayed together in hotel rooms abroad and in the US, etc. (One woman asked me if we were lovers.)

Ethan's emergence as a national and world figure reoriented our relationship, however. I was no longer a mentor, a role I to some extent had filled for him. Certainly, he had less time. But Ethan couldn't see my role on this larger world stage he now occupied. And Ethan was not naturally disposed toward being a helper, so he wasn't there for me when my marriage broke up.

Still, all in all, Ethan respected my mind, my thinking, my ideas—sometimes my suggestions. Ethan has acknowledged my central role in changing his thinking about addiction with *The Meaning of Addiction*. In this period from the 1990s through the early 2000s, when I was so alienated from the field, 12-step and disease-based as it was, Ethan's harm reduction policies offered me the greatest exposure and support.

But after the mid-1990s, I was tangential to Ethan's mission of replacing a drug policy steeped in legal regulation and criminal penalties with one based on a public health model. Ethan saw me as an impediment to his achieving rapprochement with the prevailing 12-step-based treatment system. In fact, Ethan never got support from the disease treatment monopoly, and instead received quite a bit of opposition. Meanwhile, throughout my period of DPA exile, individual DPA members continued to reach out to me sub rosa.

DPA, me, and harm reduction drug prevention

In 2015 DPA got a grant to create a drug education program for teens consistent with a harm reduction model—that is, something more balanced than the constant demonization of drugs. This was an important part of my addiction portfolio, as represented by my 2007 book, *Addiction-Proof Your Child*, and my earlier *Don't Panic* pamphlet with Marianne Apostolides. My view of addiction prevention is that there are many ways children can go wrong, and that giving them a firm foundation, based on positive values, skills, and independence, is the way for them to navigate the range of difficulties adolescence and young adulthood present, drug-related or otherwise. Zach Rhoads and I presented these themes in our 2019 book, *Outgrowing Addiction*.

In 2015 DPA hired "Drew," who had worked with students and teens on drug issues, to run its newly funded program. Drew was a friend of mine. I helped him with his application. He burrowed into the job and created an advisory board on which he included me as a central member—Drew loved my child-nurturing and strength-building approach, and he vowed to get funding to compact my *Addiction-Proof* book into a DPA pamphlet. But that didn't happen. I eventually created my own pamphlet with the material I developed for Drew, *Addiction-Proofing Your Family*, with an adolescent counselor, Kevin Gallagher.

Ethan fired Drew after less than two years. At the one meeting we had on Drew's project, with fifteen people around the table, Ethan came in, stood behind me, kissed my bald head, and said, "Who let Stanton in?" Drew invited me to the DPA conference in Washington, DC, in 2015 and gave me some featured panel slots. I made a good impression there—including a session that Ethan's long-time partner, Marsha Rosenbaum (who was also on Drew's group's board), moderated. Ethan gave me a thumbs-up after the conference, saying he had heard good reviews of my performance from his inner circle.

Shortly after, however, Drew was gone, the board disbanded and forgotten. Truth be told, Ethan had never been comfortable with what was called "harm reduction" youth prevention. For Ethan, the idea of preparing kids to take drugs, or at least recognizing that they would, was a cudgel that would be used to attack his larger goal of normalizing and regulating adult drug use.

Marsha Rosenbaum, meanwhile, developed DPA's alternative approach to drug education, called "Safety First Drug Education." Marsha—as does Carl—recommends providing adolescents with accurate information about drugs, rather than antidrug propaganda. Fair enough. But neither of them cares, or is able, to articulate an understanding of how to create a child, an adolescent, a young adult, who in turn becomes a mature adult, who is able to resist addiction, as my work does. (Marsha's course does recommend my *Addiction-Proof* book as additional reading.)

Stanton Peele, Untouchable

I can't leave the topic of youth drinking and drug use without mentioning my interaction with the former president of Middlebury College, John McCardle—actually, the lack of interaction. In 2008 McCardle organized a group of university presidents to lobby for lowering the drinking age so that the colleges could work to socialize drinking. Teaching young people how to drink on campuses (and earlier) is a favorite topic of mine. However, based on reactions to me and my work, I knew instantly that, despite his elite pedigree and great media coverage, McCardle was going on mission impossible in America. His organization, implausibly titled "Amethyst Initiative," quickly dissolved.

Sometime later I joined a panel with McCardle and other researchers and university personnel at the Purchase campus of the State University of New York. McCardle and I had corresponded briefly, after Ethan had put us in touch. McCardle was always standoffish toward me. He said nothing to me on the panel. When I approached him afterward, he walked away.

I had independent connections with a number of DPA staff members over the years—as with Marianne Apostolides and our *Don't Panic* pamphlet for parents. In 2014 Ethan's second in command, asha bandele, invited me to deliver a DPA Telephone Town Hall: "Dr. Stanton Peele on Reconsidering Addiction and Addiction Treatment." The prior speaker in this series had been Michelle Alexander, the author of *The New Jim Crow*, about the mass imprisonment of African Americans for low-level drug offenses. Carl Hart spoke next, after me, about education, where he intoned the advice to be honest with young people.

When DPA promoted my event, Scott Kellogg, an NYU clinical adjunct faculty, wrote Ethan on NYU stationary: "*I was dismayed to see that you are having an upcoming webinar with Dr. Stanton Peele on the nature of addiction and addiction treatment.*" Ethan forwarded Kellogg's letter to me with a laugh.

It was yet another demonstration of how I was connected to Ethan and DPA.

Ethan leaves DPA; the denouement of the Eldred case

Ethan himself never had me speak to his staff. Just before Ethan left DPA, in 2017, he came for the first time to my backhouse apartment in Park Slope, Brooklyn, and we reminisced. In the meantime, Ethan and the head of DPA's board, Ira Glasser, former director of the ACLU, began a search for Ethan's replacement. After almost twenty years, there was no one within DPA, or that Ethan had cultivated, to replace him. Ethan was not one to share power, or to nurture anyone to replace him. One main candidate, asha, left DPA when she was passed over.

Ethan and Ira ended up choosing as his replacement Maria McFarland Sánchez-Moreno, who assumed DPA leadership in September 2017. Maria lasted about two years, announcing that she was leaving for Human Rights Watch at the beginning of 2020. An international human rights advocate and writer, Maria—and the team of managers she brought with her—were a poor fit with DPA. Early in her tenure, Ethan suggested that Maria and I have lunch. I could tell instantly that she couldn't replace Ethan. Who could? She wasn't a brilliant speaker and fundraiser like Ethan. Within a year DPA cut a quarter of its staff and closed a number of its state offices. More fundamentally, however, Maria couldn't advance the American drug policy, addiction, and political agenda.

After Ethan had stepped down, before Maria came on board, I learned that DPA was supposedly submitting an amicus (friend-of-the-court) brief to Massachusetts' highest court supporting the brain-disease model of addiction in the Massachusetts Elder case (which Johann supported and invited me to do). I shifted into high gear, attacking this sell-out around the Internet. Eventually, DPA responded with a statement by its director of legal affairs:

> DPA has agreed to assist the petitioner in this challenge to the court's authority to order her to be drug free as a condition of probation and to incarcerate her for not remaining drug free. However, DPA is not signing onto the petitioner's brief and arguments. Rather DPA is authoring its own amicus brief—which is not yet complete—that will be filed on behalf of DPA and other amici (interested parties). DPA's brief will not focus on the brain disease theory and will be fully consistent with our support for all drug decriminalization for drug users with substance use disorder and without.

This statement had the following sequelae:

- Eldred's attorney wrote me blaming me for creating a "firestorm" that forced DPA to withdraw its support for her brief.
- Johann attacked me publicly for my role.

- Ethan told me (as DPA claims in its announcement) that DPA never intended to support the brain disease brief.
- *In fact, DPA never submitted any brief at all.*
- Sally Satel wrote an amicus brief (signed by Gene Heyman and several distinguished law professors) *opposing the disease argument and in support of imprisoning drug users to deter drug use and to force them into treatment.*
- *I submitted the only brief that (a) opposed the brain disease argument and also (b) opposed the incarceration of anyone solely due to their drug use.*
- The Massachusetts Supreme Judicial Court declined to declare the disease theory valid as grounds for avoiding incarceration for violation of probation.

Julie Eldred had been released long before this high court decision. She had spent ten days in prison before resuming her legally coerced 12-step and Suboxone treatments. Such coercion into treatment remains prevalent.

The 2020 election: Ethan's ultimate existential failures

To this day, Ethan cannot forthrightly acknowledge this series of events: that DPA failed to fulfill its purpose of supporting a non-disease basis for opposing incarceration of drug users. This is part of the legacy that Ethan has left in his wake. The chief component of this legacy, of course, is the unchallenged dominance of the disease theory for how we confront our never-ending, always-growing drug woes, most especially the decades-long accelerating epidemic of deaths among deprived white and Black Americans.

But even in the area that originally spurred Ethan, the decriminalization of drug use, embodied by America's widespread acceptance of legalized marijuana, we are taking two steps backward. Ethan, to his credit, has also sought to decriminalize all drugs, even those like heroin and meth that Ethan and other privileged people (as Carl Hart describes) don't use. In 2020, DPA sponsored (with Ethan's backing) a referendum in the progressive state of Oregon. DPA announced its passage thus: "Drug Policy Action's Measure 110 PASSES - DECRIMINALIZING ALL DRUGS in Oregon!!!"

But that law wasn't the "Decriminalizing All Drugs Act." Never mentioned by DPA is Oregon Measure 110's actual name: "Decriminalization and Addiction Treatment Initiative." The main argument for passing it was the claim that "Oregonians need adequate access to drug addiction treatment," which it was claimed that it didn't now have. The chief purpose of the Act was to divert people caught for simple possession (which was still a criminal misdemeanor) to "Addiction Recovery Centers." These centers are designed "to immediately assess the needs of people who use drugs and link drug users to treatment that is evidence-based."

Treatment for what? Using drugs. Can't they volunteer for treatment on their own should they want it? What kind of treatment will be mandated? In Oregon, and everywhere else, the vast majority of treatment is abstinence from people's drugs of choice. "Evidence-based treatment," as described, means forcing them to take Suboxone (buprenorphine and naloxone) and methadone, or MAT. Zach and my "Sundays with Stories" podcast addressed the meaning and applicability of "evidence-based." Something is lost in translation from the laboratory to the real world, as I describe in the previous chapter.

MAT now dominates the American drug treatment and legal landscape. Drug deaths haven't slowed. They've increased. In response, I and my colleagues have launched at my online Life Process Program (LPP) a coaching program for MAT recipients, headed by an LPP coach who works in the MAT field, Aaron Ferguson. Our coaches work to use the space created by prescribed opioids to help MAT recipients further their overall lives. The hope is that they can then fully emerge from addiction, *without regarding themselves as lifelong addicts,* as MAT teaches them they are.

My Advice to DPA

I have said that I am no longer welcome speaking in North America. I was perhaps premature in declaring the death of my speaking career. I contracted to make several appearances in 2020: the Annapolis (MD) Book Festival, three workshops and speeches in Canada (in Edmonton, Richmond, and Winnipeg), and, as invited by Jules Netherland, to "help educate DPA's staff" on the disease theory of addiction. *The first four were called off due to the coronavirus epidemic.* Note that none of these engagements were at an American university, treatment center, or addiction conference.

As for the cancelled events, I was disappointed not to speak in Canada, especially in British Columbia, Gabor Maté's home province.* The DPA seminar was a video conference that proceeded as planned. I tried to show DPA staff that DPA's support for the disease theory (more by inaction than action) violated their mission. Allowing the disease theory to propagate un-

---

* My Canadian workshops have now been rolled into a presentation at a virtual "Trauma and Addiction" conference in May 2021. Gabor is the featured speaker. My talk is titled: "Harm Reduction, The Disease Model, and Trauma." I wonder how that will go.

opposed *itself contributed to making drug use an aberrant and unnecessarily destructive activity.* Like former DPA board member Carl Hart, I argue that drug use and drinking have to be placed in a normal, socially regulated place in our lives. To instead demonize drugs by portraying them as beyond an individual's control, despite their ubiquity in our world, was to foster the toxic environment we now have. Today, the most vulnerable turn to drugs and, in a self-fulfilling prophecy, are often overwhelmed by them.

I have repeatedly written about the impossibility of prohibition and universal abstemiousness—i.e., "zero tolerance." I laid out my views in 2014 on how to incorporate drugs, along with alcohol, into modern human existence in another piece in *Pacific Standard*, "We Need to Normalize Drug Use in Our Society." I noted that, "after the disastrous misconceptions of the twentieth century, we need to return to the idea that drugs are an ordinary part of life experience and no more cause addiction than do other behaviors." I enlarged on this perspective in *Filter* in 2020 in a piece called "Beyond Harm Reduction: Encouraging Positive Drug Use," in which I cited cultural styles of drinking as exemplars of incorporating the use of a powerful substance in positive ways. All of this anticipates Carl Hart's *Drug Use for Grown-Ups*.

I spoke by video to DPA's policy staff. (Lest this be seen as a sign of my re-emergent influence, neither the acting nor designated future CEO participated.) In place of what DPA has been doing, I proposed ten steps for DPA's policy group to genuinely decriminalize and normalize drug use and to empower users.

Ten Steps for DPA

1. *Don't think in terms of "addicts," "alcoholics" and "treatable diseases."*
2. Regard addiction as a negative life state and a way of relating to the world.
3. Strengthen non-disease-based (i.e., things other than AA) communities.
4. Enhance people's purpose and connection—make their lives worth living.
5. Address people's basic needs: health, home, family, work, life skills.
6. *Foster people's belief that they can control their lives.*
7. Support the choice to use or not, and mindful use of, *all* drugs and alcohol.
8. Assist people who use drugs and who drink to do so safely and healthily.

9. Cease criminalizing and decrying drug use and drinking alcohol.
10. *Regard drug use and drinking alcohol as normal human experiences.*

But, despite some signs that we are moving in these directions (like Nora Volkow's late-career conversion), we are largely doing the reverse of everything on this list. And DPA was sliding down the same trail, even pushing us down it.

11

The Cultural Contexts and Politics of Alcohol and Drugs

I am as present in the alcohol/alcoholism
field as the drug/addiction one.

No one has crossed the boundaries of the addiction fields, from drugs to alcohol to love and sex to gambling. I am present in all of them, and an outsider in all of them.

Everyone knows your positions, Stanton.
— Robin Room, Ph.D., pre-eminent WHO alcohol epidemiologist,
past president, Kettil Bruun Society for Social and Epidemiological
Research, currently director of the Centre for Alcohol
Policy Research at La Trobe University, Australia

Stanton and I were both invited to talk about drinking cultures in Florence by Forum Droghe, an NGO active in the drug area. On that occasion I gave a lecture on Italian drinking culture challenging the dominant thought that affirmed the change of Italian drinking culture toward a Nordic drinking culture. I was attacked by one participant belonging to one Italian public institution followed by a heated and controversial debate in which Stanton Peele threw gasoline on the fire. After almost ten years I still meet people who were present at that seminar with a vivid memory of that moment.
— Franca Beccaria, Ph.D., past president, Kettil
Bruun Society for Social and Epidemiological
Research on Alcohol, Turin, Italy

Crossing the Boundaries of Addiction

Before me—and still largely to this day—two different groups of thinkers and researchers study drugs and addiction and drinking and alcoholism. In addition, at the time we wrote *Love and Addiction*, smoking wasn't considered an addiction. As I describe in Chapter 8, the famed 1964 *Surgeon General's*

Report on Smoking didn't label nicotine addictive—it said that nicotine was habituating. Only in 1988 did the Surgeon General "officially" apply the label in the volume *Nicotine Addiction.*

Separate movements expanded to study the range of addictive behaviors, including sex and love, et al. But I will *never* be invited to the annual conference of SASH (Society for the Advancement of Sexual Health) or other sexual addiction conferences. In order to prove their legitimacy, these are *devoted* to "proving" sex is addictive with *highly* speculative and tangential brain scans. Remember, *DSM-5* refused to declare sex addictive because, it claimed, sex doesn't produce the defining addictive brain waves, which I wrote about in national magazines *Psychology Today* (2010) and *Reason* (2014).

At the same time, I am regarded as a touchstone in the one area of behavior that the American Psychiatric Association currently regards as addictive—gambling—and have written a seminal article in that field for Canada's Centre for Addiction and Mental Health (CAMH). Although this last article appeared in this century, and in 1978 I gave the keynote address at CAMH's predecessor's (the Addiction Research Foundation's) national conference, and spoke frequently thereafter at its home office in Toronto, I am no longer welcome there.

At the same time as I crossed subject matters with our chapter, "A General Theory of Addiction," in *Love and Addiction*, I crossed disciplines willy-nilly. I leaped from epidemiological surveys of alcohol and drug use to laboratory studies of drugs with animals, to clinical research with alcoholics and heroin addicts, to naturalistic field studies of drinkers and heroin users, and to comparable research with eating and obesity, smoking, gambling, and sex and intimate relationships.

Since I respected no boundaries in my thinking, I belonged to—and was welcomed by—no group. In this chapter I discuss my work with alcohol, both clinically (therapeutically) and epidemiologically (statistically over groups and larger populations) in the United States and cross-culturally. I have largely been rejected by every group that deals with alcohol and alcoholism, in the US and worldwide, even as many of them acknowledge my role in the field.

Griffith Edwards was the long-time editor of the *British Journal of Addiction*, which became the most prestigious international journal in the field, *Addiction*. Edwards invited me to answer the question for his journal, "How Can Addiction Occur with Other than Drug Involvements?" in 1985. I say in the abstract:

> An increasing recognition of the possibility of addiction with regard to activities other than drug use seems to call for a re-evaluation of key strands of thought about the nature of addiction, namely its relationship to the biological substratum and the relevance of cultural and individual interpretation of experience in addiction.

The same year, Edwards reviewed *The Meaning of Addiction* in that journal, first praising, and then eviscerating me while changing my name from "Peele" to "Steele." Both sides of his review are included in my Wikipedia entry.

My recognition that addiction is a broader category of behavior than drugs and alcohol disproves the disease theory. Despite being highlighted in the pre-eminent international addiction journal as having revolutionized thinking in the field, I am persona non grata in *Addiction*. I describe my rejection there in the Conclusion.

The "Public Health" Model of Alcoholism

Key worldwide figures—Griffith Edwards, Robin Room, Jürgen Rehm, and Thomas Babor, from the UK, Australia, Canada, and US respectively—have created the alcohol public health model. The model claims that alcohol problems, including alcoholism, are a direct result of the amount of alcohol consumed. What an appealing, direct notion that is. It is wrong and harmful in all of its implications.

A public health advocate says, "If you drink more, you are alcoholic, even though (a) I and my friends drink a lot in positive contexts without problems and (b) consumption is decreasing in my society and problems are increasing."

I was invited to Ireland in 2018 to do a lecture and several workshops by Liam O'Loughlin (who insisted that I name-check him). Liam is committed to my approach of enhancing people's lives as the best solution for addiction and alcoholism. Moreover, he was an influencer in Galway province, which recently had seen consumption levels fall but alcohol problems increase. Liam is such a public health model believer that he repeatedly announced during my visit: "Drinking is increasing in Galway." I just as regularly corrected him, "Liam, that's not true: problems are increasing while consumption is falling."

Liam is a wonderful man, devoted to his job of supporting helpers for the most downtrodden in Galway, has friends everywhere, and has been with one partner since college with whom he has four children (the oldest in her mid-teens) to whom he and his wife are wonderful, devoted parents. Although I publicly called Liam out for his consistently misspeaking about drinking in Galway, I also described love addiction during my talk. I cited Liam and his wife as examples of non-addicted love. Liam agreed: "We're absolutely not addicted to each other! We do share a strong bond based on trust and nearly thirty years of experience that makes it feel really worthwhile being together."

Let me illustrate the positive role of alcohol in human socialization by describing dinner the evening before my 2018 presentation in County Galway. At dinner with me were Liam, another public health model advocate, my (Northern) Irish business partner Daithi Conlon, and a leading Irish cognitive behavioral psychologist and motivational interviewing teacher.

Before dinner, Liam took me to pick up another speaker at the conference to take to the hotel. *After* dinner, Liam took me to a pub for a nightcap Guinness where he ran into other people he knew and had a drink or two with them. *At* dinner, the five of us shared several bottles of wine and some Irish whiskey. At dinner, everyone told stories and made serious points, was a thoughtful listener, laughed and enjoyed themselves. (Of course, I have had similar drug experiences, including at DPA conferences.) All of us were embedded in our families and committed to our work. We drank in a supportive, mindful, and stimulating setting.

Being engaged in meaningful activities and relationships in a supportive group or community is the best guarantee of avoiding addiction.

Everything else is a stopgap measure, bound more or less to fail. Begging people not to use drugs or drink, punishing or treating them for doing so, and creating elaborate theories of the irresistible addictiveness of this or that substance are fool's errands.

How Come I Didn't Become an Addict?

People study and discuss how and why people, why *they themselves*, became addicted. I, on the other hand, relish how and why people avoid or emerge from addiction and alcoholism. I love to read about people like Lindsay Lohan's and Drew Barrymore's and Robert Downey Jr.'s unscripted recoveries; nothing pleases me more than human resilience and resurgence.

I also love to read about people who avoided addiction despite their exposure to drugs. I have taken virtually every type of drug: I took heroin with my college girlfriend's roommates, psychedelics with a friend who became a major art museum curator, and marijuana with him and a college dorm neighbor and Penn basketball player. Mary and I smoked marijuana and took LSD after our children were self-reliant. After my divorce, I smoked marijuana with my jazz trumpeter friend, had marijuana-infused candy with Ethan, and sampled my Anglo-American girlfriend Eileen's prescription Adderall, an amphetamine used to enhance concentration and intensify pleasure. I used to hang out at bars (when that was possible) with my jazz friend and a younger bartender who worked at the leading hip bars in Brooklyn (see front matter quotations) and gave me booze and beer for free.

At the dinner in Galway, I drank everything people offered. After the wine and before the Guinness Stout, the prickly, picky public health specialist who thinks that free-flowing alcohol causes alcoholism ordered an Irish whiskey. I doubled down on his order, as did everyone else at the table. Why not? I was in Ireland, the man really knew the good things in life, and I wasn't paying. In fact, I prefer to say yes when offered drugs and alcohol. Being plied by your peer group is often cited as the cause of drug and alcohol problems. Yet, that's part of my antidote for alcoholism and addiction.

- I usually use drugs when the people around me do—I never initiate drug seeking or go to a bar unless it's happy hour or to meet friends. (I do drink alcohol at home, or when dining alone, and did drugs at home with Mary.)
- I enjoy being with constructive people who have purposeful lives and positive values—like those I had dinner with in Galway, and not only then.
- I, of course, even in the darkest hours of my professional life, have always been preoccupied with my purpose and career.

I described in Filter how and why I and others drink alcohol and take drugs successfully during the pandemic; why that's a *good* thing. I am personally not an alcoholic/drug addict candidate. I realize that I have many privileges and life satisfactions, the absence of which allows—encourages—addiction and alcoholism. And how do we remedy that? Tell people never to take drugs like painkillers (I've had both of my knees replaced) or never to drink? Really? That makes sense?

My approach works remarkably well for the large majority of people who don't become addicted or alcoholic or who emerge, in the vast majority of cases, from these damaging involvements. My ex-wife Mary and Archie, both of whom have alcoholism in their bloodlines, relied on the same life techniques. Most people (like the 99 percent who *don't* have problems with prescribed painkillers) do the same. I described in *7 Tools to Beat Addiction* how the *National Household Survey on Drug Use and Health* asked about people's lifetime, past year, and current drug use.

> In 2002 [the survey no longer asks these detailed timeline questions] 46 percent of all Americans over age twelve had tried an illicit substance. However, only 15 percent have used in the past year and only 8 percent have used in the past month. More than 14 percent of Americans have tried cocaine, but fewer than 1 percent have used it within the last month. Only 1.5 percent of Americans have ever used heroin, but just one-tenth of 1 percent have used it within the past month. In other words, *of all people who have ever used cocaine or heroin, just over 5 percent continue to use it currently (the same holds for crack cocaine). But that only applies to monthly use, not even weekly or, certainly, daily use* (my emphasis).

This picture of drug use, based on the broadest government epidemiological research, is the one Carl Hart paints in *Drug Use for Grown-Ups*.

For some reason (because the percentages are so small), the Household Survey keeps eliminating categories measuring recent periods of drug use. The 1988 survey, following the height of the cocaine addiction scare, found that twenty-one million Americans had used cocaine in their lives, eight million had used it in the last year, and three million were current (last week) users, but that only 300,000 used cocaine daily or nearly every day. *Government statistics during the height of the 1980s cocaine panic thus showed that 10 percent of all then-current users, and about 1.5 percent of those who had ever used cocaine, currently used the drug close to daily.*

People are just not inclined to be addicted to drugs, or even to use them regularly, in normal life circumstances. Although many more people drink than take heroin or cocaine, these usual human processes are at work with drinking.

Sociologist Barry Glassner investigated "How Jews Avoid Alcohol Problems." Although epidemiological surveys (like Cahalan and Room, below) have always shown that Jews have extremely low problem-drinking rates, people have always loved reporting increasing Jewish alcoholism. Hearing this, Glassner searched, but wasn't able to find, any Jewish alcoholics in his midsized upstate New York city.

When Glassner questioned Jewish respondents, they described a natural process for controlling their drinking:

1. Their drinking was self-determined (i.e., they rejected culturally the disease model of alcoholism), so that Jews as a group said they only drank as much as they wanted to, when and if they chose.

2. They associated mainly with non-problem drinkers, like themselves.

3. They identified their moderate drinking with who they were, including their Jewish culture.

Returning to drugs, I described taking my girlfriend's Adderall. That drug was good! At the time I was working with people in senior care facilities, which could grind you down. I breezed through a day's interviews and therapy and felt elated going to and from the care centers. But I wasn't going to resort to the drug casually. It was too much trouble for me to obtain the drug by getting a diagnosis for adult attention deficit disorder and seeing a physician regularly to re-up my prescription. It just wasn't worth it to me, just as I wouldn't spend a lot of time at bars or drink all the time because it would cost too much money and interfere with my life in fundamental ways.

And that's exactly what Chris Johanson found. (You may recall that she and her husband, former National Institute on Drug Abuse and, before that, Michigan animal lab director Charles "Bob" Schuster, were among my few institutional supporters.) In a series of experimental sessions with students and workers at the University of Chicago, Johanson first gave subjects amphetamines. These young university people uniformly found the effects of the drugs positive, elevating. Yet, in subsequent sessions, when given the choice to take the drugs, they became less willing to do so.

Why? Despite its measured positive rewards for users, subjects found that the drug disrupted their daily routines of work and studying, which they were engaged in to further their lives and to enhance good feelings about themselves and their futures. That is, it interfered with something more fundamental for them than pleasure. So they eschewed the drug.

Glassner and Johanson, respectively, did life-observation and experimental research that fill in Gene Heyman's analyses of massive, but impersonal, surveys of Americans' drug use and the life factors that surround their use. *All* research shows that those with the most resources, the most to lose, and the strongest connections to society reject regular, disruptive, addictive drug and alcohol use. It's just common sense, the normal human balancing of pleasure and survival. And this research points the way to the best therapeutic techniques—those that enhance people's life connectedness. Understanding the relationships between these factors and addiction is the best science. *Ignoring this reality, on the other hand, is the source of our disastrous cultural attitudes toward drugs and, we shall also see, alcohol.*

You Are What You Believe

In the 1970s, '80s, and '90s, a group of brilliant British and American psychologists tested the role of people's beliefs in causing alcoholic drinking. In 1973 Alan Marlatt, an American, tested the notion that diagnosed alcoholics were set off ("lost control") by any taste of alcohol. Marlatt provided extreme alcoholics with heavily flavored drinks that either contained alcohol or did not, and informed them either erroneously or accurately that their drinks contained alcohol or did not. The subjects drank more when they *thought* their drinks contained alcohol, but not due to the drinks' *actual* alcohol content. (Such research is impermissible today.)

In the 1980s, Nick Heather, a British researcher, did studies comparing the outcomes of treatment for alcoholism based on people's beliefs about alcoholism and their self-concepts of being alcoholic. Heather found that people treated for drinking problems who endorsed the idea that one-drink meant one-drunk (which Heather and colleagues called "a cultural delusion of alcoholics") were more likely to relapse following treatment. In the 1990s, another American, William Miller, measured traits of people entering alcohol treatment and their likelihood of relapsing. He and his colleagues found that those who *believed that alcoholism was a disease* were more likely to relapse following treatment.

Heather and colleagues conducted another 1980s study of those in alcoholism treatment, in this case comparing an objective measure of people's alcohol dependence with a subjective measure. Those who *thought of themselves as alcoholics were more likely to relapse after drinking than those whose clinical profile declared them to be alcoholics*. Jim Orford, also British, did a similar study in 1986, in this case comparing alcoholic drinkers who were assigned to either abstinence or moderation treatment. Drinkers did better at moderation based on their subjective views of their drinking problems and personal preferences, more so than their objective alcohol dependence, which had no impact, indicated.

This research, taken together, showed that how people conceived of addiction and whether they saw themselves as being addicted (in this case to alcohol) were critical determinants of whether they behaved in an addicted manner—that is, *of whether they in fact were addicted*.

Jim Orford

In this chapter I describe the decades-long relationships I have had with several cognitive-behavioral alcohol-problem psychologists—Nick Heather, Alan Marlatt, Bill Miller—and yet another bête noire, Robin Room (an anti-alcohol epidemiologist). Jim Orford, a British psychologist, isn't one of them. I rarely corresponded with him. I met him once, in Bath, England, at an anti-disease conference, where we spoke together as featured speakers. Jim quite nicely came up to me to introduce himself.

Orford and I share a view of alcohol, addictive behavior, and treatment. Moreover, our careers coincide remarkably. Orford comes from a social-organizational psychology background. He applies a cultural-family-community mindset to alcohol problems. He thinks in terms of human experience:

> Getting down to the details of personal experience is, I see now, one of the continuing themes of my career. The other is a concern to understand how personal experience is shaped by, and shapes, the collective experience of the groups of people of which a person is a part. . . . Social class is traditionally more of a sociological subject of study, but it is profoundly important psychologically. As an undergraduate at Cambridge I was rather shocked to meet people who had had an even more privileged background than I had. Income and wealth inequality were actually decreasing at that time, and we believed that society would continue to become more equitable, less hierarchical. Now, post the 1980s, inequality and its social and psychological effects have been on the increase. The psychological study of inequality, one of the things that is at the heart of community psychology, should be a priority.

Orford's 1986 subjective alcohol dependence and controlled drinking research discussed above was bold work when it appeared—although, per usual, the UK was many degrees cooler in its controlled-drinking hysteria than the US. Orford (and Keddie's) piece was published in the prestigious *British Journal of Addiction* (now *Addiction*), as my work had recently (1985) been. I was never to appear there again.

Orford has worked well within the bounds of British addictionology. He certainly has been in synch with Griffith Edwards. Indeed, Orford came into the addiction field with a groundbreaking research project he conducted under Edwards's auspices, a comparison of minimal treatment, or simply advising people to cut back their drinking, versus extended treatment. Outcomes were the same in each case. The investigators did touch back with their "advice" patients over time. They found that the social stability of the drinkers was a critical element in their remission. But advising people nonjudgmentally about the consequences of their drinking and laying out alternatives for them to pursue, often with a family member (wife) present, helped as much as did receiving intensive alcoholism treatment.

This research appeared in 1977, just as I had completed *Love and Addiction* and turned my attention toward alcoholism. The "advice" study has since flowered into a widely deployed subspecies of alcohol treatment called "brief interventions" (BIs). BIs coalesced with my abiding interest in natural recovery, or outgrowing addiction (recall that Winick announced natural recovery from heroin addiction in 1962). In 1983, in the heat of the anti-controlled-drinking witch-hunt, I appeared on a panel with the leading controlled-drinking researchers (Marlatt, Miller, the Sobells, Heather) in Washington, DC, at the national conference of behavioral psychologists. I gave a keynote talk titled "Behavior Therapy—the Hardest Way: Controlled Drinking and Natural Remission from Alcoholism," in which I described how less was more.

In 1985, the same year I published *The Meaning of Addiction* and ten years after *Love and Addiction*, Orford published his best-known book, *Excessive Appetites: A Psychological View of Addictions*, which featured non-drug addictions, including food and love. Unlike Orford, I don't believe there is a "psychological view," on the one hand, and some other view of addictions. The question I have always addressed is "What is addiction?"

A Brief American History of Loss of Control in Addiction and Alcoholism

I describe in Chapters 9 and 10 how harm reduction–oriented, non-abstinence techniques are more widely accepted in America today than they were a generation ago. Yet the view that beliefs determine addiction and treatment outcomes is less accepted—is to some degree almost non-existent—even among harm reductionists. Why do even revisionist theorists reject a cognitive, social-learning vision of addiction? They are unable to escape the American visions of drugs and addiction.

The idea that people lose control of their personal volition through the consumption of alcohol or drugs is a modern creation, for which Nora Volkow is (or was, see Chapter 9) the contemporary (21st century) prophet with her shiny new brain-disease model. But that general belief about drugs goes back much farther through the twentieth century, and even earlier with alcohol, where it goes back to Temperance.

In the nineteenth century, massive amounts of opioid mixtures were consumed in the US and UK—they were given to teething children, used in patent medicines, and sold on street corners, and, at the end of the century, they were a part of every doctor's black bag. This creates a difficulty for historians who want to show the inherent addictiveness of drugs. *How, for Pete's sake, could they have been so ignorant? How could people who used substances all the time not know that the substances were unavoidably addictive, or that they were drug addicts?*

Howard Markel confronted this dilemma in *An Anatomy of Addiction: Sigmund Freud, William Halsted and the Miracle Drug, Cocaine.* For starters, Sigmund Freud and William Halsted were pioneering geniuses whose work underlies modern psychiatry and medicine. Freud, of course, invented psychoanalysis. Plenty of people question Freud's theories and therapy today. But the ideas that people's childhood experiences influence who they become and how they see the world, and that people are often unaware of the dynamics of feeling and thought that condition their actions, are an engrained part of modern consciousness.

Halsted in large part invented modern surgery. "He emphasized strict aseptic technique during surgical procedures, was an early champion of newly discovered anesthetics, and introduced several new operations, including radical mastectomy for breast cancer. . . . His operating room at Johns Hopkins Hospital was described as a small room where medical discoveries and miracles took place."

An Anatomy of Addiction thus confronts a contradiction described in its Amazon write-up: the book "tells the tragic and heroic story of each man, accidentally struck down in his prime by an insidious malady." Yet, while "Markel writes of the physical and emotional damage caused by the then-heralded wonder drug," he also details "how each man changed the world in spite of it—or because of it."

They revolutionized psychological thinking and medical practice *because* of cocaine? In fact, Freud gave up cocaine relatively early in his career due its negative effects. As I have described, this is people's standard response to cocaine and opioid problems. In my 1991 review of *The Steel Drug*, a study by Addiction Research Foundation investigators, when cocaine occasionally has a negative impact on people's lives, and they have other options, they limit or quit it:

> The large majority of those exposed to cocaine have used it infrequently. The few studies of regular cocaine users other than clinical patients find that a majority maintain controlled use, while even fairly heavy users only infrequently report addictive symptoms. . . . Twenty percent of the subjects reported uncontrollable urges to continue use. Yet, in the case descriptions of problem users, nearly all had quit or cut back without actually receiving treatment for cocaine addiction.

In 1995, the World Heath Organization conducted an international study of cocaine use which found, unsurprisingly, the same results. WHO suppressed the study.

For Freud, aside from the energy and pain relief it gave him, he "loved how cocaine made him talk endlessly about memories and experiences he previously thought were locked in his brain." Markel notes that Freud relied on his drug experiences for his breakthroughs in interpreting dreams and encouraging patients to free associate. For Halsted, a knowledge of cocaine (and morphine, which he was also thought to use) would seem helpful for his introducing modern surgical anesthesia.

Virginia Berridge noted in *Opium and the People* (1981) that, despite the near-universal use of laudanum, addiction was not associated with opiates in nineteenth-century England. Following the introduction of morphine, Berridge found "little evidence that there were large numbers of morphine addicts in the late nineteenth century." Based on such historical analyses, in 1990 I wrote "Addiction as a Cultural Concept" for the *Annals of the New York Academy of Sciences:*

> Our current conception of addiction is a historical anomaly, one that has arisen independent of laboratory or epidemiological data about drug use. This concept has never reflected actual patterns of heroin use, and it currently does no better at describing cocaine use. Neither this vision of heroin addiction nor an equally popular, complementary model of alcoholism accurately reflects data on the cause, epidemiology, life history or consistency of addictive behavior. Nonetheless, versions of addictions based on these images of narcotic addiction and alcoholism have become increasingly popular in the second half of the twentieth century and have been generalized to whole new areas of behavior, where they succeed no better at explaining the data. These concepts, moreover, have considerable potential for doing harm.

Thank God for our discovery and implementation of the idea that drugs like cocaine and opioids make us lose all control and lead us to addiction and death! Please excuse my outburst. But this is the self-fulfilling prophecy that marks modern America.

The central, crucial idea of loss-of-control as a biological imperative, i.e., addiction, was not invented with reference to drugs, however. It occurred with alcohol, at the end of the Colonial American era. Drinking was a social-controlled, cohesive force in Colonial America, often involving the tavern as a community and family center. From 1780 to 1830, this image of alcohol and drinking changed, and the disease notion was invented, then propagandized by the Temperance Movement throughout the nineteenth century, culminating in national Prohibition in the early twentieth century. It was further popularized by AA (founded in 1935, two years after the end of Prohibition) throughout the latter twentieth century, and was amplified and reified by the modern neuroscientific era, beginning in the late 1970s. From the late 1990s the chronic brain disease model was spread worldwide by the National Institute on Drug Abuse and its director, Nora Volkow, along with NIDA's junior partner, the National Institute on Alcohol Abuse and Alcoholism.

Before the modern era, people were certainly known to be addicted to alcohol and drugs. But addiction—then taken to mean having an overwhelming habit—was also applied to coffee and tea, gambling, love relationships, etc. The contemporary expansion of the application of addiction into this broader arena is thus a return to the roots of the word. The current Oxford English Dictionary definition of addiction is: "the fact or condition of being addicted to a particular substance, thing, or activity" (a definition that was impacted by *Love and Addiction*). Yet OED defines "addicted" as "physically and mentally dependent on a particular substance [which substances are those, and what happened to 'thing or activity'?], and unable to stop taking it without incurring adverse effects." But people suffer "adverse effects" when leaving a love relationship (breakups being the major cause of suicide and murder) or quitting gambling or trying to shed their iPhones. Adding to the conceptual confusion is Oxford's "informal definition" of addiction: "enthusiastically devoted to a particular thing or activity, as in, 'he's addicted to computers'." So the historic meaning and use of the term is new again. The future is itching to return to the past.

Alcohol as Evil: The Public Health Model

Alcohol cannot be portrayed in a sustained, positive way in the US, although its beneficial effects were acknowledged in the 2010 *Dietary Guidelines for Americans*, which I wrote about in the *L.A. Times*. Those guidelines declared that "the lowest mortality risk for men and women [occurs] at the average level of one to two drinks per day, [and] is likely due to the protective effects of moderate alcohol consumption on CHD [coronary heart disease], diabetes and ischemic stroke." In addition, "Moderate evidence suggests that compared to non-drinkers, individuals who drink moderately have a slower cognitive decline with age."

However, in 2020, the National Institute on Alcohol Abuse and Alcoholism lists at its website only *bad* effects from drinking, including these claims about the brain and heart:

Brain: Alcohol interferes with the brain's communication pathways, and can affect the way the brain looks and works. These disruptions can change mood and behavior, and make it harder to think clearly and move with coordination.

Heart: Drinking a lot over a long time or too much on a single occasion can damage the heart, causing problems including: cardiomyopathy – stretching and drooping of heart muscle, arrhythmias – irregular heart beat; stroke; high blood pressure.

Why in hell do people drink, given alcohol's completely negative effects, as represented by the American government? Well, people report, far and away, that they *enjoy* drinking alcohol. It is part and parcel of virtually every key ritual in religion and society (Jewish religious services, Catholic communion, Christmas, bar mitzvahs, Passover, weddings, wakes, reunions, New Year's Eve, etc.). Alcohol consumption has been a nearly universal human experience (although currently banned by Muslims* and some Christian sects, such at Mormons). It has been used since the dawn of humanity—fermented beverage alcohol has been found at the origin sites of every civilization. Today, nearly every society has salutary, joyous, and celebratory toasts.

So, would you believe that people who drink alcohol live longer than those who don't drink, even when those who quit due to alcoholism or illness are discounted (that is, using lifelong abstainers as a reference point), and these results come from government surveys of hundreds of thousands of people?

> Data were obtained by linking 13 National Health Interview Surveys (1997–2009) to the National Death Index records through December 31, 2011. A total of 333,247 participants ages ≥18 years were included. *Compared with lifetime abstainers, those who were light or moderate alcohol consumers were at reduced risk of mortality for all causes* [my emphasis]. The findings are consistent with the conclusions of the 2015 *Dietary Guidelines for Americans* and the American Heart Association.

These radical findings, based on a series of national government studies, appeared in "Alcohol Consumption and All-Cause, Cardiovascular, and Cancer-Related Mortality," published by the *Journal of the American College of Cardiology* in 2017.

Perhaps these results explain why better-off economically and better-educated people are more likely to drink. Eight in ten people in the highest income and education categories drink ($75,000 or more, college grad), while half of those with a high school diploma or less do. As a general rule, this elite group tends to do things that are good for them, and that they like. They *do*, after all, live longer than poorer, less well-educated people:

> More than 50 of America's largest cities are home to people who can expect to live at least 20 fewer years than those in neighborhoods just blocks or miles away. In Chicago, the city with the largest disparity, life expectancy varied by up to 30 years; in both Washington, DC and New York City it varied by more than 27 years.

When you go to a home or social event in a prosperous neighborhood, you are likely to be offered alcohol and to find people drinking in

---

* Well-off Muslims drink, of course; I saw them do so all the time in upscale Middle Eastern restaurants in New York.

a controlled, positive, beneficial way. *Despite its being enjoyed by a majority of Americans, particularly prosperous and healthy Americans, the government won't say a single good thing about alcohol.*

And this is due to America's temperance outlook, which will always be with us, including many researchers and often our most progressive publications. Their *public* anti-alcohol bias contradicts the behavior of these groups of well-educated, elitist individuals who enjoy drinking alcohol themselves. Their reticence is why we don't encourage, can't even recognize and identify, positive drinking habits and customs. These occur throughout the world, like a Portuguese village "where residents eat what they grow, bake their own bread (often in their village's ancient community oven), and step on grapes from their orchards to make wine."

My feelings toward this American anti-alcohol, temperance bias parallel my repugnance for the disease theory. *How can we normalize our relationship with marijuana and other drugs if we can't assimilate our longest- and best-known intoxicant, alcohol?* In addition to my 2010 *L.A. Times* article, I wrote "Bottle Battle" for *Reason* (1999), the libertarian magazine, around the 2000 US Dietary Guidelines when it was suggested that the health benefits of moderate drinking be placed on alcohol labels (*never!*). I wrote an earlier piece in that magazine (1996) on shifting American attitudes toward booze and a viral post on the *Reason* website in 2014 about prodigious Colonial American drinking titled (sardonically) "George Washington: Boozehound." I wrote about current temperance attitudes among the American elite in *Filter:* "In 2018 the Temperance Movement is Still with Us." Finally, I wrote a piece for *Filter*, "The Perpetual Pendulum of US Drinking Guidelines," when the 2020 Dietary Guidelines returned to American antialcohol prohibitionism.

My Dual Fight Against Level-of-Consumption Models and Temperance Attitudes

Related to my constant reiterations of America's strange and dysfunctional relationship to alcohol, I have a long string of academic and popular publications opposing temperance and "exposure" models of addiction. My book, *The Meaning of Addiction*, showed that many subjective and situational factors influence how people experience drugs and alcohol, including whether they become addicted. Other factors, like self-concepts about being addicted, cultural and social views of a substance and of addiction, and what a person believes about the power of a substance to control them are critical. Thus, even people taking substantial doses of narcotics for long periods of time, as chronic pain patients may do, who don't think of themselves as, or act like, addicts won't be addicted. For those who consider addiction a straightforward biological construct, my views are anathema, mad even.

Meaning was published in 1985. My Keller Award–winning article from the Rutgers Center of Alcohol Studies, *The Limitations of Control-of-Supply Models for Explaining and Preventing Alcoholism and Drug Addiction*, appeared in 1987. In *Limitations* I showed that neither addiction nor alcoholism nor societal drug and alcohol problems were neatly, or even largely, determined by how much of a substance was consumed.

In 1993, I published "The Conflict Between Public Health Goals and the Temperance Mentality" in the flagship journal of the American Public Health Association (this article was added to the APHA website in 2011). In it, I reviewed the substantial data showing that moderate alcohol consumption prolonged life by reducing heart disease, and pointed out how this information was suppressed because of American temperance thinking. In 2000, Archie and I published "Exploring Psychological Benefits Associated with Moderate Alcohol Use" in *Drug and Alcohol Dependence*, of which Chris Johanson was editor-in-chief. Robin Room wrote a contrary response, as he had done and was to do for decades to my academic pieces.

I wrote a series of popular articles over the decades about the benefits of sensibly consumed alcohol: I cited above my piece in the *L.A. Times* about the 2010 *Dietary Guidelines*, "Alcohol: The Good Side." I also wrote in 2010 in *Huffington Post* "The Hidden Health Benefits of Alcohol?" (which was among the top ten popularly accessed pieces in what was then the most popular progressive magazine online), followed by "We Don't Believe Alcohol's Good for You"; in 2014 I published in *Pacific Standard Magazine* "The Truth We Won't Admit: Drinking Is Healthy," which was in the top ten in popularity for the periodical that year.

Every academic article I published in the leading psychology and addiction journals for twenty years was a matter of strategic placement and political conflict. Every popular article roused a storm of protest and objection. Indeed, I was ultimately banned by *Huffington Post* for my anti-disease pieces. Ironically, Arianna Huffington, who is Greek, has described the warm and loving role that wine had in her life when she was growing up. I went to see her speak with Alta Ann, my older friend who had spent years living in Greece, where she drank a half a liter of white wine at lunch and dinner daily. Arianna's daughter, however, had developed a cocaine addiction at Yale (after using the drug for seven years) and turned to a 12-step group.

I questioned Huffington at this event for the publication of her healthy-living book, *Thrive*, where she was interviewed by Paul Holdengraeber. Holdengraeber had drawn her into the subject of her mother. Alta Ann wrote me the next day:

> Holdengraeber kept trying to penetrate to the reality of their relationship. But Arianna, incapable of leaving her lecturer cadence, closed him out of the picture and continued in her dramatic monologue. You raised your hand and swiftly put things into your view of it. You struck HOME but she would not admit it. You spoke of Mediterraneans, including her and her mother, learning to drink from a young age, since Arianna included wine drinking prominently in her narrative. What you said, considering her daughter's fate, threatened the dramatic masque Arianna wore. My impression was that she almost tried to banish you.

People have that reaction to me. But I never quit, do I? In 2018 I wrote in *Filter*, the digital harm-reduction publication, a review of the data, covering decades of wide-ranging research, by government bodies and others, of the health effects of alcohol, especially on mortality. The research consistently shows the benefits of alcohol. This perennial issue had been freshly raised because the World Health Organization declared in 2017 that it wasn't safe to consume *any amount* of alcohol. The year 2017 was the same year that the *Journal of the American College of Cardiology* concluded, based on the study I discuss above of a third-of-a-million Americans that covered years of their lives, that moderate drinking prolonged life.

American and temperance countries and health experts have warned against drinking for centuries. They have really never quit doing so. Yet our best-educated and well-off citizens, including all the public health specialists I know, disregard this futile, stupid message. Why do they keep drinking, and yet warn others away from doing so?

It's as though the elite want to scare off those deplorables (Hillary Clinton's term) from the good things they enjoy.

Me and Hillary

I am restricted from talking about my therapy clients. I'm going to violate that proscription in regard to an historic figure, now dead, whom Hillary Clinton credits for alerting her to the civil rights movement when she was a young conservative, thereby changing her course in life. That man, in his late seventies, consulted with me in New Jersey for a year after he had a severe health incident due to alcohol. We worked successfully on his drinking safely in social settings. One week he told me he'd miss our next session because he was joining Hillary on Air Force One. He grinned later as he described them each having a vodka tonic.

Another Bête Noir: Robin Room

In the last chapter I said Ethan Nadelmann is my longest intimate association in the addiction field. In this chapter, I will deal with a number of people with whom I have interacted longer, including Nick Heather, Alan Marlatt, Bill Miller, Peter Nathan, and . . . Robin Room.

As I moved from love addiction to alcoholism and drug addiction, I became aware of a seminal group in Berkeley, the Alcohol Research Group (ARG), spawned by social psychologist Don Cahalan. (Remember, in Chapter 8, my boss George Carcagno, at Mathematica, running into Don at a national survey research conference, where he was flabbergasted by Don's high regard for me.) Beginning in the 1960s, Cahalan applied survey research techniques to American drinking problems. Cahalan was soon to be joined as a primary force at ARG by Robin Room, an Australian graduate student who was to supplant him as head of ARG.

The 1974 publication by Cahalan and Room of *Problem Drinking Among American Men* applied modern statistical techniques to a national survey of American men's drinking. The results said nothing surprising— after all, they were just asking people (men) about their drinking. Yet their common-sense revelations were a stunning antidote to the disease theory:

- Drinking varies in large degree by people's ethnic backgrounds, with Italians and Jews having the fewest drinking problems
- Superseding background factors are current connections—people drink like those they associate with and according to other situational factors
- Since drinking is closely aligned with who people hang with and where they are in life, drinking problems can vary for the same individual, often quite radically, over relatively short spans of time
- The popular notion of alcoholism, spawned by AA and centered around loss of control, was rare in the general population; rather, people displayed a variety of drinking problems (e.g., a hangover or binge drinking on weekends) that didn't qualify as alcoholism, despite the American tendency to label all drinking problems alcoholism
- ARG surveys asked people why they drank: In large part (more than 80 percent of cases) they drank because they enjoyed alcohol's effects—drinking alcohol was a largely, almost ubiquitously, pleasurable, sociable experience for mature drinkers

I was the first person to integrate such survey findings with clinical research, beginning with my 1984 article for *American Psychologist*, "The

Cultural Context of Psychological Approaches to Alcoholism." The article, although completely outside the range of mainstream thinking, got a considerable amount of attention. This discussion involved the Rand Reports (released in 1976 and 1980), which tracked subjects treated for alcoholism at NIAAA-funded centers. Rand found the same variable time-and-situation-dependent phenomena that Cahalan and Room had earlier shown, in the Rand case with diagnosed alcoholics.

Rand thus identified a sizable group of "alcoholics" who moderated their drinking, creating a furor among—and a lashing out by—American alcoholism authorities, as represented by the National Council on Alcoholism. The NCA first attempted to suppress the report and, when it failed, instead held a highly publicized press conference on the morning of the release of the report in 1976 in which they claimed that the results would cause innumerable alcoholics to drink and to die. This is yet another example of the level of hysteria aroused when intoxicants are discussed in America. In the case of the Rand Reports, this was part of the resistance that was to set back harm reduction for thirty years.

As I discuss in Chapter 3, in 1983 I reviewed George Vaillant's *The Natural History of Alcoholism* for the *New York Times Book Review* (for which, as I wrote, Vaillant never forgave me). While defending the disease theory to the hilt, Vaillant both relied on Cahalan and Room's measures of alcohol problems and dependence and disparaged them for not recognizing the reality of alcoholism. After all, what Room and Cahalan discovered simply didn't resemble the compulsive loss-of-control and ever-worsening drinking problems/alcoholism which AA disease proponents like Vaillant term "progression" and regard as inevitable.

Soon afterward, I invited myself to ARG in Berkeley, where I was treated courteously (Robin once lent me his office to use when he was out of town) and to which I returned several times during the 1980s. During one visit, Robin invited me to breakfast with his wife, who was studying in a graduate theological program in which my *Meaning* was used as a text. Despite our breakfast conversation, Robin was and is completely uncomprehending of what *Meaning* said about addiction.

In *all of his work* Room drew a line between *subjective* drinking problems (like loss of control) and *objective* (read "real") ones, like dependence and withdrawal. Room was the apotheosis of the dualistic, mind-body distinction in human experience that you might have thought someone who went to school at Berkeley in the 1960s would be cautious of employing, and that I rejected entirely in *Meaning*. When I published my Keller

Award-winning article in the *Journal of Studies on Alcohol* in 1987, the journal felt obligated to enlist Room to counter my arguments—the beginning of decades of this pattern.

In his disputation, Room declared, up front and as his organizing principle, that dependence is simply "another name for sustained heavy alcohol use." If you drink a sufficient amount of alcohol over a sufficiently long period of time, you're dependent. This defies my ideas in *The Meaning of Addiction*. Indeed, going back to the old Cahalan and Room research, it defies the relationships to drinking problems they found there, where the highest correlation with physiological indicators of drinking problems was "psychological dependence."

Room is unmoved when I ask whether the same "do-it-often-and-long-enough-and-you're-addicted" argument applies to sex. Room, regarded as a quintessential intellectual in the addiction field, has no time for these arguments. One of his long-term reactions to me is to claim that I mistakenly opened the field to the idea of non-substance addictions in *Love and Addiction*, which I regretted in *Diseasing of America*. In fact, both books—my entire life's work—are predicated on ferreting out the meaning of addiction in essential, non-substance-caused terms in relation to the conditions of life. As I replied to Room's response to me in the Rutgers journal:

> Room is wrong, however, when he asserts that the conceptual confusion about addiction can be remedied by separating the concept into physiological and psychological components. The distinction he draws here mirrors the most mundane and traditional pharmacological thinking; moreover, as I have argued in *The Meaning of Addiction*, this whole approach is wrongheaded. It is most depressing to find as well-informed and iconoclastic a researcher and theoretician as Room held hostage by truisms that explain little about addictive behavior.

Among the seminal pieces that I wrote in the late 1980s was an article titled "A Moral Vision of Addiction," in which I dared to take the position that people's values determine when and how they become addicted and when they quit addiction. Values are a crucial lever in addiction treatment, one that we use in my Life Process Program and that forms the basis of what is generally regarded to be the key addiction treatment of modern times, called "motivational interviewing" (MI). Put briefly, MI allows people to examine their behavior in light of their fundamental values, the discrepancies with which are the best motivator for change.

I often describe my Uncle Ozzie's quitting a twenty-five-year smoking addiction when he, a staunch unionist, was confronted *one day* by a fellow worker who said, "Ozzie's a sucker for the tobacco companies." Ozzie, age 42, instantly quit smoking (he had been smoking four packs a day since he was 18; I was in graduate school when I realized that Ozzie no longer smoked). I use his example throughout my work: Ozzie, with his core identity as a radical anti-capitalist and his anti-capitalism values, couldn't justify that big tobacco had him "by the balls." He *had* to quit to survive.

Room for a time gave lectures attacking my introducing values into the addiction discussion as unscientific. Sometime after this back and forth, the first mainstream harm reduction addiction journal appeared, called *Addiction Research and Theory* (ART). ART's senior editors were John Davies, Douglas Cameron, and Ernie Drucker. I described John Davies's "myth of addiction" views in the previous chapter. Doug Cameron was a doctor who practiced harm reduction as the head of an alcohol treatment service in the UK. Ernie Drucker is an old drug-reformer friend of mine in New York. Robin was an original editor of what was at first called *Addiction Research*. I replaced him as associate editor of ART from 2002 to 2010.

Over the years I did a series of pieces for ART that reinforced my brand. In 1998, I wrote (with Rich DeGrandpre) "Cocaine and the Concept of Addiction: Environmental Factors in Drug Compulsions," which reviewed the research on animal cocaine use in laboratory settings. Room, as an editor, *loved* that piece, which supported the Cahalan and Room view of addiction as being environmentally determined. The discussion of Room's views on dependence above comes from my 2000 piece in ART, "What Addiction Is and Is Not."

Room has been wrong about every critical issue

This battle between me and Room, conducted over decades, stands for the essential struggle over the meaning and consequences of alcoholism and addiction theory and policy for the past century. Our final tête-à-tête confrontation occurred in ART in 2010, when I wrote "Alcohol as Evil — Temperance and Policy." In his response, using sociological terminology, Room regarded me as a "radical constructivist" (this sounds a bit like being a Berkeley radical of the 1960s, doesn't it?): "he seems to be adopting a *radical constructivist approach* that there is no external criterion in our field for deciding whether a statement is true or false. . . . I am a social constructivist myself, but of a *softer variety*." Translation: "Peele says that attitudes and thinking affect actual behavior and experience, while I (Room) am too grounded to believe anything so implausible."

But the scientific evidence, which I cited abundantly in my "Level-of-Consumption" piece in *JSA* and reviewed in ART, supports my views, and has confounded Room in critical tests of his and the public-health model of alcohol.

1. Room and his WHO colleagues studied the cross-cultural relevance of addiction criteria. With complete self-assurance (despite knowing of *Meaning* and responding to my Keller Award article), Room asserts that alcoholism and dependence are straightforward, invariable functions of drinking too much. Instead, their cross-cultural study found, "*contrary to expectation, descriptions of physical dependence criteria appeared to vary across sites as much as the more subjective symptoms of psychological dependence*" (my emphasis).

2. While the entire public health model is built on the assumption that drinking more leads to more problems, in the first systematic cross-cultural study of drinking problems, called the European Comparative Alcohol Study (ECAS), Room and colleagues found (as I summarized for ART) that:

   Alcohol-related problems were lowest in Southern Europe and highest in the North, despite the much greater controls the latter imposed and the lower drinking ages and far greater consumption in the former. Even more surprising was that alcohol-related mortality was also much higher in the North, due principally to the tendency in Temperance cultures to drink in heavy bursts, rather than regularly, but moderately. This leads to more accidents, violence, and suicide, and perhaps even to cirrhosis in Finland, Norway, Sweden—which consume the least alcohol—than in France, Italy, Portugal, Spain, Greece—that consume the most. ECAS found *alcohol-related mortality was six times higher* in Northern than Southern Europe: eight versus three such deaths per 100,000 for men, three versus 0.5 for women. Thus there was an *inverse* relationship between alcohol consumption and alcohol-related mortality [my emphases].

3. Room and his colleagues, when it comes to policies regarding alcohol, will assert forever that raising prices/reducing drinking is always best. Instead, ECAS found that "the association between alcohol consumption and experiencing an alcohol-related problem was stronger in Sweden and Finland than in other countries" and "that all forms of mortality analyzed (except one) respond more strongly to changes in overall consumption in Northern Europe than in other country groups." Studying the effect of EU regulations that forced Nordic countries to lower alcohol tariffs, Room and colleagues were forced to confront the reality "that a relatively large change in alcohol prices did not seem to produce a change in consumption is not something which the literature would

have predicted." Nor did problems increase as predicted. In fact, they declined in Stockholm.

These Nordic countries had assimilated positive drinking values and customs resembling those in Southern cultures. As with the non-applicability of American diagnostic criteria for alcoholism and addiction worldwide, Room and his WHO colleagues would have been better prepared and less surprised by their research results if they had paid attention to the writings of mine that Room read and dismissed. The same holds for uncovering cross-cultural differences in alcohol consumption and drinking problems and the effects of alcohol policies.

Me, and the Temperance versus Non-Temperance Cultural Split

Europe presents a laboratory for studying the discrepancies between styles of drinking. The brilliant sociologist Harry Levine identified nine temperance-based nations, five English-speaking and four Nordic countries, which corresponded closely to Northern countries in ECAS, while the Southern countries could be classified as "anti-temperance." All the key researchers in ECAS were from temperance cultures.

Enter the lone non-temperance, Italian contributor to the ECAS volume, Allaman Allamani. Allamani discussed the differences in feelings and perspectives on alcohol between temperance and non-temperance countries: "In the Northern countries, alcohol is described as a psychotropic agent. . . . It has to do with the issue of control and with its opposite—'discontrol' or transgression. In the Southern countries, alcoholic beverages—mainly wine—are drunk for their taste and smell, and are perceived as intimately related to food, and were thus perceived as an integral part of meals and family life, so that drinking is not connected to the idea of control."

In his respectful style, Allamani continued in the ECAS volume: "Many European policies have been based on the brilliant and extensive studies carried out in Northern Europe and in North America. They put great emphasis on control and restriction measures. As a consequence, alcohol studies and experiences are strongly influenced by both the Nordic and English-speaking countries. International agencies and WHO itself have possibly been influenced by this situation." Allamani's presenting those ideas in that setting was very brave. But he and his Southern colleagues have never been able to counteract the dominant views of Northern European and English-speaking countries in alcohol policy.

I threw myself for several years into this cultural gap between the Northern and Southern European visions of alcohol and understandings of drinking practices. In a series of Kettil Bruun Society presentations (Kettil Bruun was a Finnish researcher), visits, and workshop presentations, along with bombs thrown onto the KBS listserv, I fomented rebellion by the Southern Europeans in defense of their alcohol policies and way of life, all of which I described in a piece in *Huffington Post* titled, "I'm Singlehandedly Preserving the World's Wine Cultures." I felt that I was fighting alone against a huge bureaucracy.

How did I get that job?

I also befriended Franca Beccaria, an Italian sociologist. On one of a number of visits to Italy in those years, I went to Florence to speak to Allaman's students. I love Florence, which I visited first with Mary, then with Anna. Franca later had me speak at the University of Turin. I stayed at her and her husband's villa outside the city, joining Franca in picking herbs near the river for her pasta sauce. I spoke at a Kettil Bruun conference in Lucerne, on a vast lake, then drove with an Italian physician to Rome to stay at *his* villa outside the city. In Rome, I saw the largest Caravaggio (my favorite painter) exhibit ever assembled.

My favorite visit to Florence was for a conference organized by Grazia Zuffa, a former communist member of parliament, at whose villa in the hills I stayed. One evening Allaman and his philosophy professor friend visited. We had wine and cheese. Although I couldn't understand a word of the warm and energetic conversation, it was a fantastic evening that I was so pleased to have inspired. These Italian interactions were ecstatic for me.

At the conference itself, I conducted a workshop with Franca in which she reviewed the data on adolescent drinking across Europe. These data show that the claim that Southern European youths drank as badly as Northern ones is wrong (as I reviewed in the *Huffington Post*). The conference included a government representative who presented the WHO–Robin Room–Jürgen Rehm reasoning for making Southern Europe hew to Northern European and American temperance drinking regulations. The conference exploded in a giant conflagration. (See the Afterword for Franca's recollections of our times together.)

What did I do in Europe?

I was engaged in the task of recognizing and preserving Southern European—Italian, French, Greek, and Spanish—drinking against the depredations of their less healthfully drinking, but imposing, Northern neighbors. When I took Anna to Italy, Portugal, and Spain on tourist trips beginning when she was a young teenager (later, as a college sophomore, she accompanied me to Paris for my 2009 keynote address to the French national psychotherapy conference), she was served wine as a matter of course, with no age identification. My Harm Reduction International friend Pat O'Hare told me that, in the decade after he and his wife moved to Rome from Liverpool, he never saw a drunken Italian. On the other hand, when Mary and I went to Oslo for a KBS conference, we were shocked to find people lying drunk in public parks on Sunday mornings, and we were regularly accosted by public inebriates. One hostess said matter-of-factly when a drunken man entered her establishment that "he drinks like a Viking." Mary took a photo of a statue of a man lying in the street in Bergen, Norway—a kind of symbolic national monument.

What is most obvious is often ignored, in drinking behavior as in much else. (Recall my and Mary's drinking with an obnoxious American at a North Beach café in Chapter 2.) As a European researcher once told me, "All that you do is apply common sense to science!" No American has ever told me that. I quote Camus, from *The Plague* (so relevant today):

> But again and again there comes a time in history when the man who dares to say that two and two make four is punished with death. The schoolteacher is well aware of this. And the question is not one of knowing what punishment or reward attends the making of this calculation. The question is one of knowing whether two and two do make four.

Public health advocates seem unable to note the most obvious of all determinants of drinking behavior—people in a place and time, together in a group and as part of a culture, drink similarly, but very differently from those in other groups and places (as Cahalan and Room discovered in their surveys). Exploring this global reality has been the life's work of people like anthropologist Dwight Heath, whom I discuss in Chapter 8. And my job was to assert this truth, which my Italian colleagues like Franca knew and joined me in doing. Thus, Franca teamed with Finnish researchers to compare Italian and Nordic drinking. The Finns could all specifically recall their first drink, usually at a party, where they drank to extreme intoxication (a drinking style recalled by Norwegian Karl Ove Knausgaard in his brilliant, unstinting memoir, *My Struggle)*. Italians couldn't recount their first drink, which was a small amount of wine they had as young children with their families.

Contrary to the public-health consumption hypothesis, Franca showed that in those regions of Italy where the most wine was produced and consumed, where people knew and understood wine the best, drinking was most often moderate, with the fewest problems. She took me to the Piedmont region (where her husband was from), where people came to local stores to fill up large containers with fresh wine, like a filling station. This was the cultural milieu for alcohol we might emulate. Instead, WHO public health advocates were propagandizing and lobbying for Southern European countries to raise their drinking ages from sixteen years old to eighteen, the age for drinking in their temperance-based cultures (although still nowhere near our twenty-one-year-old legal age for drinking).

Franca wrote me a private email about how she and her Southern European colleagues felt like second-class citizens at KBS conferences. I encouraged her to send this email to the KBS listserv, which, after professionalizing the language, she did. Room and the other KBS leaders, deacons of cultural inclusiveness who claimed their views about alcohol were universal, were deeply embarrassed. Franca was subsequently elected president of KBS from 2011–2013. Of course, Franca's great work, her brilliance, her graciousness and people skills led to her becoming KBS president. But it would never have happened without me as a catalyst. Robin Room wouldn't acknowledge this truth if he were put on the rack.

When I was with her, Franca often decried the cultural intrusion of the Northern epidemiologists on the South. During my visit she received a flyer announcing that Rehm was coming to Italy to pressure government public health agents, based on temperance researchers' scientific claims, to eliminate youthful drinking by raising the drinking age. Included in the flyer was a picture of a group of adolescents getting drunk. Franca clucked disbelievingly when I pointed out that the picture was of Germans. We discussed how I could engage Rehm in a debate at KBS.

Room and Rehm were both at Skarpö Island in 2000 when I was invited to present my paper on the inexact—in fact, often nonexistent—tie between consumption levels and alcoholism. I cited the results from three ARG (Room's old American group) surveys in the 1980s–1990s. The data showed a decline in heavy drinking, and yet an increase in reported loss-of-control. Rehm approached me afterward to affirm my ideas and to make common cause with me on the narrow vision most people adopted on alcohol dependence and its causes. Years later, however, before she became president of KBS, when we were both at a KBS conference in Lausanne,

Switzerland, Franca approached Rehm with me in tow. She suggested that he and I debate. Rehm didn't respond. *When she became KBS president, however, Franca didn't invite me to present to KBS, let alone to debate Rehm.*

In 2018 I wrote in response to WHO's recommending zero alcohol consumption, "Five Harmful Anti-Alcohol Myths and the Evidence Against Them." I reviewed decades of government research showing life-preserving benefits of alcohol. The last myth I cited was that "Promoting alarmist views of alcohol to curtail drinking, while discounting health and cultural benefits, increases safe drinking and enhances public health." Franca wrote me, "Thank you for your perseverance, we need more scientists like you." Room wrote, dismissively, "Your views are well known, Stanton." Allaman suggested: "Stanton's position could be made public among KBS members: KBS should accept positions that are not the opinions that are currently expressed and read at KBS's site."

What I really want to know is, do WHO and KBS really expect people to quit drinking?

In Chapter 3 I discuss Hal Mulford's natural processes approach to alcohol and drinking versus the disease model: "One of them starts with nature and builds on it. The other starts with a concept and tries to make nature fit it." Hal described at the 1988 conference, Evaluating Treatment Outcomes, in San Diego, where I met him (which Robin also attended), the creation of the Iowa community counselor program.

> Recent changes in Iowa liquor control laws ended the 51-year-old state alcohol monopoly distribution system and turned the sales of bottled wine and spirits over to the private sector. The resulting increase in the availability of these beverages provided a unique opportunity to study the relationship between increased wine and spirits availability and changes in their consumption. Time series analyses of monthly sales (apparent consumption) trends showed that the increased availability had no lasting impact on consumption.

Adieu, Robin Room

It's remarkable the range of places Robin Room and I have met and venues in which we have exchanged our conflicting views. In the early 1980s, when I questioned standard definitions of addiction and reviewed Vaillant's 1983 *The Natural History of Alcoholism* in the *New York Times*, Room, as head of the Alcohol Research Group (ARG) in Berkeley, welcomed my views and my visits to ARG. Throughout the 1980s, 1990s, and 2000s he wrote uncomprehending ripostes to my journal articles. Nonetheless, we were together in 1988 in San Diego at a conference on the effectiveness of alcoholism treatment. Later that year in Sydney, Nick Heather, as head of the Australian National Drug and Alcohol Research Centre, had us both present workshops. We presented workshops in alternate years, 1995 and 1996, to the British Addiction Forum in Durham Castle in the UK.

Despite our conflicts, Room invited me to the Addiction Research Foundation in Toronto, where he became director of research, for the International Harm Reduction conference in 1994. In 1999, Room had me debate Louise Nadeau* on "The Nature of Addiction and Its Implications" at the KBS conference in Montreal. Room invited me to speak about dependence (described above) at a special Kettil Bruun Society conference when Room was head of the Swedish Alcohol Research Centre. We met on the island of Skarpö, at a retreat owned by the Swedish Alcohol Monopoly, which, as the nation's sole alcohol producer and importer, funded the Centre.

Ethan included Room and me in his Smart Family Foundation group on the future of drug policy. In this context we met in Princeton several times in 1990 and 1991, and later in New York sporadically for a few years after Ethan moved there. Ethan even had the two of us meet separately in New York to formulate a harm reduction approach to treatment. Brought along by Ethan, we met at Drug Policy Alliance conferences in Washington in the mid-1990s, where Room was uncomfortable when a reefer was passed around; marijuana was not his cup of tea. Our relationship exhausted, I haven't seen Robin for more than ten years now.

Of course, he and WHO have won in terms of convincing public health authoritiies to more thoroughly demonize alcohol.

Me, Griffith Edwards, and Virginia Berridge

Griffith Edwards is the grand vizier of British addiction and alcohol studies. He was director of the Medical Research Council–funded Addiction Research Unit from 1968 until his retirement from King's College London. He established the UK National Addiction Centre in London and was its first Chair and Director. For twenty-five years he was editor-in-chief of the journal *Addiction* while it transformed from a small British journal to the most widely read and cited substance use-related journal in the world.

---

* Louise translated my Hazelden pamphlet (since repudiated by them, as described in Chapter 7), "The Addiction Experience," into French as "L'expérience de l'assuétude." The fruit of my Italian collaborations, which I titled "The Disease Concept *Causes* Alcoholism," was translated as "La dipendenza è una patologia cronica del cervello?"

In 1985 Edwards, as editor-in-chief, reviewed *Meaning* in what was then *The British Journal of Addiction* (now *Addiction*). This was the height of attainment in the academic world. However, Edwards's review also marked my demise in that realm. He first called me a psychologist of distinction, then shifted mid-review to labeling my views, and me, a sham. That's because, at first, he addressed my dubiousness over the standard addiction concept and of treatment based on it, which Edwards shared. But I then shifted to the societal level and deconstructed the level-of-consumption model of alcohol problems. Edwards was the progenitor of the idea that more alcohol → more problems, i.e., that alcohol is bad, in a series of volumes, like the 1997 anti-alcohol tract, *Alcohol Policy and the Public Good*. In the meantime, from 1998 on, as I describe in the Conclusion, I was doomed at *Addiction*.

Earlier I noted Virginia Berridge's seminal work, *Opium and the People: Opiate Use in Nineteenth-Century England*. The 1981 edition of the book lists Griffith Edwards as co-author. The 1999 reissue has Berridge as its sole author. Berridge's book is synopsized: "At the beginning of the nineteenth century, opium was widely used as an everyday remedy for common ailments. By the 1920s, it was classified as a dangerous drug. In an examination of the social context of drug taking in Victorian England, the book explains this decisive change in attitude." Edwards contributed an appendix to the 1981 edition. Where Berridge wrote: "Addiction is now defined as an illness because doctors have categorized it thus," the reader is referred to the appendix, in which Edwards announced: "The opiates are drugs of addiction . . . anyone who takes an opiate for a long enough period and in sufficient dose will become addicted." The level-of-consumption concept of addiction!

My 1985 breakthrough piece in the *British Journal of Addiction* expressing that addiction is not automatically, or solely, linked to any one drug (e.g., opioids), or drugs at all, requires asking, "Are alcohol, cocaine, and marijuana drugs of addiction? What about nicotine and caffeine? Are shopping, eating, sex, and love activities of addiction? If you do any or all of these things regularly, will you be addicted?" Despite my exploring this crucial idea more than three decades earlier in the international addiction field's leading journal, the impact of my ideas has still not been assimilated by Room, Edwards, and their inheritors. Such a reorientation is demanded *especially* now that the American *DSM-5* and European *ISD-11* diagnostic manuals incorporate as addictions involvements other than drugs.

Why did the 1999 edition of *Opium and the People* have Berridge as its sole author? I commented on Berridge's vision of addiction (contra Edwards's) for the *Annals of the New York Academy of Sciences* in an article titled "Addiction as a Cultural Concept":

> That addiction and alcoholism had to be discovered seems bizarre and unnecessary to us, owing to the thoroughness of our indoctrination in the idea that these things are biological entities that have been independently established through clear scientific discovery and practical experience. How, then, have they been missed by so many of the world's cultures for so many centuries? After all, both alcohol and narcotics have been used widely throughout history. Yet only relatively recently, and then primarily in a few Western societies, did addiction and alcoholism come to be perceived as biological phenomena, a part of the natural landscape. How have so many societies and individuals misunderstood, ignored, or failed to perceive such obvious consequences of alcohol and narcotic consumption?

In a 2012 opinion piece in the British medical journal *The Lancet*, "The Rise, Fall, and Revival of Recovery in Drug Policy," Berridge noted, "One prominent debate in the UK last year, 'The Future of Harm Reduction and Drug Prevention in the UK,' pitched Neil McKeganey, a sociologist and prominent advocate of abstinence, against Stanton Peele, a psychologist and analyst of the 'meaning of addiction', thus epitomising the divergent positions." Interestingly, Neil and I enjoyed touring Scotland together, eating and drinking with colleagues in Glasgow and Edinburgh. Neil was the only one on the ATN list who objected when I was expelled by Nick. As for Virginia, in her books and Lancet analysis, she reflects my vision, to wit:

> Recovery is a term redolent of 19th-century temperance, with the pledge as creed and reformed drunkards as the saved.

Or, as Alan Marlatt said, "The medical model is the moral model in sheep's clothing."

My Greatest Academic Supporter, Nick Heather

I never met Griffith Edwards. In 1992 Virginia Berridge and I met at an International Harm Reduction Conference in Melbourne when Nick Heather was director of the Australian National Alcohol and Drug Research Centre (NADRC). Nick held that position from October 1978 to January 1994 (per Nick). He is now in Britain, Emeritus Professor of Alcohol and Other Drug Studies at Northumbria University. After Virginia and I did a delightful mini-tour of the Southeast Australian coast, she, Ethan, Nick, and I shared a cab to the mayor's residence for a reception.

Nick is the academic figure who has been most willing to recognize and support me. As head of NADRC he invited me to Sydney in 1988. In preparation for my visit, Heather distributed to his staff a brilliant, wonky article I wrote, titled, "Why Do Controlled Drinking Outcomes Vary by Investigator, by Country, and by Era?: Cultural Conceptions of Relapse and Remission in Alcoholism." Instead of limiting myself to reports of how many subjects moderated their alcoholic drinking in various studies, I tabulated the national and professional backgrounds of the researchers and the time periods in which they worked to explain their results. Looking at the social context of theories is called the "sociology of knowledge" in philosophy of science. True believers can't think this way. Yet it is how I approach scientific and policy questions.

A decade before the cab ride in Australia, in 1982, Nick visited with us in Morristown over the holidays, joining us for Chanukah (I gifted him a copy of *Love and Addiction*). Nick is well known for his no-nonsense demeanor, and Mary referred to him as "the dour Scotsman" (Nick wasn't Scottish, but worked at Ninewells Hospital in Dundee). Perhaps his own outsider personality allowed Nick to appreciate me. I do cherish his announcing once, out of the blue, "Stanton, you know I'm quite fond of you."

Nick saved my life on his 1982 visit. In Chapter 7 I detailed how the Mary Pendery–*Science* article inspired a *pogrom* against controlled drinking therapy. Nick (with Ian Robertson) had published, in Britain, the astounding *Controlled Drinking* in 1981. He was actually in the States when he visited us to gather information to update the paperback edition with an appendix in response to Pendery et al.'s study. In *Controlled Drinking*, Nick reviewed not only controlled drinking (CD) therapy research, but also the epidemiological studies of how people shifted drinking patterns over time (like Cahalan and Room), the Rand research and its critics, the experimental research on how street inebriates drank when they were offered alternative rewards for delaying or moderating their drinking in a laboratory, and even the history of temperance in America. It was a world-class intellectual treatment of a subject that was of crucial import to me and the entire addiction and alcoholism world.

Among Heather and Robertson's conclusions were these two, which have stood the test of time and will do so for eons:

1. Whereas American researchers, scared to death, insisted that CD therapy be applied only to "problem drinkers," not "real" alcoholics, *Controlled Drinking* "regret(ted) the tendency to relegate the new methods to a minor and ancillary role . . . as being applicable,

for example, to only those with less serious problems." Heather and Robertson thus anticipated harm reduction by showing that drinking-reduction techniques were valuable throughout the problem-drinking spectrum, including for those displaying extreme alcoholism.

2. *Controlled Drinking* summarized laboratory research with actively drinking street inebriates (research no longer permissible) as showing that even the most severely alcoholic individuals "clearly demonstrate positive sources of control over drinking behavior": i.e., addicted people respond to environmental constraints and rewards even when their addictions are at peak periods. This knowledge refutes the idea that alcoholism is due to an inherent biological mechanism that causes loss of control. It sets the stage for harm reduction by showing that improving the environments in which people live yields benefits for their drinking behavior and overall lifestyle, even without abstinence, no matter the severity of their alcoholism.

So I have always been indebted to Nick intellectually, and appreciative of his help and praise professionally and personally. But, then, it was Nick (and co-list owner, Derek Heim, another helpful British academic friend who is now editor-in-chief of *Addiction Research and Theory)* who kicked me off the Addiction Theory Network list in 2016 for reposting private exchanges around a dispute between Carl Hart and other list members. Since then, nonetheless, Nick has written praise for my and Zach Rhoads's book, *Outgrowing Addiction*, and repeatedly helped me with this book—including writing a cover blurb. Thank you, Nick! (And he and Derek have invited me to rejoin the ATN group, as I described in the last chapter, an invite that I appreciated but that I am holding off on accepting.)

While Nick was visiting me and Mary in 1982, he brought with him a copy of the just-published public-health, reduce-overall-drinking bible, *Beyond Alcoholism*, by Dan Beauchamp, which I read during his visit. Nick endorsed this model, as many other cognitive behavior therapists do (like my friend Liam O'Loughlin in Galway). Yet Nick was just then (1982) publishing research showing that those treated for alcohol problems who believe the "cultural delusion" that alcoholics lose control of their drinking after one drink are in fact more likely to behave that way: i.e., cultural beliefs create personal beliefs, and together these outstrip chemical and biological forces in addiction, consistent with my 1985 book, *The Meaning of*

Addiction: Compulsive Behavior and Its Interpretation. But Nick, like many psychologists, was incapable of generalizing the idea of social learning as a determinant of drinking behavior from the individual to the cultural level.

The year after his visit to Morristown, I joined Nick on a panel presenting to the 1983 national conference of behavioral psychologists in Washington, DC. The panel comprised leading controlled-drinking researchers worldwide, including Mark and Linda Sobell, Alan Marlatt, and Bill Miller, along with Nick. I got myself invited to the proceedings on the strength of my article in *Psychology Today* in April that year about the Pendery-Sobells conflict, "Through a Glass Darkly: Can Some Alcoholics Learn to Drink Moderately," which created a furor leading to my being banned in the American alcoholism world. In Washington, I presented a paper entitled "Behavior Therapy—The Hardest Way: Controlled Drinking and Natural Remission from Alcoholism," which I describe at my website:

> In November, 1983, under assault for CD therapy, an international group of behavior therapists conducted a panel at the annual meeting of the Association for the Advancement of Behavior Therapy in Washington DC. Stanton finagled an invitation (joining Alan Marlatt, Bill Miller, Fanny Duckert, Nick Heather, Martha Sanchez-Craig, Mark and Linda Sobell) and delivered an audacious talk equating behavior therapy and God—both tell you the hardest way to do anything. In place of standard behavior therapy protocols, Stanton described natural processes by which people achieve remission. Stanton's talk anticipated harm reduction, motivational interviewing, and just about every other current cutting-edge idea in substance abuse treatment.

Before proceeding to somewhat critical comments, I must note that Bill Miller and Alan Marlatt were large presences in my intellectual life during the early years when I was developing my views on alcoholism. I regularly cited their work in support of the propositions I put forward. Particularly important were Miller's meta-analysis (with Reid Hester) of effective alcoholism treatments (which placed AA and the 12 steps very low, and motivational interviewing, brief interventions, and the community reinforcement approach at the top) and the same authors' analysis showing that, when inpatient and residential treatment were compared, any differences favored the outpatient setting.

In the bigger picture, both Marlatt and Miller placed alcohol problems and alcoholism in a larger social and psychological framework. This includes Alan's *Relapse Prevention* (1985, 2004, with Dennis Donovan) volumes and research, which cast all addictive behavior together, his prescient work on harm reduction psychotherapy, *Harm Reduction* (1998, 2012), and

Bill's universally heralded *Motivational Interviewing* book (co-edited by Stephen Rollnick, originally published in 1991) and clinical approach. Marlatt's and Miller's work engaged crucial, nonreductive psychological perspectives on addiction that I have expanded on.

Some Things about Bill Miller

As for my personal relationship with Bill Miller—not so good. Right after my 1983 presentation in Washington during the controlled drinking furor, when I found myself in the heart of American cognitive behavioral research and researchers on alcoholism, I learned that Nick and Bill Miller were organizing a conference. I asked Nick if I might attend. He told me that Bill was in charge, and that I should ask him. Bill said no. This conference produced the leading-edge volume on alcoholism treatment.

Let me summarize Miller's distinguished career, and our relationship:

1. *Origins.* Bill Miller is a brilliant researcher, theorist, writer, and clinician. He began his career working on controlled drinking (CD) for what he would term problem drinking—as opposed to "alcoholism." Bill, cautious to his heart, didn't want to incur criticism for daring to comment on alcoholism.

2. *Conflict avoidance.* Bill is a conservative person. Bill tried to stay on the sidelines when the controlled drinking wars emerged in 1982 with Mary Pendery's article in *Science*.

3. *View of addiction.* Bill sees drug and alcohol use, including addiction, in terms of the ordinary rules of behavior, as influenced by set and setting (cognition and situational factors).

4. *View of my work.* Bill wrote me that my 1984 *American Psychologist* article, "The Cultural Context of Psychological Approaches to Alcohol," impressed him, and he included it in a binder of articles he gave students. A lay minister, Bill recommended *The Meaning of Addiction* in a pamphlet on addiction he wrote for his religious group.

5. Bill named the research group he started in 1989 the Center on Alcoholism, Substance Abuse & Addictions. CASAA's statement of purpose is to "reduce suffering related to substance use *and other addictive behaviors*" (my emphasis).

6. *Personal reaction to me.* Bill has always distanced himself from me. He doesn't react well to the personality I display in this book. Bill has never invited me to participate in any conference or project that he organized.

7. *Bill achieved star status* based on his therapy and book, *Motivational Interviewing*. *MI* is a best seller, and this approach is used throughout the helping professions. MI prompts people to explore their values and behavior so as to realize how these may conflict, which then propels their motivation to change. This approach is a well-developed version of the one I use in the Life Process Program—as I described in regard to Uncle Ozzie, whose union-based values caused him to quit smoking.

Bill was the central figure behind the most extended, expensive clinical trial of alcoholism treatment ever conducted (budgeted at $25 million, its final cost exceeded $40 million)—the legendary Project MATCH. Bill and others believed that treatment outcomes would be better if patients were matched with treatments according to their personal traits (including severity of alcoholism, cognitive level, gender, readiness to change, etc.). For example, people who thought in simpler conceptual terms might do better in AA. Project MATCH then divided a group of alcoholic subjects into one of three treatments: Miller's motivational enhancement or interviewing (MI), twelve-step facilitation, and social skills training. (Fun note: Enoch Gordis, who headed the National Institute on Alcohol Abuse and Alcoholism when it conducted MATCH, gave me his last copies of the manuals for the three treatments as we waited to meet the Queen of the Netherlands.)

Over a decade of planning, conducting the actual study, and analyses, no usable matches were discovered. Matching has now been rejected as a treatment strategy. I explained the costly failure of MATCH. As I emphasize, people do best by making their own choices in line with their values. In retrospect, it seems odd that Miller would have pushed the matching approach. Motivational interviewing is built on eliciting the individual's own motivation and choices in keeping with their values. Why would assigning people to treatment based on external criteria beat their selecting and pursuing their preferred treatment? In the end, MATCH simply reiterated the importance of *self-efficacy*, or personal agency and choice.

Another remarkable aspect of this sine qua non of research on the effectiveness of different treatments: treatment hardly mattered. MATCH subjects in twelve-step facilitation and social skills training were scheduled for twelve sessions, while those in MI were only to receive four. But subjects on average attended only two-thirds of their sessions, meaning that MI subjects had a couple of sessions. Yet the groups' outcomes were the same. A later independent analysis of the MATCH data found that the reductions in drinking MATCH laid claim to occurred almost instantaneously: "Nearly all the improvement in all groups had occurred by week one. Only 3 percent of the drinking outcome could be attributed to treatment."

MATCH's results are consistent with the analysis of alcohol treatment that I presented alongside Miller in Washington in 1983. *Yet I would never have been invited into the group of alcoholism researchers who conducted Project MATCH.* Instead, I wrote about MATCH on my own and for the addiction division of the American Psychological Association. I pointed out that subjects' socially stable status and motivation as volunteers accounted for their progress. MATCH's organizers and funding group, the National Institute on Alcohol Abuse and Alcoholism, in order to put the best light on their colossal expenditure, crowed that all of the treatments worked. This statement required them, despite the fact that subjects were the kind of alcoholic drinkers for whom Miller and NIAAA claimed harm reduction wouldn't work, to focus on subjects having reduced their drinking from twenty-five to six days a month, and drinking less on those days.

Project MATCH was touted around the horn as proving the value of accepted conceptions and conventions around alcoholism. In fact, it disproved virtually everything the NIAAA asserted about alcoholism and its treatment. Instead, as I said, Project MATCH was a radical statement undercutting these things.

Alan Marlatt, Howard Shaffer, and Morris Chafetz

As I noted, Alan Marlatt was a pioneering psychologist best known for his work in relapse prevention and harm reduction psychotherapy. Alan told me that *Love and Addiction* expanded his view of addiction so that he included food, heroin, gambling, and smoking, along with alcohol, in his relapse prevention research. In the early 1980s, as I describe in Chapter 7, he was the one psychologist who stood up with me against the assault on controlled drinking. We met speaking around the country—in his program at the University of Washington, in New York, at the DC conference of behavior therapists. Alan wrote blurbs for my books. He even wrote a letter on my behalf for a futile application I made for an academic position.

Here is the praise Alan offered about *Diseasing of America:*

> Peele makes it clear that the disease model of addiction, the ideology that currently reigns over the American addiction treatment industry, is an emperor without clothes. His approach, placing addictive behaviors in the context of other problems of living, is well documented with timely references to new scientific data. In contrast with the biological determinism that portrays 'addicts' as help-

less victims of forces beyond their control, this book empowers readers to see addiction in a new optimistic light.

I was invited to participate in a conference at Indiana University, where Alan had received his Ph.D., when the school honored his accomplishments. I moderated a harm reduction drug policy panel in Washington with Alan in the mid-1990s. That was easy for me to do, given my admiration for Alan and the closeness of our views. Alan created what was for me the most comprehensive formulation of harm reduction psychotherapy, one that could be the standard for the field today. In addition, he participated in a project that showed that wet housing (allowing street inebriates to live in residences where they were allowed to drink) was cost-effective and improved residents' health. *Moreover, residents actually cut their drinking by a third.*

My and Alan's relationship almost ran aground before his work on harm reduction due to an ethics claim I lodged against Howard Shaffer at Harvard Medical School. I have noted how my 1984 article in *American Psychologist*, "The Cultural Context of Psychological Approaches to Alcoholism," had a major impact. Shaffer, a psychologist who headed Harvard Medical School's Division on Addiction, wrote me to praise my article and to say how it had helped him in his own writing. I was well disposed toward Shaffer since he had featured the Introduction to *Love and Addiction* in his 1981 volume (with Milton Burglass), *Classic Contributions in the Addictions*. This was the first academic acknowledgement of my work.

But then I noticed that Shaffer had lifted portions of "Cultural Context" without citing me in an article he published. I pointed this shortcoming out to him. Shaffer later informed me that he would never reference me again, nor invite me to speak at Harvard addiction events he organized. Shaffer had Vaillant and Linda Sobell debate controlled drinking in one of these symposiums. Vaillant, with me safely not present, cited me as his primary example of harm reduction wrongheadedness.

Shaffer organized an annual Zinberg lecture named after my early role model, Norman Zinberg. In 1997, Shaffer had drug warrior General Barry McCaffrey speak, a ridiculously inappropriate choice I critiqued in the *L.A. Times*. Ethan was aghast at the association of an army general whom Bill Clinton had inappropriately appointed as his Drug Czar to speak. Not only that, but McCaffrey was presented with an award in Zinberg's name! Archie and I satirized an imagined debate between Zinberg and McCaffrey. Archie, who has been affiliated with Harvard's Department of Psychiatry, helped organize a protest when McCaffrey appeared. He incurred some blowback for doing so at the medical school.

Returning to 1989, I had become irate that Shaffer was boycotting *me* at Harvard for *his* sloppy use of my material. I finally filed a complaint with the Harvard Medical School ethics committee. Shaffer responded by having his attorney threaten me with a lawsuit for tortious interference with Shaffer's employment. Archie attended the resulting 1990 hearing before this committee while my attorney (Mary insisted I have one) and I were patched in by phone. The HMS committee concluded that Shaffer had indeed borrowed substantially without citing me, but that he had done so unintentionally. They did, however, chide Shaffer for undermining the due process of the committee by threatening me legally—which violated their procedures.

Marlatt knew Shaffer and was to spend a semester as a visiting professor at Harvard under Shaffer's sponsorship. Alan and I presented together at a conference in Arizona in 1989 after I lodged my complaint with Harvard Medical School. He took me aside to tell me that he was writing a letter on Shaffer's behalf. Alan sent me a copy of this letter, which said that since my work integrated data and ideas from others, Shaffer *couldn't* steal from me. Mary cried when she read it.

But that didn't end my relationship with Alan. As I said, we appeared together at DPA and other venues in the 1990s. Alan participated in my "Permission for Pleasure" conference in 1998 and contributed to the 1999 volume I edited based on the conference, *Alcohol and Pleasure: A Health Perspective*. I wrote a tribute to Alan when he died in 2011, and Ilse Thompson and I dedicated our 2014 book, *Recover!*, to Alan.

In Chapter 3 I discussed Hal Mulford's relationship to former Senator Harold Hughes when Hughes spurred the creation of the National Institute on Alcohol Abuse and Alcoholism in 1971. Morris Chafetz, a Harvard Medical School professor, became the first director of the NIAAA. *The Washington Post* reported his death in 2011: "Morris E. Chafetz, a contrarian Harvard Medical School psychiatrist who became a leading expert on alcohol abuse sought to teach Americans how to drink responsibly without shaming them into not drinking at all." (This was certainly not what Hughes had in mind!) Chafetz later wrote books like *Drink Moderately and Live Longer: Understanding the Good of Alcohol* (1995), in which he cited my work, and Morris and I did several projects together.

Thus I was amused that Shaffer was appointed to an endowed chair at Harvard Medical School in 2015 named the *Morris E. Chafetz Associate Professor of Psychiatry in the Field of Behavioral Sciences*. The description of Shaffer's interests and research pursuits read: "the social perception of addiction and disease, the philosophy of science, impulse control regulation and compulsive behaviors, adolescent gambling, addiction treatment outcome, responsible gambling, and the *natural history of addictive behaviors*" (my emphasis). One could almost write the same description of *my* interests and research, for which I am well known throughout the field.

Peter Nathan, Barbara McCrady, and the Rutgers Center of Alcohol Studies

Peter Nathan was a behavioral psychologist at Rutgers, the state university of New Jersey where I went to law school, my older daughter graduated college, and I taught a course on alcoholism and addiction as an adjunct faculty member. Peter went on to become director of the Rutgers Center of Alcohol Studies from 1983 to 1989, to be succeeded by Barbara McCrady, when I lived nearby in New Jersey. The Rutgers program is the most famous, the first, alcohol research center in the US, or the world. It was established at Yale in 1935, then moved to Rutgers in 1962.

In 1982 I delivered the keynote address, on *Love and Addiction*, to the Rutgers Center's famous summer school. The conference organizers got more than they bargained for from me, as was typically the case. From the podium I questioned the largely recovering audience about their died-in-the-wool view of alcoholism as a disease. The audience and the organizers were stunned. (I was never invited back.)

In 1989, I was awarded the Center's Keller Award for the best article in its journal over the prior two years. Barbara wrote to tell me how glad she was to see me get the award. Previously, when Peter had assumed the leadership of the CAS, he told me he'd like to hire me for a public relations position at the Center. In 1981 and 1984, as editor-in-chief, Peter had shepherded two of my articles into the flagship American Psychological Association journal, *American Psychologist*. So I knew that Peter admired my guts and point of view.

Rutgers was funded by the Christopher Smithers Foundation, named for a wealthy alcoholic. When the Rutgers journal published several articles on controlled drinking, Smithers threatened to pull his endowment. His widow, Adele, became head of the Smithers endowment, of whose recipients she was often critical. She took an intense dislike to me and had me kicked off the set of a cable television show, "Debate, Debate," on which we both were to appear. For his part, after he took on the directorship, realizing what a hot potato I was, Peter dropped any mention of involving me at the Center.

Barbara McCrady replaced Peter as acting director of the Center and led the Center for two years, while serving as clinical director at the Center for nearly twenty-five years, from 1983 until 2007. Over this time, Barbara contacted me periodically to ask me for an article I had recently written so that she might present her students with my challenging views. When Barbara left Rutgers in 2007, she went to New Mexico to become director of the Center on Alcoholism, Substance Abuse, and Addictions, succeeding Bill Miller in that position. Barbara was obviously an excellent and sought-after administrator.

In 1985, Barbara and I appeared on *Today in New York* along with a woman who headed a treatment center and Nicholas Pace, a doctor famous for attacking harm reduction. The moderator posed every question to those two—I was being set up as the fool. But I answered all the questions first. After doing so, I turned to Barbara to ask her views: she demurred, never saying a single word—she, the clinical director of the Rutgers Center of Alcohol Studies! When we met again, Barbara told me, smiling, how Pace, whenever they met, said, "Wasn't that Peele guy unbelievable?"

In 1992, I wrote an article in the journal *Addictive Behaviors* titled "Alcoholism, Politics, and Bureaucracy." I described how Peter, along with most behavioral psychologists in the alcoholism field, abandoned controlled drinking out of fear and conformity when Mary Pendery's 1982 article in *Science* demonized harm reduction. Peter Nathan was my main target, but I also focused on Barbara around an article she and Peter wrote arguing that people who did controlled drinking therapy (which Peter still performed in his private practice) put themselves in legal jeopardy.

My relationship with Barbara took a downturn after my article appeared, although that made no difference since the Center already ignored me. In 1993, however, CAS instituted a brief intervention, drinking moderation program for students. I wrote Barbara suggesting they might name the clinic after me. She replied defensively that the program had nothing to do with me, but had been started based on new data showing the value of moderation treatment. (How prescient of me, then.) Amused, I wrote Peter, who was by then at the University of Iowa:

Dear Peter:
Perhaps you are aware of developments at Rutgers since you left. The Center of Alcohol Studies has now created a brief intervention clinic that practices controlled drinking therapy! Rather than challenging client goals, the program seeks to work with them, which was the basis of our fundamental disagreement about alcoholism treatment that I expressed in *Addictive Behaviors*. Meanwhile,

> Barbara says she hasn't really accepted my approach, but rather has responded to the data Harold Rosenberg (1993) meekly reviewed. These are the same data to which I referred in my article.
>
> I'm wondering: (1) Why did Rutgers change its direction after you left? (2) Do you agree with this new direction, or do you think they have made an error? (3) Finally, don't you think that my point of view has won out, just as I predicted in my response to your and Barbara's comments on my article, when I wrote, "I fully expect that my views will be accepted eventually" (Peele, 1992, p. 89)? That has happened sooner than expected.

Peter, who had abandoned the alcoholism field after leaving the Center, didn't reply (surprise).

Before he left for Iowa, Mary and I (and her mother, who was in town for a visit) had Peter over for lunch one Sunday. He spent the entire time cynically putting himself and academia down. After he left, Mary was disillusioned and disturbed by Peter's performance. She wrote Peter saying she had always admired academia and the university faculty she encountered in college and graduate school, and how disappointing she found his visit and the fact that Rutgers and academia had never welcomed me. Peter wrote back saying he could see how much Mary loved and supported me. He was actually a very nice, if compromised, man.

After all of this, readers might be surprised (as I was!) to visit the historic timeline at the Rutgers Center's website. Covering a hundred years, extending back to the 1920s and '30s, when the school was first founded, it makes no mention of Nathan or McCrady. But it cites me as one of five entries from the 1980s: "*Diseasing of America: Addiction Treatment Out of Control* by Stanton Peele is published refuting the 'addiction as a disease' model." The first addiction specialist discussed before that point is E. M. Jellinek, the founder of the school. (You will recall from Chapter 8 that Dwight Heath ran into Jellinek and Mark Keller on the Yale campus in the early 1950s when they asked him to write up his description of drinking with the Camba Indians.) The milestone for Jellinek: "Publishes the 'Disease Concept of Alcoholism'."

Jellinek and I are joint landmarks in the Rutgers Center's historic timeline?! In *Diseasing*, I began one of the chapters describing the TV panel with Barbara and me. Did that show and my book make more of an impression on Barbara than I supposed?

The timeline also notes that in the 1990s, "Alcoholism and drug addiction began to be integrated in treatment and research." The most recent entry, under "Today," is "Center renamed Center of Alcohol & Substance

Use Studies to reflect its broader mission," the movement I had pioneered in the 1970s.

A Person Without a Home Base

Archie, in his Foreword, refers to me as an "independent scholar." That's a polite way of saying I have never had a home base (or a job). My struggles, debates, and conflicts with Room at the Kettil Bruun Society, Jürgen Rehm and the World Health Organization, Bill Miller with his motivational interviewing network and as director (succeeded by Barbara McCrady) of the Center on Alcoholism, Substance Abuse, and Addictions, Howard Shaffer at Harvard Medical School's Division on Addiction, Peter Nathan and Barbara McCrady at the Rutgers Alcohol Center—even Ethan at Drug Policy Alliance—left me with no viable institutional support or framework. I was on my own against these institutions and in the field. The only power I had was my personal presence.

Nonetheless, they all know who I am and, each in his or her own way, has been influenced by my thinking and writing. And I don't think any of them would directly deny it (well, maybe Rehm would).

So be it.

Harm Reduction in Alcohol

In previous chapters, I deal with harm reduction as it applies to drug use. This chapter deals with controlled drinking, a form of harm reduction involving alcohol with which Nick Heather, Alan Marlatt, Bill Miller, and I were involved—with great controversy and blowback in the 1980s and 1990s, and continuing even today.

Harm reduction includes *all* improvements for people addicted to alcohol or drugs. Temperance, Alcoholics Anonymous, and drug prohibition, on the other hand, are *anti*-harm reduction. All accept *only* abstinence for addicted people. Thus 12-step-inspired public health fought clean needle programs, despite their demonstrated efficacy in preventing AIDS. As I discuss in Chapter 9 around Christine Whitman, Ethan Nadelmann detailed the deadly impact of American AA and the 12 steps for drug users: "Where the 12-step thing has the most to own up to is its role in impeding harm reduction interventions to stem the spread of HIV/AIDS."

What a horrible thing, and all done in the name of public health under the aegis of the 12 steps and the disease theory of addiction!

In the case of alcoholism in the US, temperance and AA played out in ways that were similar, but different. The unrealistic goal for behavioral psychologists was to make perfectly moderate drinkers out of people with alcoholism or any form of problem drinking. In their defense, this logic was forced on Miller and other psychologists by the intense pressure of the American environment in which formerly alcoholic people who abstained, as the British Virginia Berridge described, were said to be in recovery, which was like being saved by Christianity.

Thus, controlled drinking psychologists and researchers were expected to prove that they had converted alcoholics or problem drinkers into perfectly controlled drinkers, with nary a slip. When Mary Pendery and her colleagues in 1982 attacked the Sobells' earlier research (see Chapter 7), they pointed out every case in which the subjects in the research didn't control their drinking. "Look," they said, "they weren't controlling their drinking here. The experiment, this whole form of treatment, is a failure."

What if alcoholism treatment is destructive and inhumane?
But what if those formerly alcoholic mainly drank in a controlled fashion? What if their worst drinking wasn't as severe as it had been? What if, even if they occasionally got drunk, they didn't go on drunken binges, popularly called "benders," lasting for days or weeks? What if they got drunk only in their homes, thus avoiding the dangers of fights, accidents, or sexual assaults when they were drunk in public? Didn't that count for anything? Especially since few alcoholics who enter treatment or go to AA quit drinking entirely, which certainly those treated with abstinence in the Sobells' experiment didn't do.

Alan Marlatt showed that wet housing, in which people who drank on the street were given housing where they could drink freely, produced all sorts of benefits. These benefits were for alcoholic drinkers, who now could drink safely, without fear of becoming victims of violence or robbery or of freezing or other accidents. (Remember Terry McGovern, daughter of Senator and presidential candidate George McGovern, who froze to death on the street.) Then there were the constant hospitalizations and imprisonment of such drinkers, who often showed no improvements in their lives over decades until they died on the streets.

Why wouldn't these people deserve humane treatment? And wouldn't drinking less and taking better care of themselves and living more comfortably, changes that occurred almost instantly on entering wet housing, make them more self-respecting as well as improve their lives? Perhaps Barbara McCrady would now accept this point of view, contra Dr. Pace, although it was inconceivable in the 1980s.

I was on the board of a group called Moderation Management, which endeavors to support social drinkers. Ideally, they were never to get drunk, and to drink within very low limits—for women no more than three drinks on any day, or more than nine drinks per week; for men no more than four drinks on any day, or more than 14 drinks per week. Those limits were fine, but, dear reader, there are some people not well suited to live out this kind of moderate drinking typical for social drinkers.

Are such drinkers simply to be left to die? Especially considering that, over the longer haul, studies like NESARC, which examined the lifetime drinking histories of more than 43,000 Americans, found that *most* (three-quarters) of even dependent drinkers ceased their alcoholism, largely without treatment. This finding contradicted the AA-temperance tale of the drunkard who *must* end up in an asylum, a hospital, or a graveyard. How about instead safeguarding heavy drinkers' lives as their longer-term amelioration either does or does not pan out, meanwhile making available to them positive life options and supports?

Enter Ken Anderson. Ken moved from Minneapolis, where he lived in very restrictive wet housing, to New York in the 1990s, where I met him. Ken said that *Diseasing of America*, which he read in the Minneapolis library, saved his life. In New York he joined forces with a good friend of mine, Ana Kosok, who was a formative pillar of Moderation Management (MM). But Ken chafed under the MM guidelines. Ken's style was to drink an entire bottle of liquor on one allotted day a week in his own residence. This kept him off the street and made him a solid citizen.

During all of this, in 2000 the founder of MM, Audrey Kishline, whom I also knew, quit MM, joined AA, subsequently got very drunk in her car, and crashed headlong into another car, killing the driver and his young daughter. Audrey was sent to prison. Opponents of harm reduction argued that this proved their point. It seemingly fell to me to reframe this story as a tragedy that *could have been avoided with harm reduction:* for example for *Reason* magazine, and in an interview with famed right-wing Fox News interviewer Bill O'Reilly. If Audrey could have acknowledged her drinking, instead of (now in AA) sneaking out to drink, she and others could have taken steps to avoid the life-altering horror she caused herself and others.

Fundamentally, I argued, how did this failure, of which there have been tens and hundreds of thousands in the normal course of America's dealing with alcoholism, "disprove" the benefits of harm reduction?

By the way, how did I get this job?

Back to Ken Anderson, who created, whole cloth, an organization called HAMS, or harm reduction for alcohol. Mainly online, but also in groups and through writing, Ken grew HAMS into an international HR organization. Ken produced an excellent self-help manual, *How to Change Your Drinking: A Harm Reduction Guide to Alcohol* (2010), that went beyond MM's limits. My praise appears first in the book: "HAMS is for the large majority of substance users who have problems and who remain unserved by our current Alice in Wonderland approaches."

Another friend of mine, April Smith, then partnered with Ken in 2017. I knew the two of them personally. (Before moving to Philly to join April, Ken lived nearby me in Park Slope in Brooklyn, and we periodically went to the courtyard of the church where he worked as a porter to smoke cigars.) I spent 2018 New Year's Eve in Philly with Ken and April. In 2019 I visited to support April as she led her public health class at Jefferson Medical School. Together, in 2019, they edited a book of the stories of HAMS members around the world, people who took their own individual paths to improving their lives with the support of other drinkers in HAMS and Ken and April. *Someone in the world must do this job.* Here is my praise for their book, *Better Is Better! Stories of Alcohol Harm Reduction*.

> HAMS is a group for people who want support to change their drinking. Support: not chastisement, not admonitions, not guilt tripping. Just sharing: feelings, experiences, histories, successes and failures. And that nonjudgmental approach—which is so different from AA—makes people feel better about themselves and allows them to pursue their goals better, longer, and in more areas of their lives (drinking included, but not exclusively). And what are their goals around drinking? Well, you'll have to read this book of human stories to see!

As much as the disease theory and abstinence dominate our thinking to this day, there's no question that the world of addiction and alcoholism has changed in more tolerant, useful directions through harm reduction over the many decades I have been fighting this struggle, when I often seemed to be almost alone.

Medication-Assisted Treatment Rears Its Ugly Head Again

Ken and April aren't psychologists, or psychotherapists. They help in their own fashion.

For Ken, this includes a belief in MAT, medication-assisted treatment. With alcohol, this treatment is naltrexone, which supposedly lessens people's cravings for alcohol. Ken ardently supports naltrexone therapy (which he doesn't use himself). With respect to MAT drugs for heroin and opioids, like Suboxone and methadone, it has been shown that as long as people continue to use them as substitute narcotics, they are less likely to die. Labeled and recognized as palliatives or life-stabilizing measures rather than as treatments, they have real benefits. Naltrexone (also marketed as Vivitrol, and combined with an anti-muscle spasm drug, baclofen) has never been shown to produce reliable benefits.

Charles O'Brien is, along with Nora Volkow, the doyen of chronic brain disease treatment. An O'Brien team at the University of Pennsylvania decided that naltrexone's results were unpredictable because people with different genotypes responded differently to the drug. To map this genetic nirvana, the researchers divided subjects into groups with and without a specific allele (variant of a gene) they believed was crucial to receiving naltrexone's benefits. In 2015 they published the results of administering naltrexone to alcoholic subjects on an array of measures, including amount drunk, first drinking episode, number of drinking episodes, and intensity of drinking episodes.

On every critical measure, those with either genotype reduced their drinking exactly as much, and in the same pattern, whether receiving naltrexone or a placebo. Moreover, as occurred with Project MATCH, the benefits of the treatment appeared *instantly*, with the first administration of the therapy. O'Brien and his colleagues summarized: "A significant reduction in heavy drinking occurred across all groups. Other drinking outcomes, and all secondary outcomes, demonstrated similar time effects, with no genotype × treatment interaction."

As shown throughout this book, people's self-conceptions, beliefs about alcohol and drugs, and personal motivation determine recovery from addiction. There *is* no other form of recovery than self-initiated and maintained recovery. *No drug can free us from addiction.* Recognizing this is the liberating, internal part of change. With their self-conceptions, beliefs, and motivations freed, addicted people can then hope to develop skills, establish meaningful connections with the world, and build or rebuild satisfying lives.

Have no fear, though, the O'Brien study in the prestigious JAMA *Psychiatry journal hasn't dampened anyone's enthusiasm for naltrexone treatment* (including Ken's). Naltrexone has become the new misdirection in alcoholism therapy. When another friend of mine, Gabrielle Glaser, wrote in

The Atlantic in 2015 about how ineffective AA is, she proposed naltrexone as *the answer*. Likewise, in 2015, the popular New York City public radio show *Radiolab* revealed in an episode called "The Fix" the secret, hidden discovery for curing alcoholism—yes, naltrexone. I unspooled this madness yet again in *AlterNet*.

As always, America, including its radical addiction reformers, will search for any shortcut to the task of improving the lives of people and the world in which we live, which seems a diminishing possibility and a retreating goal in our time. As perhaps impossible as it is to achieve, nothing can replace that goal for individuals, groups, and the world. As Archie and I wrote in concluding our 1991 book, *The Truth About Addiction and Recovery*, outlining the Life Process Program:

> Although the Life Process Program is oriented primarily towards self-help and effective therapy, we cannot change America's addiction problems without addressing our social and physical environment. Even the best addiction treatment will not significantly affect America's overall levels of addiction. Treatment is simply too expensive, too inexact, and too belated for therapy to do anything but apply first aid. *The only way we can really do something about addiction is to create a world worth living in* (my repeated emphasis).

Part IV

What Will Become of Me, Addiction, the World?

My entire life's purpose, ordained at the dawn of my consciousness, was to be a world figure and to change the earth. From the start (at five years old) my ideas centered on addiction.

How have I done? I'm a known quantity, a brand, one that's frequently referenced, and most of my key ideas from forty to fifty years ago have been integrated into mainstream addiction thinking. But I am still largely discounted and a pariah in much of the addiction field.

Nonetheless, I continue to provoke the field and its leading practitioners. Along with Carl Hart, I indicate that we need to develop a new relationship with intoxicants, as I describe in Filter *magazine ("Encouraging Positive Drug Use"), since our current relationship (as mediated by AA), including that proposed by reformers, is a disaster.*

In the meantime, I have survived and enjoyed myself, in cities and on beaches, in books and movies, in relationships, in writing and creating tempests. In the shifting life in the city, due to Covid-19, reading and movie-"going" now occur with Amazon and Netflix. Will there always be the ocean? For I live in Brooklyn, a beach community.

Conclusion: My Home
Ain't in the Hall of Fame

My home ain't in the hall of fame
You can go there you won't find my name.

> — Joe Dolce, as sung by Robert Earl Keen,
> "My Home Ain't in the Hall of Fame"

Standing astride a field peopled by plodding researchers, complacent clinicians, and deluded ideologues, Stanton has made his mark as a scientific theorist, a philosopher, a social critic and commentator, and a policy analyst.

> Archie Brodsky, "Stanton Peele:
> Sixtieth Birthday Tribute," 2006

When *Love and Addiction* came out in 1975, it opened my eyes completely.

> — Bruce Alexander, about Rat Park

I had severe problems with drugs for seventeen years or so. I had gone down the road of twelve-step programs, introduced to me through a drug treatment centre. In 2002, I found your book *The Truth About Addiction and Recovery* at my local library. I read it and began to implement the life process program for myself. I returned to school and became a horticulturist. My life is now rich and full, I am married and a father to a six-year-old daughter. I am fit, and I have many interests and hobbies. I just wanted to let you know what a difference you have made to my whole life. Thank you so very much.

> — John Rothfuss, Perth, Australia, 2020

Another testimony to what many of us already know. For every person like this who takes the time to locate you and write to you, there are thousands more who have experienced what he has. You're a national treasure, but what's new about that? I've been saying that for years.

> — Dan Hostetler, CEO, Above and Beyond
> Recovery Center, Chicago, 2020

The reach of online programs is unparalleled and evidence shows they can work. We will need them since we are about to witness an almost unimaginable jump in the rates of substance use and other addiction diagnoses and treatment.

> — Stanton Peele, "Online Addiction Therapy
> Can Go Viral," *The Fix*, 2013

Being banned [for dancing cheek-to-cheek with his drummer on TV] in America is the highest accolade. I admire anyone who can get up and be what they want.

> — Ray Davies (of The Kinks)

Who Loves You, Baby? (Telly Savalas, as Kojak)

In the Life Process Program we have people write a series of "memoirs." They begin by writing a narrative, including all the bad spots, of their lives, then one that highlights their successes and strengths, then one that describes their future.

I began my memoir ruminating on whether I'm a real and influential—a seminal—figure in the addiction field, or a meteor who's had a few moments casting off light as it streaks, and sinks, over the horizon.

Critics can ask, "Stanton Peele—who is he?" Or they can ask, "Stanton Peele, Mr. Outsider? Peele, who attended and taught at America's leading universities and wrote a revolutionary best seller before he was thirty; who traces his career back to Norman Zinberg, Charles Winick, Hal Mulford, and Don Cahalan, all of whom he knew personally; who knew early directors of the National Institute on Drug Abuse and National Institute on Alcohol Abuse and Alcoholism; who has years/decades-long relationships (often contentious) with central figures in the addiction and alcohol fields like Ethan Nadelmann, Carl Hart, Marc Lewis, Sally Satel, Maia Szalavitz, Johann Hari, Bruce Alexander (the inventor of Rat Park), Dwight Heath, Robin Room, Bill Miller, Alan Marlatt, Nick Heather, and Aaron Beck and Albert Ellis (the last two inventors of cognitive behavior therapy)—all of whom have given him kudos for his original ideas; who stayed at the home of the Italian head of the Kettil Bruun Society; who has lectured throughout Canada, Ireland, Australia, Italy, the UK, Scandinavia, and Hungary; who disputed with Gabor Maté in a coffee shop in Vancouver; who, while teaching at Harvard Business School, played basketball with a key editor at *The Atlantic* who later published his article debunking an alcoholism gene; who was friendly with Bill Moyers's daughter and her husband, later director of Greenpeace; who met the mayor of New York at the Brooklyn YMCA and through him the city's mental health commissioner; who, in his seventies, rushed from a symposium with the founder of the internationally lauded Portuguese drug-regulation system to a gala with Chicago mayor Rahm Emanuel for an inner-city addiction outreach program whose billionaire founder cited him from the podium; who runs an international addiction-coaching service headquartered in Northern Ireland; who is the only contemporary figure identified on the Rutgers Center of Alcohol Studies timeline; who, for Chrissake, got the last copies of the treatment manuals for legendary Project MATCH from the director of the

National Institute on Alcohol Abuse and Alcoholism (NIAAA) while waiting to see the Queen of the Netherlands—that's Mr. Outsider?"

But, although I am a successful independent intellectual, my career has been rocky and borderline. In the 1980s the director of my home state New Jersey's Division of Alcoholism called me an "embarrassment" at an NIAAA alcoholism conference. I wasn't invited to participate in or add input to the seminal alcoholism research Project MATCH—none of its organizers, who knew me, would even consider doing so! (You can see a list of my "Accolades and Brickbats" beginning on page iii and online [see References].)

Lately, I have been invited to speak in a few places in the US by a libertarian political group and on a videoconference by the leading drug policy reform group, Drug Policy Alliance (DPA), as well as a Canadian venue, along with some international venues. But, on the whole, I rarely speak in the US, and *never* at American universities or addiction conferences, even harm reduction venues.

My landmark books, *Love and Addiction* (1975), *The Meaning of Addiction* (1985), *Diseasing of America* (1989)—books that Tom Horvath (longtime head of SMART Recovery), Ethan Nadelmann, Marc Lewis, Maia Szalavitz, and the Rutgers Center of Alcohol Studies website (among others) cite as changing the way we think about addiction—along with my 1991 anti-disease self-help book, *The Truth About Addiction and Recovery*, appeared in 1975 through 1991, thirty to forty-five years ago.

Many believe that I am past my time. Yet I seem always to be relevant, increasingly so. Several writers observed of addiction during the pandemic:

Addiction in a Time of Crisis

The two keynote conference speakers (at Northern Ireland's 2019 national addiction conference), Stanton Peele and Marc Lewis, really are top of their game and their work will I believe be highly influential on addiction policy in the future. So here's a potted version of their ideas. Addiction is not "a disease" and "drugs are not addictive." Rather, addiction is an extreme manifestation of a pretty standard brain repertoire. This has been known for years and boils down to the statement "I didn't become an addict because I had something better to do." With good relationships and a purpose in life we don't become addicted to drugs. Suffer from social exclusion, low self-esteem or have ACEs (adverse childhood experiences) then we are more likely to grab forcefully onto behaviours that instantaneously bring relief from those negative emotions that burden us: anxiety, shame, boredom.

— Slugger O'Toole (an opinion portal in the UK), 2020

Why the Pandemic Will Challenge the Brain Disease Model of Addiction

Many addiction researchers, such as Carl Hart, Stanton Peele, and Maia Szalavitz, have laid out persuasive alternatives for explaining addiction that focus on an individual's adaptive response to their environment. Bruce Alexander, who conducted the famous Rat Park experiments of the 1970s and '80s—which found that rats removed from social isolation and given toys and rat friends to play with were less interested in self-administered morphine—argues convincingly that a major underlying cause of addiction is the "breaking of social links that give people a sense of belonging, meaning, and identity." Addiction to substances or behaviors (gambling, shopping, sex, etc.) is how some people adapt to this social dislocation. It is experienced by both rich and poor, though people who face economic hardships are more likely to suffer from social ones as well.

Katharine Neil Harris, the Alfred C. Glassell, III,
Fellow in Drug Policy at Rice University's
Baker Institute forPublic Policy, in Filter, 2020

Writing Popularly

I have always reached out to influence public opinion. I was active and somewhat successful in publishing opinion pieces in major publications such as the *Los Angeles Times* and the *Wall Street Journal*, among others (but *never* the *New York Times*, despite scores of submissions). I'll just cite the one of these that went most viral, and the one I am fondest of. Right after O. J. Simpson's pathetic car ride and "farewell" letter in 1994, I interpreted in the *L.A. Times* how O. J.'s note was actually an elaborate shifting of blame for murder to his dead wife, Nicole. (I wrote it on a borrowed laptop in a San Francisco hotel while at a conference with Mary.) The piece was picked up by both Howard Stern and Don Imus. In 2007, I laid out in the *Wall Street Journal* how Lindsay Lohan should "recover" by evolving her life, one of many pieces I did for *WSJ*—a prescription she ultimately fulfilled.

In 1996, I created the Stanton Peele Addiction Website with my Dutch webmaster, Arjan Sas, and began writing hundreds of blogposts there in response to readers' queries. (Using my time in this way with no direct economic benefit drove Mary wild.) By 2011 this ceased to be the best way to reach out publicly, and I started writing blogposts for the *Huffington Post*.

Huffington Post

I wrote blogposts for *Huffington Post* from 2011 through 2014, when, as I describe in the previous chapter, I was booted with no notice for running afoul of Arianna. I did about a hundred pieces, of which I'll mention four: I pointed out Donald Trump's extremely successful bullying style in 2011; in 2013 I analyzed the null impact the Human Genome Project had in identifying specific genes as the causes of various mental illnesses (it actually proved the reverse); back in 2011 I wrote "Are Addiction and Mental Illness Really Brain Diseases?" which was distributed throughout the National Institute on Mental Health; and "AA Is Ruining the World" (unwise, it turns out, given Arianna's kiboshing of my column).

Reason and *Psychology Today*

There are two popular print publications, *Reason* and *Psychology Today*, in which I've been influential for decades, where I held sway with my views of addiction, and with both of which I became an active blogger. Neither any longer accepts articles from me.

I began publishing in *Reason* in 1990, with my radical "choice" view of addiction, "Control Yourself," followed by twenty-five entries, including both articles and blogposts at the extremely popular Reason website (see References for link to the list). The last article I was to publish in *Reason* was in 2014, "Addicted To Brain Scans," which discusses the myopia with which the American psychiatric diagnostic manual (*DSM-5)* decided that one activity, and one activity only, gambling, could be addictive.

All of my articles for *Reason* were commissioned and edited by Jacob Sullum, who himself has become one of the most outspoken critics of conventional presumptions about drugs and addiction in the pages of *Reason* and in his blogposts. Jacob's 2004 book, *Just Say Yes: In Defense of Drug Use*, was a radical libertarian declaration, much of which he credited to me. I attended a book-signing party for Jacob in Greenwich Village at the home of a well-heeled libertarian supporter. I was struck by the opulence of the surroundings and the built-in support Jacob received from this philosophical/political group. Jacob appropriately acknowledged me up front in his remarks there.

In 2019, Jacob and I were co-panelists (along with Joycelyn Elders, among others) at a CATO Institute panel, "Is It the Drug? Rethinking Conventional Views of Substance Use, Abuse, and Addiction." Jacob told me over breakfast that he used my technique of asking the audience whether they had used painkillers, and with what effect. Virtually no one in our securely middle-class audience will have become addicted, even the few who say they had some difficulty giving up the drug. We combined to do that exercise together at the CATO symposium.

Jacob turned the fact of the overwhelmingly benign use of prescribed painkillers into a 2018 cover story for *Reason:* "America's War on Pain Pills is Killing Addicts and Leaving Patients in Agony." I can describe

Jacob's outlook by quoting Barack Obama, who spoke at the US governors' conference at which he was the only dissenter from the unanimous resolution to restrict painkiller prescriptions. Obama announced that he supports them in their mission to quell the nation's opioid epidemic, but he refused to support a limit on how many painkillers a doctor can prescribe at a single time:

> If we go to doctors right now and say "Don't overprescribe" without providing some mechanisms for people in these communities to deal with the pain that they have or the issues that they have, then we're not going to solve the problem, because the pain is real, the mental illness is real.

Obama's brilliant, prescient comments came in 2016, amidst a steep downturn in painkiller prescriptions and a sharp upturn in drug deaths.

In pre-reviewing his article, I chided Jacob for using the term "drug overdose" promiscuously in describing the nature of these deaths (which he changed). Jacob, during a brief period in which he was an editor at the conservative *National Review*, published an article of mine in 1994: "Hype Overdose: Why does the press automatically accept reports of drug overdose, no matter how thin the evidence?" I described the *New York Times'* shrieking front-page story on the "pure" killer drug, China Cat, when a spate of drug deaths occurred in New York. Further *Times* reports on this event, buried within the bowels of the paper, revealed that a majority of the victims *hadn't used heroin at all*, and that virtually all of them had consumed multiple drugs and/or alcohol.

"Drug overdose" is the term applied in the United States to all people who die consuming drugs, well over 90 percent of whom have chaotically consumed combinations of substances—as I had been describing for years. This error, which the *Times is* resolute in propagating (it printed no retraction or correction of its China Cat headline), along with many others about drugs, matters. Much of America's failure to reduce drug fatalities could be cleared up by the knowledge that pure drugs don't kill people. If this were understood, then the US might establish drug consumption sites, or even facilities that provide heroin, of which it currently has none. This possibility has been buried by political opposition and popular resistance, steeped in drug myths, while drug deaths spasm out of control to record levels nationwide, both before and after the pandemic. No death has ever been reported at supervised facilities in Europe.

But, as I note in Chapter 9, why would mainstream Americans care about that?

Reason Foundation runs an extremely popular website, separate from its printed magazine, with a million or more visitors daily. At one point, a young *Reason* writer, J. D. Tuccille, became blogposts editor. J. D. was a big fan of mine and ran nine of my blogposts in 2014–15, including: "The Hijacking of Sobriety by the Recovery Movement," "Government Says You Can't Overcome Addiction, Contrary to What Government Research Shows" (about the typicality of natural recovery), and "George Washington: Boozehound." Thanks to J. D. for the last title, which was my most popular blogpost at the website, with over 10,000 likes—this was a piece about the remarkable amount of alcohol Colonial Americans, notably the authors of the Constitution, imbibed.

My last such post was in 2015, when J. D. was replaced by a senior editor at *Reason*, Peter Suderman, after which nothing of mine has been published in the magazine or at its website. Indeed, I can't even get a reply from Reason now (other than apologies from Jacob).

Psychology Today's view and treatment of me is perhaps more puzzling.

I've published landmark articles in *PT* for five decades, to wit: "Love Can Be an Addiction" (with Archie, 1974); "Through a Glass Darkly" (on the attack on controlled drinking, 1983); "The Best Way to Change Is to Change" (on natural recovery in addiction and alcoholism—this article appeared in *American Health*, which T. George Harris owned for a time along with *PT*, 1983); "My Genes Made Me Do It" (with Rich DeGrandpre, 1995, about the overestimation of the genetic contribution to behavior); "Recovering from an All-or-Nothing Approach to Alcohol" (1996, attacking our abstinence fixation); "The Surprising Truth About Addiction: More people quit addictions than maintain them, and they do so on their own" (2004); and my 2010 article, "Addiction in Society: Blinded By Biochemistry," on the non sequitur in the forthcoming (three years later) *DSM-5* that there were (a) substance use disorders and (b) behavioral addictions. Well, only *one* behavioral addiction, the only addiction in the universe according to *DSM-5*, gambling.

I ended the last article, ten years ago:

Think about obsessive-compulsive disorder (OCD): People are not diagnosed based on the specific habit they repeat—be it hand-washing or checking locked doors. They are diagnosed with OCD because of how life-disruptive and compulsive the habit is. Similarly, addictive disorders are about how badly a habit harms a person's life. Whether people use OxyContin or alcohol, people aren't addicted unless they experience a range of disruptive problems—no matter how addictive the same drug may be for others. [Maia was to make the same connection to OCD in her best seller *Unbroken Brain*.]

Of course, the same criteria hold true for having sex and shopping.

Before my last article in *Psychology Today* magazine, in 2008 I initiated a blog for the *PT* website called "Addiction in Society." By 2020, I had posted over eight hundred blogs. I had 6.5 million "hits." It would be impossible to even sample my posts, but let me list six: "What Killed Anthony Bourdain?" (2018, celebrity posts get the most hits, in this case approaching a half million—the short answer is "love addiction"); "The Solution to the Opioid Crisis" (this is a direct answer to then-and-now Surgeon General Vivek Murthy); "Drew Barrymore: Sober Newlywed Winemaker" (2012, read the commenter who says it is pathetically obvious that Drew is a relapsed alcoholic!); "The Seductive, But Dangerous, Allure of Gabor Maté" (with Alan Cudmore, 2011, it has hundreds of comments, one of which I cite in Chapter 1—it's remarkable to see the hatred with which Maté supporters strike out); "The 7 Hardest Addictions to Quit— Love is the Worst" (2008, my third most popular blog, with over a quarter million hits); "Romeo and Juliet's Death Trip: Addictive Love and Teen Suicide" (2008).

In 2020, I received this note from my editor about a blogpost in which I projected AA's status in the age of the pandemic (it was removed from the *PT* website):

> Hi, Please perhaps post this elsewhere. Your views on AA are yours, not *PT*'s. If you still wish to post this on the *PT* site, please rethink the AA section.

Thus I was banned from mentioning AA by the organization that created a nationwide furor when it published my defense of harm reduction in 1983, "Through a Glass Darkly," against the AA-based assault in *Science.* Et tu, Brute?

The Sciences and reductionism

Some of my proudest publications were for *The Sciences*, the most sophisticated (and humanistic) popular science magazine. Published from 1961 to 2001 by the American Academy of Sciences, *The Sciences* featured "articles that discussed science issues with cultural relevance, illustrated with fine art. The periodical won seven National Magazine Awards over the course of its publication" (Wikipedia).

I read and loved *The Sciences* decades before publishing in the magazine. I learned from it that real scientists eschew reductionism—reducing everything to its elemental biological and physical components—since they understand what is lost in the process. In 1984, I wrote "The New Prohibitionists: Our Attitudes Toward Alcoholism Are Doing More Harm than

Good." In it, I traced the backlash against controlled drinking, represented by the Pendery group's assault on the Sobells in *Science*, to America's temperance past. In 1989 (the year *Diseasing of America* was published) I wrote "Ain't Misbehavin': Addiction Has Become an All-Purpose Excuse." In 1998, my final effort at commenting for *The Sciences* on America's dysfunctional attitude toward alcohol and approach to alcoholism: "All Wet: The Gospel of Abstinence and Twelve-Steps is Leading American Alcoholics Astray."

Numerous outlets that today present popular interpretations of science are resolutely reductive. The more they can eliminate humanity, social structure, and human decision making when dealing with behavior—including, especially, addiction—the better! In *AlterNet* in 2016 (where some people liked me), I discussed Radiolab's "finding" that alcoholism is a biological entity that has been shown to be resolved by a couple of pills: baclofen (a muscle relaxant) and naltrexone. As I always say about such declarations: "We're home free, no more alcoholism (or addiction)!"

Incredibly, the same reductive resolution is true for *humanistic* periodicals, like *The Atlantic*. In 1990 I published in that periodical "Second Thoughts About a Gene for Alcoholism: Claims of a genetic basis for alcoholism, a leading theorist argues, are not scientifically supportable and ignore the crucial link between personal values and self-destructive or antisocial behavior." That could *never* be published today, even though, as I wrote in 2011 in *The Huffington Post*, after the Human Genome Project, no scientist any longer thinks there is a gene for alcoholism. Instead, in 2015, *The Atlantic* published a piece, "The Irrationality of Alcoholics Anonymous" (by a friend of mine!), claiming the true answer for alcoholism is naltrexone.

Finally, returning to *WSJ*, I wrote "Send In the Clones." In it I explained that, even tracking identical twins raised in the same home, you don't end up with identical people—my futile, I fear, answer to the destructive fantasy that gene splicing will remedy addiction and every other lived malady that (increasingly) besets us.

Academic Peele

After leaving the Harvard Business School, my pinnacle of academic success, which occurred outside the field in which I was trained and had a degree, social psychology, I aspired to return to academia. Mary and I briefly moved to Oakland, but then returned East, where her employer transferred her. Beginning in the 1970s and throughout the 1980s, living in New Jersey, hopeful of resuscitating my academic career, I published journal articles centering on addiction.

1977. "Redefining Addiction I: Making Addiction a Scientifically and Socially Useful Concept." I began by attempting to translate the insights in *Love and Addiction* into academese, here for the *International Journal of Health Services*.

1981. "Reductionism in the Psychology of the Eighties: Can Biochemistry Eliminate Addiction, Mental Illness, and Pain?" *American Psychologist*. *American Psychologist* was the flagship journal of the American Psychological Association. It was *highly* selective, accepting one in ten submitted articles. But (per Chapter 11) I had Peter Nathan in my corner.

Reductionism is a critical label applied to the idea that translating a phenomenon from one level of analysis to another is beneficial. This idea is fundamentally flawed. Reductionists not only believe that nothing is lost by reducing a higher-level phenomenon to lower-level components or interactions, but that some kind of explanatory power is gained. In fact, essential meaning is lost by ignoring causal influences present only at the higher level. My article surveyed the reductive beliefs and practices, just beginning to permeate psychology, that cause people mistakenly to attempt to reduce psychology to biology. A premier reductionist whose work I highlighted, neurologist Richard Restak (who wasn't actually a neuroscience researcher), was famous for his claims around what was then newly emerging neurochemistry. Restak's best sellers *The Brain* (1984) and, later, *The Mind* (1988), as turned into PBS specials, popularized that claim that examining the brain would solve all of our mental health problems. Aaron Beck and renowned evolutionary biologist Richard Lewontin loved this article. Both wrote in praise of my books.

The first neurochemicals to be discovered, called endorphins, prompted this 1979 paean from Restak:

> Medical researchers tend to frown on overenthusiastic claims about "miracle cures" and "wonder drugs." Yet behind the scenes in medicine today, waves of high excitement are being generated by a group of biochemical agents called endorphins. So far, researchers have carefully avoided hyperbole in their descriptions of the endorphins. But it's hard to leave out the exclamation points when you are talking about a veritable philosopher's stone—a group of substances that hold out the promise of alleviating, or even eliminating, such age-old medical bugaboos as pain, drug addiction, and, among other mental illnesses, schizophrenia.

Here is reductionist thinking in its baldest form: we would soon eliminate addiction, mental illness, and pain through biology. As Chapter 9 reviews, this promise hasn't been borne out; rather, the reverse has occurred: as the reductionist impulse flourishes, mental disorders and addiction rampage.

1984. "The Cultural Context of Psychological Approaches to Alcoholism," *American Psychologist*. I attempted with this article to elbow my way into the academic world of alcoholism research, the one occupied by Alan Marlatt and Bill Miller, again with the help of Peter. By synthesizing clinical, epidemiologic, and cultural research into a unified vision, it gained the attention of leading figures in alcoholism research like Marlatt, Miller, and Robin Room.

1985. "How Can Addiction Occur with Other than Drug Involvements?" *British Journal of Addiction* (now called *Addiction*). As I have recounted, this was a challenge to the academic addiction field to rethink the meaning of addiction, the title of my book that was reviewed that same year in that journal by the doyen of international addiction studies, Griffith Edwards.

1986. "The Implications and Limitations of Genetic Models of Alcoholism and Other Addictions," *Journal of Studies on Alcohol* (now called *Journal of Studies on Alcohol and Drugs*). As mentioned, *JSA* was the emblematic journal of the Rutgers Center of Alcohol Studies. Getting a piece like this placed there was nearly impossible. In this article I reviewed the major genetic theories of alcoholism, showing that they were mutually incompatible and failed to account for basic facts about alcoholism.

You might ask how I became so conversant with genetics as to publish such a piece in alcoholism's leading journal. (Shucks, just gifted, I guess.) Later, when I published an article about the "discovery" of a gene for alcoholism in 1990 in *The Atlantic*, Archie had me meet with a radical Harvard biogeneticist, Paul Billings. After reading my article, he said, "You understand the basic tenets of genetics research." For example, Kenneth Blum found a specific gene allele in the brains of alcoholics he examined, which turned out to be characteristic of African American males whose corpses he studied. The standard in the field is family line studies, in which different members of a family either do or don't manifest a given malady (say, schizophrenia), for which the studied allele is correspondingly either present or absent.

1987. "The Limitations of Control-of-Supply Models for Explaining and Preventing Alcoholism and Drug Addiction," *JSA*. Almost instantly after publishing my genetics piece, I went to almost the opposite end of alcoholism research, reviewing epidemiological and policy research in the Rutgers journal. I combined drug addiction and alcoholism data, while considering historical, cultural, and psychological variables. I showed that the relationship between consumption level and addiction, alcoholism, and substance use problems, at both the individual and the cultural level, was illusory. Room, who wrote a come-lately and inadequate response, and his ilk hated this piece. Nonetheless, it won the Mark Keller Award in 1988 for the best article to appear in *JSA* in the previous year. (Impressive, huh?)

1987. "Why Do Controlled-Drinking Outcomes Vary By Investigator, By Country and By Era? Cultural conceptions of relapse and remission in alcoholism," *Drug and Alcohol Dependence*. As I describe in the previous chapter, in this article I analyzed the frame of the research rather than the elusive picture. This analysis was required to explain the wide range in harm reduction outcomes reported by different studies and researchers. Nick Heather, among others, found this article particularly brilliant.

1987. "A Moral Vision of Addiction: How People's Values Determine Whether They Become and Remain Addicts," *Journal of Drug Issues*. In which I reintroduced the radical idea that people's values are critical in whether they become enmeshed in addiction and how long they remain addicted, a lever that is used in motivational interviewing therapy and in my Life Process Program. Really, why do people decide to quit an addiction, say, smoking, when they become pregnant, for instance, or when their daughter says they'll never speak to them again after they wake from heart surgery and ask for a cigarette? Do you think a brain scan will tell you that?

This "moral" piece was so far outside the standard academic pale that it was in fact a tombstone for my academic aspirations. Here is the abstract of the article:

> Contemporary theories of addiction of all stripes rule out faulty values as a cause of addiction. Yet evidence from cross-cultural, ethnic, and social-class research, laboratory study of addictive behavior, and natural history and field investigations of addiction indicate the importance of value orientations in the development and expression of addictive behaviors, including drug and alcohol addiction, smoking, and compulsive eating. Furthermore, the rejection of moral considerations in addiction deprives us of our most powerful weapons against addiction and contributes to our current addiction binge. The disease myth of addiction in particular attacks the assumption of essential moral responsibility for people's drug use and related behavior, an assumption that we instead ought to be encouraging.

Why did I make the colossal effort of getting such articles published in leading journals? Recall that I published significant articles in the flagship journals of the American Public Health Association (on alcohol and health) and the American Political Science Association (on political identity). Remember, I published *The Meaning of Addiction* and *Diseasing of America* in the 1980s, as well as a collection of my own articles in *The Science of Experience* (1983) and an edited volume of the leading theories of addiction entitled *Visions of Addiction* (1988). All to no avail. No university would touch me.

So I—and certainly Mary—tired of my dabbling in academia with no concrete results. From time to time I've been drawn back in. For example, Roy Baumeister, a social psychologist, had written a 2011 best seller with a friend of mine, John Tierney, *Willpower: Rediscovering the Greatest Human Strength*, based on Roy's research on people's development and exercise of self-control. Roy asked me to contribute an article, which I titled "People Control Their Addictions," to a 2016 journal volume on choice and addiction that he co-edited. My piece was an answer to Nora Volkow's "Addiction is a Disease of Free Will," a 2015 blog from the director of the NIDA, before she started switching horses. It came to be cited as part of a substantial change in Wikipedia's description of addiction.

The Politics of Publication

Getting those articles published in the leading academic psychology and alcoholism and addiction journals was quite a feat. My pieces for *American Psychologist* were vouchsafed by Peter Nathan, for whom I seemed to represent a yearning to speak truth to power that he repressed in himself. Peter showed that he would never do such a thing himself by positively reviewing Vaillant's *The Natural History of Alcoholism* in *American Psychologist*, without noting the disagreement between Vaillant's data and his conclusions. (Peter later told me, with a wink, "I know what you were getting at" in my negative review of the book in the *New York Times Book Review*, for which Vaillant himself never forgave me.)

My pieces in the *Journal of Studies on Alcohol (and Drugs)* relied on crafty placement. Nancy Mello and Jack Mendelson were behavioral psychologists at Harvard who performed laboratory studies showing how malleable alcoholic drinking was, given changing conditions and rewards. As *JSA* editors who were dubious about genetic determinism, they navigated a good landing for my article. My improbable selection for the 1988

Keller Award was piloted by Harry Levine, the brilliant historian of the disease concept of addiction and the Temperance Movement, who was on the award committee.

Editors select reviewers to decide whether a paper should be published by the journal (a role I have often performed, for example, as an editor for *Addiction Research and Theory*). *I have never had a major article published without the strong objections of one reviewer.* Peter Nathan would pick three reviewers (required in such a keynote journal as *American Psychologist*) and then publish my pieces based on the two positive reviews he solicited.

My piece on sociocultural and historical variations on measured controlled-drinking treatment outcomes was published in *Drug and Alcohol Dependence*, whose longtime editor was Chris Johanson, whose research and whose history with me I have described. More than a decade later (2000) she published my and Archie's review, "Exploring Psychological Benefits Associated with Moderate Alcohol Use," an explosive topic in America. Guess who wrote a rejoinder? That's right, Robin Room, who actually reviewed the conference I organized, "Permission for Pleasure" (which he didn't attend).

A *very* odd thing happened with the review of variations in apparent controlled-drinking results in my 1987 article for Chris. The negative evaluation was a fifteen-page treatise so detailed and well-informed, and yet so reactionary, that I divined who had written it (the reviews are anonymous). He was one of the most prominent people in the American and international addiction arena, Thomas Babor. Babor was on the central committee for Project MATCH. He was the longtime American editor of *Addiction*. He was a prominent member of the Kettil Bruun Society.

I was aware of Babor, but had never spoken to him. However, walking through the hallway at the 1988 alcoholism conference at which I debated James Milam, I crossed his path. *For the only time in my life, I spoke directly to Babor:* "Tom, your review was so detailed they should have published *it*." He smiled sheepishly, acknowledging that he had written the review. We each then walked on.

I initially submitted my "Moral Vision of Addiction" to *Psychological Review*, next in importance to *American Psychologist* as American Psychological Association periodicals, but less congenial to the author's taking a point of view. After it was rejected there, I submitted it successfully for publication to the more radical, but less prestigious, *Journal of Drug Issues. Psychological Review* rejected it based on another remarkably detailed negative treatise from a reviewer. This review included this long quote from my book of a year or two earlier, *The Meaning of Addiction*, which it cited positively!

The Requirements of a Successful Theory of Addiction

A successful addiction model must synthesize pharmacological, experiential, cultural, situational, and personality components in a fluid and seamless description of addictive motivation. It must account for why a drug is more addictive in one society than another, addictive for one individual and not another, and addictive for the same individual at one time and not another. The model must make sense out of the essentially similar behavior that takes place with all compulsive involvements. In addition, the model must adequately describe the cycle of increasing yet dysfunctional reliance on an involvement until the involvement overwhelms other reinforcements available to the individual. Finally, in assaying these already formidable tasks, a satisfactory model must be faithful to lived human experience.

Around this time, Indiana University held a working conference to commemorate the University's presenting Alan Marlatt with an award for his distinguished career. Alan, a Canadian, received his Ph.D. from Indiana before moving to the University of Wisconsin. At Wisconsin he published his 1971 study in which conditioned alcoholics drank more when they thought a drink contained alcohol than when it actually did. This breakthrough study led to Alan's heading the addiction program at the University of Washington, where he spent the rest of his life.

Ovide Pomerleau was a participant at the Indiana conference. He was a behavioral psychologist in the University of Michigan's medical school. Pomerleau's research consisted of extinguishing alcohol cravings by gradually exposing the alcoholic drinkers to alcohol stimuli, like smelling alcohol, without allowing them to drink. How useful is that? When I saw Ovide at the hotel we shared, I greeted him, "I'm glad that you balanced your rejection of my article by admiring that quote in *The Meaning of Addiction*." Like Babor, Pomerleau smiled sheepishly and acknowledged his negative review of my subsequently published article.

Places I'll Never Be Accepted or Acknowledged

As I said, I persisted in the illusion that I might get an academic job through the 1980s, what with my extraordinary publication record. But that's not how academic hiring works. Departments want people who are mainstream researchers. I applied for a social psychology position I saw advertised at a mediocre university. One of the faculty members there had been a grad student of Stan Morse's at NYU. He took the trouble of writing me a response shaming me for imagining that I might aspire to having such a post, given my lack of research in social psychology.

So, with Anna, born in 1988, our add-on third child, and Mary fed up with the obvious dead-end of my academic career, I turned my mind to money-making (as I describe in Chapters 7 and 8), using my skills at Lou Harris and Mathematica and in independent survey research with health insurers. I went on to make a small fortune exploiting my addiction insights with cigarette manufacturers, alcohol producers, and the Exxon *Valdez*. Dear Lord, forgive me. Archie said that it was okay, seeing that I had nowhere else to turn and I was presenting findings and analyses consistent with my body of work and viewpoint. After Anna graduated from NYU and I bought her a condo in 2008, I created my Life Process Program, first for a residential rehab program, then as an online coaching service.

The most symbolic example of an institution that will *never* acknowledge me is the prestigious international journal, *Addiction*. Robert West is its editor-in-chief. Dr. West covers the same turf as me, including his *Theories of Addiction* (2006) and *Stop Smoking Now* (2013). In the latter, West describes addictive smoking as a brain response to nicotine and recommends nicotine replacement therapy.

There is no hope for me at this journal, despite my 1985 incursions into its pages with love addiction and *The Meaning of Addiction*. In 2016, I proposed that I describe for the journal how the field has changed in my direction in the thirty years since I last published there. I know several people on *Addiction*'s editorial board, including two "strategic advisers": Wayne Hall and Jalie Tucker. Tucker participated in the Kettil Bruun conference on natural recovery from addictions in Switzerland at which I delivered what was regarded as a rather bang-up synthesis of the proceedings. I was invited to the conference (along with George Vaillant) by its organizer, Harald Klingemann, a central European I have known for decades. I was a contributor to its frequently cited 2001 summary volume, *Promoting Self-Change from Addictive Behaviors*.

Wayne Hall replaced Nick Heather as head of the Australian National Drug and Alcohol Research Centre from 1991 to 2004. In 1998, with Wayne as director of the Centre, I co-keynoted at Australia's national addiction conference in Brisbane. My co-presenter was an Australian psychiatrist who had been an overseas adjunct to Project MATCH. The results of MATCH had just been published, and I produced my projection transparencies in the hotel overnight. I covered all of the same points as the psychiatrist. But let's say I was a little more penetrating. On the same visit, I gave the inaugural address for the Stanton Peele Lecture at Deakin University in Melbourne.

Mary enjoyed this trip very much.

So I thought to navigate through Hall to propose a review of the status of the addiction concept in a debate forum in *Addiction*. The result:

> Your proposal for a For Debate piece on the meaning of addiction was considered at this month's *Addiction* Editorial Board meeting teleconference. . . . The board thought that *your views on the topic were well known* [Robin Room's wording in rejecting my suggestion that Kettil Bruun invite me to discuss the potential benefits of alcohol; see Chapter 11] and *could be published in other outlets*. . . .
>
> I'd suggest trying the *International Journal of Drug Policy*. It publishes *more diverse and dissident views on addiction* than many more mainstream addiction journals. Its editors are *less committed to the addiction concept*. . . . [my emphases]

I reacted to Archie (copying Hall): "My views are well-known to the *Addiction* editorial board, but they won't be known to the readers of *Addiction* any time this century." Note that Hall and the editorial board seem to think that I'm not committed to the addiction concept, whereas my two previous appearances in their journal concerned my book, *The Meaning of Addiction*, and my analysis of "How Can Addiction Occur with Other than Drug Involvements?" In 2020 I wrote for *Filter* "In Defense of the Concept of Addiction." Incidentally, Archie *had* written an article for the *International Journal of Drug Policy* in 2001, entitled, "A Classic Holds Its Ground: A Review of Stanton Peele's *The Meaning of Addiction*."

Here is a 2015 analysis of the addiction concept by four European investigators:

> As Peele [1985—the authors also refer to *Love and Addiction*] summarized it, "addiction may occur with any potent experience." . . . It is of interest that until recently, mainstream addiction research has greatly departed from this broad definition of addiction that can encompass any kind of behavior whatsoever. Instead, there has been a clear tendency to over-identify addiction with substance abuse and to distinguish drug addiction in particular as a unique phenomenon, quantitatively and qualitatively distinct from behaviors and habits of everyday life. However, *recent evidence in psychology, behavioral economics, and neuroscience seems to increasingly suggest that the qualitative dichotomy is unwarranted and that addiction to drugs shares essential commonalities with motivated or goal-directed behaviors in general* [my emphasis].

After leaving Australia's National Research Centre, Hall became the inaugural director of the Centre for Youth Substance Abuse Research. I have written him about my work and my recommendations for preventing addiction in youths, but Wayne has never responded. It may be relevant that he has taken a strong position on the dangers of marijuana.

Finally, I should note the anomalous position occupied by Jim Orford in re *Addiction*. I discuss in Chapter 11 how Orford has covered the same turf that I have from a similar perspective. Jim is British and rather well-mannered—more so, say, than Nick Heather. He presents his radical positions with a composed demeanor. He is a cooperative, rather than a challenging, presence. Orford certainly has never confronted his mentor Griffith Edwards's contorted attitudes toward addiction, and especially the "consume-more-and-you-become-addicted" shibboleth, even while he hasn't joined in those. Orford published his global view that addiction isn't substance-related, "Addiction as Excessive Appetite," in *Addiction* in 2001, a decade and a half after mine appeared there. Yet Jim doesn't refer to my earlier article or to *Love and Addiction* or *The Meaning of Addiction*, seminal works in the canon of unified theories of addiction. Is Jim joining in my boycott in that journal? As a sign of the British addiction society's appreciation, Orford earned the prestigious Jellinek Award in 2010 and a complimentary profile about his career by the journal's publisher, the Society for the Study of Addiction.

Thomas Babor, Keith Humphreys, and Me

Thomas Babor (whom I confronted at the 1988 NIAAA conference—the only time we spoke) is best known for his anti-alcohol work with Griffith Edwards and Robin Room (see *Alcohol: No Ordinary Commodity*, 2003). His view of drugs is also entirely negative, as in *Drug Policy and the Public Good* (2010), for which he is lead author: "Drug use represents a significant burden to public health through disease, disability and social problems." Babor, Hall, and Keith Humphreys (who has opposed cannabis legalization in California) come to substances with an entirely different perspective from the drug policy reformers I know. I once introduced Wayne Hall and Ethan Nadelmann at a symposium Hall was presenting in New York, in which I brought up marijuana. Their meeting was uncomfortable.

Babor is concerned about research and writing on addiction. He is lead co-editor of *Publishing Addiction Science* (3rd edition, 2017), with advice for those seeking advancement in the field: "More competitive universities that value high publication numbers might urge students and junior faculty to compose theoretical papers and review articles or to write reports based on publicly sourced unpublished data" (that's a description of my acaemic career, although I don't do it to pile up "high publication numbers"). The world of addiction has exploded, Babor and colleagues note:

"During the latter part of the twentieth century, there was rapid growth in the number of people employed in the societal management of social and medical problems associated with the use of alcohol, tobacco, and illicit drugs. At the same time, similar growth occurred in the number of institutions and individuals engaged in addiction science."

Babor would *never* cite me or invite me to present my work. Indeed, as with my article in *Drug and Alcohol Dependence*, he does all he can to suppress my views—which, according to Hall, he (as an editor of *Addiction*) knows well, despite his having nowhere ever discussed them.

Keith Humphreys had replaced Babor as American editor of *Addiction*. The two are connected—Humphreys was a co-editor of *Drug Policy and the Public Good*. When *New York Times* investigative reporter Ian Urbina claimed in a front-page story that *DSM-5*'s classification of mild, moderate, and severe substance use disorders meant that minor substance use problems were now to be regarded as addictions, he called me several times for an interview. But my concern isn't that *DSM* overly classifies addictions. I'm concerned that Americans' addiction-proneness is anchored in their concept of addiction. Urbina instead got Humphreys and Babor to make his case.

As for my history with Keith Humphreys, I met him at that same monumental natural recovery conference group in Switzerland. Keith didn't actually participate, but I spoke with him and his wife at the hotel we shared. I had admired Keith's early work. Humphreys was a highly feted young star in Stanford's community psychology program, directed by Rudolph Moos. Moos's emphasis was that addiction recovery was mediated by, was expressed through, real-life, measurable changes that a person made, and not by the type of treatment that they received. I thought Humphreys expressed this perspective brilliantly in a 1993 piece in *American Psychologist* in which he detailed how government funding had shifted from providing actual assistance for people's lives (through housing, education, health, etc.) to providing ever-increasing reams of addiction treatment. Per Humphreys: "In the 1980s, the Reagan and Bush administrations reduced funding for community mental health programs and began instead to support substance abuse treatment agencies."*

This shift, as he described it, seemed to be something Humphreys regretted. So when Humphreys went from noting how real-world changes define recovery to celebrating AA, it seemed to me an extreme reversal in his thinking.

---

* Keith kindly sent me this link.

I have noted that *Addiction* big shots such as Humphreys, Babor and Jalie Tucker are Americans, and Hall and Robin Room Australians. Nonetheless, the British establishment—centered around (now-deceased) Edwards and others in the cadre of the British Society for the Study of Addiction—are resolutely (or is that simply passively, like Orford) inured to considering me a major addiction figure. Yet British (and Australian and Canadian) psychologists are as a group well-disposed toward me. It is not accidental that a major British academic publisher (as I describe at the very front of this volume and in the Acknowledgments) contracted to publish my memoir, as they have done with several important British psychologists. It was impossible for them to deal with my persona and my outlook, however. As my father Ted would say of me as a child, their eyes were bigger than their stomach. But no American academic publisher would even *flirt* with taking on my story.

Are Alcoholism Treatment/12 Steps Really Working?

In 2020, Keith Humphreys and John Kelly made news by conducting a systematic review in the prestigious Cochrane Report asserting, contrary to an earlier review, that AA works. It has been widely noted. But their analysis is simply a sleight-of-hand, a shuffling of the deck, as I indicated in my review of their analysis for *Filter. No research over many decades contests a clear picture of the results of 12-step treatment and AA*, to wit:

1983. George Vaillant's *The Natural History of Alcoholism.* I have mentioned several times my *New York Times* review of the disparity between Vaillant's data and his advocacy for AA. *But Vaillant himself found AA and 12-step treatment ineffectual.* Evaluating his 12-step treatment program at Cambridge Hospital, including compulsory AA attendance, Vaillant noted that his patients "fared little better than the natural course of the disease," including a 95 percent relapse rate and a death rate *at least as bad as for untreated alcoholics.* *"Perhaps the best that can be said for our exciting treatment effort at Cambridge Hospital is that we were certainly not interfering with the normal recovery process"* (my emphasis).

1989. On request to the Harvard Medical School, Vaillant (irately) sent me his data, which I re-analyzed in *Diseasing of America.* Those in his general sample *who went through AA and achieved remission were more likely to relapse than those who did it on their own.*

1997. Project MATCH. Twelve-step facilitation (TSF) over twelve sessions, compared with motivational enhancement over four (average attendance was two-thirds for all treatments), found no overall differences in functioning and recovery—although TSF subjects abstained somewhat more.

2003. Bill Miller and his colleagues' meta-analysis of the effectiveness of various treatments in comparison to one another, or to no-treatment groups, resulted in these "cumulative evidence scores" in favor of their efficacy:

- Brief interventions: +390
- Motivational enhancement: +189
- Community reinforcement approach: +110
- Self-help manual: +110
- Twelve-step facilitation: −82
- Alcoholics Anonymous: −94

2005. The 43,000-person national survey of alcohol and drugs use, called NESARC, *found that, although a higher percent of those who went to treatment (meaning usually 12-step programs, including AA) abstained, overall a smaller percentage achieved remission.*

2006. Original Cochrane review found: "No experimental studies unequivocally demonstrated the effectiveness of AA or [12-step facilitation] approaches for reducing alcohol dependence or problems."

2020. New Cochrane review by Kelly, Humphreys, and Marica Ferri found that "42 percent of participants participating in AA would remain completely abstinent one year later, compared to 35 percent of participants receiving other treatments including CBT." "Continuous abstinence" was the sine qua non for AA/TSF's superiority. Yet, as I noted in my commentary, *no advantages were found in either overall functioning or recovery rates in AA and 12-step groups.* Moreover, the 12-step groups didn't show more *total days* abstinent or, mysteriously, even *longest period of abstinence.* These data point to people in the 12 steps abstaining, perhaps for long times, then explosively relapsing in binges. Nick Heather reached the same conclusion, citing me.

My summary:

AA and 12-step treatment, which totally dominate the American alcoholism landscape, have never, over repeated research assessments, demonstrated an ability to reduce alcoholism or improve overall life functioning for alcoholics. While increasing abstinence rates, these approaches to alcoholism can actually lead to more, and more intense, relapses over time (due, as I have already explained in regards to relapse prevention, to its all-or-nothing view of and approach to alcoholism and treatment). The 12 steps thus produce no better, and what can often be worse, long-term life functioning.

Moreover, whatever benefits, short-term and curtailed as these are, AA and the 12 steps produce, these come at the cost of persuading people with drinking problems that they are lifelong alcoholics who can never recover fully, or on their own, which is actually the standard outcome for untreated alcoholism.

The chief author of the Cochrane review, John Kelly, is a strong advocate for the chronic brain disease theory of alcoholism and addiction.

Kelly and Humphreys would *never* share a forum with me, or mention me or my work. Why should they?

Strangely, while I was writing this, in May 2020, I received an email from Reid Hester, whose work evaluating effective treatments I cite in the timeline above.

Hi Stanton, Might you be able to attend this on Friday? I think your perspective would be helpful. Thanks. Reid

"This" was a presentation by John Kelly on the Cochrane Report to the addiction division of the American Psychological Association.

Mark Schenker, the teleconference organizer for the addiction division, responded that he didn't think that a rebuttal would be appropriate in this context. (My views weren't circulated, but John did write me a detailed response—thanks to him. Mark also generously offered me the chance to present my online LPP addiction-coaching program to the American Psychological Association's addiction division, which I subsequently did with Zach Rhoads.)

Copied on these emails, Bruce Liese, who soon replaced Schenker in his organizing role, reacted to my mentioning that I had done a rather brilliant piece at his invitation for the division in 1998 in response to Project MATCH, titled "Ten Radical Things NIAAA Research Shows About Alcoholism." Liese wrote:

Hello All and Stanton,
Yes, your piece was quite brilliant!
    But I have another recollection of time with you that still makes me chuckle. We'll have to schedule an appointment, so I can remind you in person. And no (to the rest of the group), it didn't involve intoxication, crime, wild dancing, or any other misbehavior.

— Bruce Liese, Clinical Director, Cofrin Logan
Center for Addiction Research and Treatment; Professor
of Family Medicine and Psychiatry, University of Kansas

Kelly also gave the keynote address at the 2019 twenty-fifth Anniversary Conference of SMART Recovery, the AA alternative organized according to cognitive-behavioral principles. Kelly's presentation was his standard born-again chronic brain disease/abstinence address. I am on the scientific advisory board of SMART, and I wrote my longtime colleague Tom Horvath, the former SMART president who hosted the anniversary conference, about my disappointment. Tom indicated to me that having Kelly favorably oriented toward SMART was extremely advantageous.

When I published my critique on Kelly et al.'s Cochrane Report in *Filter*, Tom excitedly wrote me welcoming my piece, saying that he would distribute it widely. I have also always chided SMART for being entirely abstinence-based—how much better is it in that regard than AA? Now, after twenty-five years, Tom has been at pains to assure Zach and me that SMART is no longer exclusively abstinence-oriented. I congratulate him and SMART. But that certainly wasn't a focus at their quarter-century anniversary celebration conference or Tom's introduction of Kelly's keynote.

I have an odd role in the addiction world.

The Big Picture

In Chapter 9, I reviewed the Global Burden of Disease Study finding that, among 196 nations, deprived and advantaged, *the US was second in disability life years lost to drugs, and thirty-ninth in DALYs lost to alcohol.* As I reacted to the Cochrane AA review in *Filter:* "*The presence of 12-step programs in every US community is not succeeding by measures of life satisfaction, survival rates, or mortality due to drugs and alcohol.*" Does anyone disagree with that?

In attempting to corroborate AA's beneficial impact on society, do Humphreys and Kelly mean to say that our bottom-of-the-tank rankings for death and disability attributable to substance use, the last twenty years of rising drug deaths, and our painful societal guilt and unhappiness over drugs and alcohol are the best we can hope for? *They do.* They are pushing as a scientific assessment what actually comprises a reversion to the drug war and temperance. The bottom line to their work is that we should push AA and the 12 steps more than we have been doing for the past half-century, while accepting that substance use is beyond control for many people—moreover, a number that is increasing. *Why is this happening now?*

My views are closely aligned with those of my most longstanding colleague in the addiction wars, Bruce Alexander. Bruce sees addictive drug use as an "adaptive" mechanism, meaning people are coping with their lives and their emotions by relying on drugs' effects, even during sustained use. (We reviewed this and other theories in Chapter 3 of *The Meaning of Addiction*.) Bruce sees the development of addiction as a modern social phenomenon, one that is worsening due to the "breaking of social links that give people a sense of belonging, meaning, and identity." And, as I said in my presentation at the 1996 DPA drug policy reform conference, treatment of addiction as a disease is *itself* a basic pillar of our becoming an addicted nation:

> Despite the coerciveness and intolerance of American drug and alcohol treatment policy, the most alarming consequence of the expansion of treatment rolls is not the external imposition of views of alcoholism, but the willingness of so many people to accept and internalize these definitions of themselves as alcohol and drug abusers and addicts. This trend will accelerate with expanding treatment.

Keith Humphreys and John Kelly, for all their renown, are at the opposite end of the spectrum from my views on addiction, treatment, and society. I—along with Bruce Alexander and Carl Hart—believe that drugs are secondary to the principal drivers of addiction: the loss, or absence, of human, social, and individual engagement and belonging. Clamoring for abstinence and more treatment through lifelong abstinence-oriented programs is firing out of the wrong end of the barrel.

Worse, those habituated to AA believe their recovery depends on the group. And, worst of all, that they lose all hope for themselves if they ever drink (remember Terry McGovern).[*]

My Case for My Nobel Prize

Another place aside from *Addiction* where I will never be welcomed is the University of Michigan, where I got my Ph.D.

Michael Lewis wrote the best seller *The Undoing Project* (2016) about the research, careers, and relationship of Amos Tversky and Daniel Kahneman. Tversky won the MacArthur "Genius" Award in 2003 and Kahneman the 2002 Nobel Prize for economics (there is none for psychology). All of this was set up, according to Lewis, by their selection to give the "prestigious annual Katz-Newcomb lecture at the University of Michigan" in 1979.

Dan Katz and Ted Newcomb created a short-lived experiment at Michigan combining psychology and sociology into one integrated social psychology program. I was among the last to gain a Ph.D. from that program in

---

[*] As this book went to press, surprisingly, Kelly (with Sally Satel) acknowledged the very points this book is at pains to make around the disease theory:

> Alex [hypothetical sufferer of the brain disease addiction] was seen as least blame-worthy when the opioid addiction was described using the biomedically loaded term ("chronically relapsing brain disease").... The problem is that the use of medical terminology led to a lower perceived likelihood that Alex could recover, greater opposition to social inclusion, and a greater perception that Alex was dangerous.

1973 (in fact it was defunct by the time I got my degree from it, as I describe in Chapter 5).

Dan Katz was my Ph.D. advisor and the chair of my dissertation committee. We had a good personal relationship, unusually close for a senior faculty member and a young grad student. I didn't know Ted Newcomb well. But when I dedicated my 1981 volume of collected papers, *The Science of Experience*, about taking a non-reductive approach to human behavior, to Katz and Newcomb, I received a handwritten thank you note from Ted, who was retired and living in California. Dan Katz died in 1998. And I must say that, however kind he was to me, he never took my work seriously enough to propose my name for the award in his name. The following analysis *is strictly my own.*

What Dan and Ted and I shared was a vision of human behavior as taking place in a social context. Newcomb became known for his studies of women students at Bennington College, which showed that their shared social environment brought their individual attitudes into close alignment (called the "proximity principle"). Dan Katz was a pioneer in studying the impact of organizations on their members (he wrote the classic textbook on the subject, *The Social Psychology of Organizations*), which was why he was able to get me a job at the Harvard Business School.

Dan Katz and Herb Kelman later studied political dynamics from the standpoint of how people conceived of themselves as citizens, that is, their political roles and identities. Stan Morse and I found that Vietnam War protesters felt that their civic duty was to protest and correct government wrongs, for which we won an award for the Society for the Psychological Study of Social Issues. In South Africa we studied the mixed-race "Coloureds" (a specific designation for a racial subgroup called "Cape Coloureds") who might have identified with Black rebellion and power, but who instead aligned themselves with the ruling whites. Finally, for my Ph.D. dissertation, we studied the South African white electorate, particularly a group born in Afrikaans homes who voted for the English-based United Party. In order to make this political transition, though, they had shifted to an English identity. Stanley and I (with Archie's assistance) published this research in the *American Political Science Review*. Dan Katz put me on a panel at the American Psychological Association's annual conference with Herb and him to discuss my and Stanley's work.

I applied this social-cultural-identity perspective to addiction. Unfortunately, Katz and Newcomb weren't tuned into America's thinking about addiction and mental illness as biomedical phenomena, whereas these are actually crucially affected by personal beliefs and cultural attitudes. This reductive approach is something they should have been aware of—it's ubiquitous—and deconstructed. Our social groups and cultural attitudes and beliefs impact the experience of addiction, causing its increasing incidence and severity, in the same way that they determine people's political identities. But such thinking was beyond their ken.

Tversky and Kahneman don't reflect this view of the interplay of social and psychological factors that Dan Katz and Ted Newcomb developed. Rather, they viewed decision-making as an entirely individual phenomenon. They asked subjects, generally students, to make quick hypothetical decisions about well-defined situations and judged their answers against the "correct" economic answers. In this light, people usually give wrong answers. Tversky and Kahneman then identified systematic judgment biases (called "heuristics") that lead people to make such inaccurate economic deductions.

Nothing actually happens in these paper-and-pencil "mind" experiments that the researchers administered; people don't actually do anything or make real decisions or purchases. My reaction is: Who thought people acted in line with formal economic models in the first place, and who cares about judgments they make about made-up people and situations? What about the troubles people encounter in how they raise their children or form relationships or engage in harmful habits? What kinds of people, under what circumstances, make *self-destructive* decisions? How do they improve, or not, in their actions and judgments? Those are, for me, crucial psychological issues.

My perspective and approach, like Katz's and Newcomb's, is anchored in the real world and is intended to be directly useful. *It was because I wanted to do such work that I rejected purely experimental social psychology programs at Stanford and UCLA that offered me fellowships in sunny California and went to Michigan.* Such real-world applications are touted for Tversky and Kahneman's work—for example, in Tversky's consulting on the army officer-selection process in Israel, or in a disciple of theirs working to gain seatbelt compliance in Canada. But these didn't stem from their own, actual research and theories; the connection seems stretched thin to me. And how crucial to human psychology are those things anyway?

Nonetheless, as I noted in my Foreword, I'm not going to win the Nobel Prize or MacArthur Fellowship. And I won't be invited to give the Katz-Newcomb lecture. Indeed, I could never get invited to speak in any forum at Michigan—remembering that psychologist Ovid Pomerleau, who deconditioned alcoholics by strapping them down and having them smell alcohol, and medical historian Howard Markel, who declared Freud and Halsted hopelessly addicted to cocaine, were faculty at Michigan's medical school, at whose animal lab I divined the nature of addiction. And, while I'm at it, Penn, where I got my undergrad degree and Richard Solomon harangued me, would never invite me to speak—despite my amusing lecture style and ability to engage an audience in discussion, as well as my pioneering, revolutionary ideas about addiction. In fact, I never get invited to speak about addiction at *any* American university or conference.

I can only hope that if Bruce or Carl or Nick wins the Nobel Prize, they'll credit me in their speeches. (I have no chance of that if Sally or Marc or Bill or Jim wins it.)

My home ain't in the Hall of Fame; you can go there, but you won't find my name.

I'm Still on the Edge

My longest running social engagements with someone in the field (after my years of dining in New York with Ethan) were my bimonthly dinners with Will Godfrey, the figure behind the cutting-edge harm reduction digital periodical, *Filter*. Will, fresh from Britain with his American wife, was introduced to the recovery field as an editor for the traditional 12-step digital periodical *The Fix*.

I wrote about twenty-five pieces for *The Fix* between 2011 and 2016. Ironically, my first piece was in defense against my being attacked in that very publication, "The Controversial Heretic Who's Taking on AA and Abstinence." My self-defense was needed because a *Fix* writer, Ruth Fowler, included me in her article (which was published at *The Atlantic* website), "10 People Who Are Revolutionizing How We Study Addiction and Recovery," where I joined Bill White, Nora Volkow, Bill Miller, and Keith Humphreys. But then an editor at *The Fix* (not Will!) tampered with the piece in that periodical to make me look idiotic.

Other prominent pieces I placed there included, in 2015, "12 Concepts of Recovery That Have Stood the Test of Time: Because one way is not the only way, *The Fix*'s Stanton Peele offers hopeful options." My, I seemed to be flying high!

Earlier, in 2013, newly separated from my rehab partners, I promoted my online Life Process Program with "Online Addiction Therapy Can Go Viral." At the time, this was a radical position: "At a time when diagnoses are set to increase, I'm working to establish online treatment. Some doubt the value of Internet programs, but their reach is unparalleled and evidence indicates they can work." Thus I previewed what became reality during the pandemic, and will clearly outlast it: "It began as a stopgap way to get through the pandemic, but both participants and providers say virtual sessions have some clear advantages and will likely become a permanent part of recovery."

In my piece, I explained my entire therapeutic logic:

> While I am a great believer in self-cure for addictions, I have also spent my career offering help to addicted individuals through writing, counseling, and treatment programs. My feeling is that people will tend to seek out the level of help they need—and they should be given a range of choices to permit them to do this. The online Life Process Program provides empowering assistance for people to do what they must ultimately do for themselves—come to grips with their addictions.

A typical LPP client wrote us:

> The goal of LPP is to make us independent, to regain control of our lives. When this is achieved, it is normal to leave LPP. Surely you understand that your business model is one in which, in a way, in order to help the customer, you actually have to work to get rid of him. Just like a doctor, or a psychiatrist.
>
> The reason groups such as AA retain their people is, as I see it, because their method doesn't really work. So people keep going back.

Or, in my view, they commit a worse sin: convincing people that AA or the group is the *essence* of their recovery, an irreplaceable part of their lives and identities.

After my earlier involvement in *The Fix*, I joined onto Will's first foray into digital publishing. Substance.com was a revolutionary periodical that Will launched in 2014, for which I became a columnist, churning out two to three articles a month. But the recovering owners of the publication soon became aware that Will wasn't running a standard 12-step rag, and they pulled the plug on him in 2015. Fairly soon after, in 2016, Will jumped to a new recovery-industry backer to create *The Influence*, again with me as a regular columnist.

Will lived in the next neighborhood over from me during this period; I was in Park Slope, Will in Boerum Hill. We settled on meeting at Vinny's, halfway between us in Carroll Gardens, where we discussed Will's conflicts with his owners. Then—you guessed it—*The Influence*'s ownership became alienated from Will and me and *that* periodical shut down in 2017. Neither my Substance.com nor *The Influence* columns are available at those sites any longer, although they were regularly reprinted in *Pacific Standard* and the AlterNet (where my interview with DPA co-director asha bandele was published as "Straight Talk from One of America's Top Addiction Specialists"). Perhaps my most prominent articles for Will's earlier publications were "My Traumatic Breakfast With Gabor Maté" and "We Need to Stop Nora Volkow from Taking Over the World."

Will then resurrected himself by creating a nonprofit organization, The Influence Foundation, with new, more harm-reduction supportive funding, to issue his current digital publication, *Filter*, with Archie as a board member and with me as a contributor. In it, Will adopts the modern harm reduction approach, where AA, the disease model, and abstinence are not the be-all of treatment; a variety of drug policy reforms—including drug maintenance and injection sites—are monitored and supported; and drug use is recognized to be an ongoing feature of many people's lives, who are not to be despised due to it, as well as of life in the United States of America.

At the same time as I wrote for Will, I also wrote for "Pro Talk," a section of rehabs.com—a well-funded site that paid well. In November 2018 I wrote one last blogpost for the site, entitled "The Addiction Therapist's Guide to the 21st Century:* You may have to unlearn much of what you've been trained to do." Shortly after that piece, my rehabs.com editor wrote me:

> I wanted to touch base with you about Pro Talk going forward. As you likely know, Recovery Brands was acquired by American Addiction Centers a couple years ago. We were told things would not change and that we—meaning Recovery Brands—would maintain our neutrality, which held true until this December. Pro Talk and Pro Corner have very successful track records; we see about 300K unique visitors each month and engagement is always very high. Readers come to Pro Talk or Pro Corner and enjoy content that is written by a trusted expert with absolutely no sales agenda. However, things will be changing going forward.
>
> AAC is now looking to use pro writers *who work exclusively in their own treatment centers or to use current pro writers who are willing to be ambassadors for the AAC brand. Going forward, all Pro Talk and Pro Corner content will be used to promote AAC treatment centers, to drive traffic to AAC's own websites, and to increase AAC census numbers* [my emphasis].

This editor then told me that she was leaving, and any connection I had with rehabs.com evaporated into the winds of history.

Me and the Future of Addiction

My, I've burned a lot of bridges, haven't I? (Someone once suggested that a burning bridge should be my coat of arms.) On the other hand, let's give me credit. *For half a century, from the time I walked into Richard Solomon's office at*

---

* My author's home page at rehabs.com has obviously been tampered with.

the University of Pennsylvania with an article I wrote for a South African liter-ary magazine when I was 24, until publishing this memoir at age 75, I've got-ten my views into print, in popular and academic publications, against all odds, personal attacks, and professional sneers and slights. The views I have expressed contradict, in fundamental ways, American visions of addiction. To what effect? The myths I constantly joust against persist; that's why they're called myths—they live on no matter what the data show or the dire consequences of ignoring reality.

And now a cadre of popular (Johann, Maia) and scientific (Carl, Marc) writers duplicate (more or less) my concerns, my insights, my understand-ing of addiction. How this all falls out remains to be seen. Perhaps I'll rest with Marc Lewis's assessment of my role: "You are the pioneer. You put these ideas out long before anyone else was thinking this way. These ideas continue to reverberate in the addiction world and influence many people, many besides me."

In the meantime, here is the first sentence of the Wikipedia entry on addiction: "Addiction is a brain disorder characterized by compulsive en-gagement in rewarding stimuli despite adverse consequences." We'll see if, and for how long, Wikipedia maintains this myopic picture.

The Earth Shifts

I wrote about Wikipedia's treatment of addiction for my memoir near the end of 2020. By the time I came to finalize the manuscript, early in 2021, I noted two (amazing?) developments.

Wikipedia now has an entry for the Life-Process Model of Addiction, to wit:

> The life-process model of addiction is the view that addiction is not a disease but rather a habitual response and a source of gratification and security that can be understood only in the context of social relationships and experiences. This model of addiction is in opposition to the disease model of addiction. The proponents of the life-process model argue that the biological mechanisms that might account for addictive behavior have not been identified and thus do not support using the term disease, preferring to emphasize the indi-vidual's ability to overcome addiction by repairing relationships and personal strength of will.[medical citation needed]

And, then, Wikipedia changed its tune on the "brain disease" of addiction:

> Addiction is a biopsychosocial disorder characterized by repeated use of drugs, or repetitive engagement in a behavior such as gambling, despite harm to self and others. According to the "brain disease model of addiction," while a number of psychosocial factors contribute to the development and

maintenance of addiction, a biological process that is induced by repeated exposure to an addictive stimulus is the core pathology that drives the development and maintenance of an addiction. *Many scholars who study addiction argue that the brain disease model is incomplete and misleading* [my emphasis].

Wikipedia then lists six references. Three involve Nick; one Sally. And one of these references is: Peele S (December 2016). "People Control Their Addictions: No matter how much the chronic brain disease model of addiction indicates otherwise, we know that people can quit addictions—with special reference to harm reduction and mindfulness."

Earlier in this chapter, I quoted two reflections on how the pandemic will affect our view of addiction. I am central in both. One was published by Will in *Filter*. Will told me he was constantly impressed by how often I served as a touchstone for cutting-edge articles in his new-line, digital periodical. At the same time, I have a team of coaches with whom I work in my online Life Process Program, which I partnered in creating in 2012. LPP has grown in popularity and utilization worldwide as the pandemic materialized.

Yet, as I indicate in Part III, I am constantly clashing with the new-wave sentiment (which is really the same as the old) that medication-assisted treatment is the "answer" to addiction. Will Godfrey regularly hears objections to my point of view, creating stress and conflict for him. And, in fact, after I published twenty-five pieces at *Filter* (including one co-authored by Zach and one with Dolores Cloward) from September 2018 to December 2020, that pace clearly dropped off in 2021. (We'll see about the future.)

One of my colleagues at LPP, Aaron Ferguson, works as an outreach manager for a national MAT provider. As MAT has grown in popularity, Aaron, Zach, and I have created an LPP track, our "MAT Empowerment Model." We coach clients involved in MAT, past and present, that MAT is a means to allow people to organize their lives and to avoid criminal activity in procuring drugs, while hopefully protecting their health. In this way, we approach MAT as one tool alongside the other tools that LPP provides. But use of such tools is *not* who they are, any more than their addictions were.

◆

Carol Beyer, cofounder of the group Families for Sensible Drug Policy, wrote in 2020: "Stanton Peele had it nailed in the 1970s. We should've listened then. The disease model has been a slippery slope for many of our families who are held hostage by an addiction treatment industry that has in effect acted as an arm of the industrial prison complex—ensnaring and diverting its victims into an abstinence-driven model where failure to adhere to compliance is sanctioned, criminalized, and shamed."

Can anyone in the field deny that *if* my point of view *had been* adopted in 1975, the outcomes for American drug use, drug treatment and policy, and ability to cope with addiction would be better than in fact they have been? (How would Thomas Babor answer this question?)

So, in my seventy-sixth year, I maintain an active—perhaps influential—therapeutic, policy, and writing life in the addiction world. And, topping off my career, I'm completing this memoir. I can still count on Archie's help.

Now, all I have to do is survive until my Nobel comes through.

The Beach and Me

The beach—from going with my family from Philly to the Jersey Shore at Atlantic City, to taking my kids to North Jersey beaches like Spring Lake from Morristown, to going to the Queens beaches with my grandkids, to visiting those beaches with Archie along, to swimming by myself at dawn at Tilden—unifies my life. I live in Brooklyn, which is contiguous with Rockaway Beach (which is in Queens). Since I've moved to my current neighborhood, I've taken to swimming at Fort Tilden (I even took Alta Ann there from Manhattan one summer evening at dusk not long before the pandemic), another stretch of the Rockaway Beach within the Gate-

Oscar, Libby, Stanton, and Sara at Atlantic City, New Jersey

Haley, Dana, Stanton, and Anna at Spring Lake, New Jersey

way National Recreation Area. The beach has no lifeguards and people swim topless. I swim in the early morning, before sunrise, after biking to catch the Q35 bus to the beach. I did this even during the 2020 pandemic summer. I *am* a risk taker.

Swimming alone in the ocean in the city of New York at dawn is divine. Of course, I also have the burden of informing scofflaws, often nice young people, that dogs aren't allowed on the beach, leashed or not, during bird mating season, as a sign at the entrance proclaims. I say, "This magnificent beach within the city of New York is largely self-policed. It depends on people of good will respecting the rules."

I never let up.

The Post-Apocalyptic Memoir

I started this memoir prior to the pandemic, but finished it holed up in my Brooklyn apartment. *What are the consequences of this new world for addiction?*

I pride myself—stake my reputation—on my prescience: I declared in *Love and Addiction*, nearly half a century ago, that addiction is a broader phenomenon than just a drug-related one, which is now recognized universally. I was a pioneering, risk-taking advocate of harm reduction, and now of normalization of drug use. I have emphasized that addiction rates and mental health can only improve if the conditions of people's lives improve, a realization now taken up by Nora Volkow.

How will the new world created by the pandemic affect addiction, as well as our lives in general? It's impossible to say what human society will look like when the dust settles. So it is hard to say how the shutdown will affect our current epidemics of addiction and drug-related deaths. But the determinants and trends I have outlined seem likely to worsen:

1. The greater health and economic impact of the epidemic on those farther down the social ladder will push more people off the livable earth and into addiction and deaths of despair.

2. Mental health indicators—including anxiety, depression, and suicide—have been plummeting. The epidemic is likely to exacerbate those trends, although perhaps a battlefield mindset will encourage people to marshal their emotional resources for survival and to become more self-reliant, including in their use of drugs and alcohol.

3. With fear, isolation, and loss of community being such profound factors in addiction, the further isolation of children, of everyone,

with social distancing and quarantining, and the ever greater funneling of our lives through electronic and digital media, seem to predict more addiction.

I nonetheless believe that, individually and as a society, we can seek intimacy, community, and purpose in new forms and new ways. In LPP, with my partners Daithi Conlon and Zach Rhoads and with my coaches Dee Cloward, Anne Earle, and Aaron Ferguson, and the Above and Beyond Family Recovery Center in Chicago, I and others are exploring new ways for people to develop insights, skills, and meaning, interact with caring people, and form communities. These are essential human experiences, alongside of which we'll have to *recognize and incorporate constructive psychoactive substance use as part of normal human experience.*

Postscript

This has been my story, and every word is true. Except that Lynne and I didn't win the Trivial Pursuit contest I describe in Chapter 5—Anna and Alex did.

But we should have won.

Afterword: Observations about Stanton Peele

I tend to have deeply engaged relationships, with men and women, professionally and personally (thus my tendency toward conflict). In this Afterword I include some views of me from my professional colleagues.

Before that, however, I want to note one relationship with a neighbor in Morris Township, NJ, where I lived and raised my children in the 1980s through the early twenty-first century. This was Stu Levitt, a former college athlete. As a student at Haverford College, not generally regarded as a hotbed of intercollegiate athletics, Stu won the 1963 javelin competition at the Penn Relays.

Personal

When I knew him, Stu was on the faculty at Brooklyn College and coached local New Jersey high school athletes. I would drop by Stu's house to play pick-up basketball at a nearby court, sometimes with my son Dana. Stu took me on punishing bike rides and cross-country skiing routes. We wrote about our exploits together for *Men's Health*, in a piece about how a well-conditioned athlete could exercise with a less fit one.

But there was a stone in our stew. Stu's wife Nina didn't accept our independent socializing—a typical attitude in our suburban community, and perhaps even more broadly throughout America. Thus, I never ate a meal alone with Stu.

In the 1990s, Stu—seeking more perfect snow and air—moved with Nina to Whitefish, Montana. I didn't hear from him for twenty-five years. I then noted a 2019 article on the Internet, "The Odyssey of Stuart Levitt" (hey, the *Odyssey* is my bailiwick!). I wrote him in late 2020. Stu responded:

> Stanton,
> I owe you a debt of gratitude for helping me improve my teaching style more than 25 years ago. I remember you suggested that I ask more questions of students and I pursued that strategy and still do when teaching or coaching. It is fun and stimulating and added excitement to sometimes dull routines. I would enjoy talking to you since my vision is poor for typing or texting.
> —Stu

Colleagues in the Addiction Field

"New York is my playground," Stanton told me. "I look at it like an amusement park, there for my enjoyment." And he does! Stanton Peele lives with zest, curiosity, and relish. He has a million interests, areas of expertise and decades of accumulated knowledge. He engages with and seizes life.

Stanton is the source of modern thought in addiction theory and treatment, and I still, after many years, see him with slightly starry eyes. But I am also privileged not only to call him a friend; he has been an incredible mentor to me.

I'm not sure if people are aware of how gracious and charming he is, in addition to being fascinating. Talking with Stanton is as invigorating as it is educational about addiction and treatment.

I first met Stanton in an online chat at SMART Recovery 15 years ago. I have since had the occasion to work with Stanton on many projects. We have hosted multiple webinars at SMART Recovery, I serve as a coach and consultant at his revolutionary online Life Process Program, and we have written several articles and blogposts together. Stanton is all about giving me and others the opportunity both to grow and to input into his process and work products.

Working with Stanton goes right to the top of my list of amazing opportunities in life, for which I will always be grateful, appreciative, and awed!

—Dolores (Dee) Cloward, SMART Recovery facilitator and
formerly online director of training and special events
and podcasts, Life Process Program recovery coach
and group leader, private recovery coach, Cincinnati, OH

I was not invited to participate in the addiction field; I forced my way into the conversation. Yet, somehow, I've made friends along the way—Stanton Peele being my first.

I sought out Stanton's point of view when I discovered that he was the only person in the addiction field making sense regarding the relationship between trauma and addiction. From that point forward, Stanton has engaged me deeply: about addiction; about society; about myself—what it means to live my most meaningful and purposeful life.

For my part, I am a unique mix of disagreeable (as per my disagreement with the dominant "brain disease" addiction narrative) and persuasive/friendly (as per my large network of family, friends, and fellow community members who know and respect me). This bodes well for me in the two domains that comprise my life's work: my intellectual pursuits and my work in a helping profession.

Unfortunately, I was once sold a story about my own best characteristics—that they were deficits that needed to be tempered—a narrative that became self-fulfilling for a time in my life.

Stanton Peele has helped me turn this story on its head. I now recognize myself as a person with strengths and potential, as opposed to a person whose challenges usurp any hope of being successful.

He never told me this, directly. Instead, he mentored me on a journey of self-discovery through a meaningful partnership that involved helping people clinically and debunking mythology through writing. He taught me to work with him in tandem (balancing our respective strengths and blind spots).

This is Stanton's M.O. He would never tell people how they ought to view themselves; only that they might reconsider putting any ceiling on their own potential to live a great life. This is a level of self-awareness that Stanton has helped me achieve, without changing anything about my authentic self.

I see Stanton as the most honest intellectual I've ever known. I am forever grateful that he is my friend, colleague, and mentor.

—Zach Rhoads, youth and family counselor, Burlington, VT,
Life Process Program coach and consultant

My assessment of you, on the Thompson Scale of Impossibility, is that you rank about 50/50: You achieve the gold standard of principle and brilliance, with the generosity of spirit, acknowledgment of vulnerability, the curiosity and discipline to listen, assimilate, and shift perspective based on your own aims and your genuine respect for others' experience. Ultimately, I believe that anyone who wants to maintain a fulfilling relationship (working or personal) with you will find their life to be enhanced. They will need to trust that you are a straight-shooter, and I know that's hard for people. You are naturally upfront and thorough, and expect the same in return. They will also have to understand that, while you may get emotionally jangled when your expectations are not being met (and shoot straight about it), you are always more than willing to hear that you might be wrong. I treasure and honor you among the people I love best—the impossible and forever friends of my heart.

—Ilse Thompson, co-author of *Recover! Stop Thinking
of Yourself as an Addict*, and co-founder
of Stinkin'-Thinkin' participatory website

Before meeting Stanton Peele I read his books and articles and I was immediately fascinated by his intriguing approach to addiction. I was especially interested by his attention to the pleasure linked to alcohol and drug consumption, an area quite neglected among scholars in the field. Then I had the opportunity to meet him on at least three occasions: one international conference, the Kettil Bruun Society Symposium 2010 in Losanna (Lusanne), and two seminars in Italy. At the University of Torino (Turin) in 2010 we organised a seminar, "Drinking cultures and policy issues: what, how, where really work?" where Stanton was provocative and participants were impressed by his thesis that Italian drinking culture should have been looked at as a good example by the rest of the world and deserved more room in the scientific debate. Then Stanton and I were both invited to talk about drinking cultures in Florence by Forum Droghe, an NGO active in the drug area. On that occasion I gave a lecture on Italian drinking culture challenging the dominant thought that affirmed the change of Italian drinking culture toward a Nordic drinking culture. I was attacked by one participant belonging to an Italian public institution. There followed a heated and controversial debate in which Stanton Peele threw gasoline on the fire. After ten years I still meet people who were present at that seminar with a vivid memory of that moment.

But my best memories are our personal talks on our walks and hikes.[*]

—Franca Beccaria, Ph.D., past president,
Kettil Bruun Society for Social and Epidemiological
Research on Alcohol, Turin, Italy

I have had the great honor to accompany Dr. Stanton Peele during several of his professional visits to Above and Beyond Family Recovery Center, where he occupied the position of Impact Board Member for several years.

I'll start by saying that Dr. Peele's fame and notoriety seem to enter the room before him and prepare those he is about to encounter for a special experience. And then he assumes his endearing smirk. He always does it and it always catches me off guard. It's his signature grin that seems to indicate he already knows what's on your mind, which he just about always does.

Next comes the unexpected and impossible-to-anticipate question. I've come to notice that his questions seem well thought out, even though they are posed quite casually, and always reveal a deeper-than-expected knowledge of the recipient or of a relevant situational matter, that makes one typically wonder, "How did he know enough to ask that question?" Mark my words, they're good ones, and then he's off to the races with his questions, his incredibly insightful comments, and his push to make you dig deeper into yourself than you were prepared to. An encounter with Stanton is always a thought provoker, and his conversations are of the highest, most entertaining, and deeply insightful quality. I love talking to the man because he is so full of surprises and interesting perspectives. I have to say that I've learned something almost every single time I've been around him, and he convinces me that he enjoys my company as well. He is not a selfish conversationalist, and I've borne witness to conversations that have leapt, cajoled, and then humorously navigated in and out of some of the riskiest subject matter that I've encountered. Being around him became an adventure for me. The man is so studied and brilliant that any subject, any inkling of an idea, or any news item or event becomes a challenge to him to intellectually decipher as long as his curiosity lasts. I love talking with him and I am quite certain that I am not alone.

I suspect that he would like to be seen as a contrarian. But I do not know him this way. I have found him to be a very natural "devil's advocate," which most people are not prepared for. I am quite certain it's his way of getting you to challenge those things about yourself—your beliefs, your community, your culture, and your government—that you might never have questioned if you had not encountered Stanton and been forced to think about them. You can then reflect on your life choices and how they stack up in your value system. That's why I love his challenges. He is always very civil and is one of the most skilled

---

[*] While staying at Franca's home outside Turin, we took a trip to Piedmont, the primary wine region of Italy, from which Franca's husband hailed. He showed us how carefully and artistically the grape vines were tied to trellises in the field.

listeners I have ever encountered. He remembers your comments and reactions through long exchanges and will bring them back up, in pristine condition, during future discussions when they are relevant. I think this is the lawyer in him, which matches perfectly the medical and psychological sides of him.

I find our exchanges invigorating and meaningful. I can't help but think, during these periodic conversations, that I occupy the same position relative to Dr. Stanton Peele that many governments, professional organizations, and legal systems have! What an honor! Although he is educated in a not-often-encountered combination of professions, they match who he naturally is perfectly.

With me, he mixes his personal life into discussions we have about a myriad of subjects (he is knowledgeable about virtually *any* subject that is introduced) in an honest, casual manner that makes what he's saying all the more genuine and real. I love it when he does this, and I've witnessed him using personal anecdotes and parables during public lectures. He is incredible in front of large audiences, one of the reasons he is such a sought after public speaker. He has a unique humility about him that he punctuates with mentions of his victories and failures, both, so that you get an honest representation of who this man really is.

Finally, we have his vast body of work to speak of, which predicted much of today's common practices in psychology. The volume of his accomplishments is staggering by any standard and qualifies him as one of the most prolific psycho-legal minds in the business. He is unmatched by anybody I have ever met.

Because of the geographical distance between us, coupled with horrendously busy work schedules, I have found myself less in contact with Dr. Peele than I would like. I would hope that one day we will be able to devote more time to each other in the service of our shared efforts and vision.

Dan Hostetler, Executive Director,
Above & Beyond Family
Recovery Center, Chicago, IL

Stanton Peele: Sixtieth Birthday Tribute

Long ago I became accustomed to seeing Stanton reading, watching TV, listening to the radio, and carrying on a conversation, all at the same time. In his thirst for life, Stanton is not the moderate drinker he holds up as a behavioral and cultural ideal. He sucks in life—and shares it with his friends—with his own unique gusto. I know of no more energetic and energizing companion at all levels at once: physically, intellectually, culturally, morally—and I don't know if any such person exists in the world. Stanton has the most well-developed and multi-faceted sense of fun of anyone I know. Traveling with him is an experience that few can withstand, or even survive.

Stanton is one of the world's great iconoclasts, contrarians, and rascals. He provokes people, often for a serious purpose, and sometimes—well, just for the fun of it.

When Stanton was a kid, a teenager, he had a friend, a kind of soul companion at the time, who had filled the walls of his bedroom with pictures of great people: athletes, movie stars, writers, artists, musicians. Sartre and Camus might have been on that wall; Picasso, Churchill might have been there. As Stanton looked at those pictures, he realized how he was different from his friend, and how he would be moving on.

As he put it, his friend had invited those illustrious people into his room, where he would be content to commune privately with them for the rest of his life. That wasn't good enough for Stanton; he was entranced by the same people, but he was determined to go out and meet them on their own ground, out in the world where you test your imagination against real challenges and constraints.

And in his way, he did go out and become one of those great people. He didn't become a basketball or rock and roll star, or an actor, or a great novelist, playwright or film director, or a business or political leader. But with those models embedded in his being, as a social psychologist and innovator in the addiction field he found his way to center court, center stage, where he could articulate and implement a large vision. Standing astride a field peopled by plodding researchers, complacent clinicians, and deluded ideologues, Stanton has made his mark as a scientific theorist, a philosopher, a social critic and commentator, and a policy analyst.

The special gift that enabled him to do this was evident back when we were students at Penn, when I overheard him talking on the phone to a graduate instructor in our social psychology course. He had asked her to try to get the professor to raise his grade on a paper or an exam, and she called to say that after going back and asking the professor a second time she had prevailed. Instead of just thanking her as most undergraduates would have done, Stanton said to her, "I know you know you didn't have to do this, and it could only be trouble for you. I appreciate and admire your integrity."

Social psychology gave Stanton the best platform for expressing his natural skill and awareness at sizing up any situation involving human behavior and understanding it in psychological and moral terms. He wrote a powerful, groundbreaking book called *The Meaning of Addiction*. For Stanton, the meaning of addiction lies in what really motivates people as opposed to what they think motivates them—the comforting illusions they use to cushion themselves from reality.

Stanton's great gift, both innate and cultivated, is to look straight at the truth with as few as possible psychological and cultural blinders.

Stanton has not hesitated to expose the large blinders worn even by people in his own field, who should know better. As I wrote in a retrospective tribute to *The Meaning of Addiction*, "Peele extends his analytical probing to the point where he undercuts his own allies—which is why, at a personal level, he hardly has any allies." That's an overstatement made for effect, but even when he does have allies, whether in the addiction wars or in the dirt trenches of community and regional environmental preservation, nothing can deter Stanton's seriousness of purpose and his willingness, when necessary, to stand alone.

—Archie Brodsky, Cofounder, Harvard
Medical School's Program in Psychiatry and the Law,
at one of the low points of my life, after my divorce

Letter from an Unknown Admirer

We've met briefly, twice. Once at an early Harm Reduction conference and once when you were presenting at Ethan's operation in NY in the very early days. But I'm good friends with Maia [Szalavitz], so I feel as though I know you better than I do because she'd talk quite a bit about you. Also, I've been reading your books since *Love and Addiction* came out in UK paperback—so since 1975? Because of that, it feels like I've known you my whole adult life.

It was clear to me that you were a dissident voice in the US drug war and—particularly when you wrote *The Meaning of Addiction* and *Diseasing of America*—that you were one of the standout voices among a tiny number of American writers at that time. I'd just finished my master's dissertation on drug policy in the late '80s, so I knew what was out there. Who else was there? Arnie Trebach [Arnold Trebach founded the Drug Policy Foundation, which gave me my lifetime achievement award in 1994 and was the forerunner of Ethan Nadelmann's Drug Policy Alliance]. Andrew Weil with *From Chocolate to Morphine?* (OK, he became a food faddist and health guru.) Norman Zinberg? And you. That was it.

So when the intellectual climate shifted and harm reduction started to become fashionable, I really expected to see you get the recognition that I thought you'd earned. But I was also conscious that you had a lot of arguments in public—and you tended to decimate your opponents. And why wouldn't you? Anyone with half a brain cell could see that most people who wrote about drugs and drug policy didn't have a clue about the subject they were writing about. And the left were even worse than the right.

Anyway, as a consequence, I've always been curious about your backstory. I'm pretty sure anybody who has read any of your books would be as well. So I'm guessing a Stanton Peele memoir would sell pretty well. [Here's hoping!]

Peter McDermott, writer and researcher

Acknowledgments

I have written fourteen books over six decades, from Love and Addiction *in 1975 to this memoir in 2020–21. Archie Brodsky has played a crucial role through all of my work.*

In 2020, Mick Jagger and Keith Richards played together (from separate locations) in the "One World: Together at Home" concert. Critical reactions were that they nailed their performance. Jagger and Richards began writing and performing together as The Rolling Stones in 1962.

Archie's and My First Published Collaboration

In the summer of 1964, after our freshman year at Penn, Archie took a Greyhound Bus to San Francisco to stay with his sister, Sara Bailis. Sara (think, someone as smart as Archie without his genius and quirks), age 24, worked at Chronicle Features Syndicate, which sent columns from the *San Francisco Chronicle* (the most famous of which were by Herb Caen) to newspapers around the country. Archie worked there as an assistant for the summer.

Later in the summer, I hitchhiked to San Francisco to spend a week visiting Archie at his sister and her husband's home.

One of the *Chronicle's* syndicated columnists was a psychiatrist who missed a deadline during my visit. I offered to fill in and wrote about a friend whose relationship difficulties were on my mind. I was 18. Archie edited what I wrote to professionalize it. He was 19. The column was published as the doctor's column.

When we returned to Penn in the fall of '64, the Stones released their single, "Time is on My Side," in the States. Archie claimed it as our theme song. We have had many chances to question our destinies since then. (Of course, so have the Stones.)

Nonetheless, this book marks Archie's and my fifty-seventh year of collaboration, almost as long as the Stones (Jagger and Richards are slightly older than we are).

When I signed on with Penguin Books in England to write *Love and Addiction* in 1970, age 24, I was completely at sea as to how I would produce a book revolutionizing the field—the idea—of addiction. It was *impossible*, really. But Archie and I completed the job five years later, in 1975, when *L&A* was published.

Writing my memoir, to be published when I am 75, has been an equally formidable mountain to climb. Who would publish, and come to grips with, my ribald personal style, my revolutionary ideas, and my history of tempestuous relationships with people and institutions? We found a seemingly eager editor at a prestigious British academic publisher, and I signed a contract. But it became clear, between the editor and the publisher's legal department, that it wasn't going to be smooth sailing. So we parted ways. Nonetheless, we did gain value from her inputs, including both modulating my descriptions of others and more thoroughly explaining my ideas.

If you have gotten this far, you will have read about the many people to whom I am indebted, some of whom have no wish at all to be cited by me, including those who would prefer to be excised from my memory. Many of them—whom I mention in the text—nonetheless provided requested documents and information, for which I thank them.

I select for special mention Stanley Morse and Dan Katz for sorting me through my Ph.D., Will Godfrey and Zach Rhoads for reading versions of this manuscript, and Nick Heather for directing me to publishers (however unsuccessfully, ultimately). Nick has provided information for this book and performed other generous acts over the decades. So, too, has Tom Horvath.

And, then, at the eleventh hour, my cousin Richard Fromberg came forward to proofread and comment on a final draft of the manuscript. What a godsend! (One little family note: Rich admired the picture that appears on the cover of this book. In 2021 I wrote him that the coat I was wearing in the picture had belonged to our grandfather, Moishe Fromberg. He was stunned.) My friends Paul Bergen and Melanie Morris contributed additional helpful proofreading and comments.

Zach Rhoads and Daithi Conlon and my other colleagues at the Life Process Program have given me a different way of presenting my views and of helping people with addictive problems. Zach, in addition, has opened a new portal for me through our wide-ranging work together, including LPP, podcasts, writing, and our other efforts to impact the addiction world.

I have been supported emotionally since my twenties by Mary Arnold and, later on, Alta Ann Morris, as described herein; my children, especially Anna Peele and her husband, Alex Clothier; and my daughter-in-law, Jackie Peele, and my grandchildren. Without them I couldn't have made it.

Thanks also to Hongxia Shaw and Yolanda Likiardopulos, two local friends and helpers who have always had my best interest at heart.

Ultimately, I have published *A Scientific Life on the Edge* via Broadrow, Archie and his wife, Vicki Rowland's, publishing outlet.

This isn't the only time Vicki has saved my life.

A Little More Manic Than Usual

In 2014 I visited Archie and Vicki in Watertown, Massachusetts, in order to digitize *Love and Addiction* for reissue as an ebook. On the way to Archie's house from the bus stop, in 80-degree weather, I asked Archie to stop by the Charles River. I jumped in for a swim.

The next day, a Saturday, late in the afternoon, shivering, I asked Vicki to turn off the air conditioner. She said, "It's not on, and it's 80 degrees." Vicki then negotiated with me to go to the hospital. I refused, and she convinced me only by saying that Mount Auburn Hospital in Cambridge had an urgent care center. But when we got to the hospital, just down the road, I was instantly sent to the ER.

After Vicki helped the emergency intake clerk register me, I was rushed to an individual room in a wheelchair. IVs were placed in each of my arms. While a Harvard Medical School infectious disease specialist was called to the hospital, emergency nurses worriedly examined my vitals. My blood pressure got down to 38/18—a tick away from death.

Meanwhile, at my urging, Vicki called Archie and asked him to come to the hospital with a couple of pizzas, with which Archie entered the room. Sitting by my gurney, Archie examined each to decide which he wanted. The doctor, assessing whether I was delirious, asked Archie, "Does he always talk this much?"

Archie looked up from the pizzas, thought for a minute, and said: "He may be a little more manic than usual."

After the antibiotics kicked in and I was off life support, I spent a couple of nights being constantly monitored in a solo room in intensive care. They were especially concerned to make sure that the infection didn't spread beyond my lower leg, where it had entered my body. Archie came by to work on the ebook; the staff kindly provided him with lunch.

Oh, what strikes people as the craziest part of this story is that when I showed up the next August, I jumped in the Charles again while Archie sat on a bench reading the *New York Review of Books*. (Archie said it was okay.)

So a special shout out to Vicki, Mount Auburn Hospital, and Harvard Medical School—even if they gave Howard Shaffer a pass.

Selected Bibliography*

Anderson, K. (2010). *How to Change Your Drinking: A Harm Reduction Guide to Alcohol* (2e). New York: HAMS.

Anderson, K., & Smith, A. W. (2019). *Better Is Better! Stories of Alcohol Harm Reduction.* Philadelphia: HAMS.

Babor, T. F., et al. (2003). *Alcohol: No Ordinary Commodity.* Oxford: Oxford University.

Babor, T. F., et al. (2017). *Publishing Addiction Science: A Guide for the* Perplexed (3e). London: Ubiquity Press.

Beattie, M. (1986). *Codependent No More.* Center City, MN: Hazelden.

Beauchamp, D. E. (1980). *Beyond Alcoholism: Alcohol and Public Health Policy.* Philadelphia: Temple.

Berridge, V., and Edwards, G. (1981). *Opium and the People: Opiate Use in Nineteenth-Century England.* New York: St. Martin's.

Case, A., & Deaton, A. (2020). *Deaths of Despair and the Future of Capitalism.* Princeton: Princeton.

Centers for Disease Control and Prevention (2018). *Suicide Rising across the US: More Than a Mental Health Concern.* Centers for Disease Control and Prevention: Vital Signs.

Chafetz, M. E., & Chafetz, D. (1995). *Drink Moderately and Live Longer: Understanding the Good of Alcohol.* New York: Scarborough.

Cohen, P. (1974). *The Gospel According to the Harvard Business School.* New York: Penguin.

Commonwealth Fund (2020). *US Health Care from a Global Perspective, 2019: Higher spending, worse outcomes?* New York: Commonwealth Fund Issue Briefs.

Danler, S. (2020). *Stray.* New York: Vintage.

Doucleff, M. (2021). *Hunter, Gather, Parent.* New York, Simon & Schuster.

Edwards, G. E., Anderson, P., Babor, T. F., et al. (1995). *Alcohol Policy and the Public Good.* Oxford, UK: Oxford University Press.

Faris, A. (2017). *Unqualified.* New York: Dutton.

Frey, James. (2003). *A Million Little Pieces.* New York: Doubleday.

Glaser, G. (2013). *Her Best Kept Secret.* New York: Simon & Schuster.

Glassner, B. (1990; 2018). *The Culture of Fear.* New York: Basic/Hachette.

Hari, J. (2016). *Chasing the Scream: The First and Last Days of the War on Drugs.* New York: Bloomsbury.

Hari, J. (2018). *Lost Connections: Uncovering the Real Causes of Depression—and the Unexpected Solutions.* New York: Bloomsbury USA.

*This is a lisitng of books mentioned throughout the text. For a complete list of references, find them online at Peele.net/ScientificLifeRefs.pdf

Hart, C. (2021). *Drug Use for Grown-Ups*. New York: Penguin.

Hart, C. (2013). *High Price: A Neuroscientist's Journey of Self-Discovery that Challenges Everything You Know about Drugs and Society*. New York: Harper.

Hart, C. (2014). *Methamphetamine: Fact vs. Fiction and Lessons from the Crack Hysteria*. New York: Global Drug Policy Program (Open Society Foundations).

Heather, N, & Robertson, I. (1981). *Controlled Drinking*. London: Methuen.

Helliwell, J., Layard, R., & Sachs, J. (2019). *World Happiness Report 2019*. New York: Sustainable Development Solutions Network.

Henningfield, J., W. Bickel, & P. Santora (eds.), *Addiction Treatment in the 21st Century*. Baltimore: Johns Hopkins

Hester, R. E. & W. R. Miller (eds.) (2003). *Handbook of Alcoholism Treatment Approaches* (3e). Boston: Pearson.

Heyman, G. (2009). *Addiction: A Disorder of Choice*. Cambridge: Harvard.

Hindy, C., Schwartz, J. C., & Brodsky. A. (1989). *If This Is Love, Why Do I Feel So Insecure?* New York: Fawcett.

Karr, M. (2005). *The Liar's Club: A Memoir*. New York: Penguin.

Kasl, C. S. (1990). *Women, Sex, and Addiction*. New York: HarperCollins.

Katz, D., & Kahn, R. (1966; 1978). *The Social Psychology of Organizations* (2e). New York: Wiley.

Khar, E. (2020). *Strung Out: One Last Hit and Other Lies that Nearly Killed Me*. New York: Park Row.

Klingemann, H., Sobell, L., Peele, S., et al. (eds.). (2001). *Promoting Self-Change from Problem Substance Use*. Dordrecht, The Netherlands: Kluwer.

Krans, K. (2020). *Blossoms and Bones: Drawing a Life Back Together*. Novato, CA: New World.

Kristoff, N., & WuDunn, S. (2020). *Tightrope*. New York: Knopf.

Leachman, C., & Englund, G. (2009). *Cloris: My Autobiography*. New York: Kensington.

Lewis, M. (2013). *Memoirs of an Addicted Brain: A Neuroscientist Examines His Former Life on Drugs*. New York: PublicAffairs.

Lewis, M. (2016). *The Biology of Desire: Why Addiction Is Not a Disease*. New York: PublicAffairs.

Lewis, M. (2016). *The Undoing Project*. New York: Norton.

MacAndrew, C., & Edgerton, R. (1969). *Drunken Comportment: A Social Explanation*. Chicago: Aldine.

Markel, H. (2012). *An Anatomy of Addiction: Sigmund Freud, William Halsted, and the Miracle Drug, Cocaine*. New York: Vintage.

Marlatt, G. A., & Donovan, D. (1985; 2004). *Relapse Prevention*. New York: Guilford.

Maté, G. (2008). *In the Realm of Hungry Ghosts: Close Encounters with Addiction*, Toronto: Knopf Canada.

McKowen, L. (2020). *We Are the Luckiest: The Surprising Magic of a Sober Life*. Novato, CA: New World.

McGovern, G. (1996). *Terry: My Daughter's Life-and-Death Struggle with Alcoholism*. New York: Penguin.

McGovern, P. E. (2009). *Uncorking the Past: The Quest for Wine, Beer, and Other Alcoholic Beverages*. Berkeley: University of California.

Miller, W. R., & Heather, N. (1986) *Treating Addictive Behaviors: Processes of Change*. New York: Springer.

Miller, W. R., & Rollnick, S. (2013). *Motivational Interviewing* (3e). New York: Guilford.

Moyers, W. C. (2006). *Broken: My Story of Addiction and Redemption*. New York: Penguin.

Murthy, V. H. (2020). *Together: The Healing Power of Human Connection in a Sometimes Lonely World*. New York: Harper Collins.

Norwood, R. (1985). *Women Who Love Too Much*. New York: Tarcher.

Orford, J. (1985). *Excessive Appetites: A Psychological View of Addictions*. New York: Wiley.

Peele, S. (1980). *How Much Is Too Much?* Englewood, NJ: Prentice-Hall.

Peele, S. (1980). *The Addiction Experience*. Center City, MN: Hazelden.

Peele, S. (1983). *The Science of Experience: A Direction for Psychology*. Lexington, MA: Lexington.

Peele, S. (1985/2015). *The Meaning of Addiction*. Lexington, MA: Lexington.

Peele, S. (ed.) (1987). *Visions of Addiction: Major Contemporary Perspectives on Addiction and Alcoholism*. Lexington, MA: Lexington.

Peele, S. (1989/2016). *Diseasing of America: Addiction Treatment out of Control*. Lexington, MA: Lexington.

Peele, S. (2004). *7 Tools to Beat Addiction*. New York: Random House.

Peele, S. (2007). *Addiction-Proof Your Child*. New York: Random House/Crown.

Peele, S. & Apostolides, M. (1996). *Don't Panic: A Parent's Guide to Understanding and Preventing Alcohol and Drug Abuse*. New York: The Lindesmith Center.

Peele, S. & Brodsky, A. (1975/2014). *Love and Addiction*. New York: Taplinger.

Peele, S., Brodsky, A., & Arnold, M. (1991). *The Truth About Addiction and Recovery*. New York: Simon & Schuster.

Peele, S., Bufe, C., & Brodsky, A. (2000). *Resisting 12-Step Coercion*. Tucson, AZ: See Sharp Press.

Peele, S. & Gallagher, K. (2017). *Addiction-Proofing Your Family*. Watertown, MA: Broadrow.

Peele, S. & Grant, M. (eds.) (1999). *Alcohol and Pleasure: A Health Perspective*. Philadelphia: Brunner/Mazel.

Peele, S. & Rhoads, Z. (2019). *Outgrowing Addiction: With Common Sense Instead of "Disease" Therapy*. Hinesburg, VT: Upper Access

Peele, S. & Thompson, I. (2014). *Recover!: An Empowering Program to Help You Stop Thinking Like an Addict*. Berkeley: Da Capo.

Perry, B. D., & Szalavitz, M. (2006). *The Boy Who Was Raised as a Dog: And Other Stories from a Child Psychiatrist's Notebook*. (2006). New York: Basic.

Prochaska, J. O., Norcross, J. C., & DiClemente, C. C. (1994). *Changing for Good: A Revolutionary Six-Stage Program for Overcoming Bad Habits and Moving Your Life Positively Forward*. New York: Morrow.

Rapoport, J. L. (1989). *The Boy Who Couldn't Stop Washing: The Experience and Treatment of Obsessive-Compulsive Disorder*. New York: Signet.

Reeves, R. (2017). *Dream Hoarders*. Washington, DC: Brookings Institute.

Rieder, T. *In Pain: A Bioethicist's Personal Struggle with Opioids*. (2019). New York: Harper Collins.

Restak, R. (1984). *The Brain*. New York: Bantam.

Restak, R. (1988). *The Mind*. New York: Bantam.

Satel, S. (1999). *Drug Treatment: The Case for Coercion*. Washington, DC: AEI.

Satel, S., & Lilienfeld, S. (2013). *Brainwashing: The Seductive Appeal of Mindless Neuroscience*. New York: Basic.

Schwebel, R. (1998). *Saying No Is Not Enough* (2e) New York: Newmarket Press.

Self, W. (2019). *Will: A Memoir*. New York: Grove.

Szalavitz, M. (2006). *Help at Any Cost: How the Troubled-Teen Industry Cons Parents and Hurts Kids*. New York: Penguin.

Szalavitz, M. (2016). *Unbroken Brain*. New York: St. Martin's.

US Department of Health and Human Services (2019). *Those Who Continue to Smoke* (Monograph 15). Rockville, MD: US Department of Health and Human Services.

US Department of Health and Human Services (1964). *Smoking and Health*. Rockville, MD: US Department of Health and Human Services.

Vaillant, G. E. (1977) *Adaptation to Life*. Cambridge, MA: Belknap.

Vaillant, G. E. (1983). *The Natural History of Alcoholism*. Cambridge, MA: Harvard.

Vaillant, G. E. (2003) *Aging Well*. Cambridge, MA: Belknap.

Vaillant, G. E. (2008) *Spiritual Evolution: A Scientific Defense of Faith. New York*: Crown.

Vaillant, G. E. (2012) *Triumphs of Experience*. Cambridge, MA: Belknap.

West, R. (2006). *Theories of Addiction*. New York: Wiley

West, R. (2013). *How To Quit Smoking*. London: University College.

Zailckas, K. (2006). *Smashed: Story of a drunken girlhood*. New York: Penguin.

Zinberg, N. (1984). *Drug, Set, and Setting: The Basis for Controlled Intoxicant Use*. New Haven, CT: Yale University.

Index

brain disease theory supported by, 33,
198-203, 216-17, 270
changing views of, 208-11, 217, 220
inner city drug deaths, 218
love addiction, beliefs of, 33-34
medication-assisted treatment favored
by, 224
neuroscientific approach to addiction, 196
recovery without treatment, acknowledgment of, 149
SP articles about, 321, 337
SP ignored by, 3-4, 8-9, 57
Voting patterns in South Africa article,
127

W

Y-Z

Made in the USA
Middletown, DE
01 July 2021

43283937R00225